D0154179

DATE DUE

GAYLORD			PRINTED IN U.S.A.

Private Equity Finance

Private Equity Finance

Rise and Repercussions

Jamie Morgan

First published 2009 by
PALGRAVE MACMILLAN

Palgrave Macmillan in the UK is an imprint of Macmillan Publishers Limited,
registered in England, company number 785998, of Houndmills, Basingstoke,
Hampshire RG21 6XS.

Palgrave Macmillan in the US is a division of St Martin's Press LLC,
175 Fifth Avenue, New York, NY 10010.

Palgrave Macmillan is the global academic imprint of the above companies
and has companies and representatives throughout the world.

Palgrave® and Macmillan® are registered trademarks in the United States,
the United Kingdom, Europe and other countries.

ISBN-13: 978-0-230-20710-3   hardback
ISBN-10: 0-230-20710-3   hardback

This book is printed on paper suitable for recycling and made from fully
managed and sustained forest sources. Logging, pulping and manufacturing
processes are expected to conform to the environmental regulations of the
country of origin.

A catalogue record for this book is available from the British Library.

Library of Congress Cataloging-in-Publication Data

Morgan, Jamie, 1969–
    Private equity finance : rise and repercussions / Jamie Morgan.
        p. cm.
    Includes bibliographical references.
    ISBN 978-0-230-20710-3 (alk. paper)
        1. Private equity–United States. 2. Private equity–Great Britain.
    3. Venture capital–United States. 4. Venture capital–Great Britain.
    I. Title.
    HG4751.M74 2009
    658.15'224–dc22   2008030082

10   9   8   7   6   5   4   3   2   1
18   17   16   15   14   13   12   11   10   09

Printed and bound in Great Britain by
CPI Antony Rowe, Chippenham and Eastbourne

Contents

Acknowledgements

I would like to acknowledge the support of the Centre of Excellence in Global Governance Research, University of Helsinki. I thank Professor Stephen Ackroyd for reading the manuscript and for some specific ideas on entitlement. I also thank Professor Heikki Patomaki and Professor Steve Fleetwood for their encouragement and for specific comments, particularly regarding Keynes. I thank Professor Paul Thompson for taking the time to read the original working paper and for passing it to his editor. I thank Professor Karel Williams and Professor Barry Gills for useful and stimulating conversation regarding finance markets. I thank Lisa von Fircks, Senior Commissioning Editor in Finance at Macmillan, and her assistant, Elodie Lecoq, for their patience during intervening illness. I dedicate this book to Laura and Alice.

> You are not the enemy of the system. You are not even a challenge to the system, as you seem to think. You have a system inherently exploitative and unjust, inherently cruel and inhumane, heedless of human values, and your job is to make such a system appear legitimate and moral by acting as though justice, as though human rights and human dignity could actually exist in that society – when obviously no such thing is possible. (Roth 1969: 262)

> Every man of ambition has to fight his century with its own weapons. What this century worships is wealth. (Wilde 1987: 489)

List of Acronyms

AIM	Alternative Investment Market
BES	Business Enterprise Scheme
BSS	Business Star-up Scheme
BVCA	British Venture Capital Association
CDO	Collateralised debt obligation
CGT	Capital gains tax
CLEC	Competitive local exchange carriers
CLO	Collateralised loan obligation
CMBOR	Centre for Management Buyout Research
DIDMCA	Depository Institutions Deregulation and Monetary Control
ECB	European Central Bank
ERISA	Employment Retirement Income Security Act
ERM	Exchange Rate Mechanism
EVCA	European Venture Capital Association
Fed	Federal Reserve Board (FOMC: Federal Open Market Committee)
FIRREA	Financial Institutions Reform, Recovery and Enforcement Act
FSA	Financial services authority
GP	General partner
IPO	Initial public offering
LBO	Leveraged buyout
Libor	London inter-bank offered rate
LLP	Limited liability partnership
LP	Limited partner
LSE	London Stock Exchange
MBI	Management buyin
MBO	Management buyout
NAIC	National Association of Insurance Commissioners
NVCA	National Venture Capital Association
OFT	Office of Fair Trading
PEF	Private equity finance
SBA	Small Business Administration
SBIC	Small Business Investment Companies
SEC	Securities and Exchange Commission
SIB	Securities and Investment Board
SIB	Securities and Investment Board
SIFMA	Securities Industry and Financial Markets Association

SIV   Structured investment vehicle
SPV   Special purpose vehicle
SWF   Sovereign wealth funds
USM   Unlisted Securities Market

Introduction

In 2007 private equity finance (PEF) became a major public issue in the UK. The main reason for this was that private equity firms had, following a longer term trend, begun to buy larger and more prominent publicly listed companies. Beginning in 2006 the GMB union raised a wide range of concerns regarding the employment effects of PEF, focusing on the example of the AA. The failed bid by a private equity firm to buy J. Sainsbury and the successful bid to buy Alliance Boots added to the publicity PEF had begun to receive. During 2007 PEF came under increasing political scrutiny. In March, the Treasury launched a review of PEF. In June the Commons' Treasury Select Committee began an inquiry into its practices. The Bank of England, meanwhile, highlighted the potential problems that PEF might cause to the finance system because of its large scale and growing use of debt.[1] The main PEF industry representative, the British Venture Capital Association (BVCA), reacted by engaging in a media campaign to highlight the positive impact of PEF on the British economy.

The argument then crystallised along two lines. On one side the BVCA, its member firms and various advocates of free market economics made the case for PEF (Linthwaite 2007a, 2007b). The US neo-conservative economist and *Sunday Times* columnist, Irwin M. Stelzer summarised this position:

> By taking over troubled companies, private equity entrepreneurs cure the problems stemming from the separation of ownership and control. They and their partners now control former public companies, and have every incentive to reward only those managers who earn their pay by increasing profits and growth rates. Enter the invisible hand, and the further long-term result might prove to be job creation and enhanced value of the pension funds and to other institutional investors who share the profits of these ventures. (Stelzer 2007)

This focus on mutual interest and broader subsequent benefits has formed the core of the case for PEF. It is one that has been put forward in the UK by the main longstanding source of academic analysis: Mike Wright and various colleagues at the Centre for Management Buyout Research (CMBOR). It is one that various other economics and business journalists, such as Anatole Kaletsky, have also contributed to. For Kaletsky the controversy has been a 'quintessential storm in a teacup' where the 'initial attacks on the private equity industry, when stripped down to their essence, amounted to a rejection of profit as the main yardstick for business success' (Kaletsky 2007). For the BVCA, the important points emphasised are that PEF acquisitions generate tax revenues to the state, that those acquisitions are employers, that the scale of employment by PEF is growing, and that investors in PEF earn returns that add to general wealth. The BVCA produces annual statistics based on voluntary reporting by its members to support its claims. These formed the basis of much of the media campaign and also the testimony of BVCA representatives to the Commons' Treasury Select Committee.

On the other side, various trade unions, some members of parliament, and some political economists have made an alternative case against PEF (Kenny 2007). Adam Lent, TUC head of economic affairs brought the union movement's point of view before the OECD. The T&G union under Tony Woodley sought to pressurise the Financial Service Authority (FSA) to improve the regulation and reporting of PEF (Hencke and Treanor 2007). The basis of the alternative case has been that PEF uses debt to buy companies. The use of debt is what enables the buyout to occur. The debt reduces the tax liabilities of the acquisition, reducing tax revenues to the state. The acquisitions are treated by the private equity firms as an opportunity to make rapid returns through the creation of debt and through selling off parts of the acquisition. The private equity firms are 'asset strippers' and the partners in the private equity firms make large personal fortunes. These too are under-taxed because they are treated as capital gains rather than income. The main emphasis is that the private equity firms get away with this because they are private and because they are secretive. They are under no obligation to publicly report their activities, which are essentially about short term profits. The private equity firms do not genuinely care what happens to the companies they buy. They do not care about the terms and conditions of employees. In fact they have strong incentives to cut costs and do so by cutting wages, reducing employment, and attacking other terms and conditions, such as pension provision. One way in which they are able to do this is through failing to recognise unions. Paul Maloney, GMB senior organiser, summarised this position:

> The case of the AA illustrates why we at the GMB union oppose the unaccountable activities of [private equity] capitalists, their tax relief on loans, and the effect they have on companies, jobs, pensions and the economy. We consider the private status of [private equity] capitalists to be an abuse of company law and of the privilege of limited liability

status... In effect it is a vehicle whereby the multi-millionaire elite are able to cream off large sums of money away from the public gaze. (Maloney 2007)

Clearly, the two sides of the argument are diametrically opposed. They are opposed in terms of actual claims concerning benefits or effects. For example, the effects on employment and tax. They also encapsulate different views regarding the legitimacy of sources of profit, value and returns.

Arbitrating between these two views is not simple. Most of the data is skewed towards the positive view because most of the data is supplied on a voluntary basis by the private equity firms. At the same time the issue itself is more complex than merely claiming that there are no potential benefits from PEF. The real issue is: what is the basis of any claimed benefit and how does this relate to the changing context in which PEF operates? Many of the new studies now being conducted on PEF have this in mind. Professor Karel Williams, for example, provided some damning testimony to the Commons' Treasury Select Committee regarding the way PEF generates returns to private equity firms and to its investors. He and colleagues at the Centre for Research on Socio-Cultural Change (CRESC) have tended initially towards an 'against' position on PEF (Froud and Williams 2007) but are engaged in follow up research. CRESC has produced a wide variety of material on the subject of 'financialisation' (Eerturk *et al.* 2008). This refers to the increasing influence of finance on economic, political and social life. Private equity firms use debt to buy companies. The company is a financial asset owned by its investors. PEF very clearly falls under the remit of financialisation and can, therefore, be usefully considered in terms of this kind of wider context. Professor Justin O'Brien (2008) takes a similar view that what is important is not just the disputed individual benefits of PEF but the overall context and ramifications of PEF. It is this line of argument of context that I pursue in this book.

What is private equity finance?

PEF is a historical phenomenon. It emerged, grew and developed as capital markets in the US and then in the UK changed and developed. Although PEF has a global presence it has been an industry focused on and through the US and the UK. To truly understand it requires an understanding of how it developed and how it grew in terms of the broader growth of capital markets in these two countries. The history of PEF has been a history of changing regulation, changing investment cultures, and changing access to debt and to sources of investment. My own interest and the ultimate focus of this study is the buyout of large companies by private equity firms using debt. A buyout using debt is termed a 'leveraged buyout' (LBO). However, the changing dynamics of PEF that have affected LBOs have not just been about LBOs. They have encompassed all the different areas of PEF. The initial growth of private equity firms and of LBOs in the US was a partial beneficiary of changes in regulation brought about to encourage investment in new business. This is the domain of venture capital. Later, the failures and learning processes of PEF resulted in a wide range of other kinds of investment activity. It is important, therefore, to have from the outset a clear sense of what the different elements and types of PEF are.

The first distinction to be made is between private equity firms and private equity funds. Private equity firms are investment and business management organisations usually comprised of a small number of executive partners and employees. Many of the firms were originally divisions of investment banks or were begun by the partners after leaving the acquisitions arm of an investment bank. Many of the investment banks still operate private equity divisions that compete with the firms. These firms solicit capital from investors and that capital is then pooled as a fund that is a separate legal entity from the private equity firm. Both the firms and the funds are usually registered as limited liability partnerships (LLPs). A partnership agreement is drawn up between the firm, who acts as the general partner (GP) of the fund, and the investors, who are designated as limited partners (LPs). This document defines the duration of the fund, usually ten years. It also defines the capital commitment of each investor, the range of permissible investments, the rights of investors to dissolve the partnership, the fees the GP is able to charge, and the duties and obligations of the GP. This legal structure has numerous advantages for the participants. It is extremely flexible enabling the parties to incorporate any criteria they desire that do not conflict with the law of the land.[2] It is 'tax efficient': the fund itself is not subject to taxation: tax is liable on investors when they receive returns. It is private, preserving the confidentiality of the financial activities of the investors. It involves limited liability: investors are only liable for the capital committed and not for the subsequent losses of any entity invested in.

The basis of the investment and of the original solicitation is that the private equity firm's partners act as 'professional intermediaries' between the investors and the investment. This is what makes PEF a specialist industry: the investment service it offers on the basis of the claimed finance and management skills of its professionals. A firm may administer several different funds. Venture capitalists specialise in investing solicited funds in small businesses of various kinds (Gompers and Lerner 2000). The business may be anything from a 'start-up', with no more than a business plan and an idea or invention, to a small firm wanting to restructure and expand. The venture capitalist takes a stake in the firm in exchange for the investment capital. The venture capitalist takes a seat on the board of the company invested in. The invested capital is usually delivered in a series of 'rounds' when certain targets or time periods are reached. Depending on the size of the investment and the terms of the initial agreement the venture capitalist may have the right to hire and fire other board members and may bring in a variety of other specialists to help in business development. The eventual aim is to 'exit' the investment through an initial public offering (IPO). Venture capital covers the whole range of types of company but is associated in the public's mind with hi-tech investment. Venture capital has historically had a high failure rate, particularly of investments at the start-up phase. Its successes, however, are high profile: Amazon, Apple, Netscape and so forth.

Private equity buyout firms specialise in investing solicited funds in LBOs (Tannon and Johnson 2005). The GP of the fund identifies potential targets for an LBO. A portion of the committed capital from the fund is used as the initial basis for the buyout. This is the equity stake of the investors in the buyout. It may be added to by an additional equity stake from other investors, including the private equity firm. The majority of the buyout is funded using debt. The GP negotiates a debt structure with investment bankers and the acquisition is used as collateral for the debt. The more debt used as a proportion of the buyout, the higher the level of leverage. The buyout typically takes the form of a majority or entire holding of the company. Buyout targets can be of a variety of kinds under a variety of circumstances. They can be divisions of larger companies (a divestment). They can be companies bought out of receivership. They can be previously nationalised or state-owned companies. They can be privately owned former family businesses or publicly listed companies. Types of LBO can be subdivided by the nature of the additional participants. If some of the original management are retained and have an equity stake then the LBO is termed a 'management buyout' (MBO). If a new management team are brought in and have an equity stake then the LBO is termed an 'management buy-in' (MBI). If the management have no equity stake then the LBO is outside investor-led. The usual LBO process is that the GP forms a holding company that administers the acquisition on behalf of the fund. The GP oversees the new management structure and engages with the new board of directors. The acquisition itself is also typically restructured, involving a combination of new investment, cost cutting, and asset sales. The GP regularly reports on the performance of the acquisition to the investors in the fund. As with venture capital, the eventual aim is to exit the investment by selling it on either as one company or several. The three main exits are an IPO, a secondary sale to another private equity firm, and a 'trade sale', usually a sale to another company operating in the same industry as the acquisition. Exit usually takes place within three to seven years, typically four.

In both venture capital and buyouts some firms and funds specialise in particular industries and particular geographical locations. The largest most prominent firms, however, tend to be general. The largest firms focus mainly on buyouts. Globally these firms include KKR, Blackstone, Bain Capital, Carlyle and TPG. British private equity firms, such as Apax, tend to operate in both venture capital and buyout markets. Most of the larger firms are also quite diversified, operating a variety of different kinds of funds. Funds of funds are solicited to invest in other private equity funds. Debt funds, buy up discounted forms of debt: the bonds of companies that are performing badly, mortgage bonds and other kinds of debt instruments that are, because of prevailing financial conditions, also being discounted. Mezzanine funds buy some of the offered debt of LBOs rather than taking an equity stake. Some firms also administer hedge funds.

The argument: private equity finance and liquidity

PEF has an intimate relationship to what is termed liquidity. Liquidity is a technical term in economics that initially describes the capacity to engage in the buying or selling of something without significantly affecting the price of the type of thing being bought or sold. It also refers to the ease with which an asset can be disposed of. A liquid asset is easily disposed of. A liquid market is one where buying and selling are quickly and easily undertaken. It also has a looser meaning where it refers to the general circumstances that facilitate transactions. This essentially refers to the liquidity of other markets: markets for debt, markets for investment and so forth. Economists tend to talk in general terms about the liquidity of the economy in all its aspects. Highly liquid markets are generally perceived in a positive way and illiquid ones in a negative way.

Liquidity too is a historical phenomenon. Financial liberalisation in the US and the UK since the 1970s has greatly increased liquidity. Within that general increase liquidity has been highly variable. This has been important for PEF buyouts because PEF solicits investment funds, accesses debt, and exits its acquisitions by a further sale. It is, therefore, highly dependent on a broad range of aspects of liquidity. This, of course, is neither a controversial nor stunning insight. However, what I want to suggest is that when looked at in terms of the dynamics of capital markets PEF buyouts exhibit a variety of tendencies. The scale of funds, the size of acquisitions, and the degree of leverage used tend to increase as liquidity increases. This is subject to the constraints of other historical factors: regulation, investment culture, banking practices, new financial innovations and so forth. But as these also change there is an interconnection between growing liquidity and growing PEF activity where available capital and credit creating resources are channelled into PEF. PEF in turn tends to respond by exploiting all available liquidity. As such, PEF can be viewed from a systemic perspective as a constitutive part of the instability of the growth of liquidity.

This places a quite different inflection on the claim that PEF turns around troubled firms than the purely positive one. PEF becomes a claimed solution to problems it helps to create. It becomes one constitutive element in the creation of an adverse economic environment based on the rapid expansion and sudden collapse of particular markets. From this perspective, PEF may well have beneficial effects on particular businesses that are bought out. At the same time, it has macro effects as it grows: it is one reason why liquidity surges and, in turn, can contribute to why liquidity collapses. This is a broad problem of and through capital markets. It is a problem for what we are used to thinking of as the real economy and also for the finance system.

Furthermore, any specific benefits created by PEF buyouts are contingent. They are contingent on context because the benefits are disputable in terms of the different parties subject to a buyout (investors, employees, etc.). They are contingent on the historical dynamism of PEF in a way that also relates to its underlying tendencies. A buyout is an investment using debt. The acquisition is an investment asset. The central focus of the process is a return to the PEF fund and the PEF firm. The buyout is a means to this end. Returns to the fund can be created using a whole variety of strategies. There is, therefore, no simple relation between a buyout and the necessity of improving the acquired business in any unequivocal way. Buyouts are not simple asset stripping ventures. They are not simple situations of cost cutting through the slashing of wages and employment. However, they are exercises in treating companies as financial instruments. They do involve the restructuring of management processes, employment relations and industrial relations. The basis on which this occurs is a form of the neo-liberal reconstruction of work. It further involves a debt structure and, as liquidity grows, larger levels of leverage for larger scale acquisitions. As such it involves debt vulnerability. One can reasonably ask, therefore: is a PEF buyout a claimed solution to problems that creates new problems? If larger scale acquisitions and higher levels of leverage only become possible as liquidity surges then the most vulnerable debt structures are created as markets become increasingly unstable and liable to collapses. The future is unwritten but it is not utterly opaque. The most recent scale of PEF activity is unprecedented. It requires no apocalyptic scenario to see that greater levels of debt linked to problems of adverse economic conditions create the possibility of debt servicing problems, with all that this entails: defaults to creditors, unemployment, insolvency and so forth.

Of course, defaults, unemployment, and insolvency may not occur. But this raises the additional question of whether any gains from PEF warrant the risk that they might. This in turn raises three ancillary issues: what are the gains from a PEF buyout? How should one view the entitlement of PEF firms to the returns they generate from buyout activity? Was the buyout necessary to any of the 'improvements' that may or may not have occurred to the acquisition? These issues raise the further issue of whether PEF should be regulated and how. All of these issues are more than just empirical matters. They are, as the different terms of debate of the two sides in the argument regarding PEF indicate, also fundamental issues about how one views economy and society. Kaletsky is not wrong to suggest that the negative case involves an attack on profit. He is wrong, however, to imply that this makes it a storm in a teacup because the attack is both unwarranted and essentially unencumbered by facts. The underlying terms of the debate involve the sources of the returns (what the profits actually involve), the wide-ranging effects of the practices, and the need to think about the norms that underpin the ability to access the returns and engage in the practices.

To recap then, the central themes I develop in the following chapters are whether PEF buyouts are:

- A claimed solution (turning round an acquisition) to problems they help to create: the instability of liquidity resulting in periodic adverse economic conditions and problems within the finance system.
- A claimed solution that creates new problems within the dynamics of liquidity and subject to the constraints of changing liquidity: the terms and conditions of work and problems of debt vulnerability.
- A claimed solution that involves issues of entitlement, gains, and regulation.

The chapters

In Chapters 1 to 4, I set out the historical development of private equity finance in the context of changing liquidity and the instability of liquidity. The chapters establish how the size of PEF as an industry has grown and how the scale of buyouts and the use of debt have been linked to liquidity. They establish how the development of PEF has involved changes in regulation and investment culture, as well as changes in the finance system. The initial development of PEF occurred in the US and in the context of the transformation of investment banking practices and the growth in the junk bond/high yield market. It came to an end with the collapse of the junk bond market and the associated savings & loan banking crisis. I explore this in Chapter 1. In Chapter 2, I set out the initial development of PEF in the UK and explain why the size of the industry did not achieve a similar scale to the US prior to the late 1990s. I also set out the conditions of the initial recovery of PEF in the US in the 1990s. In Chapter 3, I set out the context within which PEF became a more integrated industry between the UK and the US and how this led to the unprecedented growth in PEF buyouts in the twenty first century. I also place that growth within the context of the collapse of the dot.com boom, noting how venture capital activity contributed to the boom and how PEF LBOs reacted to the 'New Economy' and were ultimately beneficiaries of the collapse. In Chapter 4, on the basis of the changes explored in Chapter 3, I set out the new scale of

PEF funds and buyout activity that was achieved in the mid-2000s. I place this in the context of why the banks were prepared to offer higher levels of leverage for larger debt structures and with betters terms and conditions for the borrower. I then set out the basic problems this created, focusing on issues relating to securitisation as a main source of the growth in liquidity. This in turn gives a context for exploring the 'credit crunch' and its significance for PEF and the finance system. I have tried to make the material in Chapters 1 to 4 as accessible as possible. By the end of the chapters the reader should have a good grasp of how PEF has grown, a general grasp of how three of the major liquidity surges of the era of financial liberalism have occurred and collapsed, and also a good grasp of the standard terminology and functioning of various aspects of modern finance and capital markets (mezzanine finance, CDOs, Libor and so forth). Chapter 4 in particular should also give the reader a good grasp of the various ways in which rising leverage can also be a problem for the finance system.

In Chapter 5, I set out how PEF firms earn fees and how they use financial gearing to create a debt structure in order to undertake an LBO. Setting out this material addresses the question: what aspects of PEF cause it to expand to exploit all available liquidity? In essence this approaches the issue of the rising scale of PEF buyouts from the opposite end to that which initially motivates Chapters 1 to 4 (how liquidity expands and is channelled into PEF). Chapter 5 focuses more strongly on the challenge to the PEF firm of achieving high returns to the PEF fund and in earning its most lucrative fee (carried interest). It highlights how returns to the fund can be made through a variety of strategies (the initial gearing, special dividends, subsequent dividends paid to concentrated equity, the exit of the investment) and that those strategies do not cohere to a single overall method that requires the general partner to improve the acquisition in any unequivocal or neutral sense. By the end of the chapter the reader ought to have a good grasp of how gearing works as a technical process and the limitations that rising debt levels for larger acquisitions place on any reliance on a single source of returns to the fund.

Chapter 5 begins the process of thinking about entitlement and also begins the process of exploring in what sense a PEF buyout is a claimed solution that creates new problems. At the heart of this is the role of debt creation, debt servicing, and debt vulnerability based on rising leverage and the instability of liquidity – including future credit markets. In Chapter 6, I set out the main theorisation of PEF LBOs and also some useful theoretical insights on the instability of capital markets. It is common practice to set out theory at the beginning of a book rather than half way through. However, most of the key critical and analytical points relating to PEF LBOs and to unstable liquidity are about historical dynamics. As such, the critical comments make more sense when there is the historical material of Chapters 1 to 4 to draw on and when the basic elements of the mechanism of a buyout based on gearing and debt are already understood in a technical sense.

Chapter 6 is not, as such, an after thought, add on, or merely arbitrarily inserted. The main insights on the instability of capital markets and liquidity derive from Keynes, Minsky, Kindleberger, and Shackle and relate to the key issue of uncertainty and time i.e. the historical dynamic of markets. Their work provides useful ways of understanding why the past is not a good guide to the future. More specifically it provides a useful way to understand why relying too closely on the continuing patterns of the past results in new scales of behaviours that qualitatively change and undermine that reliance. The main source of theorisation of PEF LBOs is the work of Michael Jensen. The main focus of his work is the disciplining role of debt, the alignment of interests of the reduced number of participants after an LBO, and the wealth effects of the LBO. What I argue is that debt is not a simple source of discipline but also an opportunity. This is why it is not only the size of debt structures that rise during the growth of liquidity but also the level of leverage. Since leverage rises and also deal sizes rise, and terms and conditions of lending deteriorate for the lender, monitoring is not always and everywhere an effective mechanism – particularly in the age of securitisation. Furthermore, the alignment of interest is focused on returns to the fund and not the acquisition. Since Chapter 5 establishes that returns can be generated in various ways it does not, therefore, follow that the alignment is beneficial to the acquisition in any unequivocal sense. This is especially so if one thinks of PEF as genuinely historical or dynamic in its practices.

I argue that Jensen's work places PEF as a solution to problems of an economic system but not also as one that is a constitutive part of its problems: it is a historical phenomenon outside of history. This raises the issue of regulation because if PEF is part of broader problems then the scale and activity of PEF might better be restricted despite any specific empirical claims concerning its benefits at particular times. Thereafter, those specific claimed effects also become an issue. In Chapter 7, I look at the three main areas in which empirical claims are made for the benefits of PEF buyouts. Those are: high returns to investors, including institutional investors like pension funds from which a broad based public might benefit; employment and productivity; and tax revenue and value creation. Looking at the empirical claims is highly problematic because of limitations in the kind of data publicly available regarding PEF. Based on the available research and data for the UK, however, I argue that the empirical claims are not wholly refutable but they are partial in various ways. First, PEF buyouts have been a source of high returns, but not relatively high returns, and the returns that have been generated are contingent in two ways. They are contingent because the performance of different funds is highly variable. They are contingent because the performance of the industry is historically variable and likely to become more so at the new scales on which PEF activity has been occurring. Second, PEF buyouts do not necessarily require wage and employment cuts but they do have ramifications for the ongoing development of the employment relation and also the power relations of industrial relations. As such they can be viewed as part of the neo-liberal reconstruction of work. Crucially, the use of debt creates an additional pressure in restructuring the acquisition. A perspective that treats a unit of production as a financial instrument heightens the focus on shareholder value. Cost and particular 'stakeholder' value pressures are quintessential aspects of neo-liberalism. Third, tax is the area where PEF claims are at their weakest. The original intent of many of the tax regulations that PEF benefits from are subverted by PEF buyout activity. Tax revenues are also lower than they could be. This again raises issues of entitlement, in turn raising moral issues of economic justice and (tax) regulation.

In Chapter 8, I provide a case study of a UK PEF LBO. The buyout of Alliance Boots provides a useful contemporary illustration of the themes I develop in the previous chapters. It was a buyout of a large publicly listed company undertaken by a prominent PEF firm. The buyout was undertaken using the new large funds available to PEF and was undertaken at the height of the last liquidity surge. It involved the creation of a debt structure that was large in absolute terms and also comparatively highly leveraged. It illustrates how equity is concentrated and power distributed. As such it raises the basic question of entitlement: should PEF firms and funds have the right to do this, particularly at larger scales and focused on publicly listed companies? I argue that this is not simply an empirical question but also a moral philosophy question because the implicit 'right' of PEF is founded on a particular understanding of the right to property. That understanding combines the idea that property is a basic human right, that the state should be minimal and that the freedom of markets should be maximised. Exploring how this is so is important because it also reveals how the terms of debate regarding PEF are shaped by these commitments. Having done so, one can also look at entitlement in more specific terms, based on the idea of debt vulnerability. The buyout of Alliance Boots created a debt structure that was possible because of rising liquidity but that was also vulnerable to the collapse in liquidity. As such Alliance Boots provides a useful illustration of how PEF is itself historically dynamic. Looking at the debt structure also raises the issue of governance: why was the buyout of Alliance Boots approved? I argue that corporate governance is rarely an effective constraint on buyout activity targeted at publicly listed companies. Since it is not such a constraint the issue is again raised of whether intervention is desirable. This in effect is also a moral philosophy question because it is about the right of the state to intervene in the disposition of property and thus cuts across the idea of individual rights, the minimal state, and maximally free markets.

In the conclusion I draw the main themes together. I comment on the degree to which the arguments of preceding chapters have endorsed those themes. It is the case that no argument that highlights the importance of normative commitments can be definitive. However, I take it that on the balance of the arguments presented in the preceding chapters there is a case for considering regulation of private equity finance and that case does lean more towards the negative assessment of larger buyouts where significant levels of debt and higher levels of leverage are used. On this basis I then sketch out an integrated approach to possible regulations that could address the issues arising from the themes. These include how to control unstable liquidity, debt vulnerability, and issues arising from different aspects of entitlement. Finally I briefly address the recent approach to the regulation of private equity by the New Labour government, arguing that the approach adopted is short-sighted. Hopefully, the overall impact will not have resulted in 'that uniquely academic approach of taking a timely subject of current interest and rendering it less so.' (Hirschey 1986: 317)

1

The Emergence of Private Equity Finance in the US: Leveraged Buyouts, Institutional Investment, Junk Bonds and the Thrifts

In this chapter I begin the process of placing private equity finance (PEF) in context. Specialist firms owned and operated by general partners who act as professional intermediaries between business organisations and sources of finance emerged in the US in response to a particular set of conditions. A growing proportion of investment capital in the US was accumulating in the hands of institutions. The state was initially concerned that a failure to create a system able to effectively access this source of investment capital would be detrimental to small business growth, innovation, and ultimately economic growth. Various policies and legislative changes were instituted to address this problem. These changes, though mainly focused on PEF venture capital also provided the conditions within which PEF with a focus on leveraged buyouts (LBOs) could grow. PEF LBOs were in a sense an unintended beneficiary of these changes. Thereafter, PEF LBOs grew far more rapidly in the 1980s than venture capital because of other factors. The rise of conglomeration in the 1960s and the economic conditions of the 1970s and early 1980s provided numerous targets for PEF LBOs. Changes in the structure of investment banking and its practices and the rise of forms of financial instrument, particularly junk bonds, provided access to investors and sources for increasingly large and complex debt structures. Those structures were then tied into the willingness and capacity of the banks and the finance system to facilitate LBOs. That willingness and capacity were in turn influenced by the link between the junk bond market and the US thrift institutions. This link influenced the political dynamic of PEF LBOs. The solvency problem of the thrifts was a key issue of the time. LBOs also became an issue in their own right as they targeted increasingly large publicly listed companies and did so using more and more debt. By the end of the 1980s the collapse of the thrifts and the rise of leverage levels, affected both the state and the banks' attitude to LBOs. The result was a decline in PEF LBOs at the end of the decade.

Placing the emergence of PEF LBOs in this context of broader systemic relations begins the process of exploring the relationship between PEF LBOs and liquidity. PEF was a beneficiary of a surge in liquidity. However, that liquidity growth was unstable. What I want to suggest is that PEF is more than just a beneficiary and then victim of the instability of liquidity. It is, rather, a reason for that liquidity to grow and to grow in unstable ways. Liquidity in turn provides the impetus for PEF LBOs to grow in terms of scale and frequency. Given the availability of debt there is an inherent tendency within PEF to grow in scale and frequency.[1] In so doing PEF LBOs create potentially more vulnerable acquisitions with higher levels of leverage and also contribute to the problems of the sources of complex debt structures on which LBOs feed – adding in a sense to the context of PEF's own change in circumstances by contributing to systemic changes. PEF is, therefore, a functioning element in dysfunctional and unstable liquidity. Establishing this over the next four chapters is important because it places any further claims regarding the benefits of larger PEF LBOs in a broader context.

The emergence of the private equity firm as a professional intermediary

Private equity firms as professional intermediaries between large investors and investment opportunities in organisations seeking capital without a public offering of equity began to develop in the 1970s (Barnes and Gertler 1999: 276).[2] In 1973 the National Venture Capital Association (NVCA) was formed in the US to represent the interests of firms and to develop a consciousness of the firms as a new and distinct sector of financing. The firms were put forward as a solution to a longstanding problem first identified after World War II (Gutpa 2000: 7–8). Capital that could be tapped for investment in new and small businesses had previously been concentrated in the hands of wealthy individuals and their families but was now increasingly concentrated within institutions, even when involving the wealth of individuals.[3] Institutions included public and private pension funds, mutual funds, charitable foundations and endowments (universities etc.), insurance companies and so forth. These institutions undertook portfolios of investment and usually had a small core of staff to undertake that investment and particular rules to adhere to regarding the scale, risk and proportions of capital that could be committed. In the absence of some kind of infrastructure able to provide information to staff, able to undertake the supervision or management of the investment and able to address the rules the institutions were governed by there was a concern, for example, at the Federal Reserve, that new businesses would increasingly face difficulties attracting new investment. This concern in turn was contextualised by the Cold War. Under Eisenhower there was a general fear that the USSR might begin to outpace the US in its technological advancements.[4]

The initial solution was the Small Business Investment Act of 1958 which established the Small Business Administration (SBA) (Fenn, Liang and

Prowse 1995: 6–8). The SBA certified specialised Small Business Investment Companies (SBICs) and also provided low cost loans to those SBICs.[5] The SBICs could be either publicly listed companies or affiliates (attached to banks), but in either case were mandated to generate capital specifically to be invested in small companies.[6] For a variety of reasons SBICs were not particularly successful. Since new small business investment tends to be one whose gains are long term rather than short, SBICs were not themselves a particularly attractive public equity investment and thus faced capitalisation problems. Borrowing from the SBA merely compounded this problem. The combination meant that SBICs were more likely to focus investment on less risky small businesses with a greater likelihood of gains, thereby partially undermining the point of SBICs and of the low cost loans provided to them. In any case, SBICs did not directly address the problem of attracting investment from institutional investors.

The SBICs did, however, provide a training ground for some of the individuals who would go on to form private equity firms (Lerner and Schoar 2004: 7). The SBICs also provided the impetus to do so to these individuals and to others who wanted to avoid some of the observed constraints of SBICs. A major constraint was that the Investment Company Act of 1940 prevented managers of the class of publicly traded firms of which SBICs were a part from receiving performance based payments and stock. Pay is also a reason why many private equity firms have over the years been spun-out of venture capital and PEF units, some of them SBICs, at national, regional and investment banks – Citibank, Bank of San Francisco and so forth. The new private equity professionals avoided public listing (and walked away from the salary structure of the banks) since this meant they could maximise their own gains by PEF.[7] Avoiding a public listing also allowed them to focus directly on soliciting stable investment from large institutional investors. In the initial growth of venture capital these new professionals became synonymous with the (usually) single fund they solicited – typically from a few (3–7) investors with whom they would forge a long term relationship of trust and cooperation. Ned Heizer, for example, had directed investment in new hi-tech firms such as Memorex at Allstate Insurance in Chicago since 1960. In 1969, he spun-off Heizer Corporation and raised the largest venture capital fund of its time. (Barnes and Gertler 1999: 276).[8]

As terminology developed to capture who the new professionals were and what they did they were variously referred to as venture capitalists, LBO associates, and lead active investors.[9] From an initial *ad hoc* basis these professionals increasingly formed their own partnerships (the venture capital or more broadly private equity firm) that then had a separate legal identity from the solicited funds i.e. the investment vehicle or limited partnership (LLP) in which they served the function of general partner. The LLP fund structure in general has several implications for exposure to regulations of the Securities and Exchange Commission (SEC). The Investment Company Act 1940 was originally targeted to restrict speculative and potentially risky investment forms. This applies mainly to mutual funds – managed pools of investment capital in portfolios (like UK unit trusts). Such funds offer services to small investors as well as institutional investors and thus have large numbers of investors. They are public and tend to be open-ended. The Act, however, excluded funds with fewer than 100 investors – thus an LLP fund gains the ability to use a wider variety of investment techniques by restricting itself to fewer large investors. By also restricting the way in which it solicits funds (private solicitation by invitation to closed presentations and meetings) the LLP is also exempt from the registration and disclosure requirements of the 1933 Securities Act. The secrecy of private equity and its focus on particular clientele is thus partly a response to law.[10] The other main advantage of structuring the fund to be an LLP with a definite time span for capital commitment by the investors was to avoid the volatility in available capital conditions that public equity tended to create. This was, as the SBICs experience tended to indicate, a particular problem in venture capital where actual returns in the first years of investment may be negligible.

The emergence of the new professionals and firms did not, however, immediately result in them becoming the dominant destination for investment in venture capital and PEF (Rind 1981: 172).[11] SBICs did not simply disappear and still exist today.[12] They have, rather, slowly declined in significance in terms of proportions of capital and investment.[13] Wealthy families continued to invest through their own wholly owned venture capital organisations – Rothschild's New Court and Rockefeller's Venrock. These too, due to their limited numbers have slowly reduced in significance as the size of the industry and the number of firms has increased and wealthy individuals have become major investors through PEF funds along with institutional investors. It should also be noted that major industrial corporations, particularly, oil and major technology manufacturers operated units – usually to capture and develop related processes. As the 1970s progressed, however, industrial corporations increasingly began to work through the venture capital and private equity firms since this avoided a number of problems for the corporation: it avoided the sunk costs of acquiring and retaining specialist staff, it avoided having to justify to the board and to shareholders in what sense any given venture had succeeded and it avoided a direct relation with the invested firm that might have antitrust implications or result in expectations of additional unagreed funding commitments.[14] By the end of the decade the venture capital and private equity firms were increasingly the main destinations for investment in venture capital and PEF.[15] Such funds constituted 40% of venture capital by 1980 (Gompers and Lerner 2000: 285) and the majority of PEF in general and over the decade came to dominate the industry (Gompers and Lerner 1998: 152).

How the 1980s began

The expansion of this new industry in the 1970s was slow (Fenn, Liang and Prowse 1995: 8–11; Rind 1981: 171). Part of the reason for this was one of the general state of the US economy and of a range of further disincentives for PEF investment.[16] The decline in economic growth and particularly export growth in the US in the 1970s, Nixon's decision to abandon gold convertibility and devalue the dollar in 1971, OPEC's fourfold increase in oil prices 1973/4 and the drift into stagflation produced a period of investment pessimism. This made it difficult to solicit funds and made it difficult to realise profit from PEF because the state of equity markets made it more difficult to publicly list a venture capital nurtured firm or a PEF buyout (as an IPO) – despite the formation of the Nasdaq in 1971.[17] Small company new issues fell from a high of 698 in 1969 to just four in 1975 (Rind 1981: 171). Capital gains tax was also historically high in the 1970s – up to 49%. Furthermore, one of the key ways to generate potential returns in new business and buyouts – accumulating stock options – incurred upfront costs since these were taxable when taken up rather than when sold.

The regulation of key institutional investors and their evolved investment culture also continued to make them generally averse to PEF in the 1970s. In one sense the new funds could be attractive because acting as limited partners in the LLPs would allow them to retain limited liability. Under the Uniform Limited Partnership Act of 1916 limited partners are liable only for the sum invested in the partnership so long as they do not participate in the business.[18] Further, tax exempt investors such as pension funds stood to gain from the closed nature of the funds since if the investment in the limited partnership is not freely tradable there is no tax levied on the LLP fund itself – only on the investors when the returns are distributed (Lerner and Schoar 2004: 8). However, as Don Valentine, at Sequoia venture capital since 1971, recalls, pension funds still tended to invest highly conservatively, with around 75% of their portfolio in fixed income assets (like Treasury securities) whilst aiming for a total return on their portfolio of around 9–10% (Gupta 2000: 167). Further, the 1974 Employment Retirement Income Security Act (ERISA) 'prudent man' concept was taken to prohibit pension funds from undertaking potentially high risk investments (Gumpert 1979: 184; Fenn, Liang and Prowse 1995: 10; Gompers and Lerner 1998: 155). This interpretation tended to exclude investment in privately solicited funds – particularly new ones with no performance record, as most venture capital or PEF of the time was. The prudent man concept, along with previous legislation, also tended to exclude investment in corporate bonds that had not received an investment grading from one of the major credit rating associations (Moody's Investors Service or Standard & Poor's Corporation) or that were graded below 'investment grade' (below Baa for Moody's and BBB for Standard & Poor's) – what are collectively termed 'junk bonds'.[19] This tended to exclude investment through lending to most small and new businesses. In any case, large pension funds and mutual funds have always tended to invest in large minimum blocks in order to limit the number of individual investments that the fund administrators need to research and track. Small companies might be too small, whilst venture capital and PEF funds more broadly might absorb this capital but were usually designated high risk.[20] There was also the possibility that an investment in a long term investment vehicle that had no necessary specific investment targets would be classified as the diversion of capital to an investment advisor. This was because the very point of the PEF fund was for the professional intermediary to identify high return uses for the capital. Under ERISA an advisor must be registered and regulated according to the Investment Advisor Act of 1940. The Act 'prohibited performance-related' payment and thus, if it should be applied to PEF would produce similar problems to the SBIC restrictions in terms of personal profit for the new intermediaries (Fenn, Liang and Prowse 1995: 11).

As the 1970s drew to a close the state of the US economy prompted a similar review of the potential for small business investment as had occurred in the late 1950s. The policy changes that emerged out of that review, however, benefited the whole of PEF. The top rate of capital gains tax was reduced from 49% to 28% in 1978.[21] In 1979, after intervention from the SBA and from influential fund trustees and administrators, such as Roger Kennedy at the Ford Foundation, (Gupta 2000: 167), the ERISA prudent man concept was clarified by the Department of Labour. The prudent man rather than one acting on the basis of general understanding became one who acts on the basis of a subject specific knowledge 'in a like capacity and familiar with such matters in the conduct of an enterprise of a like character and with like aims'.[22] The prudent man thus became in essence the prudent expert able to take decisions on investments that a layman might not. This was deemed to allow higher risk investment forms (initially typically at 2–5% of the portfolio i.e. higher risk investment in proportions that are low risk to the portfolio).[23] In 1980 the Department of Labour also ruled that venture capital and PEF funds would not be classed as 'advisors', and in 1981 the Incentive Stock Option Law deferred the tax liability on stock options to the point of sale.[24]

These changes occurred in the context of another significant development which changed the environment in which venture capital and PEF funds operated. Beginning in the 1960s and developing through the 1970s the operation and organisation of the securities business was transformed. Initially, the business was highly segmented (Hayes 1979). Some investment banks provided underwriting services to large corporate and municipal (state and local government) clients. They advised on what form of financing the client should undertake – issuing stock or bonds, and in the latter case advising on what the interest rate and term of the bond should be.[25] They worked on the registration and prospectus of the new issue to comply with SEC regulations and, as underwriters, charged fees in exchange for an initial price guarantee for the issue and for bringing it to market.[26] Since these investment banks held no deposits in the sense a commercial bank does, and focused on a very narrow client base (government and the 5% of US companies that were publicly listed, had a large capitalisation, and a set of accounts that warranted an investment grade credit rating; Yago 1990), they required few staff and tended to be relatively small partnerships located on Wall Street. These first tier investment banks tended to underwrite large issues as consortia and by controlling access to syndication exercised power over both clients and the next line or second tier of investment banks that provided retail services – who mainly acted as brokers between the syndicates and either securities dealers on public markets (the exchanges) or large institutional investors with whom blocks of the issue could be placed. The first tier might also act as brokers for large institutional investors whilst the retailers also acted as dealers – buying blocks of the issue, rather than simply brokering, and then selling on at higher prices. Both employed analysts, usually within the brokerage business, who produced investment reports and notes, including market forecasts to clients, but retailers tended to require more staff, a branch operation and a more active approach to pursuing clients.

The slow economic growth and periods of recession of the 1970s caused a general slowdown in new business for the investment banks. This occurred against the background of the tendency for large US corporations to conglomerate in the 1960s. In 1950 the Celler-Kefauver Act placed new restrictions on horizontal and vertical integration by corporations and added an additional dimension to Federal anti-trust powers designed to restrict the growth of monopoly. Those powers had always been imperfectly applied but in the light of the new Act growth by merger and acquisition was increasingly through the capture of non-related businesses (conglomeration).[27] As Lazonick and O'Sullivan note:

> The 200 largest manufacturing corporations held 47 per cent of all United States corporate assets in 1947, 56 per cent in 1957 and 59 per cent in 1967... Between 1948 and 1955 only ten per cent of acquired assets were in the 'pure conglomerate' category, in 1964–71 35 per cent and in 1972–79 46 per cent. [Of the top 148 companies] the mean number of lines of business was 5.2 in 1950 and 9.7 in 1975. (1997: 16–17)

This process started to slow in the 1970s both because of recession and because the market had begun to be exhausted. The process itself created large corporations that would later be prime targets for divisional buyouts and break up of their assets. The process of conglomeration, its slowdown, and then also declining economic conditions, mainly provided business for the investment banks in the form of bond issues for debt financing (Jensen 1993: 837). Clients were increasingly aware of their value to the investment banks and increasingly tended to employ in-house finance specialists with a better understanding of what the banks did. The net effect was to increase competition between the investment banks and reduce the effectiveness of the syndicates as a way of controlling clients, second tier banks and, ultimately, overall fee revenues. This was exacerbated by the Securities and Amendments Act of 1975 which ended fixed minimum commission rates for brokerage services and resulted in both new discount brokerages and sharp falls in rates, particularly to large institutional investors and sharp falls in profits to the brokers. Other fee sources and scale of services now became important. As a result, the investment banks underwent a series of mergers in the 1970s to reduce their numbers and also to extend their operations across the range of the securities business. The 1933 Glass-Steagall Act that had separated commercial and investment banking still remained in force.[28] However, from the first tier of investment banking, banks like Goldman Sachs, and from the retail end, banks like Merrill Lynch, emerged as new broader organisations with branch offices and larger staff. As Hayes notes this was a very different kind of staff:

> [T]he major investment firms have aggressively recruited the top MBA students from leading business schools. The profile of the sought-after professional has changed over the years. An earlier interest in social and family background has given way to searches for the brightest, most articulate, and most attractive candidates available, regardless of background. In 1965, for instance, almost half of Morgan Stanley's partners were listed in the *Social Register*; from then through 1976, only 6 of the 32 new partners admitted carried this imprimatur of blueblood background. (Hayes 1979: 160)[29]

Reflected in changes like these, the banks now had a more aggressive strategy to pursue new areas of business and new clients. One new area of business was the expansion of junk bonds (Altman 1992: 78; Thore 1995: 155–62). Drexel Burnham and Lambert, formed through two mergers 1973 and 1976, pioneered the expansion of junk bond trading (Bruck 1989; Anders 1992, chp 5). As a minor part of their business many brokers had units dealing in the securities of firms that had fallen below investment grade – an increasing problem during the 1970s. Junk bonds carry a higher interest rate than investment grade bonds. The now infamous Michael Milken at Drexel marketed these downgraded bonds to clients as good investments on the basis that the spread or difference between the interest rate on the bonds and either the interest rate on Treasury Securities or the Fed Funds Rate (the interest rate for commercial banks overnight lending to each other) was higher than the genuine risk of default on the bonds – these were basically sound firms fallen on temporarily bad times (due to the overall economic environment). The bonds were thus described to clients as high yield rather than bad risk. Junk bonds typically trade at interest rates of 3–4% above graded bonds. In 1977 Milken introduced a further innovation by actually underwriting the issue of junk bonds (rather than brokering former investment grade bonds). The justification then became fourfold. The bonds were either issued by firms temporarily fallen on bad times or by a new broader range of firms with good growth prospects but who were traditionally ignored by investment bankers. The capital injected through the bond issue would provide a means for the firm to grow (either by merger, restructuring or through a buyout of one kind or another) reducing the risk of default. The bonds were not only a good investment in the sense of the high interest rate compared to the risk of default but should default seem likely the risk could be offset by buying a portfolio with a range of junk bonds – if properly constructed any given default would be offset by the high interest earned across the portfolio of bonds. Furthermore if default seemed likely the original bonds could be honoured by generating a new larger issue of bonds that generated the capital to cover the interest rate payments and/or the value of the original bonds at the point they matured. All that was required was an intermediary to offer portfolios (banks, insurance firms and mutual funds who are able to create financial products), a more 'sophisticated' network of investors (including the former), and a syndication system for junk bonds – the combination of which the investors' participation and Milken's expertise and staff could provide.

The 1980s and the dominance of non-venture PEF (the rise of buyouts)

What the changes in investment banking created then was a new infra-structure for investment that could dovetail with PEF, particularly LBOs.[30] PEF could be part of the new broader business focus of investment banking and investment banking could offer a new set of opportunities for PEF. It could provide the financing expertise and services for the debt issued by PEF for any particular deal and which would be used in conjunction with PEF's use of the capital invested in the funds. Financing could be anything from traditional underwriting to the issuing of higher risk (high yield/junk) bonds. Investment banks could also provide access to an expanded network of contacts. The effectiveness of this network would, particularly from the mid-1980s, increase the speed and flexibility of PEF LBO funds since it meant they could put together bid offers and counter-offers much more quickly than if they had to seek out debt financing sources in a series of individual solicitations (Burrough and Helyar 2004: 141). When they needed to put together a debt structure it would now be possible to do so on the basis of a couple of phone calls and a series of focused meetings. In addition to providing a nodal point from which debt structures could be put together the network could also double as an effective means of access to possible buyouts since investment banks also operated consultancy arms, had links into legal and accounting firms and worked on equity and bond issues with larger publicly listed companies (Anders 1992: 39–40). Further, it provided access to institutional investors that might invest in the original PEF funds. During the 1980s institutional investors became the largest source of investment in PEF, providing 40–50% of total commitments to PEF funds and with public and private pension funds providing the majority of that.[31] In the 1980s then, the changes in investment banking, the changes in the regulation of institutional investors, in the culture of institutional investment and in the incentives to undertake investment based on capital gains tax and on SEC regulation came together to result in a sharp increase in investment in venture capital and PEF buyout funds.[32]

Vintage year is the year in which a fund ceases solicitation and becomes operable. According to Kaplan and Schoar's data for the US (2005: 1795 and 1802) over three quarters of funds begun in the 1980s were venture capital but the size of non-venture buyout funds was significantly larger – averaging around $400 million compared to around $100 million.[33] The number of new venture funds increased sharply 1982–84 – 28 created in 1982, 68 in 1984; a peak only again attained in 1987. Buyout funds rose from six created in 1983 to a high of 29 in 1987.[34] According to Fenn, Liang and Prowse (1995: 15) the year on year commitment to funds increased for venture capital until 1984 and then stabilised. Year on year commitments to funds for non-venture capital grew until 1988. Their data, over a slightly longer period, also emphasises the scale and differences of commitments between venture and non-venture PEF:

> Cumulative commitments to private equity partnerships over 1980–94 totalled $127 billion. Of this total, $33 billion was committed to partnerships dedicated to venture capital whilst a greater amount, $94 billion, was committed to partnerships dedicated to non-venture investments. (1995: 15)

Commitments to the funds are not of course a measure of investments made by the funds. The 1994 totals to some degree reflect a residual of PEF commitments because the end of the 1980s saw a sharp fall in both commitments to new funds and to the total of actual investment by funds. The key point, however, is the greater growth in PEF buyout funds.[35]

Why did investment in non-venture capital PEF increase on a scale that venture capital did not? After all, as far as the state was concerned, one key intention of its interventions in the late 1970s and early 1980s was to produce an environment conducive to small business investment. One might argue that venture capital experienced initial increases but then suffered in comparison to non-venture PEF for three reasons. First, those few venture capital investments that were made in the 1970s were undertaken in extremely difficult conditions. Venture capitalists had to be confident in the venture for the investment to occur at all and for it to ultimately become an IPO. The success rate of actual venture capital undertaken was therefore high in the 1970s and the industry experienced a growing reputation. As Gupta (2000) also notes the culture of venture capitalists, particularly the West Coast was one of highly specialised and committed individuals with good networks of access to business academia and the burgeoning new technologies located nearby.[36] These obsessive individuals in the early venture capital firms were not necessarily all about the bottom line and their obsession tended to result in good returns in the long run. Apple and a whole host of other companies would be beneficiaries of this (Rind 1981: 171).[37] Later, however, the increase in the number of ventures and the increase in the rate they were brought to market reduced the care and the diversity of products, particularly in the key hi-tech markets (Sohl 2003: 7–8). As Jensen notes:

> Between 1977 and 1984, venture capitalists invested over $400 million in 43 different manufacturers of Winchester disk drives; initial public offerings of common stock infused additional capital in excess of $800 million. In mid-1983, the capital markets assigned a value of $5.4 billion to twelve publicly traded, venture capital-backed hard disk drive manufacturers – yet by the end of 1984, the value assigned to those companies had plummeted to $1.4 billion. (Jensen 1993: 842)

Second, the characteristics and motivations of institutional investors and investment banking were a major influence on the emerging environment for venture capital and PEF. From the point of view of these participants nurturing innovation and growing small businesses to create a long run dynamic to the economy is simply an unintended consequence of their own core concerns with returns. If there are advantages to non-venture capital funds then that is where the majority of investment will flow (Cohen 2007: 33).[38] By definition, the individual deal sizes of venture capitalists will be smaller than non-venture capital funds that focus on larger sized firms. Since any fund has limited numbers of staff it also has a limited capacity to make and monitor deals (Gompers and Lerner 2000: 295–6).[39] If a venture capital and non-venture capital fund both pursued the same number of deals based on the same criteria of effective management then, all other things being equal, the non-venture fund can use committed capital more rapidly and thus potentially generate returns more quickly as well as justify to investors a larger size of fund. This will be attractive to institutional investors because it meets their criteria for investing in large blocks and because it provides the potential for more rapid returns on any given investment undertaken by the fund – helping the trustees of pension funds to justify the reinterpretation of the prudent man concept.[40] Further, the investment banks have far more of an incentive to facilitate non-venture PEF because underwriting fees for any debt issued for the original deal (a leveraged buyout or partial investment), and the various other fees relating to consulting on aspects of the deal, and any eventual sell-on of the buy-out, are related to the total value of the different aspects of the deal – the debt issue, the later equity offering of the firm etc.: the larger the value of the deal, then the greater the total returns to the investment banks and the fewer staff required to generate those returns (increasing margins). For, example, looking back at three large LBOs from the mid-1980s (Revco, Safeway and Allied Stores) and a refinancing (Phillips Petroleum), a report to Congress found:

> The investment banks acting as advisers and financial managers for the LBOs earned fees ranging from $49 million to about $127 million for these and other services, including providing temporary 'bridge' loans... [as well as underwriting securities to finance the deals]. Similarly, other participants – primarily banks, but also attorneys, accountants and others received fees from these transactions that ranged form $38 million to about $166 million. Total fees for the deals as a percentage of the purchase price ranged from 4.5% to 7.5%. (Burnett *et al.* 1991: 9)

The third reason is that the economic environment of the 1980s was one that created obvious opportunities for non-venture capital PEF.[41] The 1980s was a period characterised by underlying economic growth, split by the recession of 1981–82 and the market crash of 1987. One major aspect of that period of growth was a general rise in equity prices and heightened merger and acquisition activity that helped fuel individual equity prices, in turn creating a sense of growing wealth and helping to motivate higher consumption. This came on the back of the growth of conglomeration by large US corporations in the 1960s. Conglomeration and merger often meant that firms had assets whose values were a significant proportion of their market capitalisation. Further, although equity prices might be rising this could be highly variable since growth by assimilation often resulted in a fall in the ratio of profits to size. Large conglomerates were thus obvious targets for partial buyouts that spun-off some aspect of their business.[42] At the same time the growth of mergers and acquisitions created a mentality amongst firms that they too could grow in this way and that if they did not they would be the target of other firms. This led medium sized firms to think about growing by merger to become larger publicly listed companies. This operated in tandem with a further incentive: for larger publicly listed firms to reduce their market capitalisation by buying back their issued equity (taking on board a minority private investor) and for publicly listed companies to seek a partner to delist the firm through an assisted management buyout.

Both directions – towards larger publicly-listed companies and towards reducing the public listing exposure for larger companies – entailed debt creation as part of the financing. As Ben Bernanke noted in his original guise as an academic economist, prior to becoming Chairman of the Fed, this made the 1980s after 1981–82 unusual as a generally upward business cycle period in which debt-asset ratios of corporations did not fall (Bernanke, Campbell and Whited 1990: 255) and in which the corporate debt-GNP ratio actually increased.[43] Between 1976 and 1990 there were 35,000 mergers and acquisitions with a total value of $2.6 trillion adjusted to 1992 dollars (Jensen 1993: 838). 'Between 1979 and 1989 there were over 2,000 leveraged buyouts (LBOs) valued in [total in] excess of $250 billion.' (Opler and Titman 1993: 1985). In terms of buyouts of publicly listed companies the total annual value of deals increased from under $1 billion in 1980 to a peak of approximately $60 billion in 1988 (Kaplan and Stein 1993: 313). PEF simply contributed to this boom. KKR provides the most prominent example.[44]

KKR and the growth in LBOs

Jerome Kohlberg and the cousins, Henry Kravis and George Roberts left the investment bank Bear Sterns in 1976 to form KKR (Bartlett 1991; Anders 1992; Kaufman and Englander 1993; Baker and Smith 1998). At Bear Sterns Kohlberg had worked on management buyouts (MBOs) of small businesses and wanted to transfer this expertise to the potentially lucrative PEF sector. KKR were one of the first private equity firms to focus on, and develop a structure and strategy for, buyouts of publicly listed companies. They undertook solicitation to create a fund, used some of the capital of the fund in conjunction with debt to undertake a buyout, and structured a separate shell company to administer the acquired company and feed returns back to the fund and its investors. The signal for KKR's interest in a given buyout opportunity was a combination of factors. The initial signal was usually whether a company was experiencing some kind of acquisition threat – usually the purchase of its stock by a competitor who intended to oust the current management. This would result in the company employing a consultant from the investment banking world with a brief to advise on avoiding a hostile takeover of one kind or another.[45] Kohlberg in particular and particularly in the early 1980s, had a good reputation and contacts in investment banking as able to provide an alternative. KKR tended to avoid hostile takeovers, partly because Kohlberg as senior partner was averse to the notion and partly because being branded a 'corporate raider' made it difficult to solicit investment from pension funds (Burrough and

Helyar 2004: 162).[46] The consultants would tend to support a buyout and KKR involvement since this would generate fees for other arms of the investment bank. This was something that the management of the potential acquisition would also be disposed towards since it could be both lucrative and offer the potential (if not always the reality) for them to maintain some control.

KKR's own interest hinged on a further four main aspects of the business. First whether the business had a wide range of assets due to previous conglomeration and merger activity that could be disposed of to pay off some portion of the debt used in the buyout. Second, whether the business's pre-buyout profits were sufficient that they could be transferred to cover some of the interest payable on the debt generated in the buyout. Interest payments on debt were tax deductible thus some of the difference between pre- and post-tax profits could effectively be transferred to debt servicing.[47] Third, whether there was clear scope for cost-cutting and revenue-increases to improve the margins of and/or expand the core business. Fourth, whether, based on the first three factors, it was possible to think of the current share price of the company as 'undervalued' since this would allow the buyout to proceed by offering a premium above the current traded share price.

These features recur in various combinations in almost all of the buyouts KKR undertook in the 1980s. The first, however, was of Houdaille Industries in 1979:

> It was the acquisition of Houdaille Industries – the first modern leveraged buyout of a mid-size public company – that woke up everyone on Wall Street. Though far from qualifying as a large corporation, [the] Houdaille [deal] was a blockbuster by the standards of the time... Perhaps more than any single transaction it set the stage for an explosion of leveraged buyouts during the 1980s. (Baker and Smith 1998: 65)[48]

Houdaille was an industrial conglomerate with a low level of debt and high pre-tax profits to revenue of around $50 million. It had been targeted by Jacobs who were buying up its available stock and the CEO, Gerald Saltarelli, had brought in Peter Sachs of Goldman Sachs to advise on how to respond. Sachs put Kohlberg and the CEO in touch and, despite Saltarelli's initial misgivings about debt financing, Sachs helped to persuade him of the feasibility of a leveraged buyout. The deal produced new innovations created by Deloitte to restructure the tax liabilities of a business and involved the creation of shell companies to administer the acquisition (Baker and Smith 1998: 71 and 73).[49] The SEC took a strong interest in the original deal but focused on adequate disclosure in the share prospectus to ensure that shareholders interest (fair value for their shares) would be met and left aside any broader issue of the potential effects of the buyout on other parties. KKR offered $40 per share, compared to the $25 it was initially traded at and the $36 it eventually closed at, and Houdaille was bought for a total of $355 million. Sachs earned around $3 million in fees, Saltarelli earned around $5.2 million on his own shares and although Houdaille did not achieve the revenues and profit levels projected by KKR,[50] asset sales and some refinancing meant that it did meet its interest rate payments and was widely considered a success by the finance industry, who had earned fees, and by management groups looking for alternatives to mergers and hostile takeovers:

> Houdaille's successful financing attracted a horde of new institutions into providing financing for leveraged deals, as an increasing number of corporations presented themselves or their subsidiaries as candidates for leveraged buyouts. In 1981 – a year in which KKR did 6 deals – just short of 100 buyouts were recorded nationwide, despite double digit inflation and soaring interest rates. In the recession year of 1982 the overall number swelled to 164. By the end of 1983 230 buyouts had closed in the US, amounting to $4.5 billion in total financing. From then until the first great buyout craze came to an end in 1990, the average annual number of leveraged buyouts rose to more than 300 per year. Throughout the period, KKR focused its efforts on relatively few but large transactions. (Baker and Smith 1998: 74–5)

As Anders states, 'Business leaders attitudes towards debt did an about face switching to a radical new tolerance of big borrowings... [and] KKR's market impact was far greater than the mere number of its deals.' (1992: 37–8). 'By 1983 Kohlberg Kravis claimed an average annual return of 62.7% for their investors.' (Burrough and Helyar 2004: 140). Accessing financing and soliciting investment for funds became easier and PEF buyout fund sizes grew. KKR undertook a series of high profile buyouts of increasingly large companies: Wometco for $1.07 billion in 1984, Storer Communications for $2.43 billion in 1985, Owens-Illinois ($4.6 billion), Safeway ($4.7 billion) and Beatrice foods ($6.2/$8.7 billion) in 1986, and Duracell for $1.8 billion in 1988.[51] Kohlberg himself was a high profile casualty of this growth – suffering a brain tumour in 1983 and following basic disagreement with Kravis and Roberts about the general trajectory towards larger and larger deals, and more aggressive investment banking strategies, his role in the partnership was ended in 1987 (Burrough and Helyar 2004: 141–5).

The most prominent deal for which the 1980s is now remembered was KKR's LBO of RJR Nabisco. As Burrough and Helyar note: it defined the 'zeitgeist of an age' (2004: xii).[52] The company was formed by the $4.9 billion acquisition of Nabisco, a food corporation, by RJ Reynolds Tobacco in 1985. Prior to any expressed interest in a buyout its 1988 share price was $55. In October 1988 the current management, led by CEO F. Ross Johnson announced an MBO offering $75 per share valuing the total LBO at $17.6 billion. The bid level was set strategically to specifically deter counter-bids from perceived possible rivals such as KKR – being more than twice the value of their largest previous deal (Beatrice). However, Johnson had miscalculated: the announcement led to the shares trading at over $77, Milken and Drexel had not been consulted on the deal and not all of the RJR Nabisco board favoured Johnson's proposal. Further, since the deal seemed to be structured to provide Johnson with an extremely lucrative stake in the buyout worth tens of millions of dollars it quickly resulted in an avalanche of negative publicity regarding Johnson's current lifestyle as CEO and his future prospects. KKR quickly put together a counter offer of $90 per share and a bidding war ensued, with Johnson and his backers eventually offering $112 and KKR $109. For a variety of reasons, the lower KKR bid was ultimately accepted by the board (Burrough and Helyar 2004: 485, 497–515). KKR's bond issue included a reset mechanism – $4 billion in bonds would reset to their original value in April 1991 – stabilising the issue and making it more attractive to investors by guaranteeing the issue against trading at lower prices in the future – allowing a stronger guarantee that the $109 share price could be met. KKR also gave stronger assurances that the food arm (Nabisco) would not all be sold off and that employee redundancies would be limited. On February 9th 1989 the buyout of the market capitalisation of the firm was completed – using an initial $16.9 billion of debt and $2 billion from KKRs own PEF funds. The overall cost of the buyout was $26.4 billion – the largest LBO until the mid-2000s. Fees alone accounted for around $1 billion:

> Drexel Burnham reaped $227 million in fees from a $3.5 billion bridge loan. It got even more from selling junk bonds. Merrill Lynch got $109 million for its role in the bridge financing. A syndicate of 200 banks collected $325 million for committing $14.5 billion of loans. Kohlberg Kravis itself collected $75 million in fees from its investors. Morgan Stanley and Wasserstein Perella got $25 million apiece. (Burrough and Helyar 2004: 508)

The RJR Nabisco buyout added to growing concerns created by the increasing prominence of LBOs. This was especially so in the wake of the October 19th 1987 market crash because the crash did not immediately result in a slow down in LBOs. The Black Monday crash had wiped 23% off the value of listed equity – creating losses for the banks and publicly listed corporations. Some corporations now looked undervalued in terms of their equity price compared to their assets. Asset stripping as a specific motive for some LBOs thus became more of an issue. Further, the larger diversified investment and commercial banks could offset their losses from the crash by earning fees from LBOs and other institutional investors might also see some of their losses offset if LBO funds posted high returns.[53] The crash thus helped to create a perception of LBOs as parasites feeding on a wounded economy. Just as importantly, the continuation of LBOs raised a central problem in a period of economic pessimism – though greater levels of debt had become an accepted aspect of business the crash was a stark reminder that debt was still debt and however innovatively it was constructed it would eventually have to be repaid.

As a result PEF and LBOs became both an economic and political issue with various dynamics. The motives and practices of the private equity firms and of the investment banks were increasingly brought into question from 1987.[54] Were they simply extracting value from firms or contributing to the improvement of individual firms and to the economic structure of the nation? The *degree* of leverage of the buyouts was a central concern since it raised questions over how the debt would be serviced in the long term and whether it affected both the stability of the acquired company (affecting employment levels and terms and conditions) and of the economy as a whole. The *nature* of the leverage was also brought into question in two ways. First, it raised issues regarding the subject of tax since PEF not only looked to subsidise debt servicing by offsetting profits against debt (aiming to reduce corporation tax)[55] but also made use of shell companies and accounting practices to reduce overall tax liabilities. Second, the use of new developments in finance – particularly the expanded use of junk bonds raised issues about the risks involved in the debt, how well those risks were understood and what effect they might have on the finance system and the state if defaults were to occur. These were precisely the same issues that were to re-emerge in 2007 in both the US and UK.

It was the issue of risk and its link to liquidity that ultimately brought the growth of PEF in the 1980s and of large LBOs of publicly listed companies to an end.

Debt structures, leverage and liquidity

PEF LBOs are undertaken with a combination of equity drawn from the private equity funds and debt. As we shall look at in more detail in Chapter 5 the majority of any buyout will be financed using debt. The amount of debt generated compared to some measure of the value of the acquisition (the ratio of debt to capital, net debt to operating profits etc.) is used to calculate the leverage of the buyout. The debt is typically divided or layered. The layering represents a descending scale of priority for the creditors if a default, insolvency or bankruptcy should occur. At the top is senior debt – usually loans arranged by one or more commercial banks.[56] Below are forms of junior or subordinated debt – mainly issues of corporate bonds, which may be junk bonds, and various forms of debt that have the potential to become equity (options or warrants, equity swaps or payment in kind on equity).[57] The debt is secured or collateralised against the tangible and intangible assets of the acquisition and an interest rate is paid on the debt, as well as, for most forms, principal payments to meet the capital sum of the debt.

Kaplan and Stein (1993) analyse a sample of 124 LBOs undertaken between 1980 and 1989 of publicly listed companies where the value of the deal exceeds $100 million. The total value of the deals is over $132 billion. They identify a series of trends based on a key switching point in 1985.[58] In terms of the levels of debt, leverage levels increased after 1985. Debt increased to an average of over 90% of the total value of the buyout.[59] The prices paid in deals tended to be higher relative to the cash flow of the firm – indicative of increased competition between private equity firms to secure a buyout. This in turn created an increased reliance on successful asset sales and/or future increases in net cash flow from the firm to service and pay down debt (1993: 325, 328). After 1985 39% of the deals had asset sales factored into the feasibility of the buyout. Further a buyout with an average debt-related obligation to pre-buyout operating cash flow would have to increase its net cash flow by 141% to meet those obligations. Buyouts were thus increasingly becoming vulnerable if they should fail to achieve their post-buyout goals.

In terms of the way debt was structured in the LBOs two main trends are identified. First, senior debt provided by commercial banks represents 70% of the total debt prior to 1985 but falls to 42% in 1985 and varies within the 50–57% range thereafter. The interest rate spread (its rate above the Fed Funds Rate)[60] paid on that debt increase after 1985 and the banks increasingly require higher principal payments on the debt, reducing the period over which the capital sum is repaid. The banks also increasingly benefited from agreed deferments on interest payments on some of the subordinated debt – essentially enabling higher initial payments to senior debt (1993: 333, 338).[61] The combination tends to indicate that the commercial banks were aware that the increase in the number and size of deals was having two effects. It was, because of competition in LBOs, increasing the relative prices paid for acquisitions and, because of those higher relative prices, it was increasing the potential that large debt levels might be difficult for the acquisitions to service. As such, the banks were aware that deals were becoming more risky and were responding by structuring their loans in more defensive ways to reduce their own risk. In so doing more of the risk (of non-payment due to defaults) was transferred to junior debt. Second, after 1985 the use of that junior debt increases markedly. The public issue of debt – corporate bonds etc. increases to over 17% of the total value of every deal in the sample and 54% of those deals involve an issue of junk bonds (of which over two thirds involve some deferred interest securities).[62] The use of forms of payment that do not involve cash also become more important, such as payment in kind. This tends to indicate that debt servicing involved longer run and more costly forms of junior debt – high interest rate junk bonds, securities that provide lenders with a stake in the firm etc.

The net effect was to create increasingly risky and more fragile debt structures. This in turn increased the potential for default on some or all of the debt, as well as increasing the possibility that the company itself would become insolvent. These potentials and possibilities were facets of the buyout in the sense that they were inherent in the debt structure and the operating expectations factored into the acquisition of the firm. But they might also be triggered by changes in the economic and financial environment that could affect more fragile debt structures and the ability of the company to service its debt (because it did not achieve expected asset sales or because its cash flow projections were unattained). Of the 41 deals in the sample prior to 1985, only one defaulted on its debt, whilst 22 of 83 did so in the following period. These were particularly associated with the issuing of junk bonds (1993: 314, 354). According to Kaplan and Stein this tends to support an 'Overheated buyout market hypothesis':

> [B]eginning in 1985, junk bond investors, attracted by the success of earlier deals, pour large amounts of money into the buyout market. This pushes up prices in general, and especially, prices in those deals in which junk bonds are actually used. Other, less aggressive classes of lenders... react defensively to the 'demand push' from the junk bond markets... Even more so than the bankers, other interested parties are also successful in extracting money from the deals up front. Ostensibly well-informed players such as management, buyout promoters, and investment bankers are increasingly able to earn compensation simply for completing a transaction, rather than having their fortunes ride on its eventual success or failure. This, instead of providing a system of checks and balances, these 'smart money' participants may be quite eager to go along, even with deals that they view as precarious. (Kaplan and Stein 1993: 345)[63]

Liquidity is usually defined as the degree to which an asset or security of one kind or another can be traded without radically altering the conditions of the market for that asset or security – typical price levels (Melton 1985: 152–3). This liquidity is sustained in turn by the liquidity of the market itself, which is based on some standard conditions. If there are numerous willing buyers and sellers and an active market (high volumes of transactions) then that market is liable to be relatively liquid and any given asset or security traded in it is liable to be more liquid than it would be under differing market circumstances. The expansion of the junk bond market can be viewed as an expansion in its liquidity. That expansion increased the availability of credit and thus had a knock on effect to the liquidity of any linked market – particularly ones that were making increased use of that credit. The stability of the junk bond market, therefore, had important ramifications for LBOs. It was not the only source of liquidity but it was a significant one.[64] It affected the form of debt being used, the overall debt structure and strategy of the financiers, and the degree to which larger LBOs could be put together under competition from rival bids. The stability of LBOs in turn, of course, affects the stability of the junk bond market because defaults affect perceptions and trading volume. What became clear at the time was that the junk bond market of the 1980s was essentially unstable and it was in the context of the unwinding of this unstable market that the growth of PEF came to an end at the end of the decade.

Unstable liquidity: the rise of the junk bond market, the collapse of the thrifts and the move to legislation

As already noted, in conjunction with other basic changes in investment banking, in 1977 Michael Milken of Drexel Burnham and Lambert began underwriting the issue of junk bonds which were marketed as high yield bonds whose actual risks were either lower than they appeared to be or could be offset by buying portfolios of such bonds or through successive restructurings of the debt. Institutional investors, due to changes in the law and in investment culture, began to buy these bonds. Events then gave this market a further push by providing a further source of demand – the thrift associations (Kindleberger 2005: chps 5, 9 and 10).

Thrift institutions – savings and loan associations and mutual savings banks – were established after the Great Depression because after the wave of bank defaults of the time commercial banks now either operated credit check systems that restricted access to mortgages for the poor and/or offered those mortgages at higher and often unaffordable interest rates.[65] The thrifts operated under a Federal mandate to supply affordable mortgages for the working class. To prevent the thrifts becoming subject to the financial instabilities experienced by banks in the early 1930s they were prohibited from high risk investments types – corporate bonds, property speculation etc. As such they relied on savings deposits to finance mortgage lending and operated an interest rate differential between the two to maintain their capitalisation – a slightly higher interest rate on mortgages than was paid on deposits.[66] In order to prevent this relation being undermined by competition for savers from commercial banks Regulation Q was included in the 1933 Glass-Steagall Act. Regulation Q placed limits on the interest rates banks could offer. In 1966 the Q differential placed ceilings on savings deposit interest rates which were 0.25% higher for thrifts on its longer term savings certificates than for the commercial banks (Glasberg and Skidmore 1997: 76).[67] However, the reorganisation of the securities and investment banking businesses in the 1970s that consolidated the banks, whilst extending their size and scope, created a new form of competition from quasi-banks like Merrill Lynch and from new commercial sources, like Sears, both of whom were not subject to the Q differential. At the same time interest rates on government securities such as Treasury Bills began to rise as the government issued more debt and the economy suffered from inflation. The net effect was to reduce the flow of new savings to the thrifts. This manifested as a fundamental problem of maintaining the capitalisation and solvency of the thrifts. The initial response was the Depository Institutions Deregulation and Monetary Control (DIDMCA) Act of 1980 which enabled the thrifts to offer credit cards and alternatives to standard checking accounts. Checking accounts had always had to be at 0% interest rates and the thrifts could now offer negotiable order withdrawal (NOWs) variations that paid interest, allowed cheques and immediate withdrawals. The Act also mandated the gradual phasing out of the Glass-Steagall interest rate ceilings (Johnson 1999: 259). Furthermore the Act increased the deposit insurance that provided a guarantee to savers that their savings were safe, designed to prevent a run on the bank. This was increased from $40,000 to $100,000.

However, savings continued to decline and the fundamental problem remained.[68] General interest rates reached 15% in 1981 (Bruck 1989: 91).[69] Mortgages interest rates were fixed for the term of the mortgage – before the 1970s era of inflation those interest rates were generally lower. Thus the total stock of mortgages held by the thrifts tended to be at lower interest rates than the current interest rate paid on savings deposits. Mortgages are of a much longer duration than any savings product sold by the thrifts. To prevent this from becoming a problem, savings levels had to be at least maintained and ideally grown – since this would facilitate further mortgage lending at a current higher interest rate that could be used to offset some of the potential capital reductions created by the historic accumulation of mortgages. The decline in savings essentially meant a reduction in the ability of the thrifts to honour savings and offer mortgages. Insolvency remained a core problem unless mortgage rates became flexible and unless thrifts could attract more savers or diversify their investments to recapitalise from other sources. This became a more urgent problem as thrifts started to actually become insolvent. In 1981 Richard Pratt, chairman of the regulator, the Federal Home Loan Bank board, testified to Congress that 80% of the 4,600 thrifts were suffering operating losses and a third were not viable (Bartley in Barth *et al.* 2004: xvi). In 1982 Congress responded with the Garn-St. Germain Act which deregulated the thrifts making them virtually indistinguishable from commercial banks (Johnson 1999: 250). The Act gave the agencies new powers to close and consolidate failing thrifts, ended deposit differentials between commercial banks and thrifts, enabled the thrifts to offer forms of variable interest rate mortgages, and allowed them to diversify their asset portfolio, allowing them to broaden their investment forms up to fixed percentages of their total assets.[70]

The content of the 1980 and 1982 Acts had a crucial impact on liquidity and the junk bond market. The 1980 Act guaranteed deposit accounts up to $100,000 but did not prevent multiple accounts. A new market therefore emerged: Savings and Loan banks began to offer $100,000 savings certificates and brokers would act as intermediaries for large investors breaking down larger sums into $100,000 units, each fully guaranteed by the state. On the basis of the 1982 Act the thrifts then began to channel this new source of capital into real estate speculation and the emerging junk bond market. Thus: 'The originally conservative residential mortgage finance industry was transformed into a free-wheeling high risk money machine, completely insured by the federal government.' (Johnson 1999: 262).

The problem then became, in various ways, the nature of the liquidity being injected into the LBO market. As Kaplan and Stein's research indicates many of the participants in LBOs became aware that the new expanded source of finance brought particular problems. A ready additional financing capacity pushed up the prices being paid for LBO acquisitions and thus reduced the capacity of the company to service its debt and prosper, thereby increasing the risk of default. Senior debt holders began to respond by structuring debt in defensive ways that actually compounded the problem and increased the reliance on forms of junior debt at higher interest rates and carrying greater risks. The private equity firms had no great incentive to draw back from buyouts and the various advisors had no great incentive to advise against larger and more costly deals because they could structure the buyout to extract more of the returns upfront. This did not mean that firms would necessarily become insolvent but it provided no check and balance on the growing fragility of the use of debt. Furthermore, the link between the thrifts, whose capitalisation was essentially federally guaranteed, the junk bond market and buyouts created a whole tier of further problems for the thrifts and ultimately for the state.

Some of what followed was predatory, some morally dubious and some simply illegal – much of the controversy was concentrated on Milken and Drexel, Burnham and Lambert (Bruck 1989). Milken underwrote issues of junk bonds bought by the thrifts, insurance companies, pension funds etc. The issues might be larger than the sums actually required in the individual buyout. This provided surplus capital to the financiers that could then reinvest it in other junk bond issues underwritten by Milken. Milken controlled the vast majority of the junk bond market – access to investors essentially came through his syndications – as such there was strong pressure on participants to comply in any given investment in order to prevent future exclusion (mirroring in a more concentrated and less salubrious way how first tier investment banks had previously controlled syndication for AAA debt):

Every business and profession has its network, through which referrals and favours are exchanged. What set this one apart was its utter dominance by a single individual. Milken and Milken alone was in a position to dispense favours. He had the product. He had the trading capital... He dominated not only the primary market (of original issuance) but the secondary market (trading). As one junk aficionado put it in a frequently uttered refrain, 'Michael *is* the market.' (Bruck 1989: 95)

Significantly, this created the power to pressurise refinancing – when it appeared a debtor might default a new issue of junk bonds would be issued at higher interest rates to ensure the interest on previous issues were met. This in turn sustained a rising junk bond market – bonds were paying relatively high interest rates, defaults seemed to be avoidable (despite the higher interest rates being paid by the borrowers) and there seemed to be a constantly growing and ready demand for the bonds. That demand was further facilitated because some thrifts were controlled by Milken associates. For example, Columbia Savings and Loan – a typical small thrift was bought by the Spiegel family in 1974. The thrift began to invest heavily in the junk bond market in 1982 – offering depositors relatively high interest long term savings products and using the capital to buy higher interest rate portfolios of bonds. The attractiveness of the savings products (partly because of the deposit guarantee, partly because of the interest rate) helped expand the thrift to become one of the largest in the market. The Milken family, through a series of trusts and associated companies owned over 20% of Columbia.[71] In similar fashion some insurance organisations offering annuity products were also controlled by Milken associates.[72] Milken, as the centre of the growing junk bond market was also in a position to direct large institutional investors to his favoured mutual funds, who would in turn invest in his bond issues. In 1983 junk bond issues grew to a then annual record $5 billion but continued to grow thereafter, quickly exceeding $30 billion (Thore 1995: 158).

The underlying problem was that a rising junk bond market and successive refinancing was tied into companies whose cash flows either could not meet the interest payments or would, if problems arose, have difficulties doing so. Furthermore, investment in junk bonds was not solving the underlying problems of the thrifts, since thrifts continued to become insolvent throughout the 1980s. Between 1979 and 1985, 300 thrifts failed (Johnson 1999: 261). But if the junk bond market (or the property market in which they also invested) should collapse there was an increasing perception that it would devastate the thrifts.[73] Further, any crackdown on the junk bond market to protect the thrifts would remove the main source of liquidity for debt financing that underpinned LBOs and thus the main strand in PEF of the time.

The problem began to manifest in early 1986 when the Fed started to increase short term interest rates after five years of general reductions. This was followed by a series of tax changes in 1986. The Reagan administration, faced with growing federal deficits, and criticism of its tax policy – that lower taxes, mainly favouring the wealthy, did not increase tax revenues – began to increase capital gains tax (though nowhere near the highs of the 1970s) and also to reduce the tax benefits of property speculation.[74] This was followed by the market crash of 1987 (and only a brief reduction in generally rising Fed interest rate levels).[75] This in turn was followed by an updating of legislation on hostile takeovers in 25 states facilitating the creation of 'poison pill' conditions attached to stock issues and purchases (Rosengren 1988; Kincaid 1988).[76]

The 1987 crash led to a growing perception that high yield bonds might well be junk and that defaults were an increasing likelihood. This caused a shift in investment towards Treasury securities and a further rise in average interest rates on junk bonds (the spread between the two rose to an average 6%, Mishkin 1992: 137). This in turn made refinancing more expensive and increased the potential for defaults – a problem that affected firms that had already been taken private and those that might be. However, though the crash reduced the market capitalisation of publicly listed corporations increasing the costs of credit for some firms it also increased the attractiveness of some potential buyouts because individual publicly listed firms might be at a low valuation compared to their capital assets. Buyouts did not therefore disappear and the junk bond market did not immediately collapse. Rather, in conjunction with buyout PEF new kinds of private equity fund began to emerge – mezzanine funds and debt distress funds. Mezzanine funds are explored in Chapter 2, debt distress funds were designed to buy up debt assets that distressed holders were forced to sell at a discount to realise capital. Three such funds emerged in the late 1980s (Fenn, Liang and Prowse 1995) and these were to become an increasingly common feature of private equity later.

The fact that defaults began to increase did begin to affect the liquidity of the junk bond market, however. The link was made between an increase in failures among thrifts and defaults on bond issues, as well as problems over property speculation. Another 769 thrifts failed between 1986 and 1989. This created a further problem – the Federal deposit insurers relied on a combination of annual levies on the banks and sales of assets of failed thrifts to pay out on the insurance. The more thrifts that failed the greater the supply of thrift assets to be sold on at a discount, further reducing their value. This, in a cycle with declining property prices and the beginnings of problems in the junk bond markets meant that the accumulated reserves of the insurers were rapidly being used up – raising the knock on problem that they too would not be able to honour deposits, which might then generate a widespread run on the banks as depositors, aware of the fragility of the thrifts and of the insurers, raced to reclaim their money.[77] Treasury intervention to guarantee the guarantors then became a necessity. It was against this background that both the junk bond market and LBOs came under broader scrutiny and Congress began to consider new legislation.[78]

The complex network of personal relations across the junk bond market had created the potential for insider dealing. In 1985 a ring of investment bankers linked into the bond market were investigated by the Securities and Exchange Commission.[79] The investigation led on in 1986 to Ivan Boesky an associate of Milken who specialised in the trading of equities that were likely takeover targets (and might experience a sudden surge in their share prices). Boesky pleaded guilty to insider dealing and agreed to cooperate on a further investigation of Milken. In 1988 Milken was charged with numerous crimes including racketeering and was eventually sentenced to ten years (of which he served two). The adverse publicity for the junk bond market and the removal of the principal motivating agent able to coordinate refinancing helped to trigger the contraction of the junk bond market. A rise in Fed short term interest rates between May 1988 and March 1989 from 6.5% to 10% compounded the problem. This was further exacerbated in 1989 by the Financial Institutions Reform, Recovery and Enforcement Act (FIRREA) which, amongst other things, banned thrifts from investing in junk bonds.[80] At the same time The National Association of Insurance Commissioners (NAIC) placed new restrictions on the ability of insurance companies to invest in junk bonds – lasting through 1991. In the first eight months of 1989 alone there were more than $4 billion in defaults (Burrough and Helyar 2004: 512). Drexel, unable to syndicate some of the bond issues it had underwritten was forced to absorb them itself. Having also paid $650 million in fines relating to the Milken investigation Drexel filed for bankruptcy in 1990.

Without refinancing and against the background of more hostile economic conditions – a further though smaller stock market crash in October 1989 and the fall into recession in July 1990 – the default rate on junk bonds increased from 4% to 10%.[81] The related collapse of the thrifts was a national disaster:

> [I]nto the early 1990s 1,273 savings and loans with assets of $640 billion failed, 1,569 commercial and savings banks with $264 billion in assets failed and 2,330 credit unions with $4 billion in assets failed. The cost of resolving this crisis in the banking industry eventually surpassed $190 billion, the majority of which was paid for by the tax payer. (Barth *et al.* 2004: xi)[82]

By 1990, the linked issues of a broad based banking crisis, higher interest rates, a fall in confidence on equity markets, and a specific bond market crisis caused a rapid contraction in available credit and in liquidity.[83] As a result the tendency towards large LBOs and the growth of large scale PEF LBO funds came to a sudden halt. Conditions were not conducive to profit and the money dried up – though not completely. The number of new funds fell to 18 in 1990 and 6 in 1991 and new commitments totalled less than $10 billion (Kaplan and Schoar 2005: 2 and 36). Venture capital also suffered, with new funds falling to a low of 18 in 1991 and total new commitments decreasing by 68% (Gompers and Lerner 1998: 163; 2000: 285). Investment by funds fell to its lowest since the early 1980s and no new large deals were done. Completed deals also ran into trouble since debt structures and refinancing now became more problematic. KKR for example, faced mounting problems over RJR Nabisco despite successfully selling off some of the food arm's assets (including Del Monte), reducing costs, and increasing cash flow to meet initial debt servicing obligations.[84] The collapse in junk bond markets meant that the original bond issue was trading at a large discount in 1990. The reset mechanism on $4 billion of this debt obliged KKR to make up the difference in April 1991 (Friday 1990: 38). KKR did manage to secure a $6.9 billion refinancing package to buy back the issue but the exchange probably represented a large write down.

Conclusion

PEF LBOs grew markedly through the 1980s. By the end of the 1980s the PEF firms, based on an LLP structure, and the PEF funds, able to access capital from a range of institutional investors, were well established in the US. The collapse in the liquidity conditions that gave rise to the growth of PEF was, then, unlikely to herald the demise of PEF in the long term. Rather the 1980s set the pattern for how PEF would grow when other conditions became conducive to that growth. By the end of the 1980s PEF firms and funds were also well established in the UK. Local conditions in the UK were, however, different than in the US. We now move on to look at the conditions under which PEF emerged in the UK and the conditions under which PEF began to recover in the US. The central issue in both is that the growth of PEF was constrained by particular conditions. In the UK in the 1980s and early 1990s PEF LBOs did not achieve the scale that they had in the US. This was also the case for PEF LBOs in the US in the 1990s.

2
Constraints on the Growth of Private Equity Finance: The Emergence of Private Equity Finance in the UK and its Recovery in the US

Private equity finance emerged in the UK at around the same time as it emerged in the US. However, PEF LBOs did not achieve the same scales in the UK in the 1980s. The main reason for this was that many of the institutional and legal changes that facilitated PEF in the US occurred later in the UK. As a result PEF in the UK was unable to solicit funds on the same scale and unable to rely on the banks and capital markets for high levels of leverage on large levels of debt. PEF LBOs remained constrained by local conditions that restricted liquidity. PEF did grow during the 1980s and did experience a reduction at the end of the decade but did not achieve the same level of notoriety that the buyout of RJR Nabisco by KKR signalled. The conditions under which this would eventually occur were not achieved in the UK until the late 1990s when many of the local liquidity constraints were addressed and the links between US and UK PEF and capital markets became more pronounced.

The development of PEF in the US in the 1990s creates a more complex version of the patterns and issues that emerged in the 1980s. The dot.com boom provided the grounds for an unstable liquidity surge in the 1990s. The associated investment bubble in capital markets was partly a product of previous venture capital activity and had definite consequences for venture capital in the late 1990s. In turn the growth of venture capital and the specific conditions of economic growth in the US in the 1990s helped to shape the growth of PEF LBOs. In the 1990s PEF buyout activity both responded to the consequences of its own unstable growth in the 1980s and responded to the new markets for investment created by venture capital and driven by other sets of changes in the 1990s. As fund solicitation increased during the dot.com boom PEF experienced a capital surplus. To a degree UK PEF was a beneficiary of the growing surplus of capital created by growth in the US in the 1990s. I explore this transfer to the UK in Chapter 3. Here I set out the emergence of PEF in the UK and then the specific conditions of growth in the US in the 1990s that account for the manner in which PEF then developed and adapted in that decade. This provides the background to the growing integration of PEF in the UK and US at the end of the decade and the subsequent unprecedented growth of PEF in the twenty first century.

The development of PEF in the UK to the mid-1990s

The growth of private equity firms as professional intermediaries and of private equity funds, finance and investment in the UK occurred based on a similar series of changes to those in the US. It has, however, involved some significant differences of context and, more importantly did not begin to achieve comparable scales until the mid-to-late 1990s – partly because of those significant differences. In the record year of the early period, 1989, the total size of UK PEF funds was less than £2 billion (Boquist and Dawson 2004: 45) and the total value of deals done was £7.5 billion (Wright *et al.* 2006: 41). Furthermore, this latter figure includes buyouts that though privately financed did not involve either private equity firms or the use of funds at all, involving rather other forms of ownership change by the incumbents, which were reliant directly on bank loans. KKR alone operated on a larger scale than the whole of the UK industry.

Ronald Cohen, one of the founding partners of Apax was amongst the most prominent figures in PEF in the 1980s and 1990s in the UK. His brief biography provides a useful introduction to the UK context (Cohen 2007: chp 1). In 1972, after reading PPE at Oxford, studying at Harvard Business School and working briefly for the management consultancy, McKinsey, he and three other Harvard alumni formed Multinational Management Group (MMG). MMG was set up as a partnership to provide business advisory services but with an aspiration to also work in venture capital and PEF. The partner's were based in their home nations – with offices in London, Paris and Chicago. In 1975, having been unable to generate any significant business, two of the partners withdrew and Cohen approached Alan Patricof, a well-known New York based venture capitalist who became their new US partner. Patricof encouraged Cohen to pursue PEF despite the lack of either an existing demand or government interest. In 1977 Cohen and several other like-minded individuals began to promote the PEF concept to business people, financial institutions and politicians. In 1981 MMG/Alan Patricof Associates raised its first fund – the APA Venture Capital Fund, for £10 million, and in 1982 the promotion of PEF was put on a formal footing with the creation of the British Venture Capital Association (BVCA) with an initial 34 members, followed by the European Venture Capital Association (EVCA), in 1983. MMG became Apax in 1991.

The formation in the UK of a formal promotional organisation for PEF – the BVCA – came a decade after its US equivalent. There were numerous reasons for this – the most significant, however, was that, despite Wilson's personal reservations concerning Clause 4 (Labour's commitment to social ownership) and his 'white heat of technology' rhetoric in 1963 there was subsequently relatively little concrete focus on the promotion of alternatives to the state as a main employer and as the driver of the economy, and little promotion of small businesses as a source of innovation and change. Britain shared with the US a historically high level of personal taxation – top rate income tax in the UK was 83%. But there was no offsetting equivalent of the SBICs and no synergy between academia, small investment and new technology of the kind that had occurred in the US – particularly on the West Coast. There was, therefore, no clear demand for venture capital that might set the PEF industry in motion. There was, as a result, no incipient market to be constrained by the recessions (1973–75 and 1979–81) and stagflation of the subsequent decade. Cohen and others were not just promoting PEF they were advocating the construction of markets in which it could function.[1]

In this respect, the UK (and Europe in general)[2] was quite different than the US. Forms of social democracy and forms of the Keynesian economic model involved a different kind of state in the UK and Europe. The US operated automatic stabilisers and had increasingly accepted the validity of a form of the Keynesian approach (Galbraith 1975: chp 3. Heilbroner and Milberg 1995) in the mid-1950s, but it did not administer nationalised industries in the way the UK did, as the UK Royal Commission Donovan Report of 1968 indicates:[3]

> The Government's involvement in economic affairs has been extended by the nationalization of a number of basic industries... The acceptance of full employment as an objective of Government policy has brought a more detailed and continuous central management of the economy. More recently Governments have accepted the further responsibility of promoting a prices and incomes policy whereby money prices and incomes should be prevented from running too far ahead of productivity. (Donovan 1971: 5)[4]

US Federal and state government were large employers (Minsky 1982: xix and chp 1) but private business and public markets were far more significant in the US. The point is not unequivocal, however, since both the US and the UK were home to large regulated conglomerates within which a large bureaucratic professional management structure had developed (Donovan 1971: 4), but business culture was more diverse in the US (Donaldson 1976: 81).[5] Both were dominated in that culture by an expectation of job security and, for management, a clear sense of a career path, and this was a main source of identity and status (Sennett 1999). But the US also had a stronger counter-discourse – the cult of the entrepreneur and of individualised success (Gupta 2000). Research and development were also dominated in each by larger organisations – and in the UK, particularly by the state. But in the US there was also a greater acknowledgment that innovation and change in economies can be driven by new and small businesses. There was a much stronger expectation in the UK and Europe that technological and economic change came at a larger scale – Mercedes and so forth (Boquist and Dawson 2004). As Cohen states, 'The entrepreneurial wave that had started in the United States had not yet reached Europe, where there was no venture-capital or private equity industry at all.' (2007: 19).

Even had there been an incipient market for ventures to back PEF faced a liquidity problem that was of a higher order than that of the US. An investment in a PEF fund is itself a highly illiquid investment since the capital is committed for the life of the fund that is created (Lerner and Schoar 2004; Huss 2005).[6] In the UK, many of the early funds were structured as investment trusts rather than LLPs because the tax status of LLPs was ambiguous. However, whether structured as an LLP or investment trust, the principle remained the same. The capital may not actually be provided until it is required by the fund to make an investment but the terms of the fund/LLPs creation require that the investor be in a position to make that provision and also mean that the capital cannot simply be withdrawn. This was one of the original attractions for PEF as an alternative to relying on capital generated by a public listing. The ability of the PEF to invest, however, and the subsequent success of any investment requires high levels of liquidity in secondary markets. Those markets are the markets creating and offering credit and the markets offering a way to dispose of the firm invested in or bought out – particularly an exchange on which they can be offered as IPOs. In the US the Nasdaq was created in 1971 – no equivalent existed in the UK. A public listing on the London Stock Exchange (LSE) required a three year trading history, a fully audited equity issue prospectus and, effectively, minimum levels of capitalisation. Venture capital tends to IPO in a series of small equity offerings – the LSE requires a minimum 25% of equity capital be issued and most new businesses would find the issuing process exorbitantly expensive and time consuming and the IPO itself would be unlikely to have sufficient prominence for success to be likely and the issue profitable.[7]

One reason for this was that British banking had not undergone the same kind of transformations in the 1970s as US investment banking. British merchant banks (Schroders, Barings, etc.), the equivalent of US investment banks, did not undergo similar transformations until 1983 and these transformations were not formalised until 1986. In the 1970s there was no immediate sign of the emergence of a complex network of deal makers able to draw institutional investors, such as the pension funds, into PEF in the UK on a large scale or to attract them to IPOs. Nor, in a related sense, was PEF an unintended beneficiary of regulatory responses to a banking crisis, such as the thrifts.[8] The UK did experience a banking crisis in the 1970s – the secondary banking crisis of 1972–74. This resulted in the 1979 Banking Act, which for the first time defined what a bank actually was and gave the

Bank of England new oversight powers. The purpose of the Act was to try to restrict the way banking type activity was growing in a way that was escaping the current regulatory powers of the state.[9] There were other changes underway that would later result in the expansion of the securities market but the point remains that in the 1970s there was no expansion of a new financial innovation able to provide a surge in credit market liquidity, such as junk bonds.

As a result, though PEF faced similar immediate issues in the 1970s in both the UK and US – inflation had made long term investments less attractive by eroding the real value of returns, equity markets tended to be suppressed, – there was less of a basis for expansion as these were addressed. The UK as with the US elected a new administration at the end of the 1970s with a fundamentally different view of how an economy functions. The Thatcher government of 1979 adopted similar initial policies to the Reagan administration of 1980. Direct taxation was reduced – top rate income tax fell from 83% to 60% and basic rate to 30% (offset by an increase in indirect taxation, such as VAT, which increased to 15%).[10] The Bank of England, as the Fed had, responded to oil inflation with higher interest rates (the base rate rose to 15% in 1979 and then 17%) and Britain entered recession at the same time as it adopted monetarism and a more free market approach to economics.[11] That approach resulted in a new industrial relations strategy and a series of legislative moves throughout the 1980s, aimed to reduce trade union power at the same time as enabling a basic shift in economic structure away from state ownership and towards privatisation.[12] It was recession, however, that provided the basic context within which both buyouts and PEF began in the UK. The Centre for Management Buyout Research (CMBOR) at Nottingham University, which was founded in 1986 has collected data on PEF and buyout activity from 1980 onwards. Wright *et al.* note that the first buyouts began to occur in the recession of 1979–82 and were mainly a result of management buyouts of small companies that were facing insolvency (2006: 38). This was facilitated in 1981 by a change in regulation enabling firms to use their own assets as security against loans for such buyouts. The majority of these early buyouts did not involve PEF funds and, like most buyouts throughout the 1980s in the UK, relied mainly on a limited supply of bank loans i.e. senior debt. By the end of the recession in 1983, however, venture capital funds, such as the first Apax fund were becoming active. New PEF firms were also being established – notably Schroder Ventures in 1985, whose UK arm was run by John Moulton (Butcher 2005).[13] Several further changes underpinned this.

Some, if limited impact, was generated by the Business Start-Up Scheme (BSS) of 1981 and the Business Enterprise Scheme (BES) of 1983. Both were initially intended to provide incentives to invest in small businesses, with a special emphasis placed on new technology – partly as a remedy for the large increase in unemployment created by the combination of recession and the government's new approach to industrial relations and social ownership. Both the BSS and BES provided tax relief (an offset against income tax owing) for up to £40,000 per annum invested in an equity share in a non-listed new and/or small company. The schemes thus seemed to fit well with the typical form of venture capital investment. However, at its height only 20% of total investment through these schemes went into new technology and into start-ups (Blackburn and Sharpe 1988: 134–5). The terms of the schemes prevented investors becoming directors of the firms in which they invested and there was an initial cap of £500,000 on the total capital that any given firm could access through the schemes. The schemes quickly became a way for the investment and tax advisors of the wealthy to limit tax exposure and a series of investment funds developed to manage their capital like any other portfolio. As a result, though £779 million was invested in 4,000 companies in the first five years of the BES, the majority was not of a venture capital kind and increasingly tended to be in established companies and property firms (Butler *et al.* 2006: 142). The schemes total generation of investment capital for small businesses was relatively small compared to the overall number and needs of small firms and also in the context of the fall-off in productive investment by the state, which it could never hope to ameliorate.[14] The regional bias in the investments, particularly those in property and agriculture, tended also to exacerbate the growing North-South divide in the UK (Harrison and Mason 2002).

More importantly, in 1980/1981, the LSE developed and launched the Unlisted Securities Market (USM) to provide an equity listing outlet for small firms lacking the capitalisation and other attributes of main listed firms. Firms could offer as little 10% of their equity capital, required only a two year trading history and did not have to provide a fully audited prospectus for the issue (Buckland and Davis 1989). When the USM was created the Inland Revenue explicitly included it under the BES. Though never achieving the scale or prominence of the Nasdaq the USM did at least provide a new outlet for any potential PEF investment and thus made it easier to market the new PEF funds as a viable investment (Cohen 2007).[15] Successful solicitation, in turn, might, to a degree, offset the lack of a consolidated investment banking network able to promote PEF and in turn, raise the profile of IPOs on the USM – creating a cycle of further investment in PEF funds. There was some scope for this since some large institutional investors had begun to invest in US PEF funds. UK pension funds and other institutions had invested $531 million in the US by 1983 (Boquist and Dawson 2004: 45). The tax status of LLPs was also clarified in 1987 and they were given the same status as US LLPs i.e. they became 'transparent vehicles' in which tax liabilities passed to the investors only if they were subject to taxation.[16] As a result an increasing number of LLPs were created.

A consolidated investment banking network and an expanded market for securities also emerged from 1983 and particularly after 1986. As with the consolidation of US investment banking in the 1970s it was a response to a longer term sequence of events (Galletly and Ritchie 1988).

The 1973 Restrictive Practices Act empowered the Office of Fair Trading (OFT) to investigate and rectify how private markets and organisations regulated themselves in ways that unfairly maintained prices and prevented 'appropriate' or 'desirable' types of competition. In 1976 the OFT began an investigation of the LSE. One issue was that the LSE was a closed market: only registered members could trade and outside firms could only own a minority (29.9%) stake in a member firm. Another issue was that British investment banking shared many characteristics with the pre-1975 US system: it was a segmented market with fixed prices. Under LSE rules brokers charged fixed minimum commission levels and there was a clear division between different functions in dealing in securities. In addition to underwriting, under LSE rules there was also a distinction between brokers (who acted for clients including the public) and jobbers (dealers who met the needs of brokers). The OFT found the LSE to be in breach of the 1973 Act and the LSE faced the prospect of litigation by a hostile Labour government that they could easily lose. The election of the Thatcher government, however, did not prove an end of the matter. Instead it changed the basis and purpose of the intervention.

The Thatcher government had a series of related sources of interest in seeing the transformation of investment banking and the securities market. British banking was a dominant force in the international lending and insurance markets but had by international standards relatively small markets trading in equity and bonds. Even by 1985 it had only 29% of the trading volume of the New York Stock Exchange. Thatcherism was ideologically committed to the growth of private enterprise and to the privatisation of state-owned industries. Privatisation would be easier if equity markets were more open and more liquid. It would also be more popular if the practice of shareholding became more widespread. This would not just make privatisation more politically feasible despite growing unemployment but would also make voters averse to voting Labour if Labour remained committed to re-nationalisation.[17] The expansion of securities markets, moreover, would also provide liquidity for private investment that could facilitate the expansion of private industry in the UK to offset growing unemployment.[18] It could also provide a more liquid market for Treasury securities issued by the Bank of England. Furthermore, the growth of securities markets would itself be a form of growth within the financial sector – and one that could capture some of the emerging international market for securities trading, transforming British financial markets from laggards to a market leader.

In 1983 the government came to an agreement with the LSE that its code of practice would be modified and then exempted from the 1973 Act. The modifications would be phased in through to October 1986 – what would become known as the 'Big Bang'. The extended period gave the LSE time to bed in the changes and the government time to develop legislation to create new regulatory and oversight structures. The 1986 Financial Services Act empowered the Department of Trade and Industry to appoint a Securities and Investment Board (SIB). The SIB then had oversight responsibilities for a series of individual regulatory bodies for different aspects and participants in trading – equity dealers, bond dealers, unit trust managers, pension funds etc. These individual bodies were essentially professional bodies. The SIB's task was to ensure that they operated according to their own best practice codes and that those codes conformed to the standards set out in the 1986 Act (which included such issues as transparency, fair dealing etc. to protect investors). This was essentially self-regulation.[19]

Over the period 1983 to 1986 fixed brokerage commissions were ended, the distinction between brokers and jobbers was ended and the restriction on outside firms owning majority shares in member firms was withdrawn. The LSE also adopted a computerised trading system based on similar principles to the Nasdaq. This allowed information to be transmitted more rapidly in real time between market participants, greatly increasing the capacity for volumes and numbers of trades to occur and for these to be tied to other computer systems whose programmes/models could support trading decisions. The net effect was to consolidate investment banking, creating a series of integrations. The end of fixed commission and market segmentation created competition. In order for the merchant banks to broaden their brokerage services and move into dealing they required greater capital. They also needed to invest in new and expensive networked computerised trading desks and new premises. The end to the ownership restriction provided a means for this to occur. International banks emerged as both new competitors to and partners for the merchant banks.[20] Chief among these were the US banks. The US banks had begun to operate in London during the growth of the Eurodollar market in the 1960s.[21] As partners and competitors to the British banks in the 1980s they didn't just bring capital. US banks could underwrite and issue junk bonds on the US markets. They also brought with them a new wave of innovations in varieties of securities being developed on US markets – particularly what has become known as mezzanine finance.

Mezzanine finance comes in various combinations (Coyle 2000) most of which rank below both senior debt and ordinary corporate bonds. In addition to ranking lower than these forms of debt, in the event of a default, they usually have no call on the tangible assets of the firm. As such they pay higher rates and involve other kinds of surety that the payment is likely to be met. One form, which itself was not new, is preference shares. These pay a fixed percentage of the value of the share as a dividend. If the firm is insufficiently profitable to pay the full sum of the dividend to all preference shareholders then they usually include a clause to rollover the sum to the following financial year. Payment in kind (PIK) bonds work in a similar fashion. They can either pay an interest rate, and if payment is not made roll over any shortfall to the principal or value of the bond when it matures, or can involve no current interest rate payment, creating instead additional bonds to the value of what would have been an interest rate payment.[22]

Most forms of mezzanine finance also involve some form of convertibility. Preference shares, for example, may be either issued with no fixed term and thus have an unlimited lifespan of dividend payments or may be issued with a date on which they are either repaid or can be converted into ordinary equity shares on the basis of some specified calculation. PIK bonds, as well as preference shares often involve warrants. Warrants are fixed term (often years) rights to buy equity in the firm issuing the bond. The shares are new issues by the firm at that time and the price for them is defined by a formula as part of the warrant. The warrant makes the bond more attractive since the bond buyer can either hold it and gamble on exercising it if the firm grows to be larger and more successful or can trade it separately from the bond. The outcome of the gamble is usually based on the 'strike price' for the warrant. The strike price is the price the holder is entitled to buy the share at, defined in the original contract. Making a gain on the warrant is thus related to the rise in equity prices above the strike price. A collapsing share value, and a long term expectation that this will continue, therefore, renders warrants less valuable or even worthless (if it is below the strike price). Strike prices to spot prices (in this case current equity prices within the period warrants must be exercised) are the basis of many derivative gambles today.

Here the main point is that 1986 was the year in which investment banking in the UK formally followed the US model and was also the year in which securities trading began to develop and expand, creating more liquid equity and bond markets in the UK. Because that development was from the very first international in terms of its participants and also intended to develop international forms of financial trading UK financial markets were highly receptive to financial innovations that created forms of trading on the basis of differences in currency levels, differences in interest rates, and that met requirements to 'insure' against those differences when making trades. As such the UK would become a main centre for currency dealing, derivatives trading, and for the creation of forms of credit to trade in other securities, including what has become known as securitisation. Derivatives and securitisation are of particular significance to the development of PEF in the twenty first century and we will look at them in Chapter 4.

In terms of PEF in the 1980s, the US banks were a main source of the financing that was available in the UK. However, when, compared to the overall financing available in the US in the 1980s it remained relatively limited. One reason for this was that despite the efforts of the BVCA, there was still little awareness of PEF in the UK. Another was that even where awareness existed institutional investors still faced various constraints. For example, the levels of investment by pension funds in the UK were constrained in three ways (Myners 2001: 181; Myners and Payne 2001: 20). First, English trust law functioned in a way equivalent to the original version of the prudent man concept in the US. This tended to inhibit allocation of pension fund capital to new forms of investment. Second, the structure of pension funds in the UK where trustees coordinate with a limited pool of consultants on fund allocation and then delegate investment to a slightly larger but still limited pool of fund managers created a conservatism and inertia in fund investment regarding forms of investment outside the current experience of the consultants and managers.[23] This was exacerbated by §191 of the Financial Services Act 1986 which required that any investment activity be by a person authorised under the Act. This placed the typical non-financially trained and certified pension trustee in an ambiguous position that seemed to require a recognised (authorised) intermediary between themselves and investment in the fund (creating additional costs and problems of sourcing). Third, though the tax status of LLPs was clarified in 1987, under the 1907 Limited Partnership Act a conflict still existed between the duty of trustees to oversee the activities of those to whom investments had been delegated and the criterion necessary for an LLP to retain its legal existence i.e. that a limited partner is one who does not take an active role (the US equivalent specified the day-to-day management). Further, the maximum number of limited partners in an LLP was fewer in the UK at just 20, than in the US, making it more difficult to accommodate several initially smaller investors. Despite these constraints pension funds did increase their investment in PEF in the late 1980s – reaching a high of 28% of the total investment in PEF in 1988. But this was and remained thereafter a small proportion of the total assets of pension funds (less than 1%).

It was for these reasons that British based private equity firms understood that most of the awareness and interest, and a significant proportion of the capital, for PEF came from the US. As such they followed the UK institutional investors to the US and engaged in the solicitation of funds there (Boquist and Dawson 2004: 50). As PEF grew in the mid-1980s overseas investment in British based funds increased, and this remained a significant source of investment throughout the 1980s.

The US banks in the UK were at least more aware of the existence of PEF than their UK counterparts. By the mid-1980s they were conversant with the format and debt structures of LBOs and were thus well positioned to provide finance (Wright *et al.* 2006: 39 and 44). As of 1986 they were well positioned to offer access to mezzanine finance to PEF buyouts as well as access to senior debt through the commercial banks. The 1987 market crash, moreover, provided a range of new targets for buyouts (as well as causing large losses to many of the traditional dealers and brokerages, which increased the numbers of mergers with US investment banks).

A new kind of private equity fund also began to emerge in the late 1980s focused directly on providing forms of debt-equity investments that could underpin PEF and leveraged buyouts. Although developed in the US – by the PEF firm Forstmann Little & Co (see Little and Klinsky 1989) Mezzanine funds are in some respects more significant in the UK because they substituted for the absence of access to other sources of finance.[24] Mezzanine funds solicit investment to be channelled into the debt structures created by buyouts. As such there is some blurring between these and more general debt funds that focus on buying the debt of firms in financial distress. Mezzanine funds provide an increase in liquidity for PEF by acting as a buyer for forms of junior debt that it would otherwise be difficult to place.

The first mezzanine fund in the UK was created in 1988. These funds began to provide an outlet for more complex debt structures involving higher cost (interest rate and dividend) forms of finance that could also be traded by the funds. These debt structures could be attractive to all kinds of PEF activity. A small firm buyout or follow on venture capital financing might use mezzanine finance because the firm is not currently profitable or because it lacks sufficient capital assets to act as collateral against all of the debt it needs to generate (remembering that mezzanine finance involves no call on tangible assets). This, for example, might also be a significant consideration for a firm that trades on the basis of human capital or intellectual property. Most forms of mezzanine finance also have a buyback condition written into them that the issuer can exercise. This makes mezzanine finance attractive for all size of buyouts since it means that the narrowing of ownership that is at the heart of LBOs need not be compromised at the same time as high levels of debt can be generated. Furthermore, since the financing comes from a private fund the overall costs of generating debt based on setting up the issue may be lower.

The net effect of these changes was a steady if small growth in buyouts and PEF in the UK to 1985 and then a further expansion in the total value of deals, their numbers and the size of some individual deals from 1986–87. That expansion, however, was never on the same scale as in the US as various pieces of CMBOR led research and other sources indicate. In the early 1980s, MBOs predominated. In two samples comprising a total of approximately 400 buyouts between 1982 and 1985 (Wright *et al.* 1996), around 75% were buyouts of small divisions of larger companies (divestments or spin-outs). A further 11% were changes of ownership in private family owned businesses where the senior generation were cashing out. The rest were firms facing insolvency. Around £5 million was the buyout price for 95% of the sample. PEF funds (LLPs) were not really a main factor in these early buyouts though some activity did derive from venture capital. The research on the UK tends to use PEF and venture capital fairly loosely – partly because the clearer distinction that could be drawn between buyout activity and buyout related funds and venture capital did not emerge in the UK (Mayer 2001: 8; Renneboog *et al.* 2005: 2). Venture capital did not have the same relation to technology in the UK – though technology industries of sorts did develop. In 1986 buyouts rose to almost 400 and continued to increase to a high of over 600 in 1990 (Wright *et al.* 1994: 22; 1996: 228). MBIs also began to occur – though these never became a majority of buyouts. Also in 1986 there were 35 buyouts whose value exceeded £10 million (Boyle 1994: 202) and between 1985 and 1989 there were 65 buyouts, out of a total of over 1,600 whose value exceeded £50 million (Wright *et al.* 1994: 28). Few of the larger buyouts were household names.[25] Many of the total of all buyouts of this period involved corporate restructuring where a division or unit of a larger firm was spunout (divested) – because a PEF fund thought it could be made profitable if run alone and then could be IPOd, because the original corporation was 'rationalising' and divisional management saw the opportunity to use PEF to seize control, because the original parent firm had entered receivership and the division could be 'salvaged' relatively cheaply, and, finally, because privatisation had created the opportunity to split formerly state owned companies into different units.[26] There were 32 privatisation buyouts in 1987 and 200 in total by 1994 (Wright *et al.* 2006: 41).[27] Before 1985 there were no buyouts of publicly listed companies and throughout the rest of the 1980s (and into the early 1990s) such buyouts never comprised more than 5% of the total of PEF.[28] The main focus was always small and medium sized firms, either privately owned or publicly listed but not targeted for or anticipating a full de-listing (just divestment).

The growth of PEF in the UK in the 1980s, then, reflected local conditions. Significantly it was always constrained by the size of the funds that could be solicited. It was 1986 before a PEF fund in excess of £250 million was closed and funds on this scale remained scarce thereafter – as the total of solicitation in the record year of 1989 (less than £2 billion) indicates. The growth of PEF was also constrained by the availability of credit for debt financing. Senior debt from main commercial banks remained a main source of financing and there was no equivalent to the development of the junk bond market in the US. Mezzanine finance and mezzanine funds offered an alternative and offered a means for complex debt structures to be created in later deals. This and the participation of American banks helped fuel the few larger LBOs of the late 1980s. As in the US these larger deals involved higher degrees of leverage and the use of more complex debt structures. Leverage in larger deals rose to 68% of the total value of the deal 1988–89 and, as in the US increasingly involved more junior debt – mezzanine finance – as well as planned asset sales (Wright *et al.* 1994: 28 and 30). For example, the largest UK buyout of the decade, the MBI of Gateway by Isosceles for £2.2 billion, used £1,765 million of senior debt and £375 million of mezzanine finance (Wright *et al.* 1994: 30; Coyle 2000: 43).

As in the US, the end of the 1980s and recession affected PEF, but the effects in the UK were in some respects different.[29] The years 1990–92 were

Britain's third postwar recession. Underlying rapid rises in interest rates – partly to try to stabilise Sterling against European currency after the UK entered the Exchange Rate Mechanism (ERM) in 1990, was the main trigger for effects on buyouts. The base rate doubled from 1989 to 15% in early 1991 and remained over 10% throughout 1992. It rose briefly again to 15% on Black Wednesday, September 16th 1992, during the failed attempt to maintain Sterling in the ERM. The surrounding events of a stock market crash, a housing market crash, unemployment of around two and a half million, sudden oil price rises (from $30 to $40 a barrel) as Gulf War preparations began in January 1991 and growing inflation, exacerbated by the devaluation of the pound after leaving the ERM, created economic conditions that affected the trading performance of all firms including buyouts. PEF faced particular issues: potential buyouts now became more expensive because debt became more expensive – new larger deals thus reduced. Some PEF firms, notably Schroders Ventures withdrew from the buyout market in the UK. Others restructured – in 1993 the European arm of Citicorp Venture Capital was bought out by its management to form CVC. Many of the American banks that had provided senior debt for such deals ceased to do so (Wright *et al.* 2006). As IPOs dried up in the recession, the London Stock Exchange closed the Unlisted Securities Market (USM) (Cohen 2007). Larger deals that had already been done with more leverage faced three problems: inability to sell off assets at the expected value that had been factored into the deal, poor sales and problems of debt servicing from revenues, and higher interest rates making refinancing more difficult. From 1990 to 1993, 355 buyouts entered receivership, others were bought out by other PEF funds (Wright *et al.* 1994: 25). This was the beginnings of a secondary market in PEF (the trading of acquisitions between funds) that would become increasingly important in the later 1990s but here emerged in the absence of IPOs and to take advantage of companies in financial distress.

The net effect was a downsizing of PEF at the end of the decade. This contraction did not involve the number of deals falling, these remained around 430 to the mid-500s throughout the early 1990s and continued to reflect the small scale focus of PEF in the UK, but the size of deals was on average smaller reflecting the contraction in the liquidity of an already illiquid market. Put another way, because PEF did not experience the kind of liquidity surge and other contributing factors that the US had in the 1980s it did not experience a spectacular and public reduction. For similar reasons it did not generate the same degree of interest in the range of issues that first emerged in the US context – tax, debt, asset sales, terms of employment etc. The difficult refinancing of Gateway by Isosceles in the early 1990s and slow demise of the company did produce media interest but not the academic scrutiny and public focus that PEF faced in the US. However, PEF had become part of the British corporate and financial landscape and was in a position to expand rapidly if other factors came into play as they did in the later 1990s. Cohen, who is a longstanding Labour donor, and, since retiring from Apax in 2005, has become one of Gordon Brown's chief fundraisers, states that the main trigger for such growth when it came was the rise of New Labour and specifically the issue of tax:

> Mrs Thatcher had opened the door to venture capital and private equity in Britain in 1979. However, for all the pro-entrepreneur sentiments of Mrs Thatcher's successive chancellors of the exchequer, they did little to actually promote entrepreneurial investment. Certainly, the Thatcher era left Britain with a far better business culture than before, and with lower levels of income tax, but we were still saddled with very high rates of capital gains tax, an unclear position about the role and status of entrepreneurs, and uncertainty about whether British financial institutions should invest in venture capital and private equity funds. It was Tony Blair's Labour government, which came to power in 1997, which gave the sector its biggest boost. (Cohen 2007: 35–6)

However, more immediately significant was the broader context of changes created by the renewed growth in the US as venture capital and PEF re-emerged as part of the New Economy and the dot.com boom. It was this growth that helped to create a more integrated form of PEF between the UK and US and helped to foster the rapid growth in PEF in the UK thereafter.

The American recovery: the rise of the New Economy

The US began the 1990s in recession. In that recession PEF activity had fallen sharply – the size and numbers of new funds reduced in 1990–91 and the number and scale of buyouts and venture capital activity also reduced (Kaplan and Schoar 2005; Gompers and Lerner 2000). As Burrough and Helyar note:

> The battle for RJR, it turned out, both defined and ended an era. KKR's winning bid of $25 billion stood for nearly a decade as the biggest business deal of all time. Several factors combined to tamp down the size of deals for several years. The great money machine behind LBOs – junk bonds – sputtered and for a time virtually stopped. Mike Milken went to jail; Drexel Burnham went bankrupt and, in the early – 90s recession, battered over-leveraged companies gave leverage a bad name. Henry Kravis ceased stalking big game, pre-occupied with the care and feeding – and debt service of RJR. Other stars of 1980s Wall Street also overdosed on hubris and disappeared. (2004: x)

Despite this, PEF did begin to recover. The initial context of that recovery was the end of the recession but more significantly the way in which economic growth developed during the 1990s. Growth in the 1990s involved the expansion of new industries as well as the creation of new relations of employment and investment and new financial innovations. The combination provided a liquidity surge. Significantly, the first major manifestation of that surge was in equity markets – the dot.com boom. But the underlying relations involved complex interactions between the results of venture capital and the opportunities open to PEF buyouts. PEF buyout investment activity over the decade was partly shaped by the consequences of venture capital. In the 1980s the growth of PEF LBOs using managed funds had been set in motion by initial changes aimed at producing economic dynamism through small firm investment. PEF buyout funds exploited those changes to focus on well established industries, particularly conglomerates.[30] In the 1990s PEF buyout activity both responded to the consequences of its own unstable growth in the 1980s and responded to the new markets for investment created by venture capital and driven by other sets of changes in the 1990s (deregulation etc.). These changes affected how equity markets grew on the basis of the new technologies and ultimately, how those markets collapsed in March 2000.

In terms of the standard definition of recession – two or more successive quarters in which GDP shrinks (i.e. negative economic growth) – the early 1990s US recession was a relatively short one, lasting from July 1990 to March 1991.[31] The immediate recovery, however, was also unusual in that GDP growth became positive but net employment did not increase.[32] This was the first indication of what was to be a key feature of growth in the 1990s – productivity tended to grow and, when it came, employment growth tended to follow an unusual pattern in terms of the quality of jobs created and the sectors they were created in.[33] Both were to reflect the growing importance of the service sector in general within the economy, and more specifically financial services and what has become known as the New Economy – telecommunications and information technology more broadly.

As Stiglitz notes, an important aspect of the recovery from the recession was an unanticipated consequence of an accounting oversight (2003: 43–4). The 1980s had ended with the financial sector in disarray. Credit was in short supply, interest rates were high (10% in 1989 still 7% in 1990), bond markets had seized up. One way in which these conditions might be overturned is if the thrifts and the banking sector in general saw their capitalisation improve. This, in combination with lower interest rates might see the banks more likely to lend and investors more able to borrow – improving liquidity and enabling growth. It is typical in times of economic downturn for capital to be redirected to safer forms of securities, such as Treasury Bonds. This tendency was exacerbated in a positive way in 1989. As part of the Federal response to the collapse of the thrifts new accounting codes were introduced to assess bank capitalisation. Capitalisation levels were linked to the kinds of assets a bank held (different kinds of securities).

Assets were graded on the basis of risk and capital reserves were required to cover any possible reduction in the value of assets. Significantly, longer term Treasury Bonds were categorised as risk free and as such no offsetting reserves were then required.

Banks, therefore, invested heavily in such bonds at a time of high interest rates. The bonds were attractive since the state does not default and because they provide a guaranteed income stream – from which the bank benefits. However, if interest rates on subsequent issues of bonds by the Treasury rise, then the market price of previous issues falls, since they are not as attractive an investment (the income stream is lower than new issues since the old issue is at a lower interest rate and new issues are preferred).[34] There was, therefore, the potential for the value of the bonds to fall and for the banks to face a genuine capitalisation problem – the bonds were not actually risk free. Fortunately, though the Fed was initially reluctant to reduce interest rates at the end of the 1980s and in 1990, despite slowing growth and then recession – interest rates did start to fall. The price of previously issued bonds thus increased – they became an even more attractive investment. The banks were then able to benefit from the original income stream at a time of uncertainty and also to sell the bonds at higher prices. The net effect was to greatly improve the capitalisation of the thrifts and the banking sector in general (Stiglitz 2004).

Furthermore, the sale of bonds and falling interest rates on new issues of Treasury Bonds made further investment in Treasury securities less attractive, turning the banks back towards other forms of investment causing the liquidity conditions of finance markets to improve. As Altman notes (1992), junk bond markets started to reorganise and restructure in the wake of Drexel Burnham in 1991. At the end of that year The National Association of Insurance Commissioners (NAIC) also reduced its restrictions on the ability of insurance companies to invest in junk bonds. Market trading of existing junk bonds started to increase. Debt funds, some of the new hedge funds, and other investors were, despite high default rates, attracted by the heavily discounted prices of the bonds. As interest rates started to fall and liquidity conditions eased new issues of bonds started to grow also, primarily to restructure the debt of LBOs. These too could be an attractive investment because the spread of interest rates on junk bonds above Treasury securities had risen to a high of 12% on the back of the collapse of the market.

The need for restructuring also resulted in a new kind of PEF fund. The collapse of PEF in the US made investors wary of being heavily committed to just one fund, since a major failure or LBO restructuring or insolvency might sharply reduce the returns on their investment. For this and related reasons private equity firms started to offer funds of funds i.e. a fund that then invested in a range of PEF funds. In principle this diversified the risk of investors. Investors also responded by themselves investing across a broader range of funds. Thus as the 1990s progressed more forms of diversification, such as funds of funds became part of PEF investment strategies (Lamm and Ghaleb-Harter 2001). The more immediate issue, however, was that as the recession ended the junk bond market was increasingly able to offer liquidity to PEF. By the end of 1991, the junk bond market had returned to around 25% of the total corporate debt market: 'After the very survival of the market had been questioned' in 1989... by the end of 1991, the size of the high-yield debt market had survived and indeed had grown to almost $209 billion. New issues totalled $10.5 billion in the first four months of 1992' (1992: 78–9).

Lowering interest rates was itself also a factor in recovery. Not just because lending conditions eased and the spread on junk bonds started to fall from its initial high, allowing further refinancing and restructuring of problematic old debt structures and allowing the potential for borrowing for new productive investment, but also because the basis of interest rate policy at the Fed started to change (Blinder and Reis 2005). Though Alan Greenspan became Chairman of the Fed in 1987, it was after an initial reluctance to lower interest rates in 1990 that Greenspan presided over a basic change in Fed conduct.[35] In the 1980s interest rate changes had been both rapid and large in size – tending to be tightly modelled to combat inflation. From 1991 the Fed started to rely less on its formal models and tended to favour lower interest rates than formal models indicated were required to reduce inflation. At the same time there was a switch to small incremental changes in interest rates.[36] These were signalled to markets in a series of oblique public statements from Greenspan regarding the current state of the economy. Whether this was initially an actual strategy or simply became one over time is in some respects beside the point.[37] What is important is that the view that the Fed was acting differently eventually began to feed through to public consciousness. This did not mean that there were no longer important periods of increasing and decreasing interest rates with both domestic and international effects.[38] However, comparatively low and relatively stable interest rates were increasingly important in various ways.

Lower Fed interest rates usually make senior and junior borrowing cheaper and can thus promote debt and investment. A sense that changes in interest rates can be more reliably forecast and that any changes will be small and incremental tends to make larger scale debt and investment appear less risky since it provides for more time to adjust to changing interest rates and to restructure debt. If interest changes also seem to be less than traditional models (based on such concepts as core inflation, the natural rate of unemployment and on data for productivity) suggest then eventually a sense arises that there will be no sudden catastrophic effects on equity and security markets by rapid and large changes in interest rates in order to rein in inflation. All these factors tend to favour more investment, the use of debt, and rising equity markets. The downside is that stability of this kind can also lead to interest rate policy failing to curb rapid expansions in markets where growth becomes a boom and a boom becomes what economists term a 'bubble' (overpriced markets unable to justify their valuation and ripe for collapse). Clearly, the notion of a bubble in any aspect of the economy was far away in 1991 but it is important to have a sense of how policy provides a backdrop to subsequent events. From the beginning of 1991 to Greenspan's retirement in January 2006 Fed short term interest rates remained consistently low, never rising above 7%, averaging less than 5% and reaching as low as 1%. From June 1989 to August 2006 there were 74 interest rate changes by the Fed of which 57 were 0.25% and 16 were 0.5%.

Lower interest rates – initially falling to 3% in the autumn of 1992: the lowest level for almost 30 years – and the gradual freeing up of lending provided general conditions in which both the economy at large and PEF might expand. The specific focus of that expansion was then also affected by a number of other changes. Although not on the scale of buyout funds, venture capital had grown through the 1980s. Since each individual investment is relatively long term many of the venture backed firms were only ready to be sold off at the end of the decade. There was therefore an accumulation of venture capital backed firms (those that had not already failed in the development stage) from the initial strong growth in venture capital in the mid-1980s, as well as a cumulative stock of venture capital fund commitments from the later 1980s – $36 billion in 1990 (Fenn, Liang and Prowse 1995: 12). Venture capital investment had created a great deal of duplication resulting in problems of competing companies trying to go public with similar technologies – computer discs etc. At the same time, many of the investments had resulted in a broadening of new information technologies – including ways of supplying telecommunication services. There were also increasingly prominent examples of hi-tech companies created in the 1970s (Apple, Microsoft etc.) whose technologies were beginning to change the way that businesses structured their supply chains and their administration. This, for example, was one of the reasons for the growth of productivity that occurred in the initial 'jobless recovery' at the end of 1991 (Stiglitz 2004). By the end of 1991, therefore, there was both a ready supply of venture capital backed firms to IPO and also an existing stock of capital in venture capital to invest. There were 635 sell-offs ('exits') of venture capital backed firms in 1991–93 – 191 in the secondary market and 444 IPOs. Approximately 30% of the total was in computer-related firms (Fenn, Liang and Prowse 1995: 22). Only 5% were in telecommunications firms – this reflects the way provision of communication services was still closely regulated and restricted. Telecommunication applicable technologies were of course developed and developing from a variety of sources.

The IPO of venture backed firms gave an impetus to renewed investment in venture capital funds and by venture capital funds. This was given an additional impetus by the reduction in capital gains tax from 28% to 14% in 1994 on investments held in small companies (Gompers and Lerner

1998: 156). The stock of capital committed to venture capital funds grew to $43.5 billion from 1991 to 1995 and whilst the number of venture capital firms offering funds initially decreased, from 664 to 591, 1990–94, the numbers then started to rapidly increase (Onorato 1997: 7). Total annual commitments to venture capital show a steady increase through the early 1990s from $3.4 billion in 1991 to $8 billion in 1995. The same figure from the total stock of capital committed was also invested in 1995. The majority of investment was directed at California and Massachusetts and was dominated by communications and software firms (Onorato 1997: 4). The Nasdaq index grew consistently in the early 1990s. In February 1971 when the Nasdaq opened, the index had been set to 100, it took until 1991 to reach 500 but doubled from this to 1000 in July 1995 (Siegel 2002: 50).[39] Thereafter its growth was exponential.

Netscape was the first major Internet IPO in August 1995. The firm was formed in April 1994 as Electric Media. The name was then changed to Netscape after a dispute with the University of Illinois – where one of the founders had originally worked on developing software. Netscape was financed by the prominent venture capitalist firm Kleiner, Perkins Caulfield and Buyers to produce a user-friendly browser system for the Internet. Initial financing was unusually short – around a year, since once the software was created there were few other development and profitability issues This was because the technology would provide a basic platform service, protected by intellectual property rights. The IPO was set at $28 per share for an issue of 3.5 million shares and closed at $52, making Jim Clark one of the founders worth $565 million at the end of that day (Samuelson and Varian 2002: 364–8). By December Microsoft was offering Internet Explorer as an alternative and this paved the way for the anti-trust litigation of the late 1990s that would help trigger problems in Internet related equities. More immediately, the IPO of Netscape created extraordinary media attention and highlighted the large and unusually rapid returns that venture capital might make on Internet-related companies. This in turn paved the way for further investment in venture capital funds.

The IPO of Netscape was not the only factor increasing the prominence of Nasdaq listed companies and tech companies in general. Netscape was part of the development of more user-friendly applications for the Internet, from which a growing number of Internet based services would develop. The form of bull market that was to occur, however, was also affected by the deregulation of telecommunications in the US (Jerram, Hodges, Turner and Kurz 1997: chapter 4). In 1984 an anti-trust action against AT&T restructured the US telephone network. AT&T remained a national long distance provider, or carrier, in competition with Sprint and MCI and local services were devolved to seven new companies (referred to collectively as the Baby Bells) each controlling a region. The regional carriers operated a series of exchanges providing the infrastructure for local calls (less than 30 miles) and which were networked to the national carriers.[40] The 1984 ruling prohibited the regional carriers from also offering cable television services. The result was competition at the national level for phone services and a series of local monopolies as well as a technological segmentation of communication service provision. The justification for the local situation was one of natural monopolies – it would be nonsensical, wasteful, and disruptive for multiple private companies to reproduce the same infrastructure. Instead, the regional carriers were subject to price controls.[41]

However, the development of new technologies including fibre optic and coaxial cabling meant that replication was no longer necessarily an issue and multiple carriers could be accommodated within a single infrastructure. Furthermore, the development of cable television and, from the early 1990s, Internet access meant that the technology of the sectors seemed to be outgrowing the segmentation of the market. The regional carriers began to lobby to be able to offer a broader range of services, arguing that computer, telephone and broadcasting technologies seemed to be converging – many of them committed to multi-billion dollar long range and large scale investment in fibre optics to replace former copper wiring systems.

Providing a system of access to technologies on a national basis for a new computer age was one of the policy platforms of the new Clinton Administration in 1993. Moreover, the National Information Infrastructure (NII) or 'information superhighway' was one of the few realisable policy commitments of the administration when the Republicans gained control of Congress in 1994 (Stiglitz 2004: 93–101). Republicans would tend to support the deregulation of regional telecommunication services on the basis that this decreased government intervention and increased competition (chiming with the lobbyists).[42] Ultimately, the 1996 Telecommunications Act, however, did little to promote actual competition despite its focus.[43] The Act required the regional carriers (termed incumbents)[44] to provide equal access to their network infrastructure to new firms (termed competitive local exchange carriers, CLECs). All carriers could (phased in over time) offer both national services and local services and also broadband Internet access.[45] The spectrum on which these services could be digitally offered was also reorganised for licensing.

A host of CLECs quickly emerged and were listed on the Nasdaq. The expectation amongst equity analysts and investors was that the successful amongst them would be well positioned to become the next wave of major US corporations, dominating, along with the large producers of computers and Internet providers, the 'information age' into the twenty first century. Venture capital, therefore, flowed rapidly into new start-ups aimed at this market. It also then flowed rapidly into Internet based companies offering software and/or services, since the 1996 Act seemed to be predicated on a rapid expansion in home and business access to the Internet as provision was commercialised. To a degree this did occur, existing providers like AOL and WorldNet expanded. Dial-up Internet access provision also rapidly expanded – by the autumn of 1996 there were 12,000 local providers and 65,000 by 1998, covering every major city (Greenstein 2007: 8). Providers increasingly began to offer low cost fixed fee contracts for unlimited access and by the end of 1996 all the major providers did so.

What also occurred was a series of mergers and acquisitions to take advantage of the new market (Grant and Meadows 279–80). Southwestern Bell (SBC), for example, acquired Pacific Telesis (an incumbent regional carrier) in early 1997, Southern New England Telecommunications Corporation in 1998 (a large CLEC) and Ameritech Corporation in 1999 (another incumbent). The combination required over $80 billion in financing and made SBC the dominant provider in 13 states, including some of the most populous and largest (Texas and California).[46] The now infamous Worldcom was created in 1995 from a discount long distance carrier (LDDS) and grew rapidly through the 1990s on the basis of a series of mergers and acquisitions, including the acquisition of AT&Ts major long-distance rival, MCI for $37 billion in 1998, as well as the acquisition of other CLECs.[47] Worldcom's value increased by 7,000% in the 1990s (Jetter 2003).

This spree of new listings and of mergers and acquisitions using debt and new share issues helped to drive up equity prices on both the Nasdaq and the traditional exchanges. 'Old economy' corporations began to take an interest in acquiring tech firms, tech firms whose share prices were increasing started to buy old economy firms, and firms in the finance sector in general expanded on the basis of their role in doing deals. The expectation of continued growth and the specific instances of mergers and acquisitions paying a premium on current share prices, further fuelled equity price rises. The more successful that technology companies and the New Economy appeared, the more attractive venture capital became and the more profitable IPOs seemed likely to be. Thus the combination of high expectations of Internet companies, based on the example of Netscape, and merger and acquisitions in telecoms accelerated a bull market creating an expanding feedback effect on venture capital from around 1995 to 2000. In 1996 the Dow index rose from 5,000 to 6,500 and the Nasdaq from 1,000 to over 1,300. Total annual venture capital commitments increased to a record $6.6 billion and $10 billion was invested (Onorato 1997: 7).

Various future problems would manifest from this bull market. Equity analysts and theorists assume that in the long run shares trade at a value reflecting the underlying performance and prospects of the firm. However this raises a number of questions for Internet firms: how does one objectively value a company with no earnings, no history and no comparable firms (Damodaran 2000 and 2001)? Amazon for example, was unusual amongst new Internet based sellers in that it generated revenues and had a clear business model. However, it was loss making at its inception and made no claim to be anything else in the first five years of its existence. Amazon was set up in 1994 receiving some business angel investment in 1995 and its first venture backing of $8 million in 1996 before going public in May 1997 with an initial IPO share price of $18. The IPO raised $49 million from a three million share issue – not a large increase over the issue price. However, by 1997 it was trading at over $50 and by 1998 $84. Using approximations of standard ways of calculating 'real' underlying share values Damodaran estimates possible values from $25 to $60 a share in 1998 and these approximations themselves were based heavily on assumptions about future earnings. Amazon would at least be able to fulfil some of its apparent potential precisely because it was a retailer of actual products and could function on the basis of economies of scale. Many other Internet start-ups were selling a concept – a business idea as a service that could easily be copied.[48] Most had little to base valuations on other than the potential for subscriptions, advertising, or hits on websites. If they were unsuccessful they owned little fixed capital and thus had nothing to liquidate, since their main asset was the intellectual capital of the founders and workforce. They thus were both a highly risky investment in terms of potential success and in terms of clawing back any of the investment in the event of insolvency (Pichinson 2002).[49] Any current valuation of them at the time of an IPO was in most respects arbitrary. Furthermore, the general increase in share valuation for tech firms and telecom firms provided one of the key sources of further merger and acquisition activity since growing capitalisation allowed further share issues and security issues and provided access to senior debt. This became a key way in which CLECs and new media companies like Worldcom maintained growth that in turn maintained share price growth. Again, the basis of valuation for these firms involved a great deal of estimation regarding future growth (as well as in some instances simple accounting fraud).

It was in this context that Greenspan first coined the phrase 'irrational exuberance' in December 1996 (Stiglitz 2004: 56). This was Greenspan's typically oblique way of referring to the possibility that equity market growth was creating a bubble effect. Interest rates, though higher than 1992, remained relatively low, having risen to 5.5% in 1994 to slow a trend devaluation in the dollar, and significantly did not change towards the end of 1996 and early 1997. In any case changes were now in small increments. Further, the overall economy was growing. Wealth effects began to fuel growing leisure, retail, and housing markets, and as a result the construction and DIY sectors and property related financial services also began to expand (Morgan 2006). Employment had grown, inflation was low and the Clinton administration was steadily reducing the budget deficit that had accumulated during the 1980s. There seemed, therefore, from a monetary point of view, either little reason or small scope for historically sharp increases in interest rates since this would have broad effects on what was increasingly an apparently healthy overall economic position. A stronger warning regarding expanding markets from Greenspan also created a credibility problem – it would be viewed as a signal for rapid changes in interest rates and there was clearly no intention, unless circumstances changed markedly, that this would be the case.[50] Markets might initially react by slowing or falling rapidly but the lack of follow through would itself create uncertainty about what the Fed was doing and this would contradict the underlying emerging ethos of its policy (stability). Problems, therefore, were simply being stored for the future. In the meantime venture capital was experiencing what PEF analysts and participants would come to call the 'halo effect' (Lamm and Ghaleb-Harter 2001). Fund investors increasingly aware of the growth in telecoms and tech companies directed more investment towards venture capital and towards funds and fund managers with a track record in these areas. This in turn created a herd effect of growing investment in these sectors amongst all venture capital and also attracted more people to start venture capital firms that would then work in this area – there were over 1,000 firms by the end of the century (Sohl 2003) and 542 new funds solicited in 2000 alone (Rand and Weingarten 2002).[51] Expansion was thus also a convergence and concentration of activity. This too would become part of the nexus of problems that would see the tech markets grow at an even more rapid rate from 1997 and would also see the dot.com boom ultimately collapse. However, it also had prior effects on PEF in general, since it created the conditions in which PEF debt funds and buyout funds operated and to which they might respond 'opportunistically' (Sood 2003).

The renewed growth of venture capital and the focus on new technologies helped to shape the future path of buyout funds. Buyout funds too had accumulated acquisitions to be sold off and fund commitments to be invested in the early 1990s. Since buyout activity in the later 1980s was of increasingly larger firms it tended to be focused on longstanding industries – ones where previous growth had come through mergers and conglomeration. Taking the largest LBOs back to public markets was extremely difficult in the early 1990s because of the scale and problems of the debt structures and because of the scale of the new equity issues they would involve (that recovering equity and debt markets might be reluctant to absorb). This added further impetus to the splitting of LBOs into smaller divisions to be sold off. There were 125 IPOs of former LBOs between 1991 and 1993, 73% of which were concentrated in retail, manufacturing and textiles (Fenn, Liang and Prowse 1995: 24).

Disposing of former LBOs and the issue of what do to with accumulated fund commitments from the late 1980s created a quandary for PEF firms. Many of the most profitable deals to be made in existing industries had already been done. Some of the deals that had been done, particularly the larger more leveraged ones had proved publicly problematic. Moreover, the 1980s had witnessed the gradual reduction of manufacturing industry as a proportion of the economy – a trend that was to continue throughout the 1990s as retail, financial services, construction related activity, and information services expanded (Morgan 2006). The combination raised the issue of how to use current funds and how to market the solicitation of new funds. Putting together larger deals was now more difficult – this was reflected in the way that though corporate bond markets, including junk bonds, had recovered – new issues within the markets (rather than trading) grew slowly in the early 1990s and much of the new issues involved restructuring. Credit markets were becoming more liquid, credit was becoming cheaper, but the banks remained wary of larger debt structures at this time. In any case highly leveraged LBOs of larger publicly listed companies were liable to generate adverse publicity and this might also make large institutional investors, particularly the state pension funds, less liable to commit to funds solicited by the major PEF firms such as KKR. Also the current management of publicly listed companies were increasingly averse to MBOs as the 1990s progressed because they were now able to generate large personal fortunes without a buyout and delisting because of the increasing use of stock options as a form of pay (Burrough and Helyar 2004: xi–xii).

Stock options are payments where the owner of the option is either given or has the right to buy, at a set price lower than the market price, shares in the firm. When the option is exercised new shares are issued to the number specified for the option. The options do not appear in the current accounts of the firm as a cost (wages/payment/compensation etc.) affecting current profitability and thus provide the capacity for the firm to provide very large payments to senior management in an oblique way. The understanding is that this gives board members a strong incentive to improve the share price of the firm by improving its underlying performance. They can be, however, also offered as part of mergers and acquisitions and as such produce a further incentive for the management of listed firms to collude in expansion by accretion rather than engage in a leveraged buyout and delisting in cooperation with the PEF firms. As Stiglitz notes: 'During the Nineties senior executive compensation rose by 442 percent in eight years, from an average of $2 million to $10.6m... by 2000 in America, CEOs were getting more than 500 times the wages of the average employee, up from 85 times at the beginning of the decade, and 45 times two decades earlier.' (2004: 124).

Of course, increasingly wealthy and powerful CEOs ultimately create a class of business people able to use their own personal wealth as part of an MBO in conjunction with the PEF firms. The CEO culture that developed in the 1990s would also facilitate this later as CEOs increasingly became tradable commodities that tended to switch between larger firms. Not only did they have reduced loyalty and identification with the traditions of any one of those firms (a dubious relation at the best of times) but they also carried inside knowledge about the asset and trading value of the firms they had worked at. The initial effect of stock options, however, was to add to the difficulty of making larger LBOs. A large LBO of a publicly listed company in a longstanding industrial sector was now more likely to be difficult to negotiate and might require a hostile takeover – which would merely exacerbate the problems of financing from increasingly cautious backers. It might also, as with larger mergers, be blocked by federal intervention based on public interest and anti-trust criteria since the Clinton administration did not take the same passive approach to these issues that Reagan and George Bush Sr had done.

The combination of all of these factors – the growth of venture capital, the rising prominence of venture capital backed firms, the difficulties of larger leveraged buyouts of publicly listed companies in longstanding industries etc. combined to produce three effects that helped shape PEF buyout activity into the early 2000s.

First, there was a renewed focus on smaller deals with less leverage. Levels were still high compared to the level of debt carried by public corporations (which tends to vary between 20 and 30% of the value of the company) but levels over 75% were now rare and many were lower – at the height of the boom in the 1980s leverage reached 85% plus for buyouts of publicly listed companies. In the 1990s the buyout of publicly listed companies dropped to less than 20 per year until 1996 and only attained the mid-1980s levels from 1998 (Renneboog *et al.* 2005: 31).[52] Even here, leverage remained lower than in the late 1980s and few of the buyouts were of household names. Moreover, the deal-making activity of the main PEF firms did not escalate in multi-billion dollar leaps as it had for firms like KKR. The emergence of one of the most prominent general PEF firms of the 1990s and 2000s illustrates this. Texas Pacific Group (TPG) was formed by David Bonderman and James Coulter who had previously worked together on LBOs for Robert Bass Group. TPG grew out of Air Partners an investment company created by Bonderman in 1992 to buy Continental Airlines out of bankruptcy in conjunction with Air Canada. Air Partners raised $66 million for a 42% stake. TPG then raised its first fund of $720 million in 1993. This was a large fund size in the context of the period – average buyout fund sizes were then less than half this. TPG undertook a series of buyouts in the mid-1990s, including $40 million for Newscope Resources Ltd and $395 million for Nestle's S. A. Wine World Estates. Even for the larger PEF firms, buyouts, as had been the dominant pattern in the UK in the 1980s, were mainly of medium sized companies or small divisions of larger companies. Billion dollar deals were rare even as fund sizes grew.

The second effect on PEF buyout activity derived directly from the New Economy. The IPO of firms providing computing and information technologies and the expectations of growth in the provision of telecommunications services through deregulation, led to both the growth and the creation of new kinds of specialised PEF firms in these areas. For example, Providence Equity Partners, founded in 1991, specialised in telecoms, and expanded rapidly in the mid-1990s (Sparks 2000). Silver Lake Partners, founded 1999, specialised in technology buyouts and quickly became one of the most prominent specialist firms (Staff Reporter 2006). The growth of the New Economy also led to the use of buyout funds by more generalist firms to buy in these areas, sometimes in cooperation with specialist firms, and for the solicitation of funds specifically for these areas. Buyout funds thus started to turn to sectors traditionally dominated by venture capital (Sparks 2000; Sood 2003).[53] Again TPG illustrates this. TPG provided backing as part of a $175 million financing for Advanced Telecoms Group, a Californian hi-tech firm still in its early stage of development and not yet IPOd (Benjamin and Margolis 2001: 259). TPG was also the first of the PEF firms to engage in a buyout of a telecom's technology firm – acquiring the modem manufacturer AT&T Paradyne for $174 million in 1996 (Sparks 2000). Of this $51 million was an equity investment from its funds and $123 million was debt – creating a debt level of 70% of the total value of the deal – a level towards the upper end of what was typical of the time. Buyout firms operating in traditional venture capital areas also began to focus on the needs of New Economy firms that venture capital could not easily meet, such as large scale investment for technology infrastructure, such as fibre optics for telecoms (Smith 2002: 67).

Third, buyout funds faced a further investment problem since not only did they have accumulated commitments from older funds but fund commitments were also growing faster than the number of viable buyouts. The total stock of accumulated funds was thus increasing. From around 1996/7 this led the largest PEF firms to diversify into Europe and particularly into the UK (Boquist and Dawson 2004). In 1996 TPG bought Ducati and also a 20% stake in Ryanair. By 1999 US based PEF funds were investing $1.6 billion in the UK, rising to $5.3 billion in 2005 with an additional $14 billion in Europe (Wright *et al.* 2006: 42). The large investment banks also started to invest in Europe through their private equity divisions. Many of them aimed at trying to emulate the growth of new hi-tech firms in the US. Morgan Stanley Private Equity, for example, was planning to invest $1.5 billion in hi-tech start ups in Europe by the end of 2000 (Reed 2000).

The expectation of PEF expanding into new territories combined with the wealth effects of economic growth and the bull market in the US meant that in many ways the investment problem of accumulated funds was exacerbated. Firms began soliciting new specialist, regional, and global funds. The marketing of these was able to emphasise that new markets like telecoms offered unprecedented opportunities based on new business models and based on the tremendous growth that prospective investors could see reflected everyday in the media and in the rising values of the Nasdaq and Dow indexes. In 1997 the US successfully sponsored a new telecom market access accord at the WTO providing the new US telecom firms with the prospect of global expansion – creating a new scale of expectation about their future profitability and about the expansion of information technologies. This both fed the bull market in the US and provided an additional underlying reason for the regional expansion of PEF funds. Furthermore, new regions offered the prospect of new opportunities for old behaviour in established industries – buyouts had been rare and large buyouts absent from Europe and the UK. UK and European firms carried, on average, less debt than their US counterparts. Moreover, global scales of investment itself justified larger scale fund solicitations. As a result, average fund sizes grew year on year, reaching $546 million in 2000 based on an increased number of PEF firms and funds. New multi billion dollar funds started to appear. These kind of funds would later be termed 'mega-funds'. At first they were of the order of a few billions but in the 2000s some would be tens of billions. In 1997 TPG's second fund was closed at $2.5 billion. Larger funds and specialised investment started to come together in the late 1990s and provided some of the few multi-billion dollar deals of that time. For example, in 1999 TPG and Silver Lake cooperated in the $2 billion buyout of the disk-drive division of Seagate Technology (Toms and Wright 2005: 284).

One of the reasons institutional investors now had the surplus capital to direct into larger funds was that bull markets and economic growth had created a surplus of capital that pension funds, wealthy individuals and other sources could commit. The problems of the PEF firms in the period 1989–91 now seemed far in the past – there had been over five years of economic growth and everywhere there were optimistic forecasts of future growth based on the emerging New Economy. Institutional investors were now less averse to directing greater absolute sums to private equity (Lamm and Ghaleb-Harter 2001). These did not hugely increase the overall proportions these institutions were now directing into private equity, since the size of assets under the management of these institutions had grown. Average total commitments remained around 3–6% from pension funds and endowments.[54] Some, however, contributed significantly more – amongst the universities Yale and Stanford were committing more than 10% of the value of their funds to private equity.

There was also a greater pool of investors to call upon – ironically because a series of economic crises around the world in the 1990s had produced a periodic inflow of capital into the US. The effect was ironic because many of the crises in markets around the world were affected by US policy in one way or another. The Fed rise in interest rates 1992 to 1994 was historically small but sufficient to trigger a devaluation crisis for the Mexican Peso – that was then pegged to the dollar. The knock on effects of that crisis affected the whole of Latin America. The East Asian financial crisis of 1996/1997, although made possible by basic vulnerabilities in the economic structure of some of the nations, was triggered by speculative investments in the Thai Baht by US hedge funds (Morgan 2003). The subsequent scale of devastation of East Asian economies has been widely attributed to the way the IMF, under US leadership, responded by trying to isolate the crisis (Stiglitz 2002). Whilst it is debatable how far one might attribute the Russian debt crises that followed to US policy, the subsequent implosion of the hedge fund Long Term Capital Management in 1998 was a specifically US problem created by lax regulation of leverage levels (Patomaki 2001). The important point is that particular economic crises tend to result in a flight of capital to 'safe havens' – Treasury securities, desirable equities listed on well established exchanges such as New York, and commodities such as gold and oil. The US has been a preferred destination since it also provides the unofficial reserve currency for the global financial system – investments there, and assets held in dollars, are seen as highly liquid (Morgan 2008). The inflow of capital, however, also has knock on effects to all markets contributing to the general bull market, as well as providing a direct source of capital for investment in PEF funds from global investors – including wealthy individuals from Arab states, the new wealthy of Russia and other more longstanding investors such as British and European pension funds. The effect then is to create a further source of growth in PEF funds, even though these were considered relatively more risky.

As a final point, bull markets and wealth effects tend also to increase the value of assets held by commercial banks, which in turn increases their capacity to lend. This helped to feed the growth of tech markets because it meant that additional financing could be accessed by venture capital and by listed firms, such as the telecoms – for infrastructure investment, expansion through investment, or simply mergers and acquisitions. As a general principle credit availability starts to rise in tandem with economic growth and the value of investments such as equities. Economic growth is also associated with lower levels of defaults on securities, which in turn reduces the proportion of losses on bank assets. Though the banks may still have been wary of the levels of leverage generated by LBOs in the late 1980s, they were by the late 1990s capitalised in a way that made securing debt financing for LBOs easier than it had been in the early 1990s. Fees and returns from underwriting, brokerage and security dealing also added to the profits of the investment banks and they started to recycle these by investing them in PEF funds of established firms and in their own PEF funds. Increasing liquidity, therefore, flowed in various ways from the growth of the New Economy.

Conclusion

By 1997 PEF buyout funds in the US were experiencing a renaissance. Fund sizes were steadily increasing, though this was not yet resulting in a sudden shift to large scale buyouts of publicly listed companies. Deal sizes were typically in the range of tens and hundreds of millions of dollars for medium sized firms and divisions of larger firms. However, in the context of accumulated stocks of fund commitments this created an investment problem for PEF. An increasing number of new specialist firms emerged at the same time as many of the larger PEF firms diversified.[55] The nature of that diversification reflected conditions in the US. Firms started to invest in telecoms and undertake smaller scale financings of new businesses in addition to their focus on established industries. They also began to shift into new territories and this in itself created the scope for further fund solicitation on larger and larger scales, tapping the growing capital created by the boom. The capacity for PEF to engage in larger buyouts that would become a major issue in the mid-2000s in the UK as well as in the US was, therefore, set in motion by many of the same conditions and events that led to the dot.com boom itself. Significantly, however, the conditions of growth of the late 1990s meant that the liquidity that grew at this time was something that did not focus quite so prominently on larger PEF LBOs. PEF benefited from the New Economy but could not exploit rising liquidity in the same way it had in the 1980s. This would only begin to occur with the collapse of the dot.com boom, by which time PEF had expanded in both the US and UK.

3
The Expansion of Private Equity Finance in the UK in the Late 1990s and the US Context of the Collapse of the dot.com Boom

The surplus of capital in the US accumulated in the context of the dot.com boom provided the impetus for PEF firms and investment to transfer to Europe. Europe was a (mainly) new target for PEF activity deriving from the US. A newly integrated Europe now provided improved liquidity conditions based, for example, on emerging bond markets. Europe, including the UK, also had relatively unexploited equity markets, which meant that there were many more currently low leverage targets for larger LBOs. The UK was the main destination for the transfer of firms and funds for a variety of reasons. The UK already had a developed PEF market and the capital markets and financial infrastructure of London provided a nodal point for liquidity that could be exploited. New Labour was also eager to attract new sources of capital and finance to the UK and provided a tax regime designed to facilitate this. A new level of internationally integrated PEF then emerged. As a result in the late 1990s PEF fund solicitation and LBO activity began to grow in the UK in the same fashion that it had begun to expand in the US. This was then briefly brought to a halt by the collapse of the dot.com boom and the market crash of March 2000. In this chapter, I set out the conditions of the growth of PEF in the UK in the late 1990s and the specific circumstances of the dot.com collapse. This was essentially the collapse of one unstable liquidity surge that was then rapidly replaced with another. Here, maintaining economic growth in the wake of the dot.com collapse combined with specific changes in banking practice to create a new liquidity surge, combining a housing market bubble and, in terms of capital investment and debt creation, a greater focus on PEF. It is in this context that PEF LBOs were once again able to attain and then surpass the scales achieved in the 1980s. I explore this in Chapter 4.

The increasingly integrated growth of PEF in the UK

In the later 1990s many of the largest PEF buyout firms in the US opened offices in London.[1] For example, TPG opened offices in 1997, KKR in 1998 and Carlyle in 1999. As Boquist and Dawson note: 'Caught between a saturated US market and the demand for continued exceptional returns, the migration was rapid and broad-based.' (2004: 41). The intention was to both use existing funds and solicit new regional funds with a focus on investment in the UK and Europe. The arrival of the US firms coincided with a rapid expansion in PEF in the UK and Europe that also encompassed incumbent PEF firms. In addition to there being good reasons for US PEF firms to diversify out of the US, various contextual factors in the UK and Europe affected both the location decision of these firms and the prospects for growth of PEF in general.

The 1992 Treaty of Maastricht accelerated the concept of Europe as a single exploitable market based on the freedom of movement of people, goods and capital. An important aspect of developing this concept was the gradual implementation of a single currency. Coordinating a single currency across member nations required the convergence of different economic indicators (inflation, interest rates, exchange rates, public spending) that might otherwise cause difficulties in transiting to and maintaining a stable Euro across different countries. It also required a single central bank to maintain the stability of the finance system and the single currency, once convergence had occurred. Thus from 1992 through to the empowerment of the European Central Bank (ECB) in 1998 and the creation of the Euro in January 1999 there was a widely understood process of unification of the economies of member states and a clear idea that the outcome would be a unified financial market.[2] This provided the basis for an organised junk bond market because that market would no longer confront the complexity of bond issues across multiple currencies within different regulatory systems. Relatedly, it would not be subject to potentially wide disparities in individual central bank activity and monetary policy – particularly interest rates that might affect the spread on bonds.

As a result, a pan-European junk bond market started to grow from mid-1997 (Arnold and Smith 1999). American investment banks, attracted by the prospect of growth in market trading in junk bonds and by the possibility of large fees, began to underwrite European bond issues denominated mainly in Sterling and European currency, increasingly the Euro.[3] In some respects this followed on from their participation in the Eurobond market of the 1970s and 1980s.[4] The American banks had the expertise in junk bonds that few European banks could muster and were at no great disadvantage due to unfamiliarity with local regulation and currency – since these were changing for everyone (de Bondt and Ibanez 2005: 176). Though the market itself did not begin to grow appreciably until 1999–2000 its very existence was a clear attraction to PEF buyout funds – even though the use of senior debt and mezzanine funds remained larger sources of finance (Biais and Declerck 2007: 7).[5] By 2001 20 billion Euros of junk debt was outstanding from prior issues. The main buyers in the market were investment funds

(41%), hedge funds (27%), commercial banks (15%) and pension funds (13%) (Biais and Declerck 2007: 5).[6] From 1998–2001, 57% of issues had been organised by Goldman Sachs, Merrill Lynch, Credit Suisse First Boston (CSFB) and Salomon Brothers (Biais and Declerck 2007: 7).

The advantages of this market were both general and specific to Europe. Generally, a large organised bond market creates liquidity and liquidity effects in various ways. The existence of an organised market provides not just a focal point for buyers but also a ready means for buyers to become sellers. High risk bonds now seem less risky. If a buyer needs cash they can offload the bond, if they decide that the bond has become a bad risk (and others have not) they can likewise sell, both without necessarily incurring a loss. Knowing that any form of junior debt that has been bought can also be sold reduces the aversion to buying it in the first place and, all other things being equal, reduces the interest rate on the initial issue that is necessary to induce buyers to buy. A large organised market, in the absence of defaults or sudden waves of selling, thus tends to reduce the spreads between junk bonds and other securities. More specifically to Europe, if that market uses a single currency that is international in scope, then payment of the bond, and payment from that initial payment to other participants, can be made without having to convert currencies. This further reduces costs for two reasons. First, there is no risk that a change in the value of the currency affects the returns to other participants when the currency is exchanged. Thus higher interest rates are not demanded to cover this risk. Second, there is no need to buy some form of insurance specifically to cover the risk of currency exchange related losses. Overall, a large organised market in a single internationally recognised currency reduces the costs of debt creation and increases the volumes of debt that can be created (Biais and Declerck 2007: 3). It is, therefore, both a source of liquidity for bonds and a source of liquidity for markets that rely on debt, such as LBOs, as Mark Patterson, CSFB's head of leveraged finance noted:

> In the US you can pick your product ... but in Europe the markets [have been] dramatically less developed. So the bank loan market has been the principal provider over the decade,' [but] the force now is the local sterling and euro junk bond market, the fastest growth sector of the junk bond market worldwide. 'That's providing the ability to do more leveraged buyouts by eliminating a foreign exchange exposure,' (Hadjian 2000: 5)

Based on CMBOR research, Wright *et al.* make much the same point:

> [L]arger UK buyouts before 1997 resorted to the US high-yield bond market. But from 1997 onwards, financial institutions became at first willing and then eager to invest in [European] high yield... Such instru-

ments enabled buyout financiers to operate with leveraged capital structures but without creating foreign exchange risks. (2006: 45)

Wright *et al.* also note that PEF activity of all kinds had already recovered in the UK prior to 1997. This slow recovery, beginning at the end of 1992, was also significant because it created a growing secondary market for buyouts. This in turn would be one of many factors that made London a more attractive location for US PEF firms.

The recovery of PEF activity in the UK occurred in the context of the stabilisation of the UK economy after 1992.[7] Economic growth increased from around 2% in 1993 to 4% in 1994 and remained above 2% thereafter. Inflation had fallen by the end of 1992 to 3.5% and remained around 2–3% through to the mid-1990s. Interest rates also fell from the highs of 1992 and fluctuated between 5 and 7% to 1996. Official statistics for unemployment fell slowly from 1993 to around two million in 1996 and in that year the housing market finally began to recover from the crash of the early 1990s.

The ongoing process of economic stabilisation influenced PEF in various ways. In similar fashion to the buyouts of the early 1980s those in 1992 were dominated by small deals from receivership. Thereafter the average size of deals rose from less than £4 million in 1992 to approximately £6 million in 1996 (Myners 2001: 165) and the focus of deals began to shift.[8] Again, as in the 1980s new deals tended to be for divisions of larger firms that were divesting. The proportion of publicly listed companies wholly bought out remained low – on or below 1% until 1997 (Wright *et al.* 2006: 43–4). Divestment reflected the basic uncertainties of the UK economy in the early 1990s – there was no initial expectation that a stable economy meant long term growth and larger companies were attempting to reduce their average costs.

From 1994, as the economy stabilised, both the size of new PEF funds and total solicitation increased. PEF firms, such as Apax and CVC, and PEF divisions of the main banks, such as Natwest Equity Partners, all grew during this period. In 1996 the total PEF market exceeded its 1989 levels for the first time (Wright, Renneboog *et al.* 2006: 24). Growth to 1996–97, however, was in most respects based on local conditions as it had been in the 1980s. Some of those conditions were, however, altered, and this was reflected in the growth of IBOs and a new period of MBIs. IBOs are where the bidding process for a buyout is dominated by investors such as the PEF firms. The current management may be retained but they are not significant holders of equity (as they would be in an MBO) – nor if any new management are brought in are they significant holders of equity (as they would be in an MBI). By 1994 CMBOR had recorded 1,000 MBIs since 1980. One reason for MBIs and IBOs in the 1990s was simple time dependence – the development of British based PEF firms meant that they now had a pool of skills that reduced their reliance on the incumbent management to set up deals and run companies.[9] Another reason was that current conditions gave PEF broader based access to potential buyouts. PEF firms were increasingly an alternative to traditional means for divestments because existing companies were less inclined to take on new acquisitions – for precisely the same reason other companies were divesting. Buyout activity, therefore, increased as a proportion of mergers and acquisitions and PEF firms established themselves as a credible substitute to the more traditional means of divestment. Since the USM had closed in 1992, disposing of buyouts increasingly relied on the main exchanges.[10] Since only larger buyouts could be disposed of this way two other alternatives remained. One was trade sales i.e. a private sale of the acquisition to another company usually operating in the same market as the acquisition.[11] The other was a secondary market where PEF firms exchange prior buyouts between themselves.

Numbers of secondary buyouts were at first still small. One reason for this was that since the company had already been bought out once and restructured it was likely that its overall financial performance had been improved in so far as that was possible. The returns on a secondary buyout would, therefore, be low compared to a new buyout unless additional debt financing could be used to generate further returns. Essentially this means paying returns to investors out of new debt – an issue I will look at in detail in following chapters. The key point here is that, compared to what would follow in future years, at this time overall credit availability for financing deals remained limited and current credit terms meant that debt was not cheap, making debt servicing more difficult. As such, there were stricter limits to the amount of debt a buyout could carry. New buyouts were therefore generally more attractive. At the same time, however, old buyouts had to be disposed of. A secondary market was one way to do this. In 1995 there were 29 secondary buyouts (Wright *et al.* 2006: 44). Though small in number, this was a perpetuation and expansion of the trading of buyouts between PEF firms that had begun in the recession as a way to resolve the problem of previous buyouts that were heading for receivership.

The London Stock Exchange introduced the Alternative Investment Market (AIM) in 1995 as a successor to the USM. AIM functioned on similar principles creating a cheaper and easier listing process than the main exchange. This was a new source of liquidity, but so was the secondary market. Moreover, the secondary market could sometimes be advantageous. A secondary buyout is a more focused process than an IPO. The firm either engages in single negotiation with a buyer or appoints an intermediary to invite bids and set up an auction based on a floor price. The process is much more easily controlled than a small IPO on a relatively new market such as AIM. As a private transaction which is not subject to the wider publication of a trading history and accounts it is also one with greater scope for the generation of further debt because there are no equity prices to be affected. That debt can be used in various ways, including paying returns to investors and the PEF firms. An active and well developed secondary market is, therefore, attractive to PEF firms – and particularly so as credit becomes more freely available and credit terms improve.

An active secondary market was just one possible reason for the location decision of the US PEF firms in and after 1997. Various others are also relevant. The UK contained far more and larger domestic PEF firms than any other European country. This didn't just create a source of competition it also provided a potential source of local knowledge for joint investment. The firms and their partners were not strangers. Apax, for example, had a US link since its inception. There had always been some US PEF presence in the UK – Citicorp Venture Capital, for example, was set up in 1981. US PEF firms as well as institutional investors had been investing in UK funds for a long time. The PEF firms themselves always operated with very few partners and as such personal networks of contacts were easily forged and maintained – a process reinforced by the US NVCA, the UK BVCA and European EVCA, as well as after 1997 the Annual Super Returns Conference, which attracted PEF participants on a global basis.

More importantly, following the Big Bang of 1986 London now contained expertise in all aspects of finance. It contained offices for the major accountancy and management consultancy firms able to offer services in assessing buyouts. It contained a high concentration of domestic and international investment banks and commercial banks offering underwriting and debt provision services. It was home to the London Stock Exchange, one of the premier exchanges in the world, as well as AIM.[12] It was, therefore, able to offer an exit for both small and large LBOs through IPOs. All of these reasons made London a nodal point for liquidity in PEF in Europe.

Another important consideration is that the economic ideology of the UK and its related corporate regulatory system was far closer to that which had developed in the US than was to be found in other European states. By 1997 Reagan and Thatcher may have been long gone but the New Democrats under Clinton and New Labour under Tony Blair were more inclined to speak the language of entrepreneurship, free markets and the need to be business friendly than were their European counterparts (Osler 2002). In the UK this translated into a hands-off approach to acquisition unless a powerful public interest argument could be made. It was, therefore, far easier to engage in PEF buyouts in the UK than in Europe in general – where stronger varieties of social democracy and corporatism still held sway. This meant that a larger proportion of buyout activity by funds with a European scope would be focused on the UK. There was also less of a cultural suspicion of the intention of foreign buyout firms in the UK than elsewhere and less capacity to mobilise opposition. In France, for example, family firms were generally averse to foreign-based buyouts (Boquist and Dawson 2004) whilst there and in Germany powerful trade unions had the potential to mobilise significant resources to oppose any buyout.[13] Trade unions had declined in power, prominence and membership in the UK in a way that made this far more difficult.[14] As such, despite the longstanding existence of the EVCA and of significant amounts of state-supported domestic venture capital activity in France and Germany, there was on the mainland a greater potential for an underlying political opposition to an internationally expansive PEF.[15] It, therefore, made political and economic sense to locate in London near one's main market, particularly since that location also shared a common language.

As Cohen notes, changes to specific tax levels and regulation played a role in the large scale expansion of PEF after 1997. Those changes were both conducive to the expansion of domestic PEF and to the location decision of other PEF firms. However, to fully make sense of the significance of specific tax levels it is useful to think of them in terms of their role in a broader tax regime and how this is part of a particular approach to finance. That approach was a constituent in New Labour's political goal of reassuring markets that they were 'business friendly' and this in turn informed their approach to 'sensible economics'. Becoming the party of 'sensible economics' was an important aspect of the reconstruction of Labour since one of the keys to their electability was not only exploiting the perception of economic incompetence (and moral dissolution) amongst the Conservatives but also providing concrete proof that New Labour was not 'old Labour'. The perception of old Labour (far more than the reality) was of a party of economic mismanagement – tax and spend and inflation and recession.

New Labour came to power in 1997. In 1998, Gordon Brown, then Chancellor, introduced 'taper relief' on capital gains tax (CGT). If investors held onto an asset for ten years they would pay a reduced rate of 10% CGT when that asset was realised or sold. The change followed broad consultation with the main business associations and was intended to provide an incentive for entrepreneurs to invest in new businesses, build them up, and sell them as profitable ongoing concerns (profiting themselves at the same time).[16] It was thus regarded as an important aspect of an overall policy to create an investment culture in Britain to emulate the expanding New Economy in the US.[17] It also followed on from a reduction in CGT by the Clinton Administration in 1997. The US Tax Payers Relief Act of 1997 reduced CGT from 28% to nearer the early Reagan level at 20% for assets held for over a year by those in the top income tax bracket.[18] From the point of view of PEF firm partners the fact that the UK level was lower could be important. The US is unusual in operating a system where citizens are taxed on their worldwide income. It also operates a general policy of offsetting equivalent foreign tax liabilities for US citizens who work abroad – thus a lower tax level in the country where the initial tax liability is incurred means the overall tax level paid, if the individual is fully compliant, will not be higher than the US level.

Given the relatively long duration that assets had to be held before taper relief applied the policy was probably less of an *initial* incentive for PEF firms to locate in London, and for new PEF funds to be set up, than Cohen recalls. It was, however, by no means irrelevant if placed in context. It certainly provided an opening for lobbying from business associations for further changes. In 1995 for example, the British private equity association, the BVCA, began to publish its own annual aggregated data trends for private equity. It went on later to use this data to produce a variety of different types of reports as a basis for presenting a positive picture of PEF and for lobbying for advantageous regulatory changes – including to taxation. Taper relief was also important in terms of what it signalled i.e. New Labour's intent to be tax-friendly to business. This had an international dynamic since finance was, and was increasingly so, a major constituent in the UK economy and one of its main growth areas. The new Chancellor was, therefore, keen not to introduce legislation and regulation that would deter a global convergence of finance activity on the UK, and on London in particular. This was then specifically codified within the Financial Services Authority (FSA) aims.

In October 1997, the Chancellor created the FSA to replace the Securities and Investment Board (SIB) that had been created in 1986. In 1998 banking and investment supervision were amalgamated within the FSA – superseding the former division of labour between the Bank of England and the SIB. This was to create a new division of labour that would be completed in 2001 when the Financial Services and Markets Act of 2000 came into effect.[19] The Act gave the FSA oversight of the market listings for the securities exchanges. The FSA thus became responsible for regulating and overseeing the exchanges and the individual financial institutions, including banks, whilst the Bank of England retained responsibility for maintaining the stability of the banking system, as set out in 1998. In 1997/8 the Chancellor also empowered the Bank of England with formal independence from the Treasury. The Bank now had sole responsibility for setting the base rate – the short term interest rate below which banks would not lend to each other – with a mandate to use this and other monetary techniques to control inflation (in line with a target set by the Treasury).

As a result, Bank of England policy increasingly resembled that of the Fed – small incremental and obliquely signalled interest rate changes. This had similar effects on attitudes to debt that had already begun to occur in the US. In the UK interest rates had reduced in the early 1990s and this had already affected debt use in PEF. As interest rates fluctuated between 5 and 7% 1993 to 1996 the use of debt in buyouts in the UK increased from an average of around 35% in 1993 to 45% in 1996 and mezzanine finance became a typical part of deal structures (Wright *et al.* 2006: 45). The use of debt, moreover, increased irrespective of the direction of changes in base rates. There was, therefore, a clear sense that debt risk was reducing and that interest rates could be expected to be generally lower and less volatile than periods in the 1980s – despite reservations regarding the economic competence of the Conservatives. Credit availability and thus an important aspect of the liquidity of PEF, was still restricted by the willingness of the banks to lend but a process of 'credit easing' was in motion. The monetary policy autonomy of the Bank of England from 1998 and the way it seemed to mirror Fed policy added to this easing because it changed expectations towards monetary policy and changed attitudes towards debt. The base rate in the UK, though usually higher than the US level has similarly subsequently avoided the highs of the previous decades. From the beginning of 1998 to the end of 2007 there were 33 changes in the rate, 32 of which were ¼% and 1 of which was ½%. Rates have varied from 7.5% to 3.5% and have averaged around 5%. Until the end of 2003 the general trend had been downwards.

If one considers the independence of the Bank of England from a propaganda point of view it was an extraordinarily successful policy since it undercut any concern that a Labour government would tend to use monetary policy in a 'politically' motivated way – creating the possibility for difficult to anticipate interest rate movements. This in turn underscored the New Labour claim to be the party of 'sensible economics' in a way that produced a concrete manifestation of its claim to be business friendly. The triumvirate that emerged in 2001, however, of the FSA, Bank of England, and a general monitoring role from the Treasury would later prove problematic – and this would manifest quite spectacularly in 2007. But in 1997/98 the main point to be drawn was that there was a clear emphasis on reassuring markets that New Labour was different than old Labour and that it was committed to attracting global finance of all kinds. One of the FSA's objectives, later affirmed in the Financial Services and Markets Act of 2000, was to be sensitive to 'the international character of financial services and markets and the desirability of maintaining the competitive position of the UK' (Myners 2001: 183). In terms of its regulatory powers within the financial sector this translated into a low key approach to all aspects of oversight and enforcement – the FSA, for example, prior to 2008 had never brought a criminal prosecution for insider dealing and favours consultation over compulsion. PEF firms are regulated by the FSA and their active partners and employees must be authorised by it to engage in investment activity.[20]

The growth of PEF in the late 1990s occurred within a specific context which is broader than simply the issue of attractive tax regulation. That context, however, affected the nature of tax regulation particularly if one thinks of that regulation as a set of interacting elements – a regime – and one thinks of that regime as a 'competitive' means to attract global investment, investors, and managers of investment. In addition to taper relief the location of PEF firms was also influenced by British non-domiciled tax regulations and regulation regarding non-residency. An individual is considered non-resident in Britain for income tax purposes if they work in Britain for fewer than 183 days in a single year or, over longer periods, they average less than 91 working days a year over four years. Though under review in 2008, previously, travelling days were not counted as working days. As a result, if one commuted Monday and Friday, which was perfectly feasible using private corporate transport networks, then only three days per working week were counted. One could thus work 30 full working weeks in London in each of four years without breaching the 91 day limit or, unlikely though it may be, a full 52 weeks in a single year without coming close to breaching the 183 day limit. Since the scope of PEF was expanding to be European there would also be numerous deal meetings and visits across Europe which could either involve full days outside Britain or count as additional travelling days. Non-residency has not, therefore, been difficult to achieve for an executive level foreign national – particularly a European national. One could, for example, live in Monaco, which has no personal income tax or CGT and has maintained a policy of non-cooperation with other states in the disclosure of the financial arrangements of residents. Over 80% of the population of Monaco is constituted by expatriates and Monaco has a transport network specifically geared to trans-European commuting.

Non-domiciled status has also had attractions. An individual has been able to register as a 'non-dom' if they are a foreign national, if a parent is a foreign national, and/or if they establish some form of ongoing connection to a foreign state, such as prior long term residence and the intention to return permanently at some future date. As a non-dom any earnings made abroad have not been counted in the UK for tax purposes as long as they remain abroad. Again, for PEF involved in pan-European business this has been extremely attractive since it simply requires split contracts and separate payments for overseas work that can then be channelled into accounts in tax havens elsewhere. The logic is that the UK potentially gains from the tax paid on earnings in the UK and simply accepts the loss of other tax revenues as the price to be paid to attract foreign firms and foreign executives. In this context it is notable that whilst Brown, as Shadow Chancellor in 1994, opposed the existence of non-dom status that opposition was quietly dropped once New Labour came to power.[21] The broader issues are whether non-dom status is a net gain in tax revenue, whether it is 'fair', and whether it is part of a broader range of tax issues relevant to PEF such as corporate taxation, tax relief on debt for corporations, off-shoring and 'tax-efficient' strategies. We will look at these issues in Chapter 7.

Clearly New Labour did not invent non-residency, non-dom status or the strategy of reducing varieties of direct taxation after the 1970s. This was a trajectory they inherited and then developed through CGT and taper relief. What made them 'new' as Labour was precisely that they did inherit these trajectories and that they applied them to the idea that a tax regime *must* be internationally competitive within a globally competitive economy. Though the point of CGT and taper relief in particular have been to promote the creation and development of new businesses of all kinds, growth in a broader sense has placed an increasing emphasis on the expansion of the financial sector and done so within a global setting where a non-interventionist regulatory approach to finance in general has been part of the ongoing attraction of London. Becoming New Labour has essentially been a process of taking the political out of the economic but this itself has been both a political strategy and a political structuring of the UK economy. In this sense New Labour also inherited, albeit quietly, the Thatcherite dictum 'there is no alternative' (TINA) as a means to justify a policy strategy.

PEF has been a beneficiary of this overall context. What this means is that the local conditions that affected PEF in the UK prior to 1997 subsequently became more globally directed local conditions. The different aspects of those conditions made London the preferred destination for US PEF once US conditions had provided good reasons for US PEF to shift abroad on a larger scale. The net effect was synergy. Expanded liquidity in the UK and Europe based on lower interest rates, credit easing, and new bond markets made raising debt for buyouts easier and increasingly so in the late 1990s. The prospect of transferring the growing New Economy and the apparent miracle of the American experience to Europe and the UK made investment – including venture capital – seem more attractive. The lower levels of previous PEF activity, particularly buyouts in the UK and Europe – meant there was more scope for new LBOs. As such, the late 1990s saw an explosion in PEF.

Initially, the UK was both the main locus of funds and the main focus of fund investments (Jenkinson 2006). Over 70% of the total of European PEF fund capital was managed from the UK in 1997 and over 50% of total PEF investment was in the UK. Thereafter, the UK has remained the main locus for the management of funds but investment has progressively spread out across Europe – 2000 was the last year in which the UK was over 50% of the market. By 2005 it was less than a third of the total, which still made it the largest single focus of PEF. In any case, the growth in the UK was on a wholly new scale when compared to the 1980s and early 1990s. New firms emerged to exploit the new conditions. For example, in 1997 John Moulton, formerly of Schroders and then of Apax, founded Alchemy. In late 1999 Bridgepoint Partners was spun out of Natwest Equity Partners. Later in 2001 Permira, under Damon Buffini, was spun out of Schroders Ventures' Europe and in 2002 Montagu Private Equity was spun out from HSBC (EVCJ 2002).

Funding was one element that increased on a new scale:

There has been a remarkable increase in the absolute levels of UK private equity funding since the mid-1990s. Independent UK funds raised

£5.8 billion in 1999, compared with £749 million just four years before. Overseas investors have been the key driver behind this growth, accounting for 70 per cent of the funds raised in the UK in 1999 by BVCA members. Analysed by type of institution, overseas pension funds committed the most, contributing some 30 per cent of the overall UK private equity market. They were followed by overseas banks (14 per cent) and UK insurance companies (9 per cent). (Myners 2001: 172)[22]

The total value and individual size of deals in LBOs were other elements that increased on a new scale. In 1997 there was £10 billion worth of LBOs in the UK and every subsequent year to 2000 was a record year (Wright *et al.* 2006: 38 & 41). In 1998 individual £100 million deals became common. Publicly listed companies were increasingly affordable and 20% of the total value of all deals in 1998 was of this kind.[23] In 1999, the first billion plus deal since Gateway in 1989 was completed with the buyout of Avecia for £1.4 billion (Wright, Burrows *et al.* 2006: 9). In the following year the Gateway deal (£2.2 billion) was exceeded by the buyout of the commercial property organisation MEPC for £3.5 billion. In 2000 there was £20 billion worth of LBOs. The total PEF market in 2000 was four times its 1995 size and 25% of the market was now LBOs of publicly listed companies.

Although, PEF expanded on a wholly new scale it still did not rival the growth in the US. In 1999 US PEF raised $40 billion and in 2000 another $60 billion (Smith 2002: 67).[24] There was a rapid increase in the numbers and value of buyouts of publicly listed companies to 74 and almost $15 billion in 1999 (Toms and Wright 2005: 292 and 294) and a rapid rise in competition for these buyouts. By 2000 *Private Equity Analyst* was estimating that there were over 7,500 private equity practitioners in the US (Gupta 2000: 2).[25] The BVCA, by contrast, had less than 400 members. In the US fund solicitation was growing faster than the use of funds. This was one reason for the flow of capital to the UK where the use of funds was still growing faster than solicitation and there was less competition. As capital flowed, interest in emulating the New Economy became an important marketing tool for PEF as well as a focus of venture capital. New Economy-type investment grew year on year from 1997. In 1999 New Economy-type companies received more PEF investment in the UK than any other group. Commenting on its 1999 *Report on Investment Activity* the then BVCA chairman James Nelson stated: 'The most striking findings in this report are not only the record levels of investment overall but the record levels of investment into high technology companies. We also saw a very significant level of new funds raised, which are intended for this sector.' (BVCA 2000: 3).

However, this focus on the New Economy needs to be seen in context. Clearly very little of the rapidly expanding activity in buyouts of publicly listed companies would be of New Economy firms in the narrow sense of Internet/computing related products and services. Only 12.5% of the

177 buyouts of publicly listed companies 1997–2003 were of this kind and many of these were later buyouts of failing listed companies. Initially New Economy firms, with the exception of some telecoms, would be far more likely to be small unlisted businesses invested in or bought by PEF for subsequent IPO. In the UK publicly listed companies were being bought with new larger funds and on the basis that smaller listed companies by market capitalisation standards (£50–£200 million) were, despite general bull markets, having difficulty raising capital from institutional investors through small share issues (Renneboog *et al.* 2005: 4). This made them more amenable to some form of buyout from the point of view of investment and growth. The management would benefit through the buyout and current equity holders would benefit from premiums paid on the shares. Business services, retail, and property related companies were main sectors for such buyouts 1997–2000.

The effect of the New Economy and PEF in the UK, therefore, is probably best seen in terms of several dimensions. PEF benefited directly from the wealth effects of the New Economy in the US, since that wealth created the capacity for a flow of firms, funds, and institutional investors to the UK and Europe. PEF benefited indirectly since economic growth in the UK followed on from US growth and UK growth provided the capacity for UK PEF to grow in general. UK PEF benefited specifically from the nature of that growth since it provided the sectors in which buyouts could occur – business services etc. UK PEF also benefited specifically from the emulation of the US New Economy since this provided the focus for investment in various forms of tech firms for IPO in extremely receptive bull markets. In this latter, minority sense, UK PEF was also part of the problematic instability of the expansion of the New Economy, since emulation was also of the self-reinforcing focus on IPOs and on finding the next Netscape that fuelled equity prices. A liquidity surge based around particular kinds of equities, but not restricted in its effects to those equities, was similarly emerging in a British and European context. What the 'real' value of those equities ought to be faced similar problems. What is interesting about this from the point of view of PEF is that the demise of the dot.com boom was the demise of one form of unstable liquidity surge that gave birth almost immediately to another from which PEF was an even greater beneficiary. It was here that the original controversies of PEF LBOs came to the fore once more and did so both in the US and UK.

The dot.com crash

As set out in the previous chapter New Economy equities began to grow rapidly in the US from around 1995. This growth became even more rapid after 1997. Between 1998 and February 2000 Internet companies alone grew to 6% of the market capitalisation of all publicly listed companies and accounted for 20% of the volume of equity trading (Ofek and Richardson 2003: 1113). Equity growth was not without some volatility – and this reflected some underlying concerns regarding equity values (Markham vol. 1 2002: 351). The Nasdaq, for example, dropped 3.2% in January 2000. It recovered in February, however, to a new record of 4,500. Similarly, the broader Dow Index fell from 11,000 to below 10,000 within February. Both, however, continued a general upward movement and the Nasdaq reached a peak at 5,048 on the 10th of March (Siegel 2002: 49) whilst the Dow recovered to over 11,000 on March 16th, after a record gain of almost 500 points in one day (Markham vol. 1 2002: 351).[26] The total capitalisation of all US publicly listed companies was $17 trillion at the peak of the combined market that year (Stiglitz 2004: 138).

This equity growth was essentially unstable but not illusory in two senses. First it was not illusory because equity growth was also based on some concrete aspects of the New Economy – such as productivity growth – and also the shift in the composition of the US economy that had arisen around it – the expansion of New Economy based services, as well as the retail, finance, and construction sectors. Real jobs were created, services and products were supplied, and revenues were generated. Growing equity prices partly reflected a growing economy. US economic growth was, however, in many ways historically odd. Consumption increased as a proportion of GDP. The US became more import dependent, with a focus on importing more consumption goods, offset to some degree by exporting capital goods. There were large numbers of 'poor quality' jobs created and a range of new 'high quality' jobs, but also a hollowing out of mid-income mid-skill employment, including lower middle management. Job security reduced even as unemployment fell. Overall wealth grew yet income inequality also increased, savings levels fell, and personal debt rose. This was the reality of the US economy that developed in tandem with the New Economy.

Second, equity growth was not illusory in the sense that it had no antecedents. It was the case that equity growth was affected by the arbitrary valuations of some equities that also affected all equities creating an upward spiral of valuations. Arbitrary, however, does not mean the process was without causes. It was not simply 'irrational exuberance' in the sense of equally absurd optimism by all investors. This kind of phrasing tends to give the impression that the outcome was a baseless deviation from the routine practice of markets, that investors were in a position to be equally informed and that general gullibility rather than specific culpability explains events.[27] Investors were investing for different reasons based on different information. The accelerating growth of the market and the collapse of it had definite causes and triggers.

One immediate trigger was the convergence of various factors in March 2000 (Ofek and Richardson 2003). During an IPO of a new firm the various participants with a stake in the firm (venture capitalists and other PEF investors and their institutional investors and the various other 'insiders' – founders, main employees etc.) rarely sell all of that stake. Equity of around 15–20% is usually issued, followed by further share issues later. The underwriter of the IPO usually requires these insiders not to cash in additional stakes for a set period of six or 12 months. This restriction is termed a lock up. Limited share issues and lock ups are useful in two ways. First, a limited IPO tends to ensure that the issue will be fully taken up. Limited issues tend to result in higher premiums to early buyers as prices rise through the day. This creates a self-fulfilling expectation of upward equity prices that makes an IPO – particularly of a fashionable form of equity in a bull market – attractive.[28] Underwriters also avoid being left with unwanted issues that they have to cover. Plus, if for some reason the issue is not particularly successful, there can still be further rounds of share issues later. Second, since lock ups help to maintain a restricted or sellers market they help to sustain the general upward momentum of the market that in turn creates an environment conducive to IPOs. Insiders cashing out their stake do not flood the market.

However, a market can be flooded if at around the same time there accumulates large numbers of IPOs, large numbers of additional share issues by previously IPOd firms, and large numbers of lock ups coming to an end. In 1999 and 2000 there were 501 venture capital backed IPOs, a large increase on previous years (Sohl 2003: 9). Many of the larger former IPOs, such as Amazon, also issued additional shares. According to Ofek and Richardson from the end of 1999 through to the summer of 2000 an increasing number of lock ups came to an end, freeing $300 billion to be cashed out (2003: 1131). Of course, an increasing supply of equity to the market is not itself necessarily a problem. It becomes one if there is less buying than selling because this changes the overall dynamic of the market. This raises the question of who is buying and who is selling? According to Ofek and Richardson all kinds of insiders were selling, including institutional investors, but the main buyers were smaller retail investors i.e. insiders were not recycling back into the dot.com market (2003: 1125). More accurately, insiders were not recycling back into the market in the same proportions that they were cashing out.

There are several aspects to this. On the one hand main institutional investors such as pension funds maintain diversified portfolios and would therefore tend not to have a high proportion of their assets allocated to a single sector. In 2000, pension funds held less than 3% of their assets in Internet shares. The levels for institutional investors as a whole were higher but still around half of what they were for holdings of non-Internet stock (Ofek and Richardson 2003: 1112). To a degree this is understandable but if tech firms, and the New Economy as a whole, were growing so rapidly and could be expected to continue to do so because the nature of the US economy was changing, why maintain smaller proportions of New Economy equities? Doing so does not necessarily imply that investors thought the New Economy and its effects were entirely illusory – they continued to invest in large venture capital funds even as they failed to recycle back into the equity market (Kaplan 2002: 13, 17 & 19). However, it surely indicates that they were aware that equities were in some sense over-valued and that the upward momentum of valuations must eventually end. One reason why insiders would be more aware of this would be the changing dynamic of venture capital in the late 1990s.

The increase in the number of venture capitalists meant that there was both more competition to back new firms and less experience and expertise applied in assessing those firms (Sohl 2003). The increase in the number of funds and their scale meant venture firms could afford to pay more for new firms.[29] This created a 'hot money' effect where the venture capitalist pays more for their stake in the firm (Gompers and Lerner 2003).[30] This was in turn focused on a restricted range of firms as venture capital herded towards previously successful firm types – Internet, telecoms etc. – and PEF firms of other kinds started to encroach on traditional venture capital territory. The combination of more money to use in investment from larger funds and the need to develop the new firm quickly to get back some of that larger payment for the initial stake and to take advantage of the bull market – especially for tech IPOs – created a rush to bring firms to market with underdeveloped business plans and product/service development. The median company age of IPOs in 1999 and 2000 was less than five years (Smith 2002: 69). In 1999 Sanford Robinson of Robertson Stephens, the specialist investment bank that advises on and underwrites technology IPOs, was already seeing the problems:

> With more money around a company might start with $5 to $15 million, and when they run out of that, they still might not be at a positive cashflow, but there's another round at a higher price, rather than lower, because they're 'on track'. Venture companies are force fed which gets them to the public market a lot sooner, since they've had $10 or $15 million pumped into them before they even go public, rather than just $1 million. I have been worried that there's too much venture capital around chasing too few deals... Somewhere between now and five years from now there will be a shakeout in the industry – maybe because the public market is going to be tougher. (Gupta 2000: 135–6)

Insiders then would be aware that more of the new IPOs were of firms in an overpopulated market and were likely to have underdeveloped business plans and under-developed products and services – and that they were being brought to market quickly, partly because there was a bull market and partly because a lot of investment had been sunk into them. Of course, one might argue that any buyer of equity in an IPO ought to be in a position to assess the underlying potential of the firm from the prospectus the issuer is required to provide. This being so one might argue that if the investor is simply buying the shares on the basis of an expectation that share prices are rising in dot.coms and are hoping to exploit the momentum of the market then if the market falls they are victims of their own ignorance and avarice. They were momentum investors when momentum failed. However, momentum investment is not irrational even if it can be based on ignorance. It is rational to follow the trend of buying in a bull market if there is no reason to think it is about to stop – as any speculative investor will aver, the skill in such markets is to cash out before the peak. If outsiders had been in a position to know insiders were cashing out then they would have had some basis for thinking the momentum would not be sustained at that time. But this was not something they were in a position to easily know. They would only find out indirectly when a convergence of IPOs share issues and lock ups meant that insiders cashing out overwhelmed the upward movement of the market. By the time outsiders were in a position to be aware of this they were already going to be the ones carrying a disproportionate share of losses from any collapse in the market. Furthermore, many outsiders were given the illusion that they were insiders because of the role of financial analysts at the investment banks.

The Glass-Steagall Act of 1933 had federally mandated the separation of commercial and investment banking. In 1956 this was extended through the Bank Holding Company Act. Insurance was also separated – creating a division of labour for the three main aspects of financial services. This prevented two things (Brown 1995: 133–5. Stiglitz 2004: 158–64).[31] First, it prevented the commercial banks risking their deposits through sudden liabilities. For example, a stock market crash might affect a large security issue that the bank was underwriting, or it might affect the value of the financial products they offered through their insurance services. Separation was thus aimed to prevent bank insolvency problems. Second, it was designed to prevent practices that would undermine the ability both to assess the creditworthiness of a firm and assess its attractiveness as an investment. For example, if a bank both underwrote the securities of a firm and provided it with loans then there was a potential conflict of interest, since it becomes in the banks interest to advise others to invest in the firm's securities to maintain the ability of the firm to service its debt. Glass-Steagall was repealed in 1999.[32] It was, however, by then essentially dysfunctional because various large financial organisations had pushed through mergers – notably various investment banks and insurers in the mid-1990s. This was followed in 1997 and 1998 by the $83 billion merger of Citibank/Citicorp and the insurer, Travellers Group, which had already acquired the investment bank Salomon Brothers and Smith-Barney, to create Citigroup (Markham vol. 1 2002: 303).[33] Citigroup went on to grow through a series of mergers to become a vast multinational financial services conglomerate.

Integrated banking served to exacerbate an already existing conflict of interest created by the increasing consolidation of investment banking services in the 1970s, which I set out initially in Chapter 1. Here the significant point concerns the role of financial analysts employed by the brokerages (Stiglitz 2004). Analysts are supposed to provide impartial assessments of current and existing stock issues based on the underlying accounts of the relevant firm, the credit-worthiness of the specific issue, and the future prospects of the firm (Morgan 2003/2007). On this basis they advise subscribing clients whether to buy a new issue, whether to buy or sell an existing issue, and whether a firm is likely to under or over perform the market. The analyst is employed by the investment bank and thus is split between talking up new issues to ensure that the bank is not left guaranteeing a failed issue and providing accurate advice to investors to maintain the analyst's credibility and status within the public domain. The brokerage and analyst are also in a position to treat different investors differently (Golding 2003: 59).[34] For example, larger repeat business investors (who may be large clients of the insurance and commercial aspects of the enlarged bank) can be given preferential treatment on the initial allocation of shares for IPOs in attractive sectors of a bull market where first day gains are virtually guaranteed. These initial investors cash out and the analyst continues to promote the stock. This can occur even if the analyst thinks the stock is overvalued because after a while s/he becomes locked in to promoting it. In 1999 a *Wall St. Journal* survey showed that around 66% of analysts' pronouncements on stocks were recommended buys, around 33% recommended holds and just 1% were sells (Barry *et al.* 2005: 171). Clearly, it is a statistical impossibility for every stock to be or likely to be in the future, outperforming the market. The promotion not only maintains the large fee incomes analysts earn – star analysts were earning $10 million plus per year – but also maintains the upward movement of equity markets and thus the momentum of investment that prevents their initial over-statement of the stock coming to the fore. There can, therefore, be a rapid slide from dubious preferential treatment to misrepresentation and criminal financial malpractice.

In this context many outsiders might easily feel like insiders in the investment process focused around IPOs and the New Economy and, whilst they may have felt that in some sense share values seemed high, they could also be reassured in three ways. First, though since early 1998 policy advisors and economists had been arguing that the Fed should increase interest rates to slow equity market growth the Fed response was not dissimilar to that following the initial surge in New Economy equities in 1996, when Greenspan coined the phrase irrational exuberance but did not move decisively to slow the market. In mid-1999 the Fed did increase interest rates but only in a series of small ¼% increments into spring 2000 that effectively offset the reduction that had occurred in the wake of the East Asian and the Russian crises. Low interest rates made borrowing to buy equities relatively cheap and the failure to raise interest rates significantly or use some other means to reduce market growth (such as raising the registration costs of IPOs) gave the impression that the market could continue to grow. As critics of Greenspan now argue, Fed policy was part of the rationale of 'irrational exuberance' (Hartcher 2006; Canterbury 2006). Greenspan gave notice in early 2000 that interest rates would continue to rise until the market slowed but given the glacial rate of change and the relative cheapness of debt, borrowing to speculate on the markets did not seem absurd. Between September 1999 and January 2000, for example, margin debt (the outstanding debt on share trades) increased 36% in the US to an unprecedented $243 billion (Markham vol. 1 2002: 303). Second, though various assessments of the 'real' value of shares, such as those applied by Damodaran to Amazon, could show that they were at the very least difficult to reconcile with current actual valuations, there was always the underlying ideological point that the New Economy was a whole new business model that would, given the chance, transform how money was made. This point could easily be confused with the notion that valuation could outstrip anything history, trading and comparison might indicate.[35] Third, there was no reason, based on the advice being given by analysts, to suggest that the upward momentum of the market was going to end and that it was time to stop momentum investing. If a market was going to grow at what seemed like an unprecedented rate there was no necessary reason from an individual point of view why one wouldn't want to continue to profit from it now. It was not irrational for individuals to want to do so, even if in an abstract sense the market itself might be seen as irrational.

In March 2000 a tipping point was reached when cashing out exceeded buying creating a downturn in the market. That was enough to change sentiments precisely because many outsiders knew they were momentum investing and that equities were overvalued. If they could not rely on a self-reinforcing upward movement in the market then it was important to sell and do so quickly before others did so. A self-reinforcing upward movement thus became a self-reinforcing downward movement. The collapse spread incrementally across different kinds of New Economy companies as Kenney notes:

> In March 2000, the Nasdaq bubble that was driven by the technology stocks began to collapse. The first to drop were the profitless e-commerce firms (Pets.com, Eve.com, Boo.com ad infinitum). They were followed by the network equipment startups (e.g. Ciena, Sycamore, Extreme Networks) and then later in 2000 by the telecommunications firms (e.g. Qwest, Winstar, Global Crossing). As their stock prices fell, venture capitalists

and corporate insiders began unloading their [additional] large holdings at any price. At the same time, stock market analysts at the large investment banks recommended stocks that they were privately disparaging. (2003: 48–9)

Curiously, a debt management consultancy working in venture capital noted of the time: 'What I hear from most VCs and financial institutions in the technology sector that turn to Sherwood Partners is "I wish we had been able to see earlier the problems that we are faced with today."' (Pichinson 2002: 10). The editor of *Venture Capital Journal* was more phlegmatic: 'Why did VCs waste so much money on dot.coms and optics deals? Because they could.' (Aragon 2002: 2).[36] Despite prior concerns, funds grew and funds were invested (Moriarty 1999: 5). The eventual outcome was a catastrophic collapse of New Economy equities and a wave of insolvencies. From early 2000 to October 2002 the Nasdaq fell by almost 78% and the Dow by just under 39% (Tran 2006: 5). Over the period there were 862 failures of Internet companies, not including mergers and pre-insolvency buyouts (Kenney 2003: 49) and 23 insolvencies of the larger telecoms, again not including mergers and buyouts (Stiglitz 2004: 92). The immediate impact on PEF was mixed. On a positive note, Cohen recalls:

Between 1995 and 2001, Apax took fifty-two companies public on the stock exchanges of Europe and the United States: averaging one flotation every six weeks for six years. In one way it was exhilarating; in another, it became a cause for increasing concern.

In the event, we were fortunate. We disposed of our hi-tech holdings just before the bubble burst in early 2000. In fact we made seven times our money – about $1 billion – in our 1995 fund, which had a lot of hi-tech companies in its portfolio. (2007: 32)

As the market crash gathered pace, however, venture capital and buyout firms who had begun to operate in venture capital markets faced new anxieties and conditions. The crash meant that firms currently being developed for IPO in the near future, on the new average five year cycle for venture capital, and firms already scheduled for IPO suddenly found themselves in limbo. This created a basic uncertainty regarding the PEF firms' current ability to generate returns to funds and investors. It also created a problem for many of the firms they were backing that were not yet profitable – since a share issue would provide some basis for cash flow. This had further knock-on effects to all the smaller early stage venture-backed firms. Investors in venture capital funds are aware that only a small percentage of venture-backed firms go on to be successful. The bull market, however, had reduced the wariness of the venture capitalists and their investors regarding the financial viability of venture-backed firms.

Here the crash had four effects. First, investors started to require more stringent checks on the financial viability of venture-backed firms. Second, where large losses were made – investors started to threaten legal action on the basis that venture capital firms and venture-backed firms had not fulfilled the requirement of fiduciary care. Third, since the majority of capital committed to venture funds, as with any PEF fund, is not usually called in until it is required for investment, the sudden need to call on new rounds of investment created a funding gap for venture-backed firms.[37] As the market crashed, banks were less willing to fill this gap and the onus for bridging finance increasingly fell on the venture capital firms (Harris 2002b). Fourth, venture capital funds started to face the prospect that investors would simply default on their commitments – either because the crash had reduced their liquid capital assets or because they viewed the venture, particularly if led by the newer less experienced venture capitalist firms, as a poor investment and they wished to cut their losses (Rand and Weingarten 2002). This placed venture capital firms in a difficult position: legal action to enforce the terms of the original contract could be expensive, time consuming and damaging to their reputation and their future prospects of soliciting funds. Further, most funds contain a no-fault clause that allows the liquidation of the partnership agreement – usually on the basis of a significant majority vote. The prospect of large legal costs and adverse publicity could easily result in this clause being activated. Any bridging finance provided to venture-backed firms would then effectively become a potential loss since there would be no additional finance from the fund and no basis for the venture-backed firm to continue. Since PEF firms are not obliged to provide accounts to anyone but their investors – the extent of these effects are simply unknown – particularly since the basis of the problem tended to militate against formal legal action. As such the extent can only be obliquely indicated by the new focus in private equity based trade publications on debt distress, on strategies to deal with investor defaults to funds when new investment is called on, and on the problems of bridge financing (e.g. Harris 2002a).[38] Clearly, the viability of some venture capital firms was placed in question and this perhaps accounts for the reduction in the number of small venture capital firms in 2001.

This also had knock-on effects to PEF buyout firms in three senses. First, as the market crash spread from the New Economy firms to all equities and the Dow index fell, the IPO of buyout firm acquisitions faced similar problems to those of venture capital. Second, some of the large US PEF buyout firms suffered direct losses because debt payments became a problem. For example, KKR and Hicks, Muse, Tate & Furst had bought the chain Regal Cinemas in 1998 with an initial combined $1 billion in equity from their managed funds and $500 million in debt (Anson 2002: 11 & 17). A further $1.2 billion in debt was generated by 2000. In December of that year, faced with poor trading revenues, falling equity prices, and a problem in meeting junior debt payments, Regal was taken over by the distressed debt firm Philip Anschutz and Oaktree Capital Management. By May 2001 KKR had written off its $492 million investment.

Third, some of the large US PEF buyout firms also suffered direct losses because they had invested in listed companies through what are known as Private Investment in Public Entities or PIPEs (Dresner and Kim 2003). These PIPEs were minority investments in publicly listed companies. The investment could either be a privately negotiated purchase of equity with additional warrants at a favourable strike price or the purchase of preference shares that convert to ordinary equity shares. The main reason for these investments was that buyout funds had grown much faster than their investments. As noted previously, the majority of committed capital from investors in the fund is not usually called in until an investment is pending that requires it. However, management fees for the fund still accrue. To cover and justify the management fees for funds some PEF firms had essentially started acting like traditional investment portfolio managers or mutual funds – calling in capital and 'parking' it (Sparks 2000). The PEF firms hoped to profit from rising New Economy equities – via the appreciation of the equity stakes they had bought and by exercising warrants at strike prices below the expanding market price of equities. Some of them may have been aware of the insider-outsider problem that was emerging in equity investments but perhaps did not expect a sudden and large scale collapse of the markets and were prepared to gamble. In other instances perhaps the insider-outsider differentiation was a highly relative one.[39] In any case the collapse of the market meant equity investments reduced in value and, as market prices fell below strike prices, any outstanding warrants became worthless. Also, when listed firms battled insolvency and sort to generate cash flow by issuing more shares, preference shares, or convertible bonds, they effectively diluted the equity (and value) inherent in previous convertible issues. This is because as the total number of shares in a fixed sum of equity increases the individual value of each share decreases.[40] The net effect, even before firms started to go bankrupt or default on bonds and roll over dividend payments on preference shares, was a net loss to the PEF firms on the investments from their funds. Amongst the largest losses were those incurred by Hicks, Muse, Tate and Furst, which invested $1.3 billion in six publicly listed telecoms (Smith 2002: 67). Four went bankrupt and the other two traded well below the price at which Hicks invested. Notably, venture capital firms and specialist technology PEF firms, such as Silver Lake, made the smallest losses and in a few cases some profits from PIPEs. Later in the crash some PEF firms tried to reduce the problem of large accumulated commitments and limited outlets by actually reducing their fund capitalisation. A survey of 15 firms in 2002 by *Venture Capital Journal* found that they had in total reduced their current capitalisation by $4.2 billion to $9.87 billion (Primack *et al.* 2002: 7).

These kinds of reduction, however, were relatively small compared to the overall accumulation of solicited funds that had occurred through the late 1990s and that actually continued into the 2000s. Funds were solicited in the late 1990s and 2000 faster than new investment could occur creating an accumulation of capital. The 19 funds of a $ billion or more in venture capital in 2000 and the larger buyout funds raised particularly by the top five firms – TPG, KKR, Bain Capital and Carlyle – had not gone away. Moreover, though total solicitation for new funds in 2000 and 2001 fell it did not fall catastrophically as it did in the early 1990s. Rather it was increasingly focused on larger funds solicited by the longstanding and most prominent PEF firms (Primack 2001). The net effect was a concentration of capital and thus investment and buying power. The initial uncertainties of public equity markets in 2000–1 meant that less of that investment and buying power was initially utilised. Numbers of venture capital investments fell back to their 1996 level (Sohl 2003: 12) and LBOs to below their 1994 level (Rozwadowski and Young 2005: 68). The number of IPOs fell precipitously.

The buyout firms, in particular, however, seemed well placed to exploit a situation in which publicly listed companies would initially be cheaper due to falls in the value of their equity. They would also be well placed to engage in debt distress takeovers. For example, though KKR and Hicks, Muse had fallen victim to a distressed debt takeover of Regal Cinemas, Hicks, Muse was also engaged in distressed debt buyouts. Hicks bought Vlasic Foods International out of bankruptcy for $370 million in June 2001 (Anson 2002: 12). Vlasic had assets of $458 million, including some well known brand names that could be sold to other foods companies, and since it was acquired out of Chapter 11 bankruptcy its new incarnation would be debt free and would have no other holders of equity.[41] Distressed debt investment could often be an extremely lucrative use of PEF funds. Furthermore, since the market collapse could not be expected to last forever buyout activity could be undertaken on the expectation that there would be a rising market at the time of a future IPO.

Conclusion

The dot.com boom was an unstable liquidity surge in which venture capital was intimately related and which had significant effects on the practices and scales of PEF buyout funds. The subsequent market crash was to spread out over 2000–02. From 2003 the number of LBOs increased rapidly in the US and also in the UK. LBOs also increased as a proportion of total PEF activity and as a proportion of total merger and acquisition activity. This was to reach new scales by 2004. Here responses to the collapse of the New Economy liquidity surge directly benefited PEF buyouts. In the twenty first century the emergence of new banking practices and new practices amongst the PEF firms enabled larger LBOs based on greater degrees of leverage. Put another way the constraints on the growth of larger LBOs that had been maintained in the 1990s, even as liquidity grew, were undone by the market crash of March 2000. Overall systemic conditions became conducive to the same kind of circumstances for PEF LBOs has had occurred in the 1980s in the US. The banks and the finance system became more willing and able to facilitate PEF LBOs. In exploiting these new opportunities PEF then contributed to the conditions that would lead to the 'credit crunch'. I now move on to look at this in greater detail in Chapter 4.

4
Private Equity Finance in the Twenty First Century: Liquidity and the Credit Crunch

The growth of PEF funds and acquisition activity in the twenty first century reached new heights in 2006 and early 2007. The scope of funds and the focus of activity had not, however, been restricted to the US and UK. It had become a more global phenomenon, based on regional and global funds. By 2007 the database of the industry advisory service organisation Private Equity Intelligence (Preqin) contained almost 10,000 PEF funds managed by more than 5,200 firms in 93 countries (Preqin 2008: 12). In 2005 $26 billion was raised for use in emerging markets defined as investments outside of the US, UK, and the core of Europe (Preqin 2006: 1). This was a 300% increase on 2004. In 2005 Permira opened an office in Japan and in 2006 TPG opened one in Moscow.[1] Many of the main firms now had Asia-focused funds and the industry based trade journals were increasingly reporting on the potential in Eastern Europe, India and China (e.g. Tannon 2006; Hane 2006; Subhash 2006).[2] Activity in Europe also grew. By 2005 the European Venture Capital Association (EVCA) database was tracking 1,600 PEF firms managing 2,600 European focused funds. From 2000 to 2005, PEF investment in Europe, including the UK, rose from 17% to 43% of the global total, whilst the proportion of solicited funds rose from 17% to 38% (Maslakovic 2006a: 1). Despite an underlying trend for activity to be more geographically dispersed, however, the UK and US continued to dominate as sources of funding and the origin of firms, and remained in combination the focus for around 60% of the total activity of PEF (Jenkinson 2006; Maslakovic 2006).[3] Global, therefore, still meant a mainly US and UK phenomena.

By 2007 PEF had grown significantly in three ways. First, there was a growth in the total number of PEF funds of all kinds (fund of funds, mezzanine etc.) and within that a growth in the number of PEF buyout funds. The growth in the number of funds became particularly significant from 2004 (Preqin 2005: 5).[4] The Preqin 2007 *Global Fundraising Review* reported a record 899 new funds had been created in 2006, but not yet closed, and that a further 500 were expected to begin to solicit capital. In the same year

188 specifically buyout funds completed solicitation and this was also a record. Second, underlying the growth in the number of funds was also the concentration of funds in larger single solicitations dominated by the main PEF firms. This trend had been developing in the US for some time but now also began to manifest in the UK (Wright *et al.* 2006: 40). In 2006, for example, the scale of mega-funds reached new levels with Blackstone soliciting a $20 billion fund and Carlyle and TPG each soliciting one of $15 billion (WSJ 2006). During the ten years to 2008 the top five US firms had each solicited over $50 billion (Preqin 2008: §4). In the UK in 2006 Permira completed the £7.4 billion solicitation of its Permira IV Fund (Quinn 2007). Apax and Alchemy were also now able to solicit multi-billion funds.[5] Overall, average fund sizes were increasing but the distribution of funds was also becoming more skewed.[6] A similar pattern emerged, therefore, as that found in venture capital in 1990s.

Third, there was a growth in the total size of private equity fund capital available. Preqin (2007) reported an estimated global committed capital for all types of funds of $607 billion for 2006 compared to $473 billion in 2003. The 188 new buyout funds that closed in 2006 raised $212 billion between them. The greatest proportion (95) and with the greatest proportion of capital ($124 billion) had a geographical focus on the US, followed by a European focus (61 and $72 billion respectively). The growth in new commitments began from 2004, following on from a slowdown from the previous peak in the US and UK in 2000–01. Notably, the slowdown was not as severe as that of the early 1990s. Furthermore, from 2000 the UK PEF firms, as with the US, solicited new commitments faster than funds made investments, producing a growing accumulation of capital. As a result, the total of available fund commitments for PEF expanded in the UK as they had been doing in the US. For 2006 Thomson Financial estimated that the available global fund commitments exceeded $700 billion. The Preqin estimate for 2007 was $820 billion (2008: 12).

By the mid-2000s the growth in the number of funds, the size of some funds and the accumulated unused capital committed to funds had radically altered the purchasing power for PEF buyouts. This was further facilitated by three other trends. First, the main PEF firms became increasingly amenable to doing 'club deals' (McCarthy and Alvarez 2006: 17). A club deal is where acquisitions are done using a combination of funds – several funds administered by the same private equity firm or more usually several funds administered by several firms. Second, funds also began to invite minority equity investment in deals, particularly from large institutional investors.[7] This was in addition to the use of equity capital from the PEF funds. Third, banks and capital markets became increasingly amenable to allowing higher levels of leverage on larger levels of debt (Acharya *et al.* 2007). Average leverage levels started to increase in both the US and UK. In the US leverage levels increased to over 75% of the total value of the deal for the first time since the 1980s, whilst in the UK they rose to over 50%, and then over 60% in 2006. The average also disguised a significant standard deviation – larger club deals under the auspices of well established PEF firms could generate higher levels of leverage still. Higher leverage levels were also associated with higher multiples or ratios of debt to the earnings of acquisitions – a standard way of measuring debt servicing capacity. The ratio of debt to earnings before interest, tax, depreciation, and amortisation (EBITDA) increased from four in 2002 to six in 2006 according to a Standards & Poor's report in November of that year.

Since more debt could now be added to equity in any given buyout then larger scale buyouts could be done with any given level of PEF fund equity. Since individual funds had on average become larger and some funds had become 'mega' then larger amounts of equity existed in individual pools of capital. Since PEF firms could call on additional minority investors to provide more capital for equity and could also cooperate with other firms to use the capital of other funds then the total pool of available equity capital for any given buyout was higher still. Of course, the range of available targets for LBO and the growth in the number of funds and firms meant also that PEF would continue to engage in the LBO of small to medium sized firms from a variety of previous ownership forms. For example, data in February 2007 from the Oxford-based research company Fast Track indicated that in terms of frequency mid-size companies dominated acquisition activity in the UK.[8] However, the large PEF buyout firms found themselves in a position to engage in LBOs of publicly listed companies on a scale that had not been the case in the US since the late 1980s and had, with a few exceptions, never been the case in the UK. In principle no FTSE 100 or Dow Jones listed company was now too expensive to be considered. Permira alone could in principle use its Permira IV Fund, in conjunction with 60% leverage, to buy a publicly listed company with a market capitalisation of over £20 billion.[9] Three $15 billion funds using 75% leverage could in principle buy a publicly listed company with a market capitalisation of $180 billion. More realistically, PEF firms could each use some fraction of the capital from their funds and combine to engage in multi-billion buyouts of prominent corporations.

Alan Jones head of corporate finance at Morgan Stanley summarises the situation:

> Morgan Stanley estimates that there are now some 2,700 funds that either have raised, or are in the process of raising, a total of half a trillion dollars... When a number of us were at the Harvard Business School some twenty years ago, there were probably only four private equity firms that had $1 billion funds. Today there are more than 150 firms of that size... And by virtue of their increasing size, and their willingness to work together in 'club' deals, they can do much bigger transactions than was ever

thought possible. With all this equity capital available, and with the help of remarkably forgiving leveraged finance markets, today's financial sponsors are able to pay much higher prices for assets than they could five or six years ago.

So we're clearly seeing private equity firms paying bigger prices, doing larger deals and, as a result, having a much more significant role in the global economy than they did ten or 20 years ago. Private equity transactions now account for a quarter of all global M&A activity – and they also account for half of the leverage loan volume, a third of the high yield [junk bond] market and a third of the IPO market. (Jones in Jones *et al.* 2006: 10)[10]

In the US the result was an increase in the number of headline-grabbing mega-deal individual buyouts. Seven of the then ten largest ever buyouts occurred in 2006 (*Thomson Financial*, 2007). TPG, for example, was involved in a variety of prominent club deals in a remarkably short period of time. In 2005, in conjunction with Silver Lake, Bain Capital, KKR and others, it bought SunGard Data Systems for $11.4 billion. In 2006 it was involved in club deals for Biomet for $10.9 billion, Univision for $13.7 billion, Freescale Semiconductor for $17.6 billion and Harrah's Entertainment for $27.8 billion (Sherman and Hart 2006: 5). In 2007 it led the club deal buyout of the Texas utility company TXU Corporation for approximately $44 billion. This deal, which was not yet fully completed in late 2007, broke the record of the previous year held by a Blackstone led consortium that had bought Equity Office Properties, a US real estate brokerage and landlord, for $39 billion. After adjusting for inflation, these deals still exceeded the level of KKR's buyout of RJR Nabisco and, according to the 2007 IMF bi-annual *Global Financial Stability Review*, helped inflate the average size of a buyout deal to $1.3 billion. Other prominent deals included those for Hertz car rental, Dunkin Donuts, and Toys-R-Us (McCarthy and Alvarez 2006).

In the UK meanwhile, the trend towards increasing proportions of larger buyouts of publicly listed companies begun in the late 1990s continued (Wright, Burrows *et al.* 2006: 8–9). In 2001 Yell Group was bought by Apax and Hicks Muse from British Telecom for £2.1 billion, in 2004 the AA was bought by CVC and Permira for £1.8 billion (Ganguin and Bilardello 2005: 413–14). There were 47 deals over £100 million in 2004 and 49 in 2005. The AA deal attracted the interest of the TUC and GMB unions. PEF activity started to become a political and employment relations issue. In 2007 the failed attempt by a CVC and TPG led consortium to buy J. Sainsbury for approximately £10 billion and the successful buyout of Alliance Boots by KKR for approximately £11 billion brought this interest to a head. Other prominent deals over the period included the buyout of Saga, New Look and Debenhams. We will look at the cases of J. Sainsbury and Alliance Boots in Chapter 8.

The late 1990s, then, had begun a period of growth for PEF LBOs that the market collapses of the early 2000s had done no more than slow. Specifically, it briefly slowed fund solicitation, though not enough to prevent the continued accumulation of unused fund capital, and it briefly slowed the IPO of buyouts. The significant question is why was PEF activity of all kinds ultimately a beneficiary of the market collapse of the early 2000s? There are several related answers to this question. As noted at the end of Chapter 3, by the end of the 1990s PEF had developed in ways that allowed it to take advantage both of rising markets and falling markets. Rising markets provided wealth effects and marketing opportunities that fed fund solicitation and created attractive IPO conditions as well as creating opportunities for particular types of investment – the New Economy and so forth. Falling markets create opportunities for buyouts of debt distressed firms and firms who are undervalued in terms of their market capitalisation. Though banks may be more or less wary of providing credit for complex debt structures and markets may be more or less liquid at any one time, PEF firms were in a position to make the claim, despite their track record of problem investments in both rising markets and falling markets (PIPES, CLECs etc.), that they were able to generate returns in a variety of market conditions. In this sense they shared a basic attribute with hedge funds.

In the first decade of the twenty first century this could seem particularly significant to institutional investors. Some institutional investors generated large losses from the market collapses of 2000–02, particularly since the collapses were not confined to dot.coms, telecoms or hi-tech equities.[11] Institutional investors also generated increased liabilities in conjunction with those losses – particularly the pension funds. Historically low interest rates and initially subdued equity markets, meanwhile, made many forms of traditional investment less attractive. New kinds of investors also emerged as sources of finance for PEF and as competitors in LBOs – hedge funds and later sovereign wealth funds. At the same time, the banks were increasingly making use of debt structuring techniques that claimed to reduce the risk involved in higher risk forms of investment, like PEF, making larger PEF LBOs seem a more viable investment once again. The banks themselves had a vested interest in promoting PEF since it provided a new motor for merger and acquisition activity from which they could generate fee income in the wake of the dot.com collapse. Due to the collapse, larger firms were now more vulnerable, and later, more amenable, to a PEF buyout than during the 1990s. The PEF firms could offer higher premiums above the current share prices of firms than in the past, 'active investors' like hedge funds could rapidly acquire a significant interest in a firm and support a bid to make a short term profit, corporate executives who had accumulated extensive share option packages could cash in some of them at a premium and still retain a greater equity stake in the new firm. Once markets started to recover debt creation had become a core constituent in market activity and a key aspect of liquidity.

All these factors helped to fuel PEF funds and enable PEF LBOs of larger publicly listed companies. They are essentially factors relating to the nature of the economy that developed in the twenty first century in the US and UK and the nature of aspects of finance that went along with that development. The significant point about this in terms of the shift to larger PEF LBOs is that they generated a liquidity surge for PEF that was itself unstable, much as it had been in the 1980s in the US. The expansion of PEF fed off that liquidity and was brought to a halt with its demise in what became known as the 'credit crunch'. Here one can view PEF once again in the context of its systemic relations. It can be viewed as merely utilising available liquidity but it can also be viewed as a reason for the unstable sources of liquidity to expand and thus, reciprocally, for PEF LBOs also to grow in terms of scale and frequency. In so doing PEF creates potentially more vulnerable acquisitions with higher levels of leverage and also contributes to the problems of the sources of complex debt structures on which it feeds – adding in a sense to the context of PEF's own change in circumstances by contributing to systemic changes. From this point of view any claims from PEF firms regarding the delivery of returns in a variety of market conditions, whilst not false *per se* (though they are certainly as contingent as the claims of hedge funds), take on a different inflection in terms of their overall benefits. We will look at this in more detail in Chapters 5–7.

The economy and institutional investment

Based on technical issues there is some dispute about whether the US entered recession in the third quarter of 2000, since the economy subsequently posted net falls in GDP in three *non*-consecutive quarters to the end of 2001. However, it is certainly the case that the economy began a downturn or slowdown in 2000 and this persisted into 2003, with unemployment rising to over 6% and net employment falling by over three million. After the initial share price collapses of 2000, the attack on the World Trade Centre on the 11th of September 2001 caused a further sudden fall in equity. The New York Stock Exchange did not reopen until September 17th and on that day the Dow fell over 7% to just under 9,000 and continued a general (if volatile) decline to Spring 2003 reaching a low of around 7,500. The Nasdaq similarly fell to below 1,500. Both began to recover thereafter and a new bull market began. Even before the bull market, however, the net effect on share prices was far larger than the overall impact on economic activity. When economic growth did fall, the amounts were small – fractions of 1%. Consumption also continued to grow. These two factors were not unrelated.

In 2001 the Fed started a process of reducing interest rates that would continue until 2004.[12] This was a response to several circumstances. In 2001 and into 2002 general uncertainty about the New Economy was exacerbated by a series of specific corporate scandals (Jetter 2003; Langley

2003). Some of the largest telecoms that had grown through mergers and acquisition based partly on new share issues and share swaps were now revealed to have few genuine assets, highly overstated revenues, and highly understated debts (Morgan 2003/2007: 109–10). As markets fell in 2000 it became more difficult for these firms to grow through merger and more difficult to hide their lack of underlying real revenue and their inability to service debt. They then had to post large losses in 2001 that caused their share prices to plummet further and this set off investigations into their accounts and the practices of their accountants and the analysts who had promoted their stock. A wave of litigation occurred against the investment banks and new conglomerate financial service organisations. These organisations had both made loans to the firms and rated their stock as a buy.[13] Enron, Worldcom and Qwest all collapsed, as did the accountants Arthur Anderson. The main banks, meanwhile, paid fines in excess of $1.4 billion.

In reducing interest rates the Fed was initially responding to the specific uncertainty regarding the New Economy and the growth that had come on the back of both the Internet and telecoms. However, though, lowering interest rates makes the use of debt to invest in shares cheaper and also reduces the debt servicing costs of corporations, with the intention of increasing productive investment and/or dividend payments, it is no guarantee that equity markets will recover quickly if a bear market is locked in and if trust in the valuation of shares is undermined. Furthermore, the 9/11 attack also brought into question the future stability of the US economy, since it raised the possibility of both frequent disruptive attacks on US infrastructure and prominent multinationals *and* the prospect of an expensive and protracted military mobilisation. With relatively low inflation the Fed thus became locked into a process of steadily reducing interest rates and this continued into 2004 when they reached an historic low of 1%. In 2003 George Bush Jr. also reduced capital gains tax on top of the Clinton reduction – this time to 15%.[14] Bush was also committed to a range of cuts to direct taxation following similar principles to the early Reagan era.

Though equity prices did not recover quickly, the overall economy did. One reason for this was that the restructuring of the economy in the US during the 1990s was one that had become particularly receptive to lower interest rates. Financial and business services had grown in tandem with the New Economy and wealth effects had created a retail boom. Low interest rates had also fed the housing market, which in turn had expanded the construction and retail DIY sectors, as well as real estate and mortgage brokering as aspects of financial services (Hatch and Clinton 2000). Cheap debt had expanded credit services. Rising house prices and remortgaging had generated equity release for further consumption, expanding the leisure sector of the economy. Changes in family dynamics had also created a growing domestic labour industry and childcare sector, as well as further demand for housing construction for divided families. Lower interest rates, whilst the housing market continued to grow and consumption continued to grow, thus meant that the economy could recover more quickly than the continued fall in share prices might indicate. The nature of that recovery would later become problematic as the dot.com bubble metamorphosed into a housing bubble.[15]

In the meantime, the fall in share prices was not without its costs. State revenues were directly impacted:

> California, the richest state in the union with an economy of $1.3 trillion, faces a $21 billion budget shortfall in 2002. Some of this is due to general recession to which the collapse of the stock market has contributed. Some if it is directly attributable to that collapse. In 2000, California received $17 billion in taxes on stock market profits, mainly from dot.coms – in 2002 that figure fell to $5 billion. Cuts in state spending of $10 billion have subsequently been announced including state worker redundancies, pay freezes, and reduced healthcare expenditure. (Morgan 2003/2007: 111)

Investments as forms of savings were also damaged:

> Three million jobs were lost at the same time as many retirees whose investment savings had vanished were seeking to return to work. In the meantime, endowments and foundations cut their spending and pensions' plans unfunded liabilities soared while corporations posted losses or profit declines due to rising contributions to their pension plans to make up for the losses in their equity investments. (Tran 2006: 6)

In this context low interest rates were a mixed blessing since lower interest rates also tend to mean lower current levels of returns on investments of all kinds. Public and private pension funds and other large institutional investors were thus provided with good reasons to allocate funds to higher risk forms of investment, such as PEF.[16] By 2005 the combined assets of pension, insurance and mutual funds for Europe and the US stood at over $40,000 billion (Maslakovic 2006b: 5). Total allocations to PEF had grown in the US to an average of 7% from around 4–5%.[17] Significantly, this is a raw average – many institutional investors, particularly pension funds, allocate nothing to PEF. The increase is thus from a smaller pool of investors. It should also be considered in terms of the initial fall in the capitalisation of some large institutional investors at the time of the market crash. This may be one reason why the decline in PEF fund solicitation was not as extreme as it had been in the early 1990s (some institutions maintained or increased their allocations at a time of lower capitalisations) and why the recovery thereafter was so marked. On a purely impressionistic basis, if one tracks the investor news in the main private equity trade journals then there is a clear sense of growing absolute levels of allocation to PEF from particular institutional investors – particularly large state and corporate pension funds (e.g. Preqin 2006b: 9). These faced increasing liabilities ('black holes') as the decade developed because of a combination of increasing life expectancies, new accounting restrictions, poorly performing investment portfolios and a persistent pattern of insufficient contributions from employers.[18]

The situation was a similar one in the UK where the bear market of 2000–03 saw the FTSE index fall by 53% from a high of 6662 and AIM fall by 82%. Interest rates fell from 6% in February 2000 to a low of 3.5% July 2003 and the housing market expanded rapidly. Large UK pension funds faced similar liability problems to those in the US, based on a similar range of factors (Morgan 2006b) and thus had good reasons to turn to alternative investment forms. This was something that New Labour was keen to promote.[19] Prior to the market crash and with the New Economy thesis in mind, the Chancellor had commissioned Paul Myners of Gartmore Investment Management to undertake a review of the various impediments to pension fund investment in PEF (see Chapter 2). The Myners report of 2001 recommended new codes of practice for trustees and new provisions for trustees that would require them to become more skilled and aware in matters of investment and finance, including PEF. The codes and provisions were reviewed in 2004 (HM Treasury 2004: 21) and informed the statutory basis of the Pensions Act of that year and the industry watchdog Opra. On the basis of Myners' previous interim report the UK finally adopted in 2001 a version of the prudent expert interpretation of the investment responsibility framework for pension funds that had been introduced in the US in 1979 (Myners and Payne 2001: 20). The ambiguous status of PEF regarding §191 of the Financial Services Act 1986, which required that any investment activity be by a person authorised under the Act, was also clarified. Under the Act and its replacement, the Financial Services and Markets Act 2000, an intermediary was not required. Furthermore, the government showed itself to be sympathetic to PEF by not pressing the point that a trustee's duty to oversee the investment activities of those to whom investments are entrusted might conflict with the LLP status (and tax position) of PEF funds.

This sympathetic position ran also to the general issue of taxation. When taper relief on capital gains tax was first introduced in 1998 an asset had to be held for ten years to qualify for the reduced CGT of 10% (from the standard 20%). In 2000 the duration was reduced to four years and in 2002 to two years. Shorter durations in order to qualify for taper relief on CGT were not aimed specifically at PEF but PEF firm general partners and fund investors who were not tax-exempt could clearly benefit from it.[20] That this was the case was underscored in regard of the Income Tax Act of 2003. §421 of the Act was intended to close a loophole that allowed high earners working in investment and finance to structure large portions of their pay (especially bonuses) as capital gains rather than income. The BVCA successfully lobbied government for a memorandum of understanding from the Inland

Revenue in 2003 exempting a PEF firm's main form of payment (carried interest – see Chapters 5 and 7). The BVCA also continued to lobby for an end to taper relief and its replacement with a universal 10% CGT (EVCJ 2003: 2). PEF firms continued to have numerous concerns regarding the way they were regulated but, as a *European Venture Capital Journal* article of the time notes, were also aware that at this time the government was committed to promoting PEF:

> Had the BVCA's permanent executive, led by [CEO John] Mackie, not put itself close to the pulse of government it would not have been able to do a combination of telling the government what it needed to hear and pure hard lobbying in order to win the concessions it sought for the industry. (Bushrod 2005: 6)

By 2005 institutional investment allocations to PEF in Europe, focused primarily through the UK, had risen to an average of 5%. As with the US, actual allocations were highly variable. In the UK PEF solicitation was now a beneficiary of both the diversion of PEF investment from the US (channelled through the large commercial banks and financial organisations) and also growing domestic institutional investment. In 2005, according to the EVCA, banks provided 31.4% of capital for European private equity funds, pension funds 25.1% and insurance funds 12.6% (EVCA, 2006). PEF funds of funds provided a further 16%.

Liquidity and debt: the banks, syndication, securitisation, and the terms of lending

The investment banks had clear motivations to encourage PEF LBOs. The bear market meant that the number of IPOs reduced and (initially) merger and acquisition activity was suppressed. The growth of the New Economy had been a significant source of fee income for the banks. Annual investment bank fees from telecoms alone had risen from $1.06 billion in 1996 to $4.14 billion in 2000 (Malik 2003: 169). Furthermore, the banks faced capitalisation issues based on the value of their asset holdings. Defaults, bankruptcies and a general bear market created problems of bad debt for the commercial banking arms of the financial organisations and poor returns for investment fund management divisions. Investment funds such as US mutual funds and UK unit trusts tend to hold 'long' positions in equities i.e. they buy shares with an expectation of rising markets. Hedge funds by contrast combine short positions (holding options on assets such as shares where the option is structured to profit from a fall in prices) and long positions.[21] Alternative investment forms that can claim to deliver returns in a variety of market conditions become more attractive to the banks because of bear markets and as a means to overturn bear markets.

This included PEF and hedge funds, forms of which the main banks operated, invested in, and promoted.[22]

By 2003 many of the large PEF firms were diversifying into hedge funds and hedge funds were diversifying into PEF LBOs.[23] The PEF firms diversified for precisely the same reason that the banks promoted PEF: hedge funds claim to be able to make returns in bear markets. As investment flowed to hedge funds, hedge fund capitalisation grew in much the same manner as PEF funds. Large hedge funds now had the capital to be major providers of credit to PEF (becoming sources for junior debt structures) and also to be collaborators in LBO club deals (Shepard *et al.* 2007). Hedge funds like Cerberus Capital thus became hybrid operations adding to the total purchasing power of PEF both as sources of credit and equity. As of 2004 there were approximately 9,000 hedge funds with almost $1 trillion in assets.[24] 'In 2004, 23 companies were bought by hedge funds in deals worth $30 billion.' (Rozwadowski and Young 2005: 70). The more important point, however, is that investment banks had a vested interest in encouraging the expansion of PEF – it provided an alternative motor for merger and acquisition activity and generated fee income from LBOs. In 2004 the main investment banks earned $2.865 billion in fees from the top ten private equity firms (Rozwadowski and Young 2005: 72). As the number and scale of PEF LBO deals increased through 2005 to 2007 total fees continued to increase as they had in the 1980s.[25]

The banks, however, did not just have a vested interest in promoting PEF on the basis of fee income. Commercial banks were also more inclined to provide higher levels of leverage on larger levels of debt because of changes in their strategies towards debt creation. The major problem for any bank in providing a large loan to a PEF firm that then passes it to a highly leveraged acquisition is that if the company that has been acquired cannot service the debt at some future point then the bank carries the loss. However, if several banks cooperate to form a consortium that provides the loan then a larger loan can be offered without any single bank carrying the whole risk. Furthermore, if the banks do not hold onto the debt but rather syndicate it then they can profit from the initial loan without carrying the subsequent risk. This can simply involve acting as an underwriter. Here the bank(s) guarantee in a manner analogous to the underwriting of bond issues, to undertake the lending themselves if the loan cannot be syndicated. The syndication involves packaging the loan as a series of smaller loans passed to other financial organisations and investors (other banks, hedge funds and so forth) in exchange for fees. The process can also, however, involve more complex financial instruments. In either case, syndication and what became known as the 'originate and distribute' lending model increasingly became key strategies in banking.

Securitisation has been a main way in which originate and distribute works. Securitisation occurs when a company separates out some of its assets and uses them to raise funds in capital markets (Raynes 2003; Schwarcz 1994). In principle the separated asset can be anything but it is usually an income stream i.e. a series of expected future payments due at given times. Typically these payments are debts owed – credit cards, mortgages repayments, car loans, LBO loans.[26] Since they involve an income stream they are termed 'receivables'. Since the asset is usually a debt owed then securitisation often originates from financial organisations, such as a bank.[27] The key step is that a bundle of receivables is sold to a legally distinct entity commonly termed a special purpose vehicle (SPV). It is important that the SPV is legally distinct because rights to the income stream need to be insulated from any insolvency or bankruptcy problems with the originating organisation.[28] This insulation is vital so that the SPV can use the assets to create a security issue that it can sell on capital markets. The assets (rights to the future income stream of payments) become the collateral that backs an issue of securities (like a bond). The issue can either be on a public exchange or, more typically, a private placement through brokers. Investors buy the securities and are in turn paid by the SPV from the income stream created by the receivables. The purchase of the securities, in turn, creates the capital with which the SPV ultimately pays the originating organisation.

A core issue in securitisation is that the receivables involve a possibility of default i.e. bad debt. The securities issued are collateralised by the receivables. Payment is based on the absence of default in the underlying asset i.e. is based on the income stream from the mortgage repayment, loan payments etc. Defaults in the underlying asset remove the guarantee of payment because the investor is being paid to carry the risk of default. The SPV must, therefore, in order to induce investors to invest, operate according to a strategy that provides investors with a sense that their level of risk is known and that the returns on investments justify the risk. This is done in four ways. First, the deal by the SPV to buy the receivables from the originating organisation takes into account the recent statistical incidence of defaults for the kind of receivables involved (for example, 1 in 10,000). The SPV then tries to negotiate an 'over-collateralisation' i.e. the initial bundle of assets is aimed to be large enough to provide an income stream that is more than sufficient to make future payments to the investors in the securities. This also protects the solvency of the SPV.

Second, the SPV splits the receivables into tranches or layers of debt. The tranches follow a line of credit seniority as with any other debt structure and the most senior level is paid first from the income stream whilst the most junior level is paid last, and is thus the first to experience any losses from defaults.[29] A credit rating for the tranches is also set. One of the rating agencies, such as Standards & Poor's, assesses how the statistically expected rate of default will impact on each tranche and a compensating rate of return is set by the SPV to induce investors to buy the securities. The lower the tranche, the lower the credit rating, and thus the higher the offered rate of return. Investors choose their level of risk by choosing which tranche to invest in.

Third, the securities in each tranche are constructed by taking strips of individual receivables (debts) and pooling them. Each security includes strips of many receivables and thus the value of any individual security should not be wiped out by the expected statistical incidence of defaults. Pooling is designed to spread the risk and impact of defaults by reducing its significance for any individual security raising, in theory, the overall credit worthiness of the securities. Fourth, the existence of a secondary market, which the underwriter is expected to help provide, in which the securities can be traded by investors, means that the investor need not be left holding securities in which they have no confidence – they are a potentially liquid asset.

The securities generated by SPVs are generically termed collateralised debt obligations (CDOs) if the underlying assets are mainly mortgage bonds, corporate bonds, credit card debt etc. and collateralised loan obligation (CLOs) if the underlying assets are mainly bank loans.[30] As Schwarcz notes, securitisation in general is advantageous because:

> One of the most important indirect benefits is that asset securitization is usually viewed, for accounting purposes, as a sale of assets and not as financing, the originator does not record the transaction as a liability on its balance sheet. Such off balance sheet funding thus raises capital without increasing the originator's leverage or debt-to-equity ratio on its financial statements. (1994: 142–3)

Securitisation is not new of course.[31] It was facilitated by the liberalisation of finance markets in the mid-1980s and was given impetus by the transformations in investment banking that encouraged financial innovation to create more complex forms of debt structures (Mathews 1994; Duffie and Rahi 1995: 5–7).[32] States with liberalised financial systems also specifically encouraged securitisation because it could be used to increase specific forms of lending which were considered politically and economically beneficial. For example, the US Secondary Mortgage Enhancement Act of 1984 enabled the securitisation of domestic mortgages with the intention of allowing more mortgage lending to occur.[33] States also inadvertently encouraged securitisation by adopting the Basel Banking Accord of 1988. The Accord, which was adopted by the G10 nations in 1992, required the banks in those nations to hold capital reserves (termed Tier 1 capital) equal to 8% of a weighted measure of its assets.[34] The weighting represented the risk level of those assets split into 5 categories. The categories ran from zero risk (Treasury securities, as in the case of the example of the US recapitalisation of the thrifts in the early 1990s in Chapter 2) to very high risk.[35] Since high risk is higher weighted the more high risk assets a bank holds the higher its actual capital reserves are required to be. Higher capital reserves mean less free capital for lending. Since the returns on higher risk assets (the interest rates the bank charges and so forth) are higher then the banks were provided with a motive to minimise their requirement to maintain capital reserves whilst maximising the proportion of higher risk assets they trafficked in. Securitisation and originate and distribute were ideal solutions because they allowed higher risk lending without the requirement for permanent large increases in capital reserves. For a bank, the primary function of securitisation through an SPV is precisely to redistribute its lending.[36] For this reason such SPV's are termed 'conduits'.

Though securitisation grew during the 1990s it grew far more rapidly in the twenty first century. This was for two basic reasons. First, the statistical modelling required to construct the securities as stripped and pooled assets to which a price (rate of return) can be applied is extremely complex.[37] As such, creating CDO/CLOs and managing SPVs was slow. The introduction of significant improvements in computing power and specialised programming subsequently made the process faster and seemingly more manageable and accurate. Second, by the twenty first century forms of securitisation had been around for a decade and more. There was a developed private placement market for them. The idea of them as a pooled risk made them an attractive investment and mutual funds, pension funds and insurance companies were increasingly amenable to buying them. The Securities Industry and Financial Markets Association (SIFMA) provide quarterly data on the total global issuance of CDOs. Figures vary depending on how CDOs are categorised but the underlying trend had been one of growth, and with a marked increase from 2004 to the first half of 2007: growing from an annual total of around $150 billion to over $500 billion (Batchelor 2008).

As Krijgsman notes securitisation created a specific opportunity to increase lending for PEF LBOs:

> Refinements in financial technology have enabled banks to increase their participation in highly leveraged private equity deals without necessarily increasing balance-sheet exposure. Securitisation instruments such as collateralized debt obligations (CDOs)... allow them to make more room on their balance-sheet for leveraged transactions. (2005/6: 13)

This increased participation had two dynamics. First, irrespective of whether the debt created in the LBO was securitised the banks were in a position because of the securitisation of other areas of lending to offer larger loans to PEF (based on consortia and then syndicated in various ways). Second, any lending for an LBO could itself be securitised. The senior debt could be passed to a conduit and reconstructed as part of a security issue, and also, any junior debt such as junk bonds, could be reconstructed within an SPV as part of a CDO/CLO. Significantly, this capacity to transfer and transform or reconstruct debt could ultimately result in lower interest rates being charged on lending based on better terms for borrowers and could add to incentives to provide larger levels of lending – which was precisely what happened in the provision of debt to PEF LBOs, particularly from 2003–04.

One way to think about how this occurs is to start from the point that the bank is not expecting to carry the long term risk of any default on its lending. However, in order not to carry this risk it must sell on its lending (which are its assets). If securitised then the assets are sold to an SPV.[38] The SPV in turn is primarily profitable because the total value of those assets is higher than the returns the SPV pays to investors in its CDO/CLOs. The total value of the assets is the sums or principals lent that are to be paid back plus the various interest rates at which those sums have been lent. The profit to the SPV is the excess in the income stream from the assets over what it pays to the investors in its securities. This is the difference between what it receives because of the higher rates of interest from the assets (plus any over-collateralisation) and the lower rates of return it pays to the investors. The point is that since the SPV has to buy the assets from the bank (the originator) it cannot pay the bank the full value of the principals of the assets and their interest rates. The bank accepts less than the full value of the lending that it would have received had it held onto the assets for their full duration but demands more than the sum of the principals (otherwise the bank would make a loss on its lending). The bank effectively discounts the interest rate payments received. It is, therefore, exchanging larger potential levels of return in the long run for smaller levels of return received upfront in order not to carry the risk of default.[39]

Smaller levels of return encourage more rapid turnover in lending in order to get more upfront payments to compensate for the loss of higher long term income streams. It can also encourage larger levels of lending to increase the absolute levels of return because of the smaller % levels that the bank receives. Since the bank is not carrying the risk of any lending that it passes to conduits it can pursue a policy of lending larger sums competitively. In terms of the relationship of the banks to PEF this can appear counter-intuitive: one might expect that bank consortia would result in a kind of oligopolistic behaviour that stabilised or slightly raised interest rates and terms of lending in ways that were collectively advantageous to the banks. Raising interest rates and then lowering the degree to which such lending was discounted when transferred to an SPV could be a profitable strategy. Imposing restrictions on debt structures to enhance the primacy of senior debt – as occurred in the PEF LBOs of the late 1980s – might also seem an advantageous strategy. However, the point of the change in the late 1980s was to protect senior debt from the potential problems created by junior debt because of high levels of leverage and the use of junk bonds. Syndication and an originate and distribute model militate this problem because the risk is being transferred.

Significantly, as the scale of PEF LBOs increased from 2004 the proportion of senior debt to junk bond issues also increased, despite the increased scale of junk bond markets in Europe and the reduction in spreads between interest rates on junk bonds and Treasury securities – which reached a historic low in 2005. Issuing junk bonds may have been getting cheaper, but so was senior debt and senior debt was available in larger volumes for any given deal than had previously been the case. In the first two quarters of 2006, for example, the ratio of senior debt to junk bonds in the leveraged loan market increased to 4:1 from 3:1 in 2005 (Stix 2006: 1).[40] In 2006 over 66% of all loans issued by the commercial banks were syndicated compared to 25% in 2001 (Jones 2007d: 20). Hedge funds and institutional investors accounted for 45% of the senior debt market through syndication (compared to 4% in 1999).

It should also be considered that higher interest rates and harsher restrictions on lending may prevent the larger deals the banks are providing the lending for from occurring. There would, therefore, be no deal to profit from. Many of the larger diversified financial organisations will not just be profiting from the loan itself. They may earn underwriting fees from their investment banking division as part of the LBO. They may earn underwriting fees from any later SPV security issue. They may have designed the SPV – either to be run as a separate off-balance sheet arm of the conglomerate or as an entity that has been sold to a third party investment organisation. They may be investors in one of the PEF funds that are undertaking the LBO. They may have a PEF division that is part of the club deal that is undertaking the LBO.

Bank syndication, therefore, need not result in a stabilisation of the terms of lending, including interest rates, but rather a competition for business because doing the deal has an overriding importance from several different causal factors. As such the originate and distribute model has built into it the potential for banks to improve the lending terms for borrowers. It provides the banks with a motive to reduce interest rates in order to capture business and to make larger LBOs viable. This, however, is only so in so far as lending can be syndicated and/or assets securitised so that the risk of higher levels of leverage can be passed on. In terms of securitisation, for this to occur investors must continue to be induced to invest in CDO/CLOs. Investors will continue to invest if the risks of the investment are justified by the returns on the investment. High credit ratings for CDO/CLO tranches are thus very important in maintaining investment. Significantly, the very basis of securitisation seemed to justify this credit-rating.

Stripped and pooled assets constructed according to statistical models of the incidence of defaults provided a means by which credit-raters could justify high credit ratings. The justifications were based on the spreading of risk and the claimed accuracy of the predictions of default rates compared to the pricing or returns offered by the securities. Moreover, the very same principles meant that a statistically large pool of lower credit rated debts could be transformed into a higher credit rated security. A highly leveraged loan, a junk bond, a large mortgage to a low income earner and so forth might all individually seem poor investments and thus below a BBB rating but many of them stripped and pooled could be a AAA rated asset. This transformation is a central way in which the SPV is able to create an advantageous spread between the interest rates on the assets it buys and the rates of returns it offers on the securities it constructs. The core point, however, is that given no reason to think that the transformation is problematic and the higher credit rating dubious, investors would continue to buy the securities – even if at the same time the banks were making it easier to borrow and to borrow larger sums. This was to become a problem for all kinds of securitisation – and particularly for mortgage securities.

There is, furthermore, a limit to the degree to which the banks can competitively push down interest rates on their lending whilst still maintaining the attractiveness of securitisation for investors. That limit is set by the way the banks own lending is limited. As part of monetary policy central banks influence a floor interest rate below which commercial banks usually cannot or will not lend to each other on a short term basis. These are the main form of interest rate referred to in the previous chapters. In the UK the Bank of England directly sets a base rate. In the US the Fed sets a target Federal funds rate and uses open market operations to enforce it. In the UK the banks lend amongst themselves on the basis of a spread above the base rate. In the US the Federal funds rate is effectively that lending rate. If the banks want to lend additional funds from the central banks they are usually charged an interest rate above the base/funds rate – typically 0.5% to 1% higher (referred to by the Fed as the discount rate).

The necessity for the commercial banks to borrow on a short term basis arises because each has to maintain sufficient liquid assets to meet day to day demands for withdrawals. Transactions by customers at different banks are effectively the transfer of funds from one bank to another and these can result in a surplus or deficit in the levels of the reserves of the bank that it has set aside to meet those demands. The banks, therefore, lend amongst themselves in order to offset these short term variations (and typically do so through their own deposit accounts held at the central bank). The rates at which they are prepared to lend create a short term interest rate. In the UK this is termed Libor – the London inter-bank offered rate. Libor is set by the British Banker's Association each working day morning when representatives of 16 leading banks make offers of amounts they are willing to lend and the interest rates they will lend at – the average is the Libor.[41] The funds are offered for fixed periods – overnight, three months etc. In the absence of problems in credit markets the overnight Libor is typically 0.1–0.2% above the Bank of England base rate. The European equivalent is termed Euribor. Libor, Euribor and the Fed funds rate set a floor below which it is ultimately not profitable for a bank to lend. All other interest rates at which the banks and other major financial institutions lend are spreads above these rates based on the duration of the loan, the credit worthiness of the borrower and the degree of any security offered by the borrower. In the absence of problems in credit markets bank prime lending rates tend to start at around 3% above these rates. All interest rates can however be competitively squeezed towards Libor.

The limit to the degree to which the banks can competitively push down interest rates on their lending whilst still maintaining the attractiveness of securitisation for investors arises in part because as the banks lending rates start to fall towards Libor the profit margins on the debts tends to fall. That margin is what the SPV uses to structure a return to the investors in its securities whilst still creating a profit for itself. In principle the assets should just become cheaper for the SPV to buy from the originator because the total value of the assets it is buying is now lower. If this is the case it should still be able to price the securities effectively. However, as the margins fall on the original debt the originator has a vested interest in not passing on the same levels of discount to the SPV. There is, therefore, the potential for a tug of war between the bank and the SPV over who will absorb the falling margins. These margins are further affected because SPVs are not a costless transformation. There are costs in setting up the SPV, administering it, organising an underwriter for the security issue, and gaining a credit rating for each tranche, and these costs must also be absorbed in the spread.[42]

Even if the SPV is actually a subordinate entity of the bank (a conduit that is only legally distinct but actually a functional element of the bank) there will ultimately still be the same end problem. As interest rates on lending fall then there is pressure to reduce the rates of return to investors in the securities. What this means is that not only does securitisation enable a continuing process of larger lending on better terms for borrowers that has built into it the tendency for more vulnerable forms of debt to be created, but also as that process develops an underlying problem is created that can eventually make it difficult to offload new security issues. This does not just apply to securitisation – the same basic relation inheres in syndication of all kinds once the process becomes competitive.[43]

Competition between the banks regarding PEF resulted in marked changes in the terms and conditions of lending from 2004 (Jones' of Morgan Stanley's 'remarkably forgiving leveraged finance markets'). The average pricing of senior debt had in any case been falling throughout the decade because of falling central bank interest rates. However, from 2004 the average pricing of debt started to fall relative to central bank rates i.e. towards Libor.[44] This was occurring as central bank rates were starting to slowly rise from the historic lows they reached in 2003–04. Senior debt on large deals now also typically included at least one non-amortising tranche (Hintze 2006). A non-amortising loan is one in which only the interest is repaid until the date of maturity of the loan – at which point the principal becomes due (often termed a 'bullet' payment). If only the interest is being paid then the PEF acquisition can service a larger debt in the short term. That servicing was also facilitated by the creative use of 'lending revolvers' (revolving credit). Revolving credit is not new – it is simply an open-ended credit facility that the borrower can draw upon. However, this can be used to meet interest payments i.e. creating debt to service debt. That lending revolvers can be used in this way is clearly problematic. If large revolvers are set up with this in mind it highlights lax oversight by lenders. It also highlights that as the size of deals rose, as leverage levels rose, and as ratios of debt to Ebitda rose, debt servicing was being seen as an issue that required contingency plans.

The key way in which debt servicing problems are signalled and the process of placing the organisation in default is begun is through lending covenants. The terms of a loan will typically contain a set of conditions requiring the borrower to act and giving the lender the right to intervene. The borrower, for example, may be restricted in terms of the levels and types of capital expenditure they can engage in or the levels and circumstances under which dividends can be paid – on the basis that either of these affects the financial stability of the organisation and thus its ability to service debt. In general terms covenants are differentiated by the nature of the conditions that create the obligation to act or intervene (Parnass 2007).

'Maintenance' covenants require the organisation not to breach given conditions (the conditions must be maintained). The main focus is financial ratios – usually a ceiling ratio of debt to Ebitda (as the measure of adequacy in debt servicing). The borrower is required to act to meet the ratio and the lender has the right to categorise the borrower as in default if it does not. Here, financial information passed to the lender on a quarterly basis will contain specific modelled tests of debt servicing that show that the borrower is and can continue to service its debt. 'Incurrence' covenants, by contrast, require only that the organisation does not actively breach specified lending conditions: in terms of financial ratios, for example, by incurring new debt without first renegotiating with the original lender and establishing that existing debt can be serviced. The ratio can be breached by factors beyond the immediate control of the lender (changing market conditions &c). The breach will still be defined within the terms of the loan as an 'event' but will not be one from which the lender has the right to immediately place the borrower in default. Furthermore, additional covenants can place a buffer around the 'event'. These include an allowable deviation from the ratio such as how far it can be breached and also the existence of additional 'covenant waivers'. Most significantly, in the absence of maintenance covenants the borrower may not be required to provide tests of its ratios *unless* there is incurrence, such as taking on new debt. The lender is then hampered in its ability to be aware of arising debt servicing problems.

From 2004 covenants on PEF LBO loans in the US began to relax restrictions relating to dividend payments and capital expenditures, began to omit maintenance covenants, provide larger buffers for incurrence covenants and make allowances for further equity and debt injections. This meant that the right of the lender to place the borrower in default was greatly reduced and their capacity to intervene if the borrower began to experience financial difficulty or was acting in a fashion that might be deemed financially irresponsible was greatly delayed. These improved terms and conditions for borrowers have been collectively termed 'covenant-lite'. Covenant-lite loans only began to spread to Europe and the UK in early 2007. The first covenant-lite deal in Europe was a refinancing by J P Morgan of the Apax/Cinven buyout of VNU World Directories (Jones 2007a) in April and the second was a new buyout of Trader Media Group by Apax, also financed by J P Morgan (Jones 2007b). There were 8 covenant-lite loans issued to large PEF LBOs in Europe and the UK in the first 6 months of 2007 and, according to Standards & Poor's, $97 billion in covenant-lite loans over the same period in Europe and the US. One third of the US market was covenant-lite over the period, compared to 7.2% for the whole of 2006 (Jones 2007c).

The net effect of covenant-lite loans is in the long term to add to the potential syndication problems created by pushing down the interest rates on lending. It is, all other things being equal, more difficult to sell on a loan where the conditions of lending hamper the ability of the lender to prevent the borrower slipping into a position of non-payment. This is particularly so if the general economic climate is one in which non-payment seems more likely. It is also the case if there is suddenly less lending capital than borrowing needs, since potential syndicate participants look elsewhere. However, covenant-lite may still have a rationale in the meantime. Some participants in syndication – such as hedge funds or other investment funds – lack the personnel or expertise of bankers in dealing in breach of covenants. Their main focus will be whether an organisation that enters default has assets to cover its senior debt commitments and also whether the organisation is sufficiently high profile to appear unlikely to become debt distressed and then insolvent. It is for these reasons that covenant-lite emerged in conjunction with larger PEF LBOs of prominent companies.

Furthermore, if the lending is securitised any resulting CLO will initially tend to offset any suspicion regarding covenant-lite conditions (as well as revolvers and non-amortising loans). The banks are not averse to offering covenant-lite because the loan is going to be passed on. Investors in CLOs are buying a stripped and pooled asset. The information required to make the investment may thus not be the same for the buyer of the CLO as it is for the issuer of the original debt or participants in straight syndication. In any case one of the initial effects of covenant-lite is actually to reduce the statistical incidence of reported defaults because the conditions under which a borrower is in default are now more lax. The rating agencies, though liable to apply a lower credit rating to the original loan if it is non-amortising or if it is covenant-lite will still be likely to apply a higher credit rating to the subsequent CLO because it is stripped and pooled. The underlying problem, therefore, remains underlying. The main reason for this is that capital markets are highly liquid: there is a large supply of capital for debt and investment. Syndication and securitisation continue to occur, PEF LBOs continue, terms and conditions of lending improve for borrowers. Levels of lending and levels of leverage continue to rise. As Jones notes the very absence of apparent problems can encourage problems:

> The one point everyone in the market agrees on is that liquidity has a lot to answer for. As far as the markets are concerned, it's a watchword for the current buoyancy of the economy (and resultant covenant-loosening). Not only are the markets awash with money, but liquidity volatility itself is historically low. The sum of which means, for borrowers, conditions over the past four years compared to the decade before have been unbelievably benign.
>
> 'Underpinning the emergence of covenant-lite is, undoubtedly, high liquidity,' says Malcolm Hitching, a partner at Herbert Smith. (Jones 2007d: 19)

In some respects this liquidity is self-reinforcing. A growing willingness to offer debt and to trade in debt creates greater levels of debt in terms of any given sum of capital – particularly as banks introduce new ways of constructing and moving debt around. Some of it, however, can also be attributed to the availability of additional sources of capital – specifically the yen carry – and also the emergence of new accumulations of capital in the form of currency reserves in particular places that can be used for investment.

Sources of capital for market liquidity: the yen carry, China and the petro-dollar; the rise of the sovereign wealth funds

Japan, though remaining the second largest economy in the world, has suffered a series of economic problems since the beginning of the 1990s, many of them related to the structure of the Keiretsu conglomerates and also to the problematic trade relation between the US and Japan. The 1985 Plaza Accord created a yen-dollar exchange rate protocol that forced the appreciation of the yen to offset the growing level of Japanese exports to the US. The result was a first wave of foreign direct investment across East Asia by Japan. In 1995 the protocol was suspended and the yen started a highly predictable depreciation against the dollar. Speculators started borrowing yen and converting to dollars. The sum could then be invested or lent to earn returns, but the underlying principle was that as the yen continued to depreciate it would require fewer dollars to buy the required sum of yen to pay back the original loan – creating a net gain. This became known as the yen carry. It was given an additional impetus by the East Asian financial crisis of 1997.[45] The crisis resulted in a major recession in Japan (industrial production fell by 9.3% 1998–2003, GDP by 1–2% per year, and the Nikkei index fell to 20% of its 1989 level). Since the Japanese banks are capitalised by their equity then falling equity values reduced their capacity to cover losses at the same time as the number of defaults on loans was rising, creating an insolvency problem for the banks. The Bank of Japan responded by allowing the banks to retain non-performing loans as deferred assets and simultaneously began a policy of negative real interest rates – reducing the central bank rate to 1% or lower. The aim was to offset deflation, stimulate the Nikkei and prevent an increase in defaults.[46] However, the resulting consistently low interest rates in Japan meant that investors could borrow in yen, convert to the dollar, earn higher interest rates elsewhere and then reconvert to yen to repay the original loan. Moreover, if the volumes of yen carry continually grow then the yen depreciates because more yen are consistently being converted to other currencies (being sold – which seemed to be the case in 2004–06). Whilst this continues the yen carry also profits from a depreciating yen – even though Japanese exports also result in increasing dollar reserves at the Bank of Japan.

As part of their use of a short (profiting from falling markets) long (profiting from rising markets) strategy, many hedge funds also structure investments in currencies and exchange rates. Shorting the yen and holding the dollar as long against the yen has been a typical hedge fund position (Allen 2007). The yen carry has produced a huge source of cheap capital for financial institutions able to access debt on a global basis. It is estimated to be a market of up to $300 billion although the scale of the yen carry cannot be directly determined because the market is informal (Lewis 2008). Even given the level of ambiguity over the full extent of the trade, the yen carry has been attributed as a main source of leverage for hedge funds, enabling them to become major investors in SPV products, to engage in buyouts and to provide sources of junior debt to PEF firms (IMF 2006: 17).

Although the Bank of Japan has, under pressure, followed a policy of intervention to prevent a rapid long term depreciation of the yen, Japan has had no motive to significantly appreciate the yen since this would reduce its export competitiveness. When the yen has appreciated it has had more to do with the long term decline in the dollar on world currency markets – something that has been occurring against the euro and sterling since the early 2000s. Strategies to maintain export competitiveness have been a main problem for Japan since the mid-1990s. One response has been a second wave of outsourcing across East Asia towards least cost labour sites – particularly China. China entered the World Trade Organisation (WTO) in December 2001.[47] China became a main focal point of both production and assembly for many East Asian corporations seeking to reduce their costs after the East Asian crisis and China has also developed its own corporations, some through joint ventures (Morgan 2008b, Belderbos and Zhou 2006).

The effect of this has been rapid export based economic growth in China and rapid growth of currency reserves in the Chinese banking system.[48] Although the US was already China's main export market China's exports to the US grew rapidly from 2001 and China quickly became the second largest exporter to the US after Canada. Significantly, the form of these exports has contributed to the nature of US economic growth and economic structure. The US has consistently imported more than it exports since the 1970s but within that relationship has increasingly become an importer of consumption goods and an exporter of capital goods (machinery and so forth). Since consumption has become an increasingly large part of the US economy and retail, along with housing and related financial services, has became a major growth sector, China has not only benefited from US consumption growth but has also subsidised it by providing a cheap source of goods. According to research by the Centre for Strategic and International Studies, China's cheap exports were making the US better off by approximately $70 billion a year (CSIS 2006). As China has grown (achieving, according to its own statistics GDP growth of at least 7% and usually more than 10% per year) and its trade surplus with the US has grown it has accumulated large foreign currency reserves. Some of these have been recycled through the purchase of US Treasury securities. By 2006 China held foreign currency reserves of $875 billion and held $263 billion in US Treasury Bonds (Morgan 2008a).

Buying US Treasury securities has effectively financed both US tax cuts under Bush Jr and expenditure on the 'War on Terror'. The effects of this new global military context have also created new sources of capital. In early 2003 as the invasion of Iraq was prepared oil prices (both Brent and US crude) rose to over $30 a barrel and though both then fell to lows of under $25 that year, the underlying trend has been upwards throughout the decade. Prices rose to $50 in 2004 and in late 2007 finally exceeded the previous inflation adjusted peak of around $90 set in 1980. This rise was not just because of uncertainty, or even actual or expected shortages in oil, although the industrialisation of China and India raised these as long term issues. The rises were also because the oil market was increasingly one in which a range of investors now operated who sought to profit from trading the commodity – previously the market was dominated by buyers for refining. The effect was to begin a process of large increases in the dollar foreign currency reserves of the oil states. OPEC generates over 40% of world oil output and, according to the US federal Energy Information Administration (EIA 2008) its net oil export revenues have been consistently increasing from 2003 from approximately $200 billion per year to $676 billion in 2007.

Projections based on an oil price consistently higher than $100 per barrel estimate revenues of around $900 billion for 2008. If one uses $100 per barrel as a floor price then the total known reserves of all the oil exporting nations are worth approximately $104 trillion (Jen 2008). Total annual revenues for all oil exporting nations have, on this basis increased to around $2 trillion per year.

Both China and the oil exporting nations have been accumulating foreign exchange reserves faster than they have been able to use the capital in their domestic economies. China has been trying to avoid additional inflation. The OPEC nations have small populations, and despite attempts to undertake large scale domestic investment programmes to reduce the long term dependence of their economies (particularly in the United Arab Emirates) on oil (and gas) exports have still only been using fractions of the capital. In recent years this, particularly if one also adds in a range of other nations accumulating foreign currency reserves based on trade surpluses of one kind or another (and the revenues captured by 'high net worth individuals' who monopolise some resources), has created a growing pool of capital available for overseas investment. Significantly it has not been possible to recycle this capital simply by buying traditional forms of fixed income investments such as Treasury securities. In 2006 alone the foreign exchange reserves of China and the oil exporting nations grew by more than $1.2 trillion whilst the combined EU, UK and US issue of state securities was just $461 billion.[49] The net effect has been to add to sources of global investment capital for other markets and purposes. One manifestation of this has been the growth of specific state vehicles for investment that have become known as sovereign wealth funds (SWF) (Morgan 2008c). Little is known about the actual capital assets of some SWF – particularly the Chinese variants and some of the Middle East funds – and many of the estimates of the sum of their assets and how they are held are based on limited disclosures and/or tracing the investments they have made in countries that require public disclosures. On this basis, in 2007 the main SWFs were estimated to control $2.5 trillion in worldwide assets. Research by Merrill Lynch estimates SWF total assets will grow to $8 trillion by 2011, research by the IMF estimates a growth of assets to $12 trillion by 2012 and research by Morgan Stanley generates the same figure for 2015. In terms of PEF, prior to the credit crunch of mid-2007, SWF had begun to function in ways analogous to hedge funds. They invested in PEF funds, they had invested in PEF firms, they had become buyers of debt and they had also begun to be participants in PEF deals and competitors for publicly listed companies. In so doing, they also became a subject of national security concern because some of them are owned by non-democratic states and because their motives for investment might be other than for profit – securing access to sensitive technologies and so forth. This has brought PEF firms acting in conjunction with SWF into conflict with national security oversight bodies – particularly the Committee on Foreign Investment in the US (Cfius) (Kirchgaessner 2008). As the credit crunch took hold it also resulted in various initiatives, particularly through the G7, to make the practices and intents of SWF more transparent. In more general terms, however, the SWF are just one manifestation of the growth in liquidity from which the credit crunch developed. The very existence of the crunch, moreover, has forced the US state in particular to be more accommodating in its approach to SWF because the funds became one of the few sources of readily available capital to meet some of the problems the crunch created.

The credit crunch and the collapse in liquidity

From 2004, changes in the terms and conditions for larger PEF deals clearly indicate that completing the deal had overriding significance. Banks were willing to offer better terms and conditions on larger deals with greater levels of leverage because they were not as concerned by problems of bad debt and defaults as they had been previously. This was partly because debt could be syndicated and securitised. But it was also because economic growth had essentially continued through the market collapses of 2000 to 2003 and by 2004 equity markets were also recovering. Default rates are lower during periods of economic growth and rising markets. This has a self-reinforcing effect on debt provision that tends to maintain low default rates. Low default rates create the statistical background on which confidence in higher risk investments is maintained – they are tolerable risks because they are in a sense not 'high risk'. This in turn feeds the liquidity of markets by encouraging a supply of capital to them. As a result interest rates on lending began to be squeezed towards Libor, spreads on junk bonds fell to lows against Treasury securities. Debt thus became cheaper and at the same time more freely available. Since the banks were syndicating loans and securitising all forms of debt the margins of profits to the banks from issuing debt were also falling, creating a further impetus to increase their lending. Lending spread both in terms of scale and, in more general terms, who could and would be lent to. This applied to all forms of financial organisations and all forms of lending – PEF, mortgages, credit cards, car loans and so on.

Low interest rates allow credit access without generating high debt servicing costs. This in turn creates lower default rates reconfirming the tolerable risk of the investment. The inherent problem is that the self-reinforcing nature of the process is based on the availability of capital and the liquidity of the markets. The process itself tends to accumulate larger levels of debt on better terms and conditions. But larger levels of debt still have to be serviced and as debts rise, servicing costs rise unless terms and conditions continue to improve. There is a limit to which they can do this without the provision of debt becoming unprofitable. Moreover, at some stage investors will start to see this and their idea of tolerable risk will change creating a change in the availability of capital and the liquidity of markets. Once something triggers this change the basis on which higher levels of leverage were generated and on which syndication and securitisation could be undertaken are undermined. Just as in the case of the dot.coms, the change is not indicative that there has been a deviation from rational behaviour in efficient markets. This would imply that suddenly realising the scale of the problem was also a return to an ordinary state of affairs – a re-imposition of 'fundamentals'. However, as Chapters 1–3 indicate, there is no ideal time where there is an ideal state of rational behaviour where every act is informed by what is most efficient. There is rather a change from one set of behaviours that have an underlying set of rationales to another. The reason for the change is precisely the accumulation of problems created in the first set of behaviours and the conditions under which they occurred.

That there were problems and that they were accumulating did not go unnoticed by the main central banks and global institutions. However, the approach adopted was similar to that employed by Greenspan in 1996 and 1999. They focused primarily on warnings regarding the desirability and sustainability of trends. For example, in April 2006 an IMF private equity intelligence report highlighted that growing levels of leverage in LBOs was creating debt servicing issues as well as fuelling higher prices for mergers and acquisitions. The frequency of warnings increased in 2007 and there were numerous ones in June of that year. Ben Bernanke, now Chairman of the Fed, stated that banks needed to re-evaluate the way they were providing loans to finance LBOs since prevailing liquidity conditions could alter. The Bank of England *Quarterly Review* noted that highly leveraged loans and increasingly lax terms and conditions raised the possibility of a major default if financial conditions became less benign and interest rates continued to rise. Rodrigo de Rato at the IMF stated that LBOs threatened financial stability. Significantly, each warning was also balanced by reassurance: the overall system is essentially robust and thus a particular problem need not become a general one either for a domestic economy or the global economy. That each warning was also softened by a reassurance was because each spokesman was aware of the rhetorical power of his position. A strong statement of doom could easily precipitate changes in behaviour that could result in the outcomes they were seeking to forestall. However, each reassurance – problems are typically not realised as crises, tensions trade through, any landing is liable to be soft rather than hard – also weakens the capacity of the warning to be a decisive break on the accumulation of problems. The banks, seemingly, had no clear motivation to reverse the trends in their lending, and investors, initially, had no clear reasons to cease to participate in syndication, securitisation and so forth. Credit markets were liquid, and though interest rates had started to slowly rise from the historic lows of 2003–04 they were still low and were moving in quarter % points. The situation was much like that during the dot.com bull market where rising markets may seem somehow difficult to justify but whilst they continued to be profitable there seemed no reason not to be one of those profiting. Moreover, even if one were inclined to heed the muted warnings of the main institutions, one of the central tenets of the reassurances was that financial markets had become more sophisticated – risk was better understood, and financial innovations were now more effective at spreading that risk. CDO/CLOs and the existence of complex forms of derivatives – particularly credit default swaps (CDSs) were often highlighted as reasons why risk was better understood and more effectively managed.[50] The focus of warnings was mainly on the growing levels of leverage in the assets that became CDO/CLOs and not on the role of CDO/CLOs.[51] This was curious since it tended to neglect the way the two are inter-connected and tended to emphasise the potential for problems in the 'real' economy. This was despite that many of the warnings started from acknowledging the underlying problem was one of lending and thus of capital markets.

In the event the first manifestation of the underlying problems did not occur in terms of the level of leverage in PEF LBOs. There was not a major default on the debt servicing obligations of one of the prominent buyouts. The first manifestation occurred, rather, in the US sub-prime mortgage market. This manifestation catalysed a collapse in the housing market bubble in the US and created a chain reaction effect through the financial system and the main drivers of economic growth in both the US and UK. It also had various effects throughout the global economy, beginning from its effects on liquidity and credit creation.

A rising housing market, low interest rates, and the broad range of effects of securitisation, encouraged mortgage lenders in both the US and UK to extend the range of their lending: offering better terms and conditions to a wider pool of borrowers. A sub-prime borrower can have one or several of the following characteristics: they are low income earners, cannot definitively verify their income over time (they are self-employed), require a mortgage that is a high multiple of annual income (over three) and are looking to borrow a high proportion of the cost of the property being bought (greater than 70%, often 90–100%). In the summer of 2007 there were 50 million active mortgages in the US, of which approximately 7.5 million were sub-prime. Sub-prime lending was thus 15% of the total number of mortgages. In terms of value, there was approximately $10,000 billion in outstanding mortgage lending. Approximately $1,300 billion of sub-prime lending had been transferred to CDOs.

The viability of some sub-prime lending relied heavily on a rising housing market and the capacity to remortgage. Prior to the height of the housing boom a sub-prime borrower was typically charged 3% more than a prime borrower and usually required a large deposit against the value of the property. However, as the boom developed new lending business for variable interest rate mortgages was created by providing mortgages with an initial interest rate discount lasting between six months and two years. Mortgage sellers earned commission on the basis of the value of new business and thus were given strong incentives to exploit increasingly lax lending conditions – borrowers were allowed to self-certify their income and were allowed to borrow increasing multiples of that 'income' to buy property that required the lender to provide a greater proportion of the total cost of the property. The introductory interest rates meant that this debt would probably be serviceable during the period of the discount. During that time the seller has already received their commission. Furthermore, the seller need not necessarily fear being blamed for a subsequent surge of defaults at the end of the discount period. At the end of the period a rising housing market would mean that the borrower now owned an asset worth more. They could remortgage accessing another discount rate and release some equity that, in principle, might be banked to help service the debt.[52]

It is important to note that sub-prime is a highly variable category and that a broader range of borrowers become sub-prime as a housing boom develops – there was $600 billion in sub-prime lending in 2006, the highest level reached during the boom (also the year in which the issue of CDOs peaked).[53] Since a housing market boom means property prices are rising faster than incomes, more and more people *must* buy property at greater multiples of income in order to gain access to the property ladder. Moreover, some borrowers at all levels of the ladder will choose to leverage themselves even further than is necessary to buy property, in order to buy the most desirable property they can 'afford'. A rising housing market means that 'better' properties may become even less affordable later. A rising housing market also means that buying now at higher levels of leverage makes property more affordable in the future if the market continues to rise – precisely because the equity in the property can be realised. A rising housing market creates incentives to reinvest realised equity in buy-to-let properties, since the returns on property are higher than savings deposit interest rates. The problem is, therefore, not simply one of a limited incidence of misselling and of reckless provision of what became known as 'Ninja' loans (no income no job no assets). It is rather the confluence of a broader range of aspects of a system based on lending liquidity.

The essential problem is that the absolute levels of debt are rising. For the mortgage providers this debt is an asset i.e. a source of income. It can be securitised and thus passed on. For the owner, the debt is offset by the rise in the value of the property. For both the lender and the borrower the debt can appear manageable. However, the debt must still be serviced from income for it to be genuinely manageable. Mis-selling to low income earners and other vulnerable categories is simply the most immediate and egregious manifestation of the essential problem of debt. As debt rises debt becomes less manageable. As debt rises debt servicing becomes more reliant on favourable credit conditions and thus on liquid markets. As debt rises the providers of that liquidity become increasingly aware that the only thing maintaining debt servicing is the liquidity they are providing. A situation then arises that is analogous to that of the momentum investor in the dot.com boom. Do I continue to participate or do I anticipate problems and exit? The nature of the warnings offered by the central banks and the claims made for new financial innovations could only serve to delay a decision until a tipping point was reached.

That tipping point was reached in the summer of 2007 when it became clear that the US housing market had slowed and the bubble might collapse. Home sales fell by 12% in the second quarter of 2007 and the average time a house spends on the property market increased to 8.7 months – the highest in 15 years. Data for the first two quarters of 2007 revealed that mortgage delinquency rates were also rising to mid-1990 levels. A borrower is categorised as delinquent when 30 days in arrears, seriously delinquent after 60 days, and is subject to foreclosure on the loan after 90 days – when legal proceedings begin to seize the property and force a sale (which occurs in around 40% of cases when proceedings are begun).[54] By mid-2007 approximately 10% of sub-prime loans were delinquent, though less than 10% of that 10% were in the process of foreclosure – a fraction of the overall housing market. However, it was clear that the combination of a slow rise in Fed interest rates from 2004, which was gradually squeezing the floor on mortgage interest rates upwards, and the rising levels of absolute debt being carried by mortgage borrowers, were together starting to affect the rise in house prices and the capacity of borrowers to service debt.[55]

For buyers of CDOs this initially meant that the income stream on which a CDO relied could not be relied upon. This was more of an immediate problem for the holders of the most junior forms of the tranches. But the problem that defaults were slowly rising and seemed likely to continue to do so also indicated something fundamental about CDOs that affected how one thought about every tranche. The idea that spreading each individual debt across several securities reduced its impact on any given security, creating a less risky security, only works if the cause of any default in the underlying asset is genuinely individual rather than systemic. CDOs spread risk if the statistical incidence of defaults is low. CDOs make sense on the basis of past circumstances only if those circumstances are stable and continue. However, the very existence of securitisation promoted more lending at better terms and conditions for borrowers generating higher levels of debt. The existence of CDOs tended to change the characteristics of the system that justified buying the CDOs. The prior statistical incidence of default as a way to create a credit rating and set a price for a CDO thus became deeply problematic. This realisation meant that holders of CDOs faced a dual problem. An uncertain housing market meant that the returns on their investment were threatened. At the same time, the changes that an uncertain housing market indicated meant that there was currently no way of adequately quantifying the value of a CDO at all.

There was also the additional problem that the credit rater who assesses a CDO had always confronted a conflict of interest because they were paid by the originator and not the investors. As such, to secure repeat business, they would be liable to provide the highest possible grading for any given tranche. But it is important that this problem does not obscure the more fundamental issue. All forms of complex financial instruments are constructed on the basis that risk is mathematically tractable – that one can calculate a set of probabilities that give some credence to investment decisions and give some reason for expecting particular levels of return on investments. Uncertainty arises when the past becomes a poor guide to the future. In a sense the past is always a poor guide to the future if one reduces the future to what can be described in an equation. But this becomes a particular problem when the underlying aspects of a system that are changing become sufficient to qualitatively change outcomes. Part of changing outcomes is, however, not just the underlying factors such as growing levels of debt and terms and conditions. It is also the way that perceptions of those factors affect behaviour that in turn influences the nature of ensuing events.

CDOs were in fact more of a problem than any as yet realised level of default in any of the income streams they held might indicate. Not all CDOs contained sub-prime mortgages. Not all debts that had been stripped and pooled were of the lowest credit rating grades. The problem was that the realisation that CDOs could not be realistically valued started to have an effect on how CDOs were viewed that in turn guaranteed that any attempt to state the value of CDOs as part of the capital asset value of an organisation, any attempt to use CDOs as collateral for other forms of borrowing, and any attempt to trade CDOs would face problems. As such CDOs became a fulcrum for problems across the financial system.

The first manifestation of this occurred in June 2007. Hedge funds are typically highly leveraged and use assets, such as securities, as collateral for their borrowing. Bear Stearns' High Grade Structured Credit Strategies Enhanced Leverage Fund and its High Grade Structured Credit Fund had used CDOs it valued at $800 million as collateral on around $6 billion in borrowing from Merrill Lynch and several other large banks (Pittman 2007). Its Enhanced Leverage Fund had since lost 20% of its value and Merrill took control of the CDOs in order to sell them and recoup some of the losses on the lending it had made to both funds. Investors in the funds also began to claw back their capital and as the size of the funds shrank the funds found it more difficult to meet margin calls on their investments. Bear Stearns was forced to provide a guarantee of $3.2 billion as a credit line to the funds as they sold off all of the investments they had made using the leverage. The collapse of a large hedge fund is a notable event – smaller hedge funds collapse frequently but multi-billion dollar ones (such as Long Term Capital Management in 1998) only rarely.

However, the major concern in terms of the collapse was that offloading a large number of CDOs would test the liquidity of the market for them.

Though one of the features of securitisation is that the underwriter undertakes to provide a secondary market CDOs had not developed a particularly active one. Investors tended to buy them and then use them as collateral for additional borrowing more than they traded the actual CDOs. The experience of Bear Stearns focussed attention on the valuation of CDOs and on their use as collateral. There was no apparent market for them at the current valuation. This immediately raised the concern that all forms of financial organisation that were using CDOs as collateral were both holding an asset that may be worthless to them (based on defaults in the underlying asset – particularly sub-prime mortgages) and worthless as a form of collateral against their borrowings. CDOs suddenly became a financial problem rather than a sophisticated innovation that solved problems. The market for new issues of CDOs/CLOs started to dry up. Investors in financial organisations that had invested heavily in CDOs started to look for ways to withdraw their capital. Lenders became reluctant to accept CDOs as collateral. The credit rating of CDO security issues started to be downgraded. The credit rating of financial organisations holding CDOs started to be downgraded. The share price of any organisation linked to CDOs started to fall.

This became a problem for the mortgage providers and then also for all of the banks. The first line of US mortgage provision is divided between large national mortgage providing banks such as Countrywide, smaller regional providers, and specialist providers – particularly sub-prime lenders. There is also a second line of provision designed to maintain the liquidity of mortgage lending: the federally backed Fannie Mae and Freddie Mac who buy up mortgages and issue bonds (that in turn may be further securitised as CDOs).[56] In order to finance lending, the first line of lenders use a combination of deposits by customers and short term borrowing from the commercial paper (CP) market. CP is the issue of an iou to a financial organisation such as an insurer who provides a low interest short term loan, up to 180 days.[57] When there are no problems in credit markets, average interest rates on CP tend to be 2–3% below the bank prime lending rate and thus close to Libor, making CP a cheap and usually easily renewed form of credit. However, fears over the US housing market and over the value of CDOs caused the CP market to grind to a halt in July. More than 50 specialist sub-prime lenders had gone bankrupt by the end of August because of defaults by borrowers and because of an inability to rollover the lender's own debts by reissuing CP backed by their mortgage book (Jagger 2008). Also in August, Countrywide, the largest mortgage lender in the US reported that 5% of its borrowers were delinquent and its share price fell over 30% on the basis of rumours that it could not rollover its CP borrowing and that it faced capitalisation problems. Under pressure from the Fed the Bank of America stabilised Countrywide's capitalisation by investing $2 billion in it for a 20% stake. Fannie Mae and Freddie Mac, meanwhile, faced problems in generating capital to buy up mortgages and problems in selling on bonds and both started to post quarterly losses. Problems at Fannie Mae and Freddie Mac effectively slowed down the distribution of mortgage lending and thus further reduced the capacity of lenders to lend.[58] As the numbers of mortgage providers and their capacity to lend reduced those mortgage providers responded by making the terms and conditions of lending worse for borrowers: both as a defensive measure to exclude lending to those who were a bad credit risk and as a means to claw back losses. The terms of lending thus deteriorated faster than the slow rise in Fed interest rates from 2004 might indicate. This meant that the problem of remortgaging at discount rates became more acute for sub-prime borrowers and that the costs of taking out a mortgage more generally also rose.[59] This in turn would set off a cycle of further rises in delinquency and sent the housing market into a definite decline.[60]

Changes in perceptions of CDOs thus fed back into the way credit was created producing tighter lending conditions that exacerbated the levels of defaults within CDOs based on mortgages. Expectations that a falling housing market would in turn produce more defaults in the coming months further undermined CDOs. From July 2007 housing market analysts were anticipating that defaults would occur at an increasing rate in the second half of 2007 and in 2008. Over 2.5 million adjustable rate mortgages constituting about $700 billion in lending were due to come to the end of a discount period in 2008. On 19th July 2007 in the first of his twice yearly reports to Congress Bernanke set out a Fed estimate that defaults on sub-prime could exceed $100 billion. Also in July 2007 J P Morgan estimated that sub-prime defaults would amount to $60 billion for 2007 and, in a worse case scenario, $230 billion for 2008. Such estimations increased fears over CDOs. Financial organisations came under pressure to report their exposure to CDOs and any losses they had yet incurred. As quarterly figures became due from different organisations it became difficult not to provide some account of exposure and losses.

From July the main US commercial banks started to report that they expected their levels of bad debts to increase and that they expected this to have some effect on earnings. However, the first major acknowledgement, after Bear Stearns, of problems from CDOs by a bank came in Germany on August 2nd when IKB Deutsche Industriebank announced it had $12 billion invested in CDOs with an exposure to US sub-prime mortgages and that its losses on them may rise to $5 billion. IKB shares fell by 30%. The prospect of the bank becoming insolvent and the potential for this to cause panic withdrawals resulting in a run on the bank caused the state to intervene. The state-backed bank KfW, which had a 38% stake in IKB stepped in to guarantee IKB's obligations. On August 9th France's largest bank BNP Paribas temporarily closed three of its funds that had large investments in CDOs in order to prevent investors withdrawing their capital.[61] The capitalisation of the funds had fallen by 25% in two weeks. BNP halted redemption on the basis of two arguments. First, the CDO market had become dysfunctional and it had become impossible to currently value the funds assets. Second, panic redemptions simply guaranteed that the funds would collapse and was therefore detrimental to the interests of other investors in the funds. BNP shares fell 3%.

The action by BNP Paribas was the catalyst for a sudden collapse in inter-bank lending in the UK, Europe and the US. The CP market had become dysfunctional meaning that financial organisations were now looking for alternative sources of borrowing because they could not easily rollover their existing borrowing. The securitisation market had become dysfunctional, meaning that banks were not going to be able to move their current (some of it high risk) lending off balance sheet. Syndication had suddenly become difficult, meaning that large loans made for mergers and acquisitions and LBOs (mostly agreed before the summer at favourable terms and conditions to the borrowers) could not be shifted off-balance sheet. This increased the proportion of many of the major banks high risk lending that was suddenly immobilised on balance sheet. At the same time, the equity prices and thus market capitalisation of some of the major banks was starting to fall.[62]

Looking ahead the banks realised that this threatened their Tier 1 capital ratio set by the Basel Accord. Maintaining Tier 1 capital ratios was vital. Failing to do so at a time of potential market crisis meant that reserves could not meet any possible losses. Given the circumstances, falling below the ratio would be a market signal that the solvency of the bank was threat-ened creating the potential for a catastrophic fall in equity values creating further Tier 1 capital problems. The banks, therefore, had individual motives to hoard capital and also to increase their own borrowing. Each bank was also aware that the other banks had some exposure to CDOs and some poten-tial for large losses – creating further possible Tier 1 capital problems for those banks. Each bank, therefore, had reasons not to lend to other banks knowing that they may need the capital later and that other banks may be disinclined to lend to them later. Individual motives thus created a collec-tively harmful situation. The supply of funds in the inter-bank market fell precisely as demand for funds rose. Lending in the inter-bank market – a key element in the liquidity of the finance system became dysfunctional. The net effect was a rapid rise in Libor and Euribor as well as a collapse in US inter-bank lending. On the 10th of August the overnight Libor rose to 6.5% at a time when the base rate was 5.75%, Euribor rose to 4.6% against a European Central Bank (ECB) target of 4% and the actual US inter-bank rate rose to 5.75% compared to the Fed funds rate of 5.25%.

The central banks felt compelled to respond on the basis that the problem could be expected to get worse if they did not. Central banks are always engaging in open market operations to manipulate liquidity in the banking sector and influence interest rates. They sell securities on capital markets effectively withdrawing capital from the banks and reducing liquidity, since the buyers are bank customers and the payment flows from the bank to the central bank. They offer funds for auction to banks and accept various kinds of assets owned by the banks as security, increasing liquidity. By reducing any sums offered to markets as previous sums become due they again reduce liquidity. On the 10th of August the main central banks, excluding the Bank of England, but including Australia and Japan, offered over $300 billion in funds to the banking sector. The Fed provided $60 billion compared to a typical daily level of $5 billion, the ECB provided Euro 95 billion. Not only was the scale of intervention large but the rates at which they were offered were low – the ECB offered unlimited funds at its target base rate of 4% and the Fed did not impose its discount rate. The Bank of England initially took no action on the basis that injecting liquidity into the market at favourable rates was not yet justified and would tend to sanction the lending strategies that had created the underlying problems (what is termed a 'moral hazard' argument).

The Bank of England, however, was ultimately forced to respond by increasing its offers of capital in order to ease liquidity problems.[63] It and the other main central banks became locked into a cycle of offering large sums to the banking sector in order to control surges in Libor, Euribor and the US interbank rate. As the year progressed the main central banks offered funds at below their punitive discount rates, began to accept a broader range of assets as security (including in the US, CDOs) and began to do so based on a coordination of injections of capital across the main central banks.[64] The effects, however, consistently proved to be temporary. The essential problem was one that the central banks could not easily address. Large scale debt had already been created and distributed through syndication and securitisation. No amount of new capital injections would make, for example, existing CDOs attractive. There was no secondary market and any existing CDOs were of indeterminate value even before defaults began to affect a specific CDO. The losses they represented would simply have to manifest before capital markets recovered. The only way central banks or states could address this would be to absorb existing CDOs into the state, and though the US began to tacitly do this through its open market operations a wholesale explicit policy of doing so by any of the major liberalised economies would be an expensive and potentially politically suicidal acknowledgement of the failures of financial liberalisation.[65] This was particularly so in the US where the main problems were focused and where the housing market decline was producing very visible effects on the most vulnerable sectors of society.

In the meantime the Fed started to cut the Funds rate and later the Bank of England began to cut the base rate.[66] But again, lower interest rates could not consistently feed through to ease liquidity problems in the financial sector (and thus reduce Libor and other lending rates) whilst the banks had good reasons to hoard capital and restrict lending and whilst other sources of lending, such as CP markets, remained reluctant to lend to financial organisations with an exposure to CDOs. Rather the persistent detachment of Libor from the central bank rates indicated a basic problem with the effectiveness of monetary policy.[67] It was being asked to do something for which it was not designed. Moreover, it was being asked to balance several problems with one failing policy tool – interest rates. Inflation was starting to rise based on global forces: rising oil prices, rising iron, steel and cement prices, rising food prices, particularly grain and rice, and rising prices for consumer goods from China. Lowering domestic interest rates might fail to affect actual lending interest rates and produce no easing of credit conditions. Growing inflation, meanwhile, was beginning to trigger Fed and Bank of England model conditions for higher interest rates – even though higher domestic rates could have no effect on the main reasons why inflation might rise.

As central banks continued to fail and Libor remained erratic, the essential problems of the finance system remained unaddressed. The underlying problems, then, persisted and the longer they persisted then the more new elements they accumulated as events unfolded. A high and erratic Libor for example, is itself destabilising because spreads from Libor provide the basis for most contracts in capital markets including the basis of derivatives. A high and erratic Libor thus makes all contracts both expensive and uncertain.

Another core issue that developed over time was losses within the banking sector. Clearly, the banks originate and distribute model had not insulated them from risk in quite the way it had initially appeared that the policy would. This was for two reasons. First, banks, unable to resist the apparently favourable returns on CDOs, bought them and held them as forms of assets. Although it may have the appearance of hubris this was an entirely consistent policy in the sense that securitisation was intended to created securities of a higher credit rating than the original lending. Second, banks had various relations to forms of investment funds that created additional exposures: primarily through hedge funds and SPVs.

In terms of hedge funds, since CDOs were being used as a form of collateral for leverage by hedge funds they created an exposure for the bank offering the loan. Since banks underwrote and operated hedge funds the existence of the funds, which may not be on balance-sheet, created an obligation if they suffered financial distress – as in the case of Bear Stearns. Several other major banks, including Goldman Sachs, were forced to recapitalise hedge funds.[68] This was because many hedge funds invested heavily in CDOs and then used the CDOs as collateral for further leverage. Hedge funds were then hit in two ways. First, CDOs made actual losses through defaults and CDOs could not be traded. Second, the other investments made using the leverage (and other sources of leverage such as the yen carry) suddenly became unprofitable – the emerging credit crunch made capital markets suddenly volatile undermining the basis of most short-long strategies. This was a particular problem for computerised trading model funds (Quants), which started automatic cycles of selling every time certain floor prices were reached – multiple sellers doing the same forced down the values of particular equities and securities.[69] This created further losses and difficulties for highly leveraged hedge funds in meeting their margin calls. Only the most liquid and profitable of hedge fund assets could be sold and as such they were selling their best assets whilst being forced to hold onto their worst (CDOs). Narrowing capitalisation and dysfunctional credit markets prevented them from renewing leverage and this in turn helped send the yen carry into reverse because the reduced borrowing of the yen was one reason why it suddenly started to appreciate (causing further losses because hedge funds also shorted the yen). Over the final two quarters of 2007 the major hedge fund indexes indicated that most varieties of funds posted losses.[70]

In terms of SPVs, the banks who had created them as conduits were exposed to CDOs in several ways. The primary way an SPV generates a return is by managing the spread between the receivables and the CDOs. However, an SPV can also use the CDOs as collateral to borrow. SPVs typically do so by accessing the CP market and then using the borrowed capital to invest in longer term higher return securities – such as additional CDOs (creating multiple CDO chains termed CDO^2 and so forth). These SPVs are referred to as Structured Investment Vehicles (SIV). Several of the large banks had exposure to such SIVs.[71] Citigroup in particular operated a number of SIVs.[72] Barclays designed and guaranteed SIVs for other organisations.[73] The guarantee is termed a 'liquidity backstop', which is a commitment to meet up to 25% of the capitalisation of the SIV if it faces liquidity problems (such as dysfunction in the CP market). The SIVs faced essentially the same problems as the hedge funds: the underlying assets used for collateral became problematic, sources of credit were cut-off, and at the same time most of their investments ceased to be profitable. A dysfunctional SPV or SIV that is effectively part of the bank would ultimately be brought back on balance-sheet by the bank. The CDO commitments that had been transferred would thus be reabsorbed.

Through these and other avenues many of the major banks were aware that they had a core of definite exposures to CDOs, based on the investments they held and on the use of CDOs as collateral by borrowers. They would also be aware that they had a series of potential exposures, based on their relations to other off-balance sheet investment funds. This created a quandary for the banks. There was no market for CDOs and no adequate way of valuing them. Since they could not be sold they would not appear in any final year accounts as a definite loss (unless a particular CDO was destroyed by defaults). Since there was no market for them they could not be valued on the basis of what they could be sold for (what is termed a 'mark-to-market' valuation). Under such circumstances banking accountancy regulation allows the banks to use internal models to estimate the value of an asset.[74] Accountants only sign off on the banks accounts at the end of the financial year.[75] Its quarterly accounts are works in progress. An asset that is not sold but that is reduced in value is subject to what is termed a 'writedown'. The banks faced the problem that CDOs were going to involve large writedowns. But they had no vested interest in modelling the value of CDOs in a way that would maximise that writedown in any particular quarter. Full writedowns and acknowledgements of exposure to CDOs would likely trigger the requirement that the bank post a profit warning according to the regulations of both the New York and London exchanges. Stating the worst case scenario would result in rapid falls in share prices and, in addition to all the other problems this causes for CEOs and executives, likely create new Tier 1 capital problems. Instead the banks started a process of gradually reporting writedowns and levels of exposure to CDOs. Even so, these writedowns were large – multi-billions of dollars.

The approach was more than an accounting finesse since as time passed and the US housing market worsened (and problems started to mount in other debt markets such as car loans and credit cards)[76] more defaults occurred and the modelled valuation of CDOs necessarily fell. But it was also a strategy of wait and hope that somehow markets would become more liquid – perhaps because the central banks were offering more funds and lowering interest rates. Yet at the same time each bank continued to act on the basis of protecting Tier 1 capital and thus continued to perpetuate the absence of liquidity. This process of gradually introducing bad news and hoping for the best whilst contributing to a worsening situation actually had a reverse effect, creating a general suspicion regarding just how large the banks' eventual losses would be and just how much each of the central banks knew but were not saying. This in turn caused a general reduction in share prices in the banking sector and created an atmosphere ripe for manipulation where speculators short banking stock and then disseminate rumours that a particular bank is in trouble causing the stock to fall. Bank strategy thus made conditions worse for banks and perpetuated the crisis.

In September and October all the major US banks reported large writedowns, and losses based on CDOs, bad debt and failed syndications. However, each simultaneously initially reported positive net revenues or break even positions for the third quarter – giving the impression that they would still generate profits for that quarter and the year as a whole. This was so even for those posting the largest writedowns: Citigroup and Merrill Lynch. On October 1st Citigroup announced $6 billion in third quarter losses and writedowns but net revenues of $2.2 billion (a fall of 60%). On October 5th Merrill Lynch initially announced $5 billion in losses and writedowns and a barely positive net revenue. On October 24th Lynch adjusted this to $7.9 billion in losses and writedowns, constituting a negative net revenue (essentially a loss) of $2.3 billion – the first such loss in its history. On October 30th the CEO of Merrill Lynch, Stan O'Neal resigned, followed by the CEO and Chairman of Citigroup, Charles Prince, on November 4th. Later the CEOs of UBS and of Bear Stearns would also lose their jobs. Prince's resignation was precipitated by the investment analyst, Meredith Whitney's report to investors on November 1st that Citigroup's capitalisation was probably £30 billion below its Tier 1 level. Citigroup shares fell by 7% and had fallen 30% over the year – a loss of $80 billion in market capitalisation. The Dow Jones index fell 360 points on the back of the news and the inter-bank lending rate in the US once again surged, causing the Fed to offer $41 billion in funds for auction. By the end of the third quarter, and with some banks, such as UBS, adjusting their writedowns several times, the major banks had reported a combined writedown of over $50 billion.

The heightened effect on the Dow of the report on Citigroup, however, emphasised the scepticism with which the reported accounts of the banks were being viewed. Analysts were aware that the total value of outstanding CDOs exceeded $1 trillion and that SIVs alone (whose total known capitalisation was $375 billion in July 2007) had generated significant leverage in CP markets that, given the short term basis of that market, were constantly becoming due. On this basis, Bob Janjuah, an analyst at the Royal Bank of Scotland, was in November projecting potential eventual losses to the banks of $250 to $500 billion (Ashton 2007).[77] As bank shares continued to slide and inter-bank lending rates remained high lending conditions across the US economy began to deteriorate inviting recession because the US economy had become increasingly dependent on debt creation for growth. The housing market decline and the credit crunch reduced employment in financial services by over 140,000 over 2007 and there were net falls in employment in some months in the third quarter and across the fourth quarter, but it was early 2008 before consumption started to fall and growth slowed in the US effectively became recession. Significantly, since the major growth areas of the US economy had increasingly focused around housing, financial services, construction, retail and ultimately continued consumption – tighter credit markets essentially produced a self-fulfilling process of reduced growth. Thereafter tighter credit markets and reduced growth would essentially mean an expanding range of defaults far beyond subprime borrowers in all kinds of credit markets.[78]

As the prospect of expanding defaults grew a new source of concern emerged. In early December Moody's announced a review of the main bond insurer organisations (MBIA, Ambac, Security Capital Insurance and Financial Guaranty Insurance) on the basis that widespread defaults and thus large payouts by the insurers could exceed the capital reserves of those insurers. The insurers were themselves AAA rated, if downgraded by the raters on the basis of their capital capacity to meet the crisis then this would create a market signal that all forms of insured debt were insecure – setting off a wave of further problems in debt markets – corporate bonds etc. Over the third quarter of 2007 the spread on corporate bonds over Treasury securities had risen rapidly and new issues of corporate bonds had hit historic lows.[79] The bond insurer problem simply exacerbated this. Since the bond insurers guaranteed $2.4 trillion of debt on a global basis the problem caused ripple effects across the provision of all kinds of debt – increasing both the insurance costs of debt and the terms and conditions borrowers faced and security issues needed to offer.[80]

By the end of the fourth quarter of 2007 the banks were reporting writedowns and losses of over $190 billion on a global basis and the problem had expanded far beyond mortgage related CDOs and CDOs in general. Most of the major US banks (with the notable exception of Goldman Sachs) posted negative net revenues for both the final quarters of 2007 and reported multi-billion dollar expected writedowns for the first quarter of 2008.[81] By April 2008, following the collapse of Bear Stearns and a series of other major capitalisation problems with SIVs and hedge funds the IMF was forecasting total losses from the crisis of around $945 billion – three times the largest estimate for losses from the collapse of the thrifts in the 1980s and far in excess of the eventual losses from LTCM, Enron, World.com etc in the 1990s and early 2000s. Recession in the US raised the possibility of a knock on recession across the global economy, despite the optimistic thesis that the size of the global economy in comparison had become such that it had 'decoupled' from the US. The US economy in 2007 was still 30% of the total size of the global economy. The Japanese economy was still less than half the size of the US economy, and China's economy was around the size of the Californian economy. Moreover, Japan remained mired in a general economic stagnation, China remained highly dependent on US (and EU) demand and the very basis of the crisis was a collapse in liquidity on a global scale that would have profound effects on consumption in the US and EU.

In the UK the main manifestations of the credit crunch focused around the exposure of the banks to CDOs and the extent of individual banks' reliance on CP markets. The crunch itself followed similar patterns to those set by the US because the UK and the US are the most prominent exponents of a liberalised financial system and are the main focus of capital markets: they are at the core of liquidity and thus also at the core of liquidity problems. Both have benefited from being the main focus of capital markets but both are also pre-eminently vulnerable to problems created in them.[82] Particularly since both also had created growth models focused around rising housing markets and consumption (though the UK to a lesser degree). The highest profile manifestation of the credit crunch in the UK was the collapse of Northern Rock. Northern Rock converted from a building society to a public limited company bank in 1997 and began to rapidly expand its mortgage business in 2002. At the beginning of the crisis Northern

Rock had £24 billion in customer savings deposits and £97 billion in mortgage lending. As it expanded over 70% of its new lending was financed by CP markets and it followed a strategy of securitising its lending allowing a rapid turnover in new lending. Its use of CP was more than twice that of any other bank or building society (Bradford and Bingley at 35%). It was, therefore, far more vulnerable to freezes in CP markets that would leave it unable to meet its current CP obligations and/or fulfil its lending plans. It also faced problems because rising base rates were reducing the margins on its assets (as income streams), which was a particular problem because Northern Rock had captured over 8% of the mortgage market by offering preferential terms and conditions and by targeting sub-prime borrowers. In June and July Northern Rock posted profit warnings and started to have difficulty negotiating rollovers for its CP. Its share price started to fall. On August 22nd it reported that it had £275 million invested in US mortgage securities, including CDOs. Its share price continued to fall. On September 5th Northern Rock alerted the Financial Services Authority (FSA) that it was facing serious liquidity problems and had almost £3 billion in CP that was about to become due. The bank's board began to seek assistance from other banks. On September 10th an initial interest from Lloyds in a takeover came to nothing when the Bank of England initially baulked at providing a credit line guarantee for a private takeover.[83] The Bank of England sent in analysts to assess the solvency of Northern Rock and on September 13th, after consultation with the FSA and Treasury, and agreed to act as a lender of last resort – providing Northern Rock with an unlimited credit facility at 1% above the base rate. News of the action set off a run on the bank and began a downward spiral in its share price (falling from £6.39 to £4.38 September 14th and to 90p by the end of 2007) and a continual increase in its calls on the Bank of England credit facility (to over £20 billion). It also resulted in a Treasury Select Committee inquiry into the role of the FSA in monitoring Northern Rock's lending strategy and the Bank of England's culpability in creating a run on the bank – given that one of its main functions is to maintain financial stability. The run and the damage done to Northern Rock's share price set off a wave of speculative attacks on other banks equity as hedge funds took short positions on them. Northern Rock was ultimately nationalised. Its collapse was an additional factor that heightened concerns over the stability of the banking and finance system in the latter half of 2007 and thus helped to feed the changes in behaviour that exacerbated and perpetuated the credit crunch.

The credit crunch and PEF

The credit crunch had multiple effects on PEF activity. Its first effect was to freeze the syndication of the senior debt of a whole series of large buyouts. The introduction of better terms and conditions for borrowers over the period

2004 to early 2007 had reduced the margins from which returns could be generated in syndication and securitisation. The credit crunch brought securitisation to a rapid halt and gave investors motives to pick and choose which syndications to participate in. As liquidity dried up hedge funds in particular then faced problems in generating leverage to invest in syndication. Covenant-lite loans rapidly became unpopular forms of investment and the main banks found themselves with numerous lending commitments stuck on their balance sheets. This was initially referred to as a 'backlog' – Dealogic put the total at approximately $500 billion in the first week of August.[84] The 'backlog' meant that no new lending for large deals was likely to be forthcoming. In Early July, for example, CVC shelved plans for a Euro 13 billion LBO of the Franco-Spanish tobacco company, Altadis. Several protracted deal negotiations and bid auctions collapsed as the summer progressed.[85] For example, the proposed sale of Cadbury's drinks division (including Dr Pepper and 7-Up) by bid-auction between two PEF club consortia – Bain Capital, Thomas H. Lee and TPG versus Blackstone, KKR and Lion Capital – collapsed in August at the second round stage after the bank consortia organising the sale and the PEF firms came into dispute. The bank consortia of Morgan Stanley, Goldman Sachs and UBS reduced the offer of the level of leverage they would finance from 9.5 of Cadbury's Ebitda to 8.5. On October 10th Cadbury formally announced that the auction process would be replaced by a spinout and IPO.

Problems of syndication meant that deals just completed confronted restructuring pressures as the different participants came into conflict over terms and conditions. In July, J P Morgan abandoned plans to syndicate $12 billion in lending made to Cerberus as part of an LBO of Chrysler. Instead, J P Morgan absorbed $10 billion of the loan and the parent company Daimler agreed to retain a $2 billion 19.9% stake in Chrysler. One key element in the degree of latitude different participants can have in pressurising an advantageous restructuring is the issue of any proven 'material adverse change' in the financial health of an organisation undergoing acquisition. In late August, for example, Carlyle, Bain Capital, and Clayton Dubilier & Rice forced a restructuring of their LBO of H D Supply, which was being divested from Home Depot. The basis of their claim was that the declining housing market was and would affect sales revenue. As a result Home Depot cut the sale price by 18% to $8.5 billion and agreed to finance $1 billion of the debt by retaining a 12.5% stake (Owers 2007).[86] As August came to a close Goldman Sachs, Morgan Stanley, Citigroup, Lehman Brothers and J P Morgan, who between them had provided the offer of $37 billion of lending for the TPG led buyout of TXU for approximately $44 billion offered to pay a $1 billion break out fee to rescind the offer before the final negotiation for TXU was complete. The banks were nervous because they had been unable to syndicate the deal based on its current terms and conditions. TPG and the rest of the club consortia, however, were under no legal obligation to accept a break out payment because no material adverse change had occurred to TXUs business. On September 7th the shareholders in TXU voted by 95% majority to accept the TPG LBO and the TPG consortia rejected the banks' offer.

Similar problems emerged in syndication for the £11 billion buyout of Alliance Boots and the recent $24 billion buyout of First Data, both of which were covenant-lite. On September 13th the bank consortia behind the First Data deal (CSFB, Deutsche Bank, Citigroup, HSBC, Lehman, Goldman Sachs and Merrill Lynch) began a process of discounting the $14 billion senior debt and offering further inducements to possible syndicate participants. They offered a 75 cent loan on each dollar value of participation to finance syndication and discounted the cost of the debt to 95 cents in each dollar value. They followed this strategy because once the loan was syndicated the participants would be carrying the primary risk and the nature of the debt held on the banks' own balance sheets would be transformed from single large sums to several smaller ones where the further risk of default on the original large lending (based on attractive terms and conditions to the PEF firms) would be held by the syndicatees. The debt would also be reduced by at least 25% making additional room for the TXU lending that several of the banks' had been involved in.

As failed syndications started to be absorbed onto the balance sheets of the banks this increased the level of their higher risk assets and thus increased the pressures on their Tier 1 capital ratio. This in turn created greater pressures on them to discount the original lending in order to kick start syndication. This, in conjunction with the rising costs of credit compared to the rates at which they had undertaken to offer lending, meant that great swathes of their lending for LBOs would involve writedowns and eventual losses. After sub-prime defaults and CDOs, syndication problems created the next largest source of initial writedowns and losses amongst the main banks. At Citigroup LBO lending writedowns were actually larger in the 3rd quarter than those for sub-prime losses ($1.4 billion compared to $1.3 billion). Merrill Lynch by comparison posted smaller writedowns of $463 million on LBO lending and Bank of America $247 million. By early 2008 the IMF was estimating that direct losses on leveraged loans could reach $10 billion and that losses on CDOs/CLOs could reach $240 billion.

As credit conditions worsened, buyout activity continued to slow. According to Thomson Financial global figures for August were 64% down on the previous year. This trend continued through the latter half of the year in both the UK and US. The effect was particularly significant in reducing larger buyouts of publicly listed companies since these required the largest scale of financing. Since PEF activity had become a major source of merger and acquisition activity, this too reduced. Since merger and acquisition is a source of average upward movements in share prices the slow down in PEF became a contributory (though by no means main) factor in the subsequent slow down in equity markets. The collapse in some kinds of equities created particular opportunities for PEF. The most notable examples of this were the injections of new capital into the main banks by sovereign wealth funds. On November 27th Citigroup announced that the United Arab Emirates SWF, ADIA, was buying $7.5 billion in convertible bonds at a fixed annual interest rate of 11%. The bonds will convert to a 4.9% shareholding. The level of the holding probably indicated the bank wanted to avoid any intervention from Cfius regarding national security issues, whilst the remarkably high interest rate probably indicates how few options Citigroup had in attempting to improve its capitalisation. The deal was followed by a similar one between UBS and the Singapore SWF, GIC, announced December 11th. GIC bought SwFr 13 billion in convertible notes at 9% for a 9% stake. This was followed a few days later by a deal between the China Investment Corporation and Morgan Stanley, buying $5 billion in stock at 9% for a 9.9% stake. Essentially the SWF were engaging in PIPEs, and other PEF firms began to follow suit in early 2008. Washington Mutual, for example, agreed a $7 billion capital investment (in common stock and preference shares) from a TPG led consortium (Jagger 2008). In December 2007 Blackstone announced that it had raised a $1.3 billion fund specifically to invest in debt distressed discounted securities, including CDOs.

Conclusion

It is clearly the case that PEF was not the immediate trigger for the credit crunch. However, it is also true that the growing scale of LBOs and the relation between LBOs and lending were identified by the central banks and main global economic institutions as problematic. The basis on which the effects of expanding PEF were identified as problematic does not simply disappear because PEF was not the immediate trigger of the subsequent credit crunch. Social causation is more complex than that. Still it remains that there was also no major default from a large PEF buyout in the US or UK in the latter half of 2007 as credit conditions worsened. As such, it could easily be argued that the tendency for PEF to grow in scale is more benign than concerns over levels of debt and so forth might indicate. However the vulnerability of current large PEF LBOs to debt levels is something that will be tested by subsequent adverse economic conditions. It is these that will affect the revenues of acquisitions and thus debt servicing. The economic slowdown resulting from the credit crunch only began to take hold towards the end of 2007. If economic conditions worsen at the same time as credit markets remain tight then debt vulnerability will contribute to higher levels of defaults. Larger PEF LBOs seem likely candidates for defaults under these conditions. Again, such conditions may not arise but this in itself is not an argument that justifies a form of finance that creates vulnerabilities *if* such conditions arise.

What should be clear from Chapters 1 to 4 is that PEF exists within a set of liquidity conditions. Since the 1970s liquidity has expanded and contracted in unstable ways. At the same time the underlying trend has been for financial liberalisation to expand the absolute scale of liquidity. In the UK, for example, the value of shares traded on the London Stock Exchange increased 1,500% from the Big Bang to 2005 and average daily trading stood at around 27,500 in 1986 and 350,000 in 2006. There are now trading indexes, exchanges, formal and informal markets in bonds, currencies, and a host of other securities as well as numerous forms of derivatives. Each operates in terms of vast scales of trade. In April 2007, for example, daily foreign exchange trading in London stood at $1.2 trillion. Capital markets and financial markets have grown exponentially. Within that growth PEF has grown and contracted as the liquidity available to it has grown and contracted.

In 2007, as in previous periods, the collapse in liquidity also reduced the scale of activity of PEF. Since funds still had accumulated capital and because falling markets produce debt distress PEF firms could both engage in alternative forms of investment (PIPEs), and continue with smaller scale buyout activity that did not rely on large scale lending.[87] They could also begin new solicitations to specifically target economic sectors and economic forms that were suffering financial distress of one kind or another. From the point of view of PEF, this is simply good business sense – seeking new avenues of profit. From the point of view of the economics of PEF it has a certain narrow consistency with the idea that a PEF firm buys up or invests in a failing organisation and helps turn it around. But it should also be clear from Chapters 1 to 4 that PEF is not just responding to circumstances around it. It is part of the confluence of factors that create those circumstances. It is, therefore, a solution to problems it helps to create. Historically, then, the emergence and growth of PEF in the US and UK can be viewed as part of the instability of liquidity. One can also look more specifically at how the structure of PEF firms and funds also create the tendency towards larger levels of debt and higher levels of leverage, in PEF LBOs. I now turn to this subject in Chapter 5.

5
The Role of Fees and Gearing in Leveraged Buyouts

In Chapters 1–4, I looked at how liquidity expands and how this affected the development and scale of PEF. In this chapter I look at the matter from the opposite point of view: what aspects of PEF cause it to expand to exploit all available liquidity? The basic answer to this question is that the fee structure of PEF funds and the range of available strategies open to PEF firms in undertaking an LBO and then managing an acquisition create motives to do so. In order to generate high returns to the fund that justify some fixed fees and enable the firm to earn the key performance based fee – carried interest – the PEF firm has a motive to increase the levels of debt they use and to focus on larger LBOs, creating more leverage.

In placing the expansion of private equity finance in context in Chapters 1–4, I suggested that PEF can be viewed as a contributing element in the liquidity growth upon which it feeds. As such it could be viewed as a claimed solution to problems that it actually helps to create. In this chapter I begin to extend this perspective. PEF may also be viewed as a claimed solution that creates additional problems. It creates problems related to debt structures and the vulnerability this can then create for acquisitions. It creates problems in terms of how one equates the financial performance of the PEF firm with a broader sense of the performance of the acquisition. These points, in turn, raise the issue of whether PEF is a claimed solution to problems that could be resolved in its absence. These points will be taken up in various ways over the subsequent chapters.

Fees

As I set out in the introductory chapter private equity firms raise capital from investors in a series of separate funds. Both the firms and the funds are typically set up as limited liability partnerships (LLPs). The capital for a fund is directly solicited rather than raised on public markets.[1] Potential investors are invited to a private presentation by the firm and the firm engages in a series of these presentations on what is colloquially termed a 'road show'. The fund is marketed on the basis of a specific focus for investment: a geographical area (East Asia), an industrial sector (telecoms), or forms of investment (creating a buyout fund, funds of funds, mezzanine funds, debt funds &c). The firm typically sets a target total for the fund and closes when that total is reached – although changes in liquidity conditions during solicitation may cause the total to be amended upwards or downwards. Investors commit capital the majority of which is only supplied when required. The fund is a closed end investment and thus has a limited lifespan. This is usually ten years. The investors are the limited partners (LPs) and the firm is the general partner (GP) of the fund LLP. The GP manages the fund on behalf of the LPs. LPs are provided with periodic updates on investments and the performance of the fund but do not take an active role in the day-to-day management of investments.

The PEF firm often commits some of its own capital to the fund. This commitment is rarely a large proportion of the fund. The commitment may be as little as 1% and is rarely more than 10%.[2] The firm, therefore, does not derive the majority of its revenue and profits from returns on a capital investment in its own funds. Rather it derives most of its revenue and profits from its role as GP. If we focus on buyout funds the firm's main sources of return are generated in three ways (Tannon and Johnson 2005; Jenkinson 2006).

First, the firm charges a percentage fee for its management role as GP of the fund. The fund involves start up costs, general administration costs, and also various forms of legal and regulatory compliance costs. Since the LPs cannot undertake a direct management role in the fund without it losing its LLP status, these costs provide the initial basis for the GP to charge management fees. The further justification is that the GP's expertise is pivotal to the appropriate use of the fund capital. Since management fees are a percentage of the total of the fund the absolute size of fees tends to rise as funds grow in scale. The percentage charged does vary and is typically lower for larger funds but a 2% fee per annum for the duration of the fund has not been unusual (Jenkinson 2006; Fenn, Liang and Prowse 1995: 38). On this basis, the management fee for a £500 million fund would be £10 million per year, constituting a total of £100 million for the standard ten year fund duration. The management fee for a mega fund of £5 billion would be £100 million per year, constituting a total of £1 billion for the standard ten year fund duration. On a cumulative basis the management fee accrues to a significant fraction of the original size of the total capital commitment to the fund. A lower rate of 1% on a mega fund of £5 billion would still constitute a total of £500 million in management fees, whilst a rate of 0.5% would constitute a total of £250 million and a rate of 0.25% would constitute a total of £125 million.

Clearly there is a great deal of latitude in terms of the potential significance of management fees. One reason for this is that there are few limits to the specific terms of the LLP fund contract between LPs and GPs.[3] Larger more established PEF firms with a track record of good returns on their investments might be able to charge higher fees. The motivation to do so may be partly offset by their ability to solicit larger funds. Fees may also be negotiated in different ways during different phases of liquidity. For example, during the downturn of the early 1990s some firms offered variable fees and, over and above start-up costs for the fund, calculated them based on invested capital rather than committed fund capital. As such management fees began to accrue from the point the fund became active rather than the vintage year in which solicitation closed. The central point, however, is that management fees produce a significant source of return for the PEF firm and can, when applied to the full duration of the fund, be extremely lucrative despite the relatively low percentage at which they are applied. Moreover, they apply irrespective of the success of any given investment undertaken by the GP.

Second, once the fund becomes active and begins to undertake investments the firm also charges additional fees on the basis of its specific investments. A buyout fund will levy a series of fees on the companies it invests in and/or acquires. These fees are of various kinds. When a company is acquired the PEF firm sets up a shell company to manage it on behalf of the fund. The GP may then charge the acquisition a monitoring fee through the shell company. This monitoring fee would again be an annual percentage. In this case, the fee would be based on some underlying aspect of the accounts of the acquisition. As with the fees charged to the fund the absolute returns to the PEF firm will increase as the scale of operation increases. The LBO of large companies with greater revenues will produce greater levels of monitoring fees. The GP may also charge transaction fees. For example, if the debt structure of the acquisition is restructured the GP may charge a fee for administering the process. Some of the initial cost of setting up the LBO may also be transferred to the acquisition.[4] For example, the costs incurred in employing consultants to aid in targeting, assessing, and negotiating the LBO may be transferred. This transfer of costs enhances profit to the PEF firm as a proportion of fees that the firm charges in its role as GP.

Thirdly, the PEF firm derives a final profit share from the fund based on the returns from investment. This is termed 'carried interest' and is typically set at 20% of net returns. That is, 20% of all profits realised by the fund and its participants. Carried interest is either paid to the GP subsequent to each individual investment or on the basis of the whole portfolio. In either case the carried interest is initially calculated on an incremental basis as returns on investments flow back to the fund.[5] The increments are adjusted in different ways, based on a series of clauses that apply to the two different systems of calculation. If carried interest is calculated on the basis of each specific investment there is usually a mechanism to allow for loss making investments. The losses are subsequently factored into the GPs entitlement to carried interest, reducing that entitlement overall. This prevents the GP from concentrating solely on the most lucrative investments being made and delaying the realisation of any losses on other investments to the end of the life of the fund. If carried interest is calculated on a whole portfolio basis then investors must receive back the sum of their capital commitment before the GP is entitled to carried interest as returns flow to the fund from the investments. For both the individual investment and whole portfolio system of calculation there is also typically a 'hurdle' clause set out in the LLP partnership agreement. The hurdle is a specified percentage level of return to investors that must be exceeded on investments before the GP is entitled to carried interest. The hurdle is usually set at a level higher than the return level on traditional investments – perhaps 10%. Carried interest is the main way in which PEF firms generate returns to themselves through their role as GP. The typical carried interest level of 20% is high when compared to the fees and charges levied by portfolio managers in unit trusts, mutual funds and such, which are typically set at 0.5–1% of the value of investments, but it is comparable to that charged by hedge funds. PEF firms justify the level of carried interest on the basis that it is performance based and on the basis that the GP only becomes entitled to it if, where a hurdle is applied, the fund outperforms traditional forms of investment. Relatedly, GPs often refer to carried interest in terms of the entrepreneurial role of 'sweat equity': the time effort and risk they have undertaken to generate economic 'value'.

The structure of fees provides strong incentives for PEF firms to increase the size of buyout funds. The larger the fund size then the larger the primary annual management fee. A larger fund size enables larger single acquisitions, increasing the absolute size of any series of additional fees for that acquisition, and also enables a greater number of acquisitions to be undertaken increasing the potential for additional fees. The profit from PEF increases for the firm as the scale of activity increases. Moreover, profit will tend to increase at an increasing rate for management fees and additional fees, if these are fixed percentages and the percentage levels do not reduce appreciably as scales of operation increase. This is a likely conjunction because both are influenced by liquidity conditions. During periods of greater liquidity the firms need not mark down fee levels appreciably to attract investment in larger funds. Larger funds mean higher value individual LBOs.

There is, therefore, a clear relationship within the management fee structure of PEF for the scales of PEF to grow in order to exploit liquidity conditions. That relationship also inheres in carried interest, albeit in a more convoluted fashion. Carried interest is earned on net returns to the fund. It is a performance based fee. At 20% it is a large fee. The conditions of the LLP fund contract will not make it easy for the firm to be entitled to that fee. Overall returns to the fund must, therefore, be high. A buyout acquires a firm and restructures it. It thus would seem to have a focus on improving the performance of the acquisition in order to generate returns to the fund that entitle the GP to its performance based fee – carried interest. However, there is a danger here of confusing two different aspects of performance. The GP is ultimately interested in the performance of the acquisition only in so far as it contributes to achieving a performance based fee in terms of the performance of the fund. The performance of the fund is the trigger for carried interest. The key focus of performance is as a financial measure of the return to the fund – a quantity. It does not necessarily follow that this is actually generated by any neutral notion of improved performance by the acquisition because returns to the fund from the acquisition can be generated in various ways. What is improved performance by the acquisition is in this sense contestable. How performance is understood relates to the way in which returns to the fund are generated and carried interest is achieved.

Achieving carried interest is in many respects easier as liquidity conditions improve. This is because greater liquidity enables higher levels of leverage at better terms and conditions for the borrower. As I set out below, this in turn enables the GP to more effectively concentrate equity through financial gearing as an acquisition is undertaken and then also to take advantage of credit markets to use debt creatively to channel returns to the fund. Liquidity simultaneously enables larger LBOs and also a more effective channelling of returns to funds. Achieving carried interest provides the PEF firm with strong motives to exploit all available liquidity. As fund sizes grow exploitation will occur on the basis of larger LBOs. This is because the GP of a buyout fund must undertake a series of LBOs over the ten year duration of the fund in order to use up the committed capital in the fund.[6] This places pressure on the GP to engage in a manageable number of LBOs where the duration between the acquisition of a company through an LBO and its sale is minimised.

Financial gearing: concentrating equity as a first stage in accelerating returns to investment

The goal of the GP in a buyout fund is to identify companies that can be bought and then used as a means to generate returns to the fund. Those returns must be sufficient to recoup the committed capital of the fund investors and then exceed this to generate a level of return to investors that also exceeds the hurdle and enables the GP to earn carried interest. GPs typically look to do this on the basis of a four year time horizon. This means a company is bought and held as an investment for four years before being disposed of. The duration can, however, vary from two to around seven years depending on the nature of the acquisition and the plans of the GP.[7] The basis of a buyout is the use of fund capital to create an equity stake in an acquisition and the use of debt that generates a level of leverage. The first task of the GP is, therefore, to assess what level of debt a potential acquisition can service and how the current earnings of that acquisition can be channelled to accelerate the rate of return to the fund. This assessment provides the initial basis for consideration of the viability of an LBO as an investment for the fund.

If we take four years as the time horizon on which the GP is working then a useful starting point is to ask what level of committed equity from the fund can be repaid on the basis of the buyout in four years and what level of debt would be required to enable this repayment to occur? The level of debt the firm can service and the amount of invested equity it can repay in four years is a highly contingent problem since it involves various unknowns regarding future revenues of the company and market conditions. One can, however, begin from the current accounts of the firm and assume that there is no change in the firms underlying performance, sales etc. This will give a base line answer concerning serviceable debt and repayable equity. This in turn will give some initial idea of how the LBO might be financed using equity and debt. If we assume the company is publicly listed then it is a combination of equity from the fund and debt that will be used to buy the current market capitalisation of the firm.[8] One is then looking at how to replace the market capitalisation with equity from the fund and with debt.[9] The initial calculation can be done using price/earnings ratios (p/e).

A p/e ratio is a measure of how many years are required to recoup invested equity. A ratio of 4 would be four years. Most companies have a p/e ratio far in excess of 4. For the purposes of simplification let us say the GP is planning a buyout of a publicly listed company whose market capitalisation is £2 billion. The company is in the unusual position of having no current debt, has cash deposits of £100 million, and property and other capital assets of £500 million. Further, the company's current annual after tax profit is a relatively healthy £160 million. Its current p/e ratio is:

£2 billion divided by the after tax profit of £160 million, which = 12.5

The GP is thus looking to reduce the p/e from 12.5 to four. This would 'concentrate' the equity because it would mean all the equity in the company would be paid in four years. All other things being equal this concentration requires that there be less equity in relation to earnings. Equity must, therefore, be reduced at the same time as the buyout is financed.

To reduce the p/e to four or less the general manager can plan to use up the cash deposits, realise the disposable assets and create debt. The £100 million cash can be used to buy back shares reducing the market capitalisation to £1.9 billion. The capital assets, particularly property, can be sold and then leased back generating a further £500m, which will ultimately finance part of the buyout. This will ultimately reduce the market capitalisation to £1.4 billion. The GP can then plan to generate debt. Let us say he plans to take out debt against the firm of £1.1 billion. This will reduce the market capitalisation of the firm to £300 million. Ostensibly the p/e ratio would now seem to be:

£300 million divided by £160 million, which = 1.9.

This would mean that a £300 million equity stake could be repaid from the earnings of the firm in just 1.9 years. However, since interest will have to be paid on sold and then leased back capital assets and on debt then the firm will have additional annual debt servicing costs. For the sake of simplification, if we assume interest rates of 5% then those costs will be:

5% of £500 million = £25 million
5% of £1.1 billion = £55 million

This provides a total debt servicing cost of £80 million per year. If one subtracts this from earnings of £160 million then after tax net profits reduce to £80 million. The adjusted p/e would then be:

£300 million divided by £80 million, which = 3.75.

As an initial calculation then the GP knows that on the basis of the current accounts of the firm the fund can commit £300 million in equity and create £1.1 billion in debt and use these in conjunction with assets sales to finance the buyout of a company with a market capitalisation of £2 billion.

Of course, since the buyout precedes the sale of assets or access to the acquisitions cash deposit: initial debt would be higher – though this additional debt would be likely to be short term. Furthermore, as Chapters 1–4 illustrate, the actual debt structure of a buyout will in reality be far more complex.[10] The debt will typically be split into senior and junior elements. The senior element will be provided as fixed term loans by the banks, some of which may be syndicated. Junior debt will consist of different kinds of securities: preference shares, corporate bonds, payment in kind bonds and so forth. It may also include liens. Liens are rights to specific property where that property is used as security against a loan for a given period. Most forms of junior debt liens are secondary liens i.e. rights that are subordinate to some other debt that is already secured on that property: as such they pay higher rates of return. Within both senior and junior debt there may be a series of tranches following the overall line of credit seniority. Some senior debt tranches may be amortising, where the principal is also incrementally repaid during the life time of the loan, and some may be non-amortising involving a final bullet payment of the principal when the loan matures. Since buyouts tend to be finalised on relatively short time scales, particularly where there has been competition between different club deal consortia, there is usually insufficient time to arrange a public issue for securities. The initial round of junior debt is, therefore, typically financed through private placement. This typically involves mezzanine funds, funds of funds, sovereign wealth funds and hedge funds. Again, since time scales are short the senior debt may also involve bridge financing offered by the underwriting banks in order to expedite the buyout. The underwriting bank consortia may also provide a revolving credit facility. The interest rates of the various tranches will likely be set as spreads over Libor and the extent of the spread will be wider the more junior the debt. Since junior debt is more expensive, the GP will usually try to maximise the use of senior debt. A more realistic version of our example £1.1 billion debt would, therefore, look something like:

Senior debt:
Fixed term loan 1 (amortising) five year duration: £300 million at 2% over Libor
Fixed term loan 2 (amortising) six year duration: £250 million at 2.5% over Libor
Fixed term loan 3 (non-amortising) seven year duration: £200 million at 3% over Libor
Fixed term loan 4 (non-amortising) eight year duration: £150 million at 3.25% over Libor
Subtotal: £900 million

Junior debt:
High yield/junk bonds ten year duration: £100 million at 5% over Libor
Mezzanine finance ten year duration: £100 million at 5% over Libor + convertibility rate
Subtotal: £200 million

Total debt: £1.1 billion

If one were to take Libor at a conservative 4% for the first year of the term of the lending then the cost of debt servicing in that year would be:

Fixed term loan 1: £18 million
Fixed term loan 2: £16.25 million
Fixed term loan 3: £14 million
Fixed term loan 4: £10.88 million

High yield/junk bonds: £9 million
Mezzanine finance: £9 million

Total: £77.13 million

If one then factors in rent on sold and leased back assets at £25 million the firm has a total debt to service of £102.13 million. This would reduce after tax net profit to £57.87 million, plus any additional charges based on the use of any revolving credit facility. In terms of the standard debt servicing measure using pre-tax and pre-adjustments to earnings (Ebitda) then gearing has created a debt ratio of around 1.6.[11] Leverage as a proportion of the total value of the deal is, meanwhile, if one excludes asset sales, around 50%. This is a relatively modest figure by large LBO standards and particularly during periods of greater liquidity. This highlights the importance of asset sales in terms of the ability to concentrate equity without generating higher levels of leverage. The fewer available asset sales that can be factored into a buyout the higher the likely level of leverage (measured as a proportion of deal value) will be when equity is concentrated.

Whether one uses the more realistic construction of a debt structure or a simplified version the essential insight regarding the use of debt and the concentration of equity remains the same. Before planning to do anything else to the prospective acquisition the GP knows that he can recoup £300 million in invested equity for fund investors within four years and transfer £1.7 billion of the finance costs of the buyout to that acquisition. Given that the debt can be serviced from earnings and that equity can be returned to fund investors from earnings then the GP knows that the primary cost of the buyout – its £2 billion market capitalisation can be covered. It is, first and foremost, this that makes the prospective acquisition a viable investment target. Using the simplified version of the debt structure 'viability' is compatible with transforming the finances of the firm from a situation with no debt, after tax profits of 12.5% (£160 million from £2 billion), assets of £500 million and £100 million in cash, to one of reduced net profits of £80 million, no assets, no cash deposits, £1.1 billion in new debt and ongoing annual debt servicing commitments of £80 million that may fluctuate as interest rates change.

It should be noted, however, that in terms of the LBO of publicly listed companies the GP has not planned to do anything that the Plc could not have done itself. All that has occurred is that the finances of the firm have been restructured to increase the rate at which the equity in the firm is returned. This is the basis of gearing. The core strategy involved is to affect the relation of equity to debt and thus reduce the p/e ratio. Absolute returns on the business need not be higher they need simply be concentrated in fewer hands. The initial difference between private equity and public equity in engaging in such gearing is that private equity engages in a buyout and delists a publicly listed company, whilst in public equity gearing would be to buyback shares and simply reduce the amount of public equity of the firm (its market capitalisation).

Still, the LBO has done what a publicly listed company is unlikely to do: radically concentrate equity through leverage. The leverage has been created to channel returns to the fund. As Chapters 1–4 indicate, as liquidity improves there is a tendency for PEF firms to use an increasing amount of leverage in larger deals. One reason for this is precisely that it enables the more effective concentration of equity and enables it for larger and larger firms where the absolute size of the revenues being captured will be higher. The use of gearing is thus one facet of why PEF expands to exploit available liquidity and why more debt will be generated, subject to current servicing conditions, when lending conditions allow.

The very process of a leveraged buyout, therefore, immediately raises questions concerning the meaning of performance. Gearing has made the LBO possible and has accelerated and concentrated the returns to equity. This is channelled into the fund. The GP has thus begun the process of meeting his performance based criteria for the fund. But it is an open question as to whether this is compatible with a broader notion of the performance of the acquisition. The debt it is carrying may well be currently serviceable. But this raises two initial questions. First, will credit conditions vary and will this make servicing the debt more difficult? As Chapters 1–4 indicate, this is an ever-present problem and it is more of a problem for larger LBOs using more leverage. Second, will the market conditions of the acquisition change, in turn affecting revenue? The GP may well have clear plans to improve the organisation of the acquisition and improve its profitability in one way or another. However, the GP has no control over the business cycle. He may be committed to making the acquisition more able to resist economic downturns by reducing costs, improving margins and focusing on core business – hoping to improve customer loyalty etc. But there are limits to how far one can do this. Furthermore, those limits are influenced by the constraints created by debt. Debt servicing creates a vulnerability to the business cycle because it reduces the levels of net revenue in excess of servicing costs. Using Ebitda as a measure of profit simply disguises this. If net revenues are low then there is little leeway before the firm enters a loss making position and an economic downturn makes this more likely.

Using debt as part of a buyout, therefore, creates the basic problem that enhancing the performance of the fund can come at the expense of reducing the viability of the acquisition. This, however, is not how advocates of PEF LBOs view the situation. The main theorist of LBOs, Michael Jensen, reverses this logic and argues that the existence of debt is actually a discipline on the function of the acquisition because there is no margin for error. We will look at Jensen's argument in more detail in Chapter 6. What I want to suggest here is that if one takes the point that PEF LBOs are often articulated as solutions to the problems of companies that are ailing in one way or another, a clear counter-argument is that PEF is a solution that creates new problems: specifically that of debt and the vulnerabilities that debt creates.

Maximising returns to the fund and achieving carried interest

What Jensen's point does indicate, however, is that gearing alone is not all that the GP is thinking about when undertaking an LBO. Gearing is a starting point. If we return to our original example, a £2 billion buyout that returns the initial committed equity of £300 million from the fund in four years has not actually generated a net return to the fund. If one factors in management fees it has actually made a loss. Of course the GP is also planning to sell the acquisition at the end of the four years, through a trade sale to a company working in the same sector, through the secondary market to another PEF, or as an IPO. Given that the initial equity has been covered then the sale is liable to be a significant net return to the fund. There is, therefore, no necessary great pressure on the GP to significantly improve the revenues of the firm. However, if the GP can succeed in improving the revenue position of the acquisition then this will have two effects. First it will enhance the earnings side of the p/e ratio. This will increase the returns to the equity committed from the fund during the time the acquisition is held.[12] Second, it will, all other things being equal make the acquisition a more attractive prospect for subsequent sale. On both counts returns to the fund are likely to be improved.

Three additional points follow. First, it is unlikely that the GP planned to commit the minimal amount of equity from the fund that we derived from the initial gearing calculation. Large buyout funds, particularly mega-funds, have a great deal of committed capital to utilise within ten years. Given that the first couple of years of the fund will involve finding initial targets and the final years of the fund will also involve winding up existing investments then the total committed capital must be utilised within six to eight years. PEF firms are themselves LLPs with few GPs. There is, therefore, limited manpower to undertake investment. As a consequence there is a pressure to both use committed capital in greater than minimal portions and to seek out larger acquisitions. Thus, although leverage rises during liquidity surges the GP will also look to use fund capital in large chunks. In smaller deals the GP may look to finance up to one third of the deal using fund equity. In larger multi-billion deals this may be far less, since the committed fund equity can still be large. The point, however, is that the initial p/e ratio created through gearing will likely be greater than 4. Raising earnings will help reduce it and guarantee that the equity capital committed from the funds is repaid. This reduces the reliance of the GP on a favourable sale (at the same time as making it more likely) and improves the likelihood that carried interest will be earned.

Second, though the GP seems to have a vested interest in improving the revenue position of the firm this, if we return to the idea of performance, does not create a neutral or objective sense that the performance of the acquisition will be improved. The revenue position of the firm can be enhanced in various ways. Some of the debt financing could be earmarked for investment: new technologies, new machinery, new production processes, new premises, renovations and so forth. These could result in increased productivity improving margins on revenue and reducing margins on costs. Costs and revenues could also be enhanced in other ways. Wages could be reduced. This is unlikely to be a matter of simply cutting current wage rates. Rather employment relations could be restructured. High cost non-core activities (payroll, some aspects of administration, IT etc.) could be outsourced, reducing costs and reducing the labour force. More low skilled staff, less senior staff and contract workers could be used. Employment contracts could be rewritten to allow flexible working patterns, the gradual reduction of core wages in favour of performance fees could be implemented and other terms and conditions could be phased out for new workers (defined benefit pension schemes and so forth). At the same time, and in conjunction with capital investment, productivity could be increased, perhaps by reducing labour and/or requiring each worker to do more and more of different tasks. The point is there is scope within the idea of improving the financial position of the firm to ask the question: improve for whom and on what basis? We will return to this matter in more detail in Chapter 7.

Improving the financial position of the firm, when the GP has a time horizon of four years is more than just an issue of improve for whom and on what basis. It is also about the sustainability of those improvements. New employment contracts and changes in employment relations can reduce the commitment of employees as expressed in their 'psychological contract'. This in turn can erode the amount of additional unpaid commitment workers invest in their work. For some kinds of business organisation this can have long term detrimental effects on business performance and thus on financial performance – particularly services based on human capital. Outsourcing can produce similar problems (call centres etc.). These are just two of several ways in which improving the accounts of a firm on a short time horizon for resale can produce an artificial sense of positive performance gains. Work is measured by the financial accounts of the organisation but cannot be reduced to those accounts without barbarising the complex relationships that underpin business success in the long term. The GP does not have to think in terms of that long term.

Third, the idea of the long term beyond the four year time horizon creates additional conflicts in the decision making process for the GP. Though the GP seems to have a vested interest in improving the revenue position of the firm this can be offset by other factors. Greater leverage and improved liquidity conditions mean that larger levels of debt can be created. This in turn creates the opportunity to use the debt structure to specifically channel returns to the fund. This may be in the form of special dividends paid to the equity holders in the acquisition. The payment of special dividends became a common private equity practice for larger LBOs during the last liquidity surge. The dividends are created either in the initial debt structure of the acquisition or in any further refinancing. Refinancing may be to take advantage of cheaper debt as liquidity improves. The GP may be, for example, activating a clause in the junior debt that allows the securities to be bought back. The GP can then replace the junior debt with cheaper forms of senior debt. If this is the case the payment of special dividends may in part be derived from debt servicing savings in the new debt structure. There is, of course, always the temptation to increase the absolute size of debt to take advantage of current lending conditions. If so, such dividends effectively mean that not only is the acquisition being mainly bought with debt that can be transferred to the acquisition, but also additional debt is likely to be created to guarantee returns to the fund investors, irrespective of how the acquired business then performs.

This is not a simple process by which the acquisition is loaded with debt it cannot service. Rather it is the temptation created by greater liquidity to refinance and increase leverage, affecting debt servicing ratios. Improved lending conditions allow for larger scale debt and thus debt structures that are more vulnerable to changes in the business cycle. In a sense the GP is in a position to gamble that the business cycle will not experience a downturn and that his current plans to restructure the acquisition will enhance the acquisition's revenue position. If so debt will continue to be serviceable until the acquisition is disposed of. This is a gamble worth taking since achieving carried interest requires high returns to the PEF fund. Those returns are unlikely to be generated within the lifetime of the investment in the acquisition purely through improving the revenue position of the firm. This is partly because net revenues are initially reduced by the LBO process because of the need to service debt. It is also because as the scale of LBOs increase and larger absolute volumes of fund capital are used there is a greater absolute size of capital to be returned to the fund. Failure has greater effects on the returns to the fund. Special dividends can generate large sums of capital very rapidly that can then be directed back to the fund. This is another way in which the GP is induced by the fee structure of PEF to exploit all available liquidity.

The LBO of Debenhams illustrates some of these issues. CVC, TPG, and Merrill Lynch Private Equity won an auction for Debenhams in 2004. They then undertook a sale and leaseback in March of that year, raising £430 million of which £130 million was returned to the investors. In May 2005 they then refinanced for a further £1 billion, all of which was returned to the investors. At the same time Debenhams cut margins to suppliers, and reduced capital spending. The firm was floated as an IPO in May 2006 at £1.95 per share, but a series of poor performance figures saw its share price drop to £1.30 by the 1st week of July 2007, giving the firm a market capitalisation of around £1.1 billion – considerably less than its current debt.

There are then in combination four ways in which the GP can look to channel returns to the fund and achieve carried interest. First, the basic gearing procedure of the LBO concentrates equity and accelerates the rate of return on that equity. The revenues of the acquisition are channelled and focused on the capital committed from the fund. Second, the cost/revenue basis of the acquisition can be restructured using a series of different strategies.

These can be used to increase rates of return to the fund investors who hold the concentrated equity. Third, the GP can use the debt structure, particularly through refinancing, to create special dividends. Fourth, the GP then looks to sell the acquisition on.

That the GP can rely on some combination of these four is an important point because they do not easily cohere. The GP will be looking to sell the business on in around four years. By that time the business may have been merged into others or split into several separate entities. In either case, the ideal aim is that final sale(s) ought to exceed the original cost of acquisition and cover the combination of the debt used in the purchase, the fees generated to the GP by the fund, and a return to the investors that exceeds what they would have earned from alternative investments. This outcome, however, is by no means certain. A secondary buyout by another PEF firm provides the buyer with strong incentives to push down the purchase price. Moreover, for larger acquisitions that could have been floated on public markets, a secondary buyout might indicate that the GP had failed to improve the acquisition in a way that would make it attractive to public investors, which may be precisely why another fund has a strong negotiating position. The price of IPOs, meanwhile, are not just a product of the performance of the business in isolation but are also related to the number of IPOs occurring at that time (more tends to reduce the price) and whether a bull market is occurring – neither of which can be known four years in advance.

The most primitive aspects of gearing make a business less attractive for resale on the basis of its accounts. If resale means that the debt carried by the firm is replaced by equity through flotation then the holders of the new equity have effectively subsidised the previous gearing procedure. If sold on through either a secondary buyout or prepared as an IPO carrying its debt then there is the problem that assets have already been sold and leased back, debts and servicing commitments already created, and net profits, ceteris paribus, reduced. Not only are the 'fundamentals' of the business less stable but the gearing itself creates a barrier. If the debt carried by the firm is passed on in the resale and the original leased assets not recovered then the gearing procedure cannot be repeated in the same way. Taking on debt and management of leased assets become issues of refinance not fundamental financial engineering. This would be a secondary form of gearing.

The limiting factor on what another private equity firm will pay in a secondary buyout is not just the accounts of the business but also the environment within which refinancing can occur. The buyer may have a certain degree of negotiating power if the business is already leveraged. But the secondary buyout may still be for more than the original buyout if additional debt can be loaded onto the firm. To a degree, the firm is simply a convenient vehicle for this. That said, in either a shift to secondary gearing or the substitution of equity the transfer of the acquisition through resale is on the basis of, if all else is the same, precisely the weakened fundamentals of the business because the firm has carried the servicing costs of the debt for four years. Gearing has been a way of enabling a rapid extraction of value based on a technical strategy that is first and foremost about the mathematics but in terms of ultimate importance is about the conditions that make that gearing possible and the consequences that flow from it.

This raises the important issue of how far costs can be cut and revenue can be enhanced in order to both service and reduce debt and how far the GP is genuinely relying on this to be the means by which the majority of the returns to the fund are generated. There is no definitive answer to this question in the sense one cannot simply say that the GP must improve the acquisition in order to generate high returns to the fund and achieve carried interest. The returns to the fund can be based on a combination of the four ways in which returns are generated. All are effectively contingent. The background to that contingency is liquidity. How much debt and on what terms and conditions can the GP access? What are the prospects for refinancing at any given time? How conducive are secondary markets to the resale of the acquisition? What is the current state of the business cycle and how does this impact on revenues? These are factors that affect how much debt the LBO involves, how debt is structured, and whether that debt can be serviced.

Conclusion

Since there are various ways in which high returns to the PEF fund can be generated it cannot simply be asserted that high returns to investors is a signal of the success of the acquisition. Even if the business is sold for more than it was acquired for this also cannot be taken as a definitive signal of the success of the acquisition. Even an improvement in the current revenue position, measured using either Ebitda or measured using net revenues from the new post-acquisition lower profit level, cannot be taken as an unequivocal signal of the success of the acquisition. The different financial indices that these are based upon are not their own explanation. Each involves a context. From this point of view each PEF LBO can only be assessed on a longer time line and on the basis of the specifics of the case. There is no simple financial measure one can use to say that PEF is about and can easily claim to be about enhanced performance of acquired businesses. One can, however, draw the conclusion that PEF is a claimed solution to the problems of the businesses it buys that also involves a series of new problems. The buyout process creates a debt structure. The internal dynamics of the fee arrangements of the PEF firms and the way that returns can be generated in different ways for the fund create incentives to exploit all available liquidity. That is why it is not just the absolute scale of debt that increases during a liquidity surge but also the level of leverage. Liquidity conditions can create a gambler's scenario based on strategies for financing, refinancing, and terms and conditions. The gamble for the GP is how to generate high returns to the fund and achieve carried interest. Since leverage levels rise during liquidity surges then clearly debt creation becomes a more prominent strategy. The use of special dividends seems to confirm this.

It is also worth noting that the gamble is not one between equal parties. PEF practitioners sometimes describe an LBO is analogous to taking out a mortgage and using the borrowed capital to improve the property before selling it on (for example, Little and Klinsky 1989: 71). This is not a wholly inaccurate analogy. However, as the role of the housing market bubble in the credit crunch set out in Chapter 4 indicates, the choices made in regard of property and the potential profits generated from property are more complex than the simple equation of debt → investment → improved equity would seem to imply. Moreover, in one sense the analogy is misleading. If I buy property, I do not buy it with debt that the property repays and from which I am insulated. A PEF LBO transfers debt to the acquisition but concentrates and extracts revenues as returns. The failure of the acquisition may be an investment failure for the fund, but it is not a liability for the fund or for the PEF firm. Moreover, if special dividends have been generated early on in the four year time line then it may well be that guaranteeing returns to the fund is one reason why the acquisition then failed. This reinforces the point that PEF is a claimed solution that creates new problems. One can reasonably ask here whether it is necessary to generate debt in order to address any claimed problems of a business. Put another way was a PEF LBO a necessary solution? This brings us back to the point made at the end of Chapter 4 that even if defaults are avoided, debt creation is a vulnerability.

PEF practitioners are not altruists. They do not undertake LBOs as a public service. The motive, even in MBOs, though this may be ameliorated in smaller scale transitional buyouts involving family succession, is profit for the fund and the PEF firms. Improving the business is a contingent issue and is not the ultimate concern of the GP. It is simply one means to generate returns to funds and achieve carried interest. This then raises the corollary question of whether this extraction needs to occur in order that any business be 'improved'? This is not to suggest that the business may not survive the extraction. As Chapters 1–4 indicate, although there have been periods of higher defaults and refinancing problems for PEF there has been no cataclysmic collapse of LBOs, large or otherwise. In a sense the question becomes one of both risk and entitlement. Should PEF be allowed to risk the long term future of companies – particularly large publicly listed companies that are main employers? Have PEF firms done anything to entitle them to the potentially large returns earned by GPs through undertaking

LBOs? These are questions in addition to the core issue of Chapters 1–4 that PEF helps to create the conditions to which it then becomes a solution. These are questions I will be addressing in Chapter 7 as both conceptual and empirical questions. To expedite this I now move on in Chapter 6 to look at how PEF LBOs have been conceptualised and theorised.

6
Theories of Leveraged Buyouts and Theories of Market Instability

In Chapter 5, I focused on the internal dynamics of why private equity finance expands to exploit available liquidity. In so doing I made the point that it can be seen as a claimed solution that creates new problems. Those problems included complex debt structures and rising leverage. In this chapter, I look at the theorisation of PEF LBOs. I do so with a focus on Michael Jensen's work because he has been the outstanding scholar in this field. His work is the foundation of all other theories of LBOs. Others tend to absorb his key insights and appropriate his key concepts.[1] Jensen's approach begins from the way the possibility of an LBO is signalled creating a market for corporate control. The initial basis for this signalling became his free cash flow theory. His work, however, is important beyond free cash flow as a market signal. For Jensen, debt is not just a necessary adjunct of an LBO. It is also a positive disciplining force that helps make PEF a desirable model of business organisation. I argue, however, that one can deconstruct Jensen's approach to show that it is less coherent than it initially appears. Moreover, Jensen's approach also involves a series of normative commitments that rely on a basic understanding that PEF responds to historical dynamics but is not itself shaped by them. I argue that if one thinks of PEF as a constitutive part of the growth of unstable liquidity then PEF is also historically dynamic. In so far as this is the case, debt ceases to be an unambiguous source of discipline. In order to facilitate this argument I also formalise some of the ideas developed in Chapters 1 to 4 regarding liquidity by drawing on the relevant work of Keynes, Minsky and Kindleberger. Doing so broadens the focus of the theoretical analysis of PEF that Jensen has pioneered. This broadening is an important preliminary in placing the empirical arguments regarding PEF in a different context than the unremittingly positive one provided by Jensen and other proponents of LBOs.

LBOs as a solution to free cash flow

The original argument for LBOs was US based and grew out of a more general tradition of work on conflict of interest and corporate control, first highlighted by Adam Smith in *The Wealth of Nations* and then explored in behavioural economics in the 1960s (Hirschey 1986: 317). The historical context was one in which the particular circumstances of growing equity ownership in the US had separated equity ownership and corporate management in a way that gave equity owners little scope or incentive to monitor management and gave managers reasons to centralise control as they expanded the business to feed dividend payments:

> Throughout most of the twentieth century, American public stockholders have made no direct contribution to decisions regarding the allocation of corporate revenues. Nor have they hired, fired, rewarded or punished the corporate managers who made these decisions. Ostensibly the board of directors represents stockholders' interests in these matters. But it is well known, historically, that the top managers of American corporations, not the stockholders, have chosen the board of directors, and that it would be very expensive for stockholders to mount a proxy contest to replace top management... The market in industrial securities evolved in the United States to effect the separation of stock ownership from strategic control because it offered households liquidity while not requiring commitment. American households became willing to hold stocks in publicly-traded corporations only because their 'ownership' stakes did not entail any commitment of their time, effort or additional funds to ensure the success of companies. A general willingness to leave control over the allocation of corporate revenues with managers stemmed from the prior revenue-generating successes of publicly-listed corporations under management control, and in part from the limited liability protection that public stockholders enjoyed... The separation of stock ownership from strategic control, as it occurred in the United States, encouraged both the continuous growth of industrial corporations and the centralisation of strategic control so that these companies grew larger and larger as unitary strategic entities. (Lazonick and O'Sullivan 1997: 15)

In the mid-1970s and early 1980s Michael Jensen and others developed the concept that public companies incurred 'agency costs' (Jensen and Meckling 1976; Jensen and Ruback 1983; Jensen and Zimmerman, eds. 1985). According to Jensen *et al.*, managers were agents of shareholders whose function was to generate returns to those shareholders. In public corporations managers had an incentive to generate sufficient returns to pay satisfactory dividends but had no specific interest in maximising the corporation's performance to generate greater revenues to return to shareholders. Management compensation was not strongly related to the returns to shareholders and management were not directly hired or fired by shareholders. Moreover, management had a vested interest in retaining profits from the corporation for reinvestment because this way of financing growth did not require them to rely on capital markets. Using external sources could create more public monitoring of management and of the corporation's performance and strategy.

For Jensen these 'interest misalignments' become particularly significant as public corporations grow in size and the industry they operate in 'matures'. Large corporations dominating longstanding industries are organised in ways where management themselves face intra-managerial agency costs due to hierarchies based on divisional structures. Despite such organisational inefficiencies, as dominant forces in longstanding industries these corporations tend to generate large revenues and cash flows, and these revenues can experience surges due to particular industry-specific circumstances – such as rising oil prices creating windfall revenues to oil companies in the 1970s. Large banked cash balances can then emerge. This and the existence of large revenues and cash flow tends to feed growth by merger, and in the context of US anti-trust law, conglomeration. Increasing size and conglomeration dilute efficient control of corporate performance in a centralised management system. Moreover, large cash flows produce incentives for high levels of investment in research and development. In mature industries much of this research and development is superfluous and, in any case, wasteful because it is poorly monitored and poorly scrutinised in terms of its market potential. There is no great incentive to channel higher revenues into dividends since this creates higher future expectations. There is, however, an incentive to misuse corporate funds to subsidise extravagant management lifestyles based on tenuous justifications – luxurious homes in various locations for corporate entertaining, private aircraft fleets for business travel etc.

The agency costs argument was, then, originally focused on a particular characterisation of dominant public corporations: large, wasteful, and typically conglomerated. The argument was that these corporations were ones that could make better use of cash flow by returning more of it to shareholders. They were corporations whose performance could be improved and that would probably benefit from shrinking. For Jensen it was with these specific characteristics in mind that takeovers in the form of LBOs provided a particular solution. Jensen argued that high levels of 'free cash flow' particularly in the context of large diversified/conglomerated firms were a signal to outside investors that some or all of a corporation could profitably be acquired. 'Free cash flow' was defined in technical terms as 'cash flow in excess of that required in order to fund all projects that have positive net present values when discounted at the relevant cost of capital.' (Jensen 1986: 323; 1988: 28). Decoded, this simply means cash flow in excess of productive/profitable investment and other justifiable utilisations by the corporation. The existence of this free cash flow acts as a signal creating a 'market for corporate control' in which 'alternative management teams compete for the right to manage corporate resources' (Jensen 1988: 23). For Jensen, an LBO is a preferable solution within the competition for corporate control because it has strong motives to create 'value'. This is because leverage/debt creates a disciplining effect. He terms this the 'control hypothesis' for debt creation (1986: 324; 1988: 31).

The control hypothesis argues that debt is a far more binding promise to distribute returns from a business than is any undertaking by the management, in the absence of an LBO, to improve future dividends. High leverage creates debt servicing costs. The holders of the debt receive guaranteed returns. High levels of leverage tend to require that the financial performance of the firm be improved in order that the debt can be serviced. The existence of the debt creates a further monitoring function for the holders of that debt. Covenants will require that the firm can periodically prove it is capable of meeting its debt servicing commitments and that its credit rating is warranted. Debt servicing reduces free cash flow and as such reduces the discretion of management and management's opportunity to engage in wasteful investment and frivolous uses of corporate funds for personal ends. In the context of PEF, however, there is no implication that management compensation will be reduced. Rather the opposite: depending on the variety of buyout the management will either be part of the team who undertake the buyout, including the original PEF firm, or will be brought in by the PEF firm. They will either have an equity stake in the acquisition, with all the benefits of the concentration of equity through gearing, or will have a lucrative performance based contract. In Jensen's schema this creates an 'incentive realignment' between management and equity owners i.e. the conflict of interest from which agency costs originally derive is removed. All sides are now committed to improving the financial performance of the acquisition – 'value' is raised to return to equity holders and to satisfy debt servicing. Within this process the PEF firm, through the participation of its general partners as active representatives of the PEF fund, provides a focused group of monitors with a degree of expertise and access that ordinary institutional investors and small shareholders in a publicly listed company simply would not have.

Jensen's original theory is simple and elegant. It is, however, more problematic than purely parsimonious.[2] A useful place to start in establishing this is by looking at the way free cash flow is defined. The definition is set up as though it were an unproblematic and unambiguous means of calculation: free cash flow is that in excess of all projects and uses that have net *present* value. Looked at more closely, however, this is not deterministic based on any indisputable single formula for calculation but rather determined by the way one assesses the future. This is because free cash flow is derived by looking at current uses of resources and making decisions about their appropriateness. There is here a tendency to confuse the source of some of the investment that is undertaken and the concept of free cash flow. The main source that Jensen focuses on in his original theory is the existence of high levels of retained profits as well as banked cash balances.

It is because retained profits are coupled with high proportions of investment to revenues within a general context of mature industries with low growth that they are seen as a form of excess. But this does not make free cash flow an unproblematic concept.

It is certainly true that there have been numerous clear cut cases of waste in large corporations based on management excess and poorly considered investment, including research and development. Here, egregious examples can readily be addressed by better monitoring. However, there is also a good deal of ambiguity in the majority of productive investment decisions. There is no algorithm for productive investment and thus no genuine way of calculating the net present value of what is essentially going to be determined by future events. One can look at current investment and ask questions about whether it appears to have been properly costed and whether it has been directed by a fully reasoned projection about future business possibilities. It may well be that what appears wasteful or superfluous would not be if properly costed and understood in terms of future business possibilities. It may well be that there are simply unintended consequences and unknowns relating to the investment and the future which mean that apparently superfluous investment will pay off. The latter point of course is no basis to conduct a business that must consider margins of profit and loss now. The point, however, is that demanding discipline in how investment is justified is quite a different thing than being able to calculate free cash flow as a definite figure. The definite figure assumes some unambiguous means to identify some uses of resources as unequivocally unproductive now and in the future.

In a PEF context the definite figure also assumes that the PEF firm *is* simply looking for a means to cut unproductive uses of resources that are unambiguous. If they are in fact ambiguous then one cannot assume any simple relation between cutting waste and superfluous investment *and* creating free cash flow by calculating a net present value. The numbers won't just speak for themselves – there will rather be a line of debate about what productive and necessary investment is *and* what the best use of resources is. This returns us to the territory covered in Chapter 5. The PEF firm's first concern is concentrating equity through leverage. Its first question is what level of debt servicing can the firm carry? Jensen sees no contradiction here with an improvement in the performance of the firm that is acquired because the new ownership structure is intent on creating 'value' and is disciplined to do so by its debt servicing and by its 'incentive realignment'. One cannot, of course, ignore that new investment is often a key aspect of post LBO business strategies. In Jensen's terms, since the investment is now part of a larger debt structure it too is disciplined by its relation to external monitors rather than being the undisciplined product of retained profits. However, a tension will always exist between leverage as a discipline and leverage as a constraint on investment. This need not imply that investment will necessarily be lower but something must give in order that debt can be serviced and this may be jobs or wages, terms or conditions of employees. Ultimately, since free cash flow is created by constrained decisions about what uses of resources are valued and for what purposes, free cash flow is actually more appropriately termed 'liberated capital'. Liberated capital is generated from the redistribution of resources and in a PEF context this is directed primarily at debt servicing. It is not a neutral process based on an easily applied calculation. The concept of free cash flow, then, quickly escapes the boundaries set for its meaning by Jensen.

What Jensen is actually concerned with in the original free cash flow argument is the critique of an organisational form – the conglomerate – and critique of the use of retained profits as a source of investment. His commitments are implicitly that smaller less diversified organisational forms are more efficient and that capital markets are more appropriate sources of finance for investment. Neither commitment requires the free cash flow argument follow the definitional form he uses. What free cash flow does is make the argument appear less normative and more empirical in the vein of positive economics.[3] Liberated capital could still be an empirical argument but it would be one that at least acknowledged the normative nature of an empirical argument. Jensen's argument is essentially that PEF LBOs are an economic and social benefit in the context of conglomeration. Leverage is not just a convenient means for equity to be concentrated but also a beneficial aid to organisational restructuring. He is quite clear about this but less clear that the empirical argument about leverage and the role of debt involves basic assumptions about how an economy should be ordered. This becomes more apparent when his original argument is broadened in later accounts of PEF and LBOs. A number of specific points of critique build to this point regarding how an economy is ordered.

Incentive realignment and human nature

As Chapters 1–4 indicate, not all LBOs have involved large corporations or conglomerates and not all LBOs have followed on from the identification (however problematic) of free cash flow (Opler and Titman 1993; Opler 1992). PEF LBOs have covered a wide range of industries, organisational forms, and circumstances. Publicly listed and private companies including small and medium sized firms looking to expand, family companies seeking a way for the older generation to cash out whilst the succeeding generation retain some management involvement, firms suffering from debt distress and seeking to avoid bankruptcy: all have been targets of PEF LBOs of one kind or another. As such, the free cash flow argument concerns a subset of a broader phenomenon. Jensen is, of course, aware of this (1986: 324 & 328). As such in subsequent work he argues that the case for LBOs is broader than simply the existence of free cash flow as a signal for LBOs in the context of conglomeration (Jensen 1989a, 1989b & 1989c). His and our interest is still mainly in large LBOs and in publicly listed companies. Within this context he makes the point that the existence of a signal may be a reason for an LBO to occur but there is also a case for PEF LBOs because they are a source of economic efficiency in general. Here free cash flow becomes less central to his argument. Instead he begins to emphasise the general benefits of LBOs by reiterating the function of a PEF firm as a more focused group of owners and monitors creating an 'incentive realignment' that motivates improved business performance. LBOs are a solution to the agency problem in a way that is not reducible to the issue of free cash flow.

This idea of alignment assumes that organisational efficiency is created at the top of those organisations and is motivated by new higher levels of 'compensation'. Organisational inefficiency is not just about size and divisional structure it is about basic human motives to excel. Management will care about creating 'value' because they are now significant recipients of that value. Essentially this is an argument that suggests firms can optimise but will only do so because managers can be induced to optimise. In some respects it seems curious that a manager who earns $1 million a year has no incentive to seek an efficient organisation whereas one who might earn multiples of that salary through a PEF LBO will. Empirically there seems no way to directly test this tacit assumption about human nature. If the original organisational form was a large conglomerate then engaging in asset sales and splitting it into smaller units may account for the higher returns and better financial performance. Equally, if the firm is of some other organisational form, involving any one of a number of reasons for a PEF LBO, then any improvements in financial performance could be related to any of the various factors that the LBO addressed. One could of course counter that the reason that the organisational form was addressed was because the new owners stood to make large gains through the concentration of equity and this was the reason for the LBO. But this is not an argument for optimising as an aspect of human nature of quite the same kind as incentive realignment implies. Incentive realignment implies that the only reason to engage in marginal improvements in financial performance is the existence of commensurate marginal improvements in personal rewards. What actually happens in an LBO, however, is that a large share of the returns from an organisation are captured through the concentration of equity. This is not directly about margins but rather about absolute control of proportions of returns. It is in the process of generating those proportions that the organisational structure is initially affected and it is because of the ramifications of the debt structure that further changes may occur. These are not marginal issues of compensation. Furthermore, if incentive realignment was genuinely tenable, the monitoring function of other participants would be redundant as a form of discipline. Monitoring would be about cooperation and the contribution of ideas to create a performance enhancing synergy – discipline would be a misleading metaphor. The marginal basis for optimisation founded in human nature would not require it.

What Jensen is actually pointing to is a systemic defect in corporate governance. The CEO and other executives who earn large salaries lack job insecurity. Advocating PEF LBOs on the basis that they generate incentives for financial performance is, from this point of view, arguing for a complex solution where simpler ones might exist. The question then becomes how does one generate job insecurity amongst CEOs in such a way as they value retaining their already large salaries and benefits? Answering this question is not part of Jensen's concerns or of others who have considered the role of PEF LBOs of publicly listed companies because the system is taken as a given to which PEF responds. Curiously, both the PEF response and the subsequent development of the corporate system have taken the same tacit line on human nature. As I discussed in Chapter 2, one of the reasons for the slowdown in PEF in the 1990s was the growth in new kinds of compensation packages for CEOs and boards. Stock options, bonuses etc, were put forward as ways of creating incentive realignment in a public forum. Stock options, of course, create new problems: they create accounting problems, they dilute existing equity when they are exercised, and executives tend to argue that performance is relative to current markets (if the market is falling then not falling by as much is success that should be rewarded). The underlying argument remains, however, that the only reason to engage in marginal improvements in financial performance is the existence of commensurate marginal improvements in personal rewards.

At first sight this just seems a scaling up of the way ordinary employees are now treated and thus seems consistent both as a systemic practice and as an insight into human nature. Performance based pay has become a common feature of modern employment contracts. However, performance based pay for ordinary employees can be used as a way of reducing their share of the overall value of the firm. Over time basic pay as a proportion of the revenues of the firm can be lower and the performance based component that is related to the improved financial performance of the firm need not rise commensurately to reflect the growing differential in basic pay (particularly when other issues like pension payments are considered). One of the reasons for the improved financial performance of the firm may be precisely this. Here, an employee's situation is the reverse of that for management who now command greater shares of the value of the firm through the concentration of equity. A consistent view of human nature would treat all humans in the same way, if nature was what was at issue. Yet from the perspective of an ordinary employee the notion that a top executive earning $1 million plus benefits was not sufficiently motivated to improve the financial performance of the firm would seem nonsensical. In any case, the incentive basis of the alignment for management is not in the context of job insecurity. In a PEF LBO management are likely to also be equity owners, they do not fire themselves. If anything they are more secure than their public counterpart. An ordinary employee, however, confronts basic job insecurity. Here incentives are mainly stick rather than carrot and this puts a quite different inflection on tacit assumptions about human nature. This reflects the marginalisation of employee relations in ideas about incentive alignment: performance related compensation for employees can be the illusion of an alignment. What it can disguise is a new kind of disjuncture regarding an us and them.

Incentive realignment, monitoring, and debt

One might argue that segmenting Jensen's argument misses the point that it is the overall structure of PEF that makes its role a potentially beneficial one. It is important, however, to unpick its various inconsistencies because it is the individual inconsistencies that show that the overall structure is less coherent and thus less persuasive than it appears. That said, Jensen does place the incentive realignment aspect of PEF LBOs firmly within the context of his debt control hypothesis. Irrespective of free cash flow as a signalling device, the subsequent generation of debt in an LBO creates an important source of discipline. This has various ramifications for different kinds of monitors. PEF firm professionals act as general partners to the PEF funds. In conjunction with retained or co-opted management they act as the first line of monitors, typically as key personnel on a new board operating through the shell company set up to administer the acquired firm. They in turn provide detailed and regular financial updates to fund investors. Fund investors rely on their own financial experts to decode and assess these updates. Thus, the management monitor the acquired firm, general partners monitor management and limited partners monitor general partners. The focus of all of these monitors is the financial performance of the firm as a means to ensure returns to the fund within a definite time line. From the point of view of the control hypothesis, since the firm is leveraged, then the existence of debt provides the basis of a disciplining procedure for monitoring: can debt servicing costs be met and how can debt servicing costs be exceeded to achieve returns?

However, one cannot make the simple assumption that the control hypothesis indicates that the financial performance of the firm must be improved and that monitoring is necessarily focused on this through incentive alignment. Again this returns us to a point made in Chapter 5. The incentive alignment of participants is to maximise the returns to the fund. It is the financial performance of the fund that is of primary concern – the financial performance of the acquisition is a means to this end. The financial performance of the fund is what is ultimately being monitored. Some participants may have more of an emotional investment in the acquisition than others – particularly if the PEF involved succession or an MBO. But that emotional investment is itself monitored and disciplined by the relation of the acquisition *as an acquisition for the fund*. The assumption that debt carried by the firm disciplines the way the firm performs is additional and not primary to the core relations in PEF LBOs. This is because levels of debt and debt servicing costs are not simply initial ways to achieve control of the firm where it is then the financial performance of the firm that guarantees returns to the fund. Just as important are the conditions under which debt can be accessed and debt can be restructured. These are matters of the overall liquidity context of PEF and these are historically dynamic. That is why the scale and numbers of LBOs, particularly of publicly listed companies, varies. If, as Chapters 1–4 illustrate has been the case, debt providers become more willing to provide debt at particular times then levels of leverage can rise so long as debt servicing remains possible. If interest rates fall then debt can be refinanced producing higher levels of leverage at lower overall costs. Neither requires an improvement in the financial performance of the firm – they can actually reduce it – but both enable special dividends to be paid to the fund. As I set out in Chapter 5, there is an inbuilt attraction to doing this for PEF LBOs based on the time horizons of their investment. Debt is, therefore, not necessarily a disciplining force only. It can simultaneously be a source of temptation as liquidity conditions change.

The idea that the PEF LBO is an economic good because it is forced to seek efficiency is thus a questionable one when debt is placed in a dynamic context of changing liquidity conditions and when one places this in the context of the structure of a PEF fund and the purpose of the PEF firms. Since there are cycles of liquidity, if PEF LBOs push the boundaries of leverage then the acquisition becomes vulnerable to insolvency. Monitoring by PEF participants need not prevent this because incentive alignment is ultimately focused on the fund. Clearly, debt providers are not necessarily effective monitors either, if they were then liquidity surges in capital markets would not translate into liquidity surges in PEF LBOs that then result in levels of leverage that are vulnerable to collapses in capital markets. Debt generated in the here and now reaches into an unknown future. The fact that debt can currently be serviced does not mean that this situation will continue. The end of the 1980s and the collapse of capital markets in 2007 clearly illustrate this. Moreover, competition between debt providers and the inurements fostered by financial innovation can reduce the commitment and capacity of those providers to act as monitors: bank syndication involving originate and distribute strategies, CDOs, covenant-lite models, the use of 'revolvers' &c highlighted in Chapter 4 all clearly illustrate. One might also note that mezzanine finance in PEF buyouts may also be provided by mezzanine funds solicited and administered by the same PEF firm. The relation between incentive alignment, monitoring, and the control hypothesis is, therefore, at the very least ambiguous. Asserting control may simply become opportunity exploitation in some circumstances and damage limitation in others. In terms of monitoring this raises the classical philosophical problem set out in Plato's *Republic* of who guards the guards?[4]

The problem of debt as control and the question of how efficiency is situated

Thinking about the control hypothesis in terms of its time relation is also useful when assessing what leverage means for efficiency. In Jensen's account, a highly leveraged buyout has few margins for error in its business plan and operating performance. If an investment or business strategy are not working out this is quickly signalled through difficulties in meeting debt servicing obligations. This creates an immediate pressure for adjustments to investment and business strategy. A listed company, by contrast, has lower levels of debt and higher levels of equity on public markets. Though its profits may fall and its equity price decrease it does not face the same pressure to adjust its strategy. In Jensen's understanding leverage is, therefore, more conducive to organisational efficiency (1989c). Leverage does not just reduce inefficiency it steers efficiency.

The problem here is that high leverage can easily lock the firm into a short term approach to investment that actually undermines organisational efficiency in the long term. Many forms of innovative investment and business strategy involve disruption that may have immediate adverse effects on financial performance. These forms are not just restricted to industrial sectors that very obviously require high levels of research and development (such as technology sectors) but can occur in any industry where a firm wants to be a 'market leader'. The argument that PEF narrows ownership is sometimes used to make the case that this creates a clearer vision of the future of the firm that is not pressured by variations in share price. But again leverage is not just discipline it is a constraint. The PEF firm may actually be steered away from long term investment strategies with long term payoffs. Here the publicly listed firm may be at an advantage in having the leeway to consider the long term and resist pressures to forego innovation.

More accurately, perhaps, both the PEF acquisition and its publicly listed counterpart face different manifestations of a common constraint. As the material in Chapters 1–4 should have made clear, one of the major changes in economics and finance since the 1970s has been that financial markets – markets trading and offering capital in the form of equity, debt etc. – have become more liquid. There have been various surges in liquidity but at the same time an underlying growth in liquidity. The numbers and varieties of investors and of tradable entities, and the volumes of trades, have all increased. Within this process, the 1980s saw the emergence of the concept of 'shareholder value' and it is the pre-eminence of value creation stemming from this that Jensen has in mind when he writes of LBOs as a solution to the failure of value creation in some public corporations.

Value creation has a definite context in terms of highly liquid equity and debt markets. A publicly listed company may have a kind of leeway to pursue the long term that a highly leveraged PEF acquisition does not. But for the publicly listed company the pressure of debt is replaced by the pressure of volatile share prices. In an abstract sense greater liquidity is usually viewed as a positive aspect of an economic system. But in terms of the information and rumour sensitive nature of equity markets where there are many alternative investments its effect on the firm is to situate its operating strategy to meeting dividend payment expectations. Those expectations emerge on a time line related to past performance and a series of ratings by financial analysts. The dot.com bubble and the telecoms expansion were simply more pathological forms of this. The underlying issue is that volatile share prices have become the language of shareholder value and shareholder value has become the primary means of assessing firms. Placating fears over realising shareholder value with an eye to reducing the volatility of share prices can also steer the public firm away from long term investment strategies with long term payoffs.

In both cases the firm is being steered away from some forms of strategy that may incur initial high costs that affect the current balance sheet. In a dynamic sense creating value for shareholders in publicly listed companies, and, in PEF, creating value for fund investors and to satisfy debt providers, are issues of value *distribution* as much as they are value creation. Just as in the case of liberated capital and in the case of financial performance and monitoring, there is a blurring between absolute and relative issues. What both PEF and publicly listed companies share in the case of efficiency considerations is a common context in which the role of the firm as a productive unit is subordinated to the role of the firm as a financial instrument. One cannot, therefore, sustain the point that leverage is more conducive to organisational efficiency. Rather, Jensen's point that debt can be a useful signal concerning organisational efficiency indicates a deeper affinity between all forms of productive unit. It indicates how efficiency has become conditioned by finance and how finance steers investment and affects business strategy on a short time horizon.[5] One might respond that PEF has a longer time horizon than current share prices because a PEF fund operates for ten years and acquisitions tend to be held for an average of four years. But the debt steering aspect of the control hypothesis will operate on shorter timescales since senior and junior debt servicing will be monitored on at least a quarterly basis and any publicly traded bonds will face market responses on even shorter timescales. In any case four years is still short when one thinks of the time line of major innovation and research and development changes that have restructured industries and economies.

I am not suggesting here that the fact there is a relation of subordination between capital markets and product markets is new. Veblen recognised this relation long ago:

> The goods market, of course, in absolute terms, is still as powerful an economic factor as ever but it is no longer the dominant factor in business

and industrial traffic, as it once was. The capital market has taken the first place in this respect. The capital market is the modern economic feature which makes and identifies the higher 'credit economy' as such. (1958: 75)

What the 1980s and the subsequent period has witnessed however has been a growth in liquidity and forms of unstable liquidity. These have heightened the pressures of finance on production. What is efficient is subject to this pressure and thus no more neutral than the question of how free cash flow will be determined.

Debt as the efficient solution when control fails to be efficient

Jensen's final argument regarding the control hypothesis is that leverage is efficient even when firms fail (1989b). This is for two reasons. First, high levels of leverage mean that buyouts become insolvent more quickly. This death of the firm argument shares a focus on haste with the argument for organisational efficiency. There are few death throes for the highly leveraged firm. There is, however, the potential for a rapid resurrection. The main reason for this is that the narrowing of ownership of equity and of primary responsibility for debt will tend to make it easier for a new company to be carved out of a failing one without the need for recourse to the courts for the recovery of assets. In the original argument this is particularly so where strip financing had been applied to the debt. Strip financing is where investors in the LBO hold equivalent proportions at different levels of seniority of the debt. Creditors would have a definite claim on different aspects of the debt at different levels and would all have equal call on the different levels because of the nature of the strip process. This would prevent the conflicts of interest that creditors usually face in an insolvency situation. Liquidation of the firm is more likely to be avoided and agreement reached on some kind of asset rehabilitation, restructuring, or sell-on. Some form of going concern is more likely to emerge and emerge more quickly than would be the case for a public corporation.

The problem here is that the benefits of leverage are set up as a solution to the problem that leverage actually creates. If there had been no PEF LBO there would be no need for an efficient way to dispose of the ailing acquisition. The notion that it is an economic good that a firm avoids a long drawn out process in the bankruptcy courts that may ultimately end in liquidation is a curious one in this context. It is equivalent to being press-ganged into an A&E ward and then assaulted by a doctor. Publicly listed counterparts to a PEF LBO are not leveraged to the same degree as the LBO and would not be as vulnerable to insolvency and bankruptcy in times of adverse economic conditions. To focus on speed and efficacy of the resolution of forms of debt distress is, therefore, to focus on the wrong aspect of the issue. The more appropriate aspect concerns how the acquisition came to be leveraged in such a vulnerable way. One could of course argue that the point is subsidiary. PEF LBOs are not undertaken with an eye on insolvency but rather with an eye on financial performance. However, the very fact that the argument was worth making indicates the underlying problem of debt and financial vulnerability that is created by PEF LBOs.

LBOs as good governance and creative destruction

For Jensen, leverage and the possibility of the insolvency of the acquisition are acceptable risks. This was so in early 1989 before the final collapse of the junk bond markets and the wave of bond defaults that followed and it was so (in terms of a different emphasis) in the aftermath and thereafter. Two of his 1989 contributions were interventions into the public and political discourse regarding the economic benefits of LBOs. In a letter to the *Wall Street* Journal he states: 'The evidence of the past fifteen years of higher leverage in the US is favourable. Managers, bankers, scholars and government policy makers must continue to learn, tolerate mistakes and even encourage the innovation so vital to the restoration of a competitive corporate sector.' (1989a: 5). In a statement to Congress, which was then considering responses to the increasing scale of prominent buyouts by KKR and other PEF firms that were using increasing levels of leverage he states:

> As major innovations in corporate organization continue, mistakes will be made. This is natural and not counterproductive. How can we learn without pushing new policies to the margin? The surprising thing to me is that there have been so few major mistakes or problems in a revolution in business practice as large as that occurring over the last decade. Many of the proposed changes in public policy towards these transactions threaten to stifle this recreation of the competitiveness of the American corporation. (Jensen 1989b: 44)

In retrospect these statements can appear extraordinarily blithe. They can also appear prescient if one takes the view that late and ill-advised regulation exacerbated the illegal aspects of junk bond market and investment bank practice, which then had knock on effects to PEF. This was an argument pursued, for example, by both Yago and Barth (1991, 2004) at the Milken Institute. There is some credence in it from the point of view that intervention to curtail a problem always has consequences. Terms like 'late' and ill-advised' provide grounds for debate. However, the terms of the debate are also set by how one views relative issues of causation. At the core of this is the distinction between arguing that state intervention to prevent a disaster is a trigger of underlying vulnerabilities, created by opportunistic behaviour, and arguing that state intervention is the material cause of the problem. If one always took the latter point then the opportunistic behaviour of agents would carry no responsibility. Pushed to its logical conclusion the point would also entail that there would be no case for state intervention and ultimately no state at all in the economic realm. If one does not push the point this far one is still closer to the non-regulation end of the spectrum in terms of understanding issues like deregulation and markets. This in turn structures one's approach to questions such as what is appropriate regulation (created through 'deregulation-reregulation' processes) and how should an economy be ordered? That structuring, furthermore, is also a commitment to the idea that markets efficiently structure themselves *and* that they then efficiently unwind the problems that they may manifest, which is of course a contradiction in terms of uses of the term 'efficiently'.

What Jensen's two statements also share is the idea that the benefits of PEF are in some sense an economic necessity or at the very least economically desirable. They are a useful adjunct as part of the wider function of a liberalised economic system. It is this point that Jensen takes forward in the 1990s. Here he makes the argument that PEF LBOs should be viewed as part of the typical cycles of the capitalist system. He argues that they are aspects of what Schumpeter in *Capitalism, Socialism and Democracy* regarded as 'creative destruction' (Jensen 1993/1999: 2). Jensen situates PEF within a third wave of industrialisation from the 1970s onwards (6–13). Economic policy liberalised. Large inefficient corporations were dismantled. Those that were not dismantled faced new pressures and disciplines from increasingly liquid capital markets based on financial innovation and from the threat of takeover. Debt provided new discipline. Even the failures of the time were in a broader and long term sense useful. Problems in bond markets (which were overstated) were learning processes and created new approaches and innovations improving the understanding and spreading of risk. Asset stripping was also the freeing of assets for alternative uses. The downsizing of manufacturing, though painful, also released labour from unproductive sources where competitive advantages had been eroded. Relatedly, the role of PEF in the 1980s and then the effects of the subsequent recession in the early 1990s were useful ways of hastening 'exit' where overcapacity had accumulated.

Written in the early 1990s, before being revised for republication in 1999, one focus of the argument is that the recession of the early 1990s was affected by the 'politics of finance' (52): the reregulation of the thrifts etc. Jensen's primary concern is how one should better understand the complex relationships between organisational efficiency, finance, and governance (51–2). Interestingly, he sees greater market liquidity as a useful means for PEF to occur but also as a problem for governance in public corporations. In so far as PEF is less liquid as an investment and as an ownership strategy than public listing it can be seen as in some respects superior. Here governance provides another way to talk about incentive alignment, control etc because governance is defined as a means to discipline the organisation to generate value (47–51). The original argument, therefore, is both posed in a different context – a historical dynamic within which problems emerge and are resolved – and within a different set of key terms (governance, creative destruction) that sit alongside the original terminology. The argument reaffirms the role of PEF LBOs. Jensen summarises this nicely in his contribution to a symposium on PEF in 2006:

> To sum up, then, the structure and conventions of private equity have provided US capital markets with a way to recreate old-fashioned active investing... In the process, the private equity firms have invented – or perhaps 'rediscovered' is a better word – a better way to run a group of different businesses, one that is very different from how the typical US public company is run. The differences are so striking that I like to define private equity firms as 'organizations that run governance systems that run businesses'.
>
> The result has been enormous increases in corporate efficiency and value. Looking back we can now see that LBOs played a major role in restoring the profitability and competitiveness of American business in the 1980s... It was essentially the leveraged restructuring movement of the 1980s and the pressure for value maximisation that came with it, that launched the remarkable increase in the productivity of US industry in the '80s that has continued pretty much to this day. (13–14)

There are various ways one might critique Jensen's association of PEF LBOs with good governance and creative destruction. One would be to point out that Schumpeter develops the idea of creative destruction in quite a different context (1952: 81–6). Schumpeter's argument was first published in the 1940s and focuses on corporations prior to World War II. His point was that large monopolistic and oligopolistic firms are misunderstood by a great deal of economic theory because that theory lacks a dynamic context and compares real firms to a timeless and static ideal of pure competition. Large monopolistic and oligopolistic firms are in fact subject to an invisible competition in a dynamic sense based on consumer demands, new technologies etc. From a historical point of view, those firms had also contributed to the remarkable improvements in the 'standard of life'. Schumpeter's interest in dynamism was then also an interest in the vitality of large corporations. Schumpeter, though broadly liberal by inclination, was also ambivalent from the point of view of historical expectation as to whether cycles of creative destruction would continue. For example, the fourth edition of the text concludes with a reprint of his last public address. The final paragraph contains the statement: 'Marx was wrong in his diagnosis of the manner in which capitalist society would break down; he was not wrong in the prediction that it would break down eventually.' (1952: 417).[6]

There are limits, however, to the effectiveness of trading arguments regarding textual authority. Jensen's use of Schumpeter is to make the point that one must understand aspects of an economy in a dynamic and historical sense, which is an important insight. Moreover, Jensen could easily draw on Schumpeter's *History of Economic Analysis*:

> If an economist investigates... by methods that meet the scientific standards of his time and environment, the results will form part of the scientific fund of economic knowledge, irrespective of whether he wishes to use them for recommending regulatory legislation or to defend speculation against such legislation or merely to satisfy his intellectual curiosity. Unless he allows his purpose to distort his facts or his reasoning, there is no point in our refusing to accept his results or to dent their scientific character on the grounds that we disapprove of his purpose. (1997: 10–11)

The point I want to pursue is not so much disapproval of Jensen's purpose but rather to show how advocating PEF LBOs entails certain assumptions that structure his approval. Jensen's assumptions are in this sense *purposive*. Placing PEF LBOs in the context of creative destruction situates PEF as an emergent solution to the problems the system itself created. In so far as his point is historical and contextual there is some commonality here with the way I set out the material of Chapters 1 to 4. There is, however, a quite different understanding of PEF in terms of history and context than I would draw. In Jensen's argument PEF becomes a component in a general system or historical period but not one whose tendencies are also causally implicated in its problems as a system. There are mistakes and there is learning but the basic model (incentive alignment, debt control etc.) is positive.[7] However, as the previous arguments on monitoring, control and debt show, when one thinks of PEF as occurring within the development of liquidity, and specifically of debt, it has tendencies that need not be seen as abstract economic goods. The curious thing about Jensen's argument is that the model of PEF it propounds is a timeless and static one. History is something it intervenes in rather than is shaped by. Yet one can read both Chapters 1–4 (particularly 1 and 4) and Jensen's third industrial revolution as accounts of how liquidity grows, how liquidity is unstable, how PEF exploits debt and debt providers have good reasons for colluding in that, and how the accumulation of debt becomes both a problem for individual firms (since all debt must be paid eventually) and for the system (because debt creation is part of the reason why liquidity collapses). If one thinks of PEF in this way then it ceases to be a static model that is within history but not of history and ceases to be merely (or mainly) a solution. It becomes part of the problem that is unstable liquidity and its exploitation.

Thinking in these terms gives a different emphasis to the idea of creative destruction. In Jensen's version, the historical argument is one that militates against the regulation of PEF. But one could as easily think of PEF as part of the broader problem of how to reduce tendencies for debt and liquidity instability. This in turn leads to the question whether any actual empirical benefit of PEF – a specific advantage – is also a solution to a problem that need not exist. This requires one to think of the problem of appropriate regulation at the opposite end of the spectrum to that Jensen's argument tends towards. In general, resistance to the idea of greater emphasis on regulation has a simplistic and a sophisticated form. The simplistic form is a variant on the efficiency contradiction: markets are efficient and efficiently resolve their own manifestations of inefficiency. The variant is that regulation should be resisted because it is a permanent solution to a temporary problem.

There are two obvious counters to the simplistic form. First, one is not fixing something that fixes itself. If 'fixed' were to have any genuine purchase as a concept then it would mean that the problem did not recur. And yet it has and does – debt and leverage rise, systemic instabilities come to the fore and when they do so they risk crisis. Relatedly, if the splitting of the conglomerates in the 1980s was a solution to the problems accumulated in the 1960s then why did the 1990s create yet more mergers and acquisitions and still higher levels of management compensation? It is only by focusing on the particular manifestation that the problem can seem temporary. The tendency for the problem is a permanent aspect of PEF, as it currently operates, and of the system at large. Second, regulation is no more permanent than is deregulation – the real issue is the learning process of attempting to achieve appropriate regulation that controls the identified underlying problems.

This raises the more sophisticated form of argument for the resistance of regulation. The sophisticated form is that regulation is always retrospective whilst problems are prospective. Here, the move to regulate also motivates creative responses that subvert or bypass it and thus regulation does no more than help to shape the next phase or manifestation of the problem. In some respects this is a difficult argument to counter since it has such clear historical resonance. One need only think of responses to the Basel Accord. However, though historically resonant – the nature of that resonance disguises a confusion regarding what regulation is capable of and how history is being used in the argument. Regulation is, of course, about the last manifestation of a problem but this does not mean that regulators cannot be as creative in thinking about possible ways to subvert that regulation as those who will seek to do so. These can then become part of the regulation. The real issue is not that regulation is retrospective – at least not in so far as this is an argument for not regulating – but rather that the future has unknowns and any (in)action has unintended consequences. Resistance to regulation *per se* is, therefore, not so much an historical argument about how regulation is constrained to be retrospective but is rather an historical argument that experience has shown that any unfolding series of human events is ultimately found to be complex. For this to be an argument against regulation, however, it would have to be the case that the unfolding is of a different simpler and safer form if one does not regulate. Given that the very reason for regulation has been to attempt to restrict, constrain or forestall problems and crises, and given that one of the main planks of the sceptical argument regarding regulation is that it seems to fail to do so (creative individuals subvert its good intentions), even the arguments against regulation start from the implicit assumption that the absence of regulation would not be a safer situation. It is a basic contradiction in the sceptical argument that it seems to rely on a negative view of unrestrained human nature and its systemic consequences.

The residue of the argument then becomes one of a counsel of despair: the problem is complex and it is difficult or impossible to design effective solutions to complex problems. This, however, simply brings the argument full circle – the real issue is the appropriateness of degrees of regulation and regulation-deregulation as a learning process. It is not the case that a complex problem requires a single complex and all pervasive solution – a Big Bang of law and an elegant theory of everything. Ironically only a pristine version of the efficient markets hypothesis actually entails this conceit. As long as one has clear ideas of what the overall intent of regulation is, there is no reason why regulation cannot be a learning process of small incremental steps each targeting a particular problem and from which something more complex can evolve. Regulation would then be something rather different than a permanent solution to a temporary problem – it would be continuing contingent solutions to a continuing complex subject. We will return to this point in the concluding chapter.

Why is liquidity unstable? From Keynes to Minsky and Kindleberger

One of the central points I made over the course of Chapters 1 to 4 is that leverage levels rise as liquidity surges and that changes in the use of debt then affect the conditions under which debt is created and offered. This is one of the contributing reasons why liquidity is unstable. What it suggests is that there are periodic quantitative and qualitative changes in conditions. This in turn entails that the past is not always a good guide to the future in human affairs, including economics. There are two dynamics to this. First, it is in some respects because humans use the past as a guide to the future that problems are perpetuated and exacerbated. We tend to continue to behave in similar ways as though underlying conditions were not being affected by the time line of our behaviour and its accumulated effects. Second, humans are capable of realising that their behaviour is changing the conditions within which they act. They then begin to act differently – perhaps following new collective trajectories. In so doing they break the continuities that maintained the very possibility of using the past in some limited sense as a guide to the future. The relation between these dynamics implies that activity has some kind of rationale and is always situated to conditions but that it is at the same time operating in terms of a certain degree of flux. Absolute stability in human affairs is not normal. The ongoing course of human affairs involves relative degrees of uncertainty. This has important ramifications because most forms of financial activity rely on forecasting the future. Within that activity, specific forms of financial instrument rely on a determinable future – at least in the sense that reasonable probabilities can be calculated. Rating agencies rely on this, as do investment bankers when setting the rates for a security issue. It is the very basis of the concept of risk as a technical term in finance. The irony is, as Chapter 4 in particular illustrates, relying on a calculable concept of risk is itself a contributory factor in creating uncertainty because it creates behaviours that both assume the past is a good guide to the future and sets in motion changes in the scales of activity that ensure that it is not. From this perspective, for example, CDOs were a liquidity time bomb.

These are ideas that would be all too familiar to John Maynard Keynes. Keynes took an early interest in the significance of probability for the conduct of human affairs (Skidelsky 1994: 56). This interest began in terms of his doubts regarding G. E Moore's approach to ethical decision making in *Principia Ethica* but developed into something of more general significance regarding behaviour in his own *Treatise on Probability*. For Keynes definite calculable probabilities (tractable ranges of possible outcomes) were an unusual subset of how we face and forecast the future in ways that affect our conduct. Calculable probabilities rely on regular outcomes that we infer from the frequency of their occurrence. These provide 'certainties' that help guide our judgement. However, most circumstances are more ambiguous. Frequencies can simply be averages that disguise that conditions are not stable. Even if conditions are stable they may not remain stable. At the same time we still think about the future and provide reasons and rationales for how we are going to act based on the past. We do this where there are no calculable forms of probability to guide us. We do this in ways that confound calculable probabilities. We do this on the basis of uncertainty.

This insight was to form a central thread in Keynes' major work *The General Theory of Employment, Interest and Money*.[8] The most relevant aspect of that thread is set out in Chapters 11 and 12 of the text and concerns investment, the marginal efficiency of capital and the role of expectations in investment behaviour. Keynes defines the marginal efficiency of capital as the expectation of a yield from a capital asset compared to its current supply price.[9] It is deemed efficient to invest in a capital asset if its expected return exceeds the current supply price and exceeds alternative uses of the capital used to make the investment in the capital asset. For Keynes conditions in the recent past hold a disproportionate weight in our expectations about the future. We tend to act as though those conditions will not alter. At the same time that tendency to act is based on the degree of confidence we have in the way we have formulated the judgement. As Keynes puts it:

> The *state of confidence*, as they term it, is a matter to which practical men always pay the closest and most anxious attention. But economists have not analysed it carefully and have been content, as rule, to discuss it in general terms. In particular it has not been made clear that its relevance to economic problems comes in through its important influence on the schedule of the marginal efficiency of capital. These are not two separate factors affecting the rate of investment, namely the schedule of the marginal efficiency of capital and the state of confidence. The state of confidence is relevant because it is one of the major factors determining the former. (1936: 149)

Keynes illustrates the key role of confidence and rationales of behaviour using equity markets. He first notes that shares trade every day but that genuinely significant information about the companies traded is less frequent. The majority of day-to-day changes are, therefore, ephemeral and speculative. This in turn is linked to the general level of ignorance of the average investor. As a result markets tend to follow a collective mass psychology that can, based on triggers, shift from optimism to pessimism but can also be relatively stable in one direction because the recent past influences current behaviour. These markets are not irrational they are, as instances of mass psychology, simply not founded in ways amenable to definite calculation. Moreover, the intervention of the professional investor armed with specialist knowledge and insight is not a break on this system. This is because the goal of that professional investor is to profit from the movement of the markets. As such the skill of the professional investor is in interpreting the conventions that are affecting mass psychology and exploiting them: knowing when and how to invest and when to withdraw that investment. Again, the decision making process is not groundless. Nor are the concerns and discourse or language of the investor unrelated to numerical issues of costs, revenues, yields, dividends and so forth. These may be part of the way in which his skills are applied to knowing when and how to invest and how to interpret and anticipate market psychologies. But the process is not a bloodless one of straight calculation and highly probabilistic outcomes where regularities can be assumed to continue based on the frequency of their past occurrence. Rather the anticipation of events can also be the construction of them where both are ultimately about the exploitation of opportunity. For Keynes' this creates two effects. The first is a rational absurdity: 'We have reached the third degree where we devote our intelligences to anticipating what average opinion expects the average opinion to be.' (1936: 156). The second is the potential for irrationality from the point of view of social welfare: 'There is no clear evidence from experience that the investment policy which is socially advantageous coincides with that which is most profitable.' (1936: 157)

What Keynes' work highlights is the key role of expectations in behaviour. The grounds of that role are ultimately attempts to construct rationales that stretch into the future and that are based on the goal of realising yield from investment. Time and uncertainty are at the heart of Keynes' thinking. Unfortunately for Keynes' legacy these are precisely the aspects of his work that were eviscerated in the widespread adoption of a Keynesian approach to economics, particularly the version that developed out of Hicks' IS/LM approach to macro equilibria (Heilbroner and Milberg 1995: 40–2). Economic theory has always had a difficulty incorporating time into its models (Shackle 1990). In most economic theory time is simply the periodisation of activity. In most economics the future is like the past in the sense that it can be mathematically modelled in ways that translate uncertainty into probability (Nielsen and Morgan 2005).[10] Jensen's concept of free cash flow as net present value discounted at the relevant cost of capital is an example of this.[11] Discounting is a standard economic technique of working back from a known future to the present. This simply elides the distinction that Keynes' wanted to make between uncertainty and the special sub-set of probabilities that are (temporarily) tractable. The elision loses any possibility of understanding why – with, in our case, special emphasis on financial economics and on the construction of financial instruments or innovations – relying on certainty by any other name is a dangerous way to think about economy.[12]

If expectations play a key role in behaviour then they also play a key role in liquidity conditions. As Chapters 1–4 illustrate, particularly Chapters 3 and 4, it has been the stability of the expectation that current trends can continue that has perpetuated and exacerbated unstable liquidity surges. It has been the change in sentiment regarding rationales of behaviour that have caused instability to manifest as sudden reversals. Keynes has relatively little to say regarding liquidity in the context we are interested in. He does make some reference to the role of debt in investment. Here he makes the point that lenders and borrowers have a specific motive to take opposite views on interest rates. The more 'risky' a venture is then the greater the doubt in the mind of the borrower that he will realise a return on his investment. This results in a motive to maximise the difference between a possible high yield and a lower interest rate (on the basis that some investments will not come off and these can be cross-subsidised). The more 'risky' a venture is then the greater the expectation in the mind of the lender that the borrower's investment will not realise the expected yield and that a default will occur. This results in a motive to increase the rate of interest charged. For Keynes, economic growth tends to reduce both the lender and the borrower's sense of risk making each sense 'unusually and imprudently low' (Keynes 1936: 145). The implication is that a boom period causes the two different spreads on interest rates to converge generating further growth in liquidity.

This idea of expanding debt and liquidity plays a key role in the work of Hyman Minsky. Minsky was a student of both Schumpeter and Wassily Leontief and described himself as a 'financial Keynesian' (Papadimitriou and Wray 1997: 4). Minsky's work is in essence a highly original elaboration of Keynes' insights on time and uncertainty (Sethi 2002: 520; Wray 2002: 1231). His starting point is that: 'any economic theory which separates what economists are wont to call the real economy from the financial system can only mislead and bear false witness as to how the world works.' (1982: vii). The financial system can as a set of institutions be analytically distinguished from other aspects of the economy. However, the financial system is also integrated into all aspects of the economy and is central to the way they function – how they grow and how they suffer periodic crises. The basis of the relations is institutionally specific and as such related to time and place.

Minsky's particular interest was in understanding how the US economy that emerged after World War II differed from that of the Great Depression. For Minsky, the US economy was initially more robust because government spending and employment created more effective forms of intervention and stabilisation (1982: 12). However, Minsky was also of the opinion that the finance system in general was prone to evolve in ways that accumulated the potential for crises. He termed this the 'financial instability hypothesis'. In a capitalist economy where investment can be undertaken using debt there is a complex interaction between the debt providing institutions and the expectations and behaviour of market participants. The net effect of this interaction is a steady growth in the fragility of organisations. Economic growth tends to result in increasingly optimistic expectations about future growth and the returns on investment. This in turn also leads to the expectation that lending is secure because defaults will be avoided. Growth thus leads investors to be more likely to borrow and leads financiers to be more likely to lend. This tends to shift the nature of the financing of growth across three categories: hedge, speculative and ponzi (1982: 22–33). Hedge finance is where both the principal and interest can likely be paid based on extrapolating current operating receipts or income. Speculative finance is where the interest only can likely be paid from extrapolating operating receipts or income. Ponzi finance is where meeting debt servicing relies on further refinancing or on continuous rises in the valuation of an asset class (housing, equities & c). Growth tends to result in more investment being undertaken in the second two categories because these are associated with greater levels of return whilst market conditions remain good. There is, therefore, both a change in the quantity and quality of debt as more aggressive investment strategies are pursued.

What this suggests is that in the absence of some intervention process to control liquidity any set of apparently 'stable' institutional arrangements in a capitalist economy will accumulate underlying vulnerabilities that may then result in a reversal of the behaviours that maintain growth. Paradoxically, time and uncertainty introduce a kind of structural inevitability into a decentralised capitalist economy: the realisation of the ever-present potential for crisis based on new elaborations of persistent tendencies and interests (Minsky 1993 and 1996). For Minsky the clear conclusion was that a capitalist economy does not stabilise itself: regulation of market participants and an appropriately designed set of institutions for intervention are necessary. As a Keynesian this extended also to a reaffirmation of the role of government as a counter-cyclical balancing force (1986).

Though Minsky acknowledges that financial markets have become a 'world' phenomena (1987: 1884; 1990: 1221)[13] most of his work precedes the transformations that have made it such an issue and also tends to focus on the US in isolation.[14] Others have applied his work in a more international context (Bellofiore and Ferri 2001). The Bellofiore edited collection, for example, includes discussions of the East Asian Financial crisis and also the collapse of the LTCM hedge fund in 1998.[15] Perhaps the most prominent and detailed application of Minsky's approach has been in the several editions of Kindleberger's *Manias, Panics and Crashes*. Kindleberger illustrates the way that financial markets have, in ever more complex ways, facilitated liquidity bubbles in particular types of assets and capital markets. In accordance with Minsky's financial instability hypothesis he states:

> The expansion of credit is not a series of accidents but instead a systematic development that has continued for several hundred years as the participants in financial markets sought to reduce the costs both of transactions and of holding liquidity and money balances. The form each even takes seems accidental... [but] Monetary expansion is systematic and endogenous rather than random and exogenous... The efforts of central bankers to limit and control the growth of the money supply have been offset in part by the development of new and very close substitutes for money. (2005: 57)

Kindleberger pays particular attention to the way that specific crises are triggered. He distinguishes between the role of *causa remota* and *causa prox-ima*. *Causa remota* are the underlying conditions that give rise to the potential for crises: specifically the complex interactions of credit creation. *Causa proxima*, meanwhile, are the specific triggers that realise that potential.

Conclusion

The insights and terminology of Keynes, Minsky and Kindleberger provide a useful framing device for reiterating some of the arguments I have made in regard of PEF in this and previous chapters. One of the core problems with the way Jensen frames his theory of PEF LBOs is that LBOs are within history but not of history. This is a form of the problem that Keynes' identified: the significance of time and uncertainty are elided from how we think about economy. For Jensen PEF is not viewed as part of the accumulation of problems to which it then becomes a claimed solution. LBOs are seen as a functional solution to systemic problems but are not also situated as an evolving part of the functioning of the system itself. There is, therefore, no possibility of thinking of them in broader terms as part of the potential dysfunction of an apparently functioning system. Minsky's key insight is that finance and production cannot be seen in isolation. I would emphasise that this is particularly so as the ownership of production becomes increasingly pressurised on the basis of its role as a financial instrument. Minsky emphasises that the real economy and the finance system are integrated. The two develop together over time. As they do so there are changes within both. In terms of PEF there are changes in the terms and conditions of credit based on, and reinforcing, changes in liquidity. There are then changes in the scale and type of activity that PEF engages in. PEF is not static and the financing of PEF is not static. Changes within both can be part of the *causa remota* of financial instability. They can also be *causa proxima*. The level of leverage can play a role here in various ways. Leverage and absolute debt levels provide sources of concern for financial institutions and analysts (central banks, the IMF, OECD etc.). As concerns they can be converted into warnings that affect the perspectives and behaviour of market participants in ways that reach far beyond it significance and impact on PEF. It may, however, be that warnings provide no immediate break on the tendency for liquidity to surge. This has often been the case in the context of a modern highly decentralised financial system where there are good short term reasons to continue with current behaviours and no strong expectation of decisive intervention from central banks. It may then be that the very continuation of liquidity growth creates debt structures apt to default and that such a default sets of a change in expectations and behaviours. In Chapter 4, for example, concern over PEF LBOs and leverage resulted in warnings. These perhaps went some way to making concerns more visible but they were not a *causa proxima* of the credit crunch. Nor were CLOs. CDOs and sub-prime markets were the *causa proxima*. PEF LBOs, however, played a constitutive role as a *causa remota*. They were a reason for liquidity to surge and, in exploiting that surge, exacerbated it and its eventual problems. One manifestation of this has been the subsequent large writedowns on LBOs loans and failed syndications by the banks. The PEF firms did not carry the losses created in this way. PEF is in some respects, as it increasingly claims, recession proof as a means to create returns for investors and for general partners. But it might also be viewed as a recession proof industry that can be a causal factor in recession.

What I have tried to do here is broaden the focus of the theoretical analysis of PEF. How we view LBOs should not just be informed by narrow empirical arguments but also by the way the argument is first set up. In Chapter 5, I asked whether PEF as a claimed solution created new and avoidable problems. I also raised the issue of what performance and efficiency mean and how these terms are conditioned. In this chapter, I have essentially placed these kinds of concerns in the context of the broader thematic question of whether PEF is a solution to problems it helps to create. Hannah Arendt considers the tendency not to ask such framing questions as symptomatic of the modern age, to which she responds: 'What I propose, therefore, is very simple: it is nothing more than to think what we are doing.' (Arendt 1958: 5). This is less patronising than it sounds. It is a key constituent in any complete analysis of a problem. It is about how and in what sense we recognise something as a problem. Still, Schumpeter was certainly correct when he stated that one does not de-legitimate the empirics of an argument by questioning its purpose. What one does do, however, is show that it can be looked at in a different way. Here we have done that by looking at liquidity and by looking at debt and by looking also at the basic coherence and adequacy of Jensen's argument about debt, discipline, and PEF in general. I now move on to look at some of the specific empirical claims made for PEF regarding its economic benefits.

7

The Empirical Arguments for Specific Benefits of Private Equity: Returns to Investors, Employment, and Tax

Private equity finance can be viewed as a claimed solution to problems it helps to create and it can be viewed as a claimed solution that creates additional problems. Both these arguments rely on its relation to the overall environment: its relation to capital markets and its relation to the economy in general. Both are focused on the implications of the growth in scale of PEF as a historically developing phenomenon where there is an interaction between the potentials of the overall environment and the internal tendencies in PEF buyout behaviour. They are conditional arguments regarding the negative consequences that flow from those potentials. There is a great deal of 'what if' about them. They can seem overly complex and overly concerned. This is particularly so if one can counter in narrower ways that PEF creates specific benefits that offset any other concerns. These are specific empirical arguments. There are three main areas of such argument that have been important to the public relations role of the main PEF associations and that have been sources of dispute taken up in research on PEF. First, there is the claim that PEF funds are a source of high returns to investors in the funds. As such they are an important means by which pension funds, insurers etc. meet their obligations. Second, there is the claim that the image of PEF LBOs as primitive asset strippers is undeserved. A buyout is focused on turning around an acquisition and thus ultimately creates healthier businesses with higher revenues and more employment, and can do so without slashing wages or imposing onerous new conditions on labour. Third, there is the claim that PEF's reputation for contributing little to the tax revenues of the state is undeserved. PEF creates 'value' as such it contributes to economic growth and thus does contribute to tax revenues in various ways.

What I want to suggest is that there is more to these argument than a simple refutation of the three points. A simple refutation would in any case be quite difficult because there is a fundamental data problem in analysing PEF. Firms and funds do not face the same requirements for public disclosure of their practices and accounts that a publicly listed company must meet. The majority of information regarding PEF is based on voluntary disclosure. It is disclosed to the main PEF associations and to a select number of data bases, such as CMBOR. The data is then aggregated and the confidentiality of the firms and funds is maintained. It is based on this kind of data that the empirical arguments are made and disputed. This does not make the data worthless but it does make it difficult to verify and it does make it difficult to generate more complete pictures based on fuller disclosure by all firms and funds. That said the three empirical claims can be addressed in the following ways. PEF has created high returns to investors, but it has done so in a variable way that is also not relatively high when taken in context. PEF has not had devastating effects on employment, but it can be interpreted to have worked in conjunction with basic changes in the ideological construction of employment relations that have affected the power relations of work and that have affected the longer term issues of terms and conditions. PEF does contribute to tax revenues, but its contribution is far smaller than it could be and raises various economic and moral issues regarding tax efficiency.

Does private equity in actual fact create high returns to investors?

In Chapter 1, I explored how private equity finance was a beneficiary of various changes intended to access the growing accumulation of investment capital in the hands of institutions. Since the 1970s PEF has essentially become an asset class for investors. It is seen as one element in a diversified portfolio of investments designed to generate an overall positive rate of return. In standard approaches to investment analysis different asset classes and different investments within each asset class have different levels of risk associated with them. Private equity has always been considered a relatively high risk investment. As such the proportions of capital committed to PEF from mutual funds, pensions funds etc. has always been relatively low, even in periods of growth for PEF. PEF is considered high risk in three ways.

First, as I set out in Chapter 5, the overall fee structure of private equity is comparatively high compared to other investment asset classes. As such the overall returns extracted from given investments must also be high in order to offset these fees and maintain a high net return to the investors. Second, the capital invested is relatively illiquid – once committed to the fund and then used for some investment purpose it cannot be withdrawn. As such, one cannot anticipate events by identifying emerging problems and then shift committed capital away.[1] Third, the capacity of PEF to undertake an LBO investment relies on the liquidity of capital markets – specifically credit markets. PEF can still operate in economic downturns through debt distress investment etc. but at the same time PEF also relies on the availability of credit on favourable terms. This kind of environment cannot be guaranteed to persist through the ten year life cycle of the investment in a typical fund.

There are various statistical measures one might use to assess the level of returns to investors that PEF generates. The main two measures are direct expressions of the return to investment net of fees to the general partner and PEF firm. These are the internal rate of return and the multiple of the investors committed capital. Two are indirect measures. These are exit values and the failure rates of acquisitions. Both the direct and indirect measures are worth considering for different reasons. The direct measures indicate the high degree of variability and contingency in returns. The indirect measures are worth considering because they provide a context for thinking about how returns are generated in different ways over time. This helps to make sense of the contingency of returns. The contingency of returns is another way of making sense of PEF as a dynamic (rather than static) element in the liquidity of markets. Both the direct and indirect measures indicate that PEF is a source of high returns to investors but that this is not a simple matter of vindicating any claim that PEF buyouts are a source of exceptionally high profits to investors.

With the assistance of Thomson Financial the main PEF associations publish a range of statistics based mainly on information voluntarily provided by members. An exit value is the sum realised on an acquisition when it is sold. The associations provide information on exit values as quarterly or annualised aggregated data that is then broken down into different economic sectors of buyout activity. This preserves the privacy of their members. The information is also classified into different forms of sale: IPOs, secondary buyouts, and so forth. The longstanding and comprehensive project at CMBOR provides similar data. More specific information regarding individual deals can be gleaned on a shorter time horizon from the industry trade journals. The magazine *Buyouts*, for example, has both a public and private exit column detailing forthcoming sales. Exit values can provide an indirect indicator regarding the scale of likely returns to investors rather than the net or proportional levels of returns on investment. They are an indicator of scale rather than proportions of return for a variety of reasons. The raw exit value of an individual buyout is not the total value extracted from the acquisition over the life of the investment. It does not include the ordinary dividend returns to equity over the life of the investment or any special dividends generated through refinancing. It does not account for fees to the GP. There may also be a number of accountancy adjustments that need to be made to both the original valuation of an acquisition and the net value of the sale, based on 'fair-value' related accountancy issues (Pwc 2007). As such exit value is not a net measure of returns to investors. In many respects, higher values may indicate no more than a trend increase in private equity activity and, within that, specific periods of increase in the size of acquisitions under management during times of growing liquidity.

As one might expect total exit values have grown in the UK since the growth of integrated PEF from 1998. Further, total exit values grew significantly from 2004 to early 2007. Annual total exit value was just under £5 billion in 1998 and grew to approximately £11 billion in 2002 (CMBOR 2005).[2] Annual total exit value grew from approximately £18 billion in 2004 to £27 billion in 2006 before declining in 2007 (Barclays Private Equity 2008).[3] Accordingly the scale of returns to investors has clearly increased during this period. Significantly, exit values as a percentage of the estimated total values realised from buyouts have declined since the late 1990s from over 70% of the total to around 50% (Wright *et al.* 2006: 49). This decline, as CMBOR data also indicates, coincides with the growth of refinancing and asset sales.

The point I want to emphasise here is that though exit values are an indicator of scale of return they are important also because they coincide with other changes that indicate something about the likely sources of return. The greater use of refinancing and of asset sales can be understood in three ways. First, both provide means to enhance gearing: refinancing can lower the costs of debt servicing and asset sales can assist in concentrating equity. Second, both can provide guaranteed and immediate sources of return to the fund. Third and relatedly, the growing liquidity of some secondary markets (credit and commercial property markets) make refinancing and asset sales more attractive at the same time as the proportion of returns on the exit of firms is likely to be declining. From 2000 to 2003 an IPO would be liable to be more difficult and less lucrative – hence the growth and continued growth of secondary buyout markets set out in previous chapters. From 2003, the combination of an equity bull market and increased competition for LBOs of all kinds increased the premiums paid to shareholders/owners (the additional capital required to secure the buyout), tending to reduce the margins on exit values.

One can also look at the failure rates of acquisitions as an indirect measure of returns on PEF investment. All other things being equal one would anticipate that higher failure rates would mean lower returns to investors. Lower failure rates are thus an indicator of the likelihood of returns to investors and thus of a lower 'risk' factor in the overall investment. However, context also plays a role here because both lower failure rates and the implications of higher failure rates for the investment affect both the relationship of returns and the significance of that relationship. The failure of the acquisition, for example, may be due to the way equity was concentrated and/or special dividends generated during a time of liquid capital markets. As such, there may have been rapid returns to the fund prior to the failure. Since, the late 1980s not withstanding, higher gearing and greater leverage levels on larger acquisitions are a relatively recent phenomenon in the UK and the adverse capital markets that might set in motion rising failures are even more recent, the level of failures related to higher gearing and the use of refinancing remains a future unknown. One should also consider that although equity is at the bottom of the order of priority of creditors in an insolvency or bankruptcy situation, equity owners may still recover a proportion of their committed capital. Again CMBOR research highlights this (Wright, Jensen *et al.* 2007: 1). Between 1985 and 2005 there were 12,267 UK buyouts of which 1,431 were placed in receivership – a failure rate of approximately 12%. Five of the seven largest failures occurred during the Market collapse of 2000. As one might expect the failure rate over the full period has been highly variable. It decreased year-on-year from 2000 as interest rates fell. Most importantly, the average recovery rate on the invested equity subsequent to receivership was 62%.

The point, then, is that failure rates are not a clear indicator of definite losses to investors. This, as with the issue of exit values has implications for the context in which one understands returns. From an investors point of view it indicates that the failure of an acquisition does not translate into an absolute loss on the investment. This places a question mark over the monitoring role of LPs in the fund of the kind I highlighted in Chapters 5 and 6. This is not because LPs have an interest in the collapse of the acquisition or are in some sense absolute sense 'negligent' in their monitoring. Rather it is because the combination of equity recovery rates, the availability of rapid sources of return, and the recent low and falling statistical incidence of failures in the context of increasingly liquid capital markets creates a decline in the perception of risk of LPs that in turn facilitates the use of strategies that create more vulnerable debt. The existence of a dividing line between the failure of the acquisition and the failure of the investment is, therefore, an indicator of the likelihood of returns to investors of a complex kind. Its complexity has the potential to undermine the viability of the acquisition in a long term sense within the dynamics of capital markets. This in a sense reiterates the point of Chapter 5 that fund investors can be part of the process that encourages the exploitation of all available liquidity for the purposes of returns to the fund.

Exit values and failure rates are particular kinds of indirect indicators of returns to investors that indicate that one can anticipate scales of returns and the likelihood of returns. This still leaves the question: what is the level of returns to investors in a PEF fund? Clearly, institutional investors are not fools and PEF has been around a long time – certainly long enough for institutional investors to have some measure of its worth, including in different capital market contexts. There may be specific reasons why investment in PEF has grown and grown at particular times but the very fact that investment has continued tends to indicate that it has been a source of high returns – at least from the best performing funds.[4] This, of course, is not particularly surprising given the variety of strategies to generate returns set out in Chapter 5. However, as Jenkinson notes (2006: 29), public knowledge of the actual performance of individual funds in terms of returns is limited. Public disclosure is not a legal requirement for the firms. In the absence of this disclosure levels of return can be considered in three ways. First, in terms of how they are calculated and whether different averages of fund performance meet the claimed or target returns set in PEF fund solicitation. Second, whether in fact what is known of performance indicates that PEF funds outperform alternative investments – the typical comparison being public equities. Third, whether the unprecedented changes in PEF activity in the last decade has implications for returns.

Funds report performance based on two different measures. First, they report performance on the basis of the internal rate of return (IRR). IRR is calculated as an annualised rate and is defined as the net return to investors after carried interest and other fees are accounted for. However, because it is an annualised rate, the IRR is not initially an actual calculation of what investors receive. The fund is a ten year commitment and in the first few years very little actual capital will be returned to investors. Until the fund's lifecycle is actually completed, the IRR is initially wholly, and later partly, an estimation based on an accountancy assessment of the prospective value of the investment.[5] This is termed 'residual value' and ultimately reflects projections based on the plans of the GP that have not yet been realised. The second measure is the multiple of the original investment that is then returned to the investor. During the life of the fund this too is a combination of the actual capital returned and of the estimation of residual value. It is the sum of these two as ratios to committed capital.

In soliciting funds PEF firms tends to set target goals of 25% for IRR and two for multiples of committed capital. The main source of information for Europe, including the UK, is the annual Thomson Venture Economics (TVE) survey produced with the EVCA and based on a data set of 956 reporting funds.[6] As Jenkinson reports the average IRR for all private equity over the period 1980–2004 was 9.5% and the average multiple was 1.32. For buyouts as a category the figures were 12.3% and 1.37 respectively. Within the average moreover, for all types of PEF the top 25% of funds achieved 23.3% and 1.84 – indicating a high degree of variation in averages of fund performance.[7] For buyouts as a category the figures for the top 25% of funds were 28.7% and 1.89. Significantly then, PEF does not seem to have consistently achieved the high levels of returns it tends to set as target goals. The figures, however, as claims of net returns, are still high – certainly high enough to exceed a typical carried interest hurdle of 10%. Though PEF may seem to be underperforming its claims it still appears to be a high performance asset class.

'Appears', however, may be the operative word in several senses. The typical lifetime of an investment in a PEF fund is ten years. The investment itself is relatively illiquid in the sense that committed capital cannot easily be withheld or withdrawn. One question, then, is: what might the returns on the capital be over the given period had it been invested in another asset class? Most studies have focused on the US and compared relative returns with public equity investment. Most of those studies have focused on PEF funds that have closed i.e. completed their term of operation – typically those before 1996. The findings of studies have been highly variable. However, no study has found that PEF actually outperforms investment in public equity in any spectacular sense. For example, Stephen Kaplan, one of the most respected and longstanding academics in the field (a former graduate student of Jensen's) found that over 1980–95 the average return to investors in buyout funds net of fees to PEF firms was approximately the same as that of an investment in the S&P 500 (Kaplan and Schoar 2005). However, the best performing funds did exceed that level. Another study by Philippou and Zollo (2005) questions the basic standard methodology of performance calculation used to derive average IRRs. Based on three key adjustments to method (particularly the use of aggregate cash flow rather than weightings of committed capital) they find that previous claims that private equity outperformed public equity investment over the life of the investment were reversed. Between 1980 and 1996 it actually underperformed the S&P 500 by 3.3% per annum.[8]

No similar studies are available for the period after 1996. But here a different factor also comes into play – many funds created after 1996 would still be operative in the first decade of the twenty first century. As such some proportion of reported returns in private equity association statistics using IRR and multiples of committed capital will be in actual fact residual values rather than achieved returns. They are accountancy fictions. Since the size and number of funds has increased markedly in the last five years and much of the early period of returns calculations for funds is residual values, then arguably a significant proportion of recent statistics on returns to investors are essentially projections. For them to be realised, then, GP plans must likewise be realised. This is partly a matter of how successfully they restructure acquisitions. But it is also partly a matter of the external environment in two senses. First, the finance environment that facilitates restructuring and refinancing as sources of returns. Second, the state of secondary buyout markets for PEF exits and the state of equity markets for PEF exits. The former is highly reliant on credit markets for a new round of gearing. The latter influences the exit value of IPOs.

Time relations are also important when one considers how rapidly PEF has grown since 2003–04 – particularly the growth in the numbers of firms and funds set out in Chapter 4. The success of any given PEF investment in terms of the returns to the fund have been historically variable and also highly variable between the best and worst performing funds. Performance relies heavily on the skills of the GP of the PEF funds and their advisors and consultants. GPs and their advisors are responsible for identifying potential acquisitions, developing profitable debt structures in conjunction with concentrated equity, and then creating further opportunities for returns through refinancing. Whatever stance one ultimately takes regarding PEF this is still an extraordinarily complex task. Moreover it is multiply complex in a way that other forms of investment portfolio management are not. One cannot simply hit the industry benchmark through convergent behaviour in a way that is possible for other financial actors – who for example buy and sell equities on public markets. Whenever herding has occurred in PEF it has usually been a disaster – as it was in the run up to the collapse of the dot.com boom. The success of individual funds can be far more variable than the equivalent variation between typical investment management of other kinds. Since solicitation is for funds whose duration is around ten years and the number of funds and firms has grown it is likely that many of the GPs now administering funds and overseeing acquisitions are an unknown quantity with limited experience.

The essential point to emerge from this combination of factors is that whether in fact *relatively* high returns are provided by private equity to institutional investors is both contentious and itself subject to change. As I noted earlier, institutional investors are not fools and private equity has been around long enough for institutional investors to have some measure of its worth. That said, it appears that private equity often underperforms its own typical solicitation claims, and due to the large variation in performance of funds, has done so in a highly variable way. Moreover, much of the current claims of high returns are questionable as actual achieved claims – as projections they are future dependent. One might note in this context that the corollary of the concepts of risk that underpin the relatively low proportions of capital committed to private equity by institutional investors is the existence of a real investment environment within which returns are dynamically variable. Institutional investors are aware of the variability in fund performance, are aware of the issue of the role of the executives as GPs, and are aware of the issues of liquidity and the external environment. This is precisely why private equity is deemed high risk. It is also why the main response to the market collapse of 2000 was a concentration of capital in mega funds administered by longstanding and prominent PEF firms. Here, it is important to note that categorising private equity as high risk has not prevented the proportions of capital committed to such funds from increasing. Institutional investors appear to have placed a degree of trust in past reputation in an industry which is radically expanded and where the future may have different conditions than the past because of that expansion. It is reputation and the claims made in solicitation that maintained the flow of capital to funds into 2007. It is liquidity and low returns elsewhere that provided the source and impetus for the capital. This re-raises the issue of whether the concept of risk as a technical term is adequate.

As I set out in Chapter 4 and reiterated in Chapter 6, there is no reasonable way to reduce to a calculation issues of the open and multiply interacting effects of different elements in a system. The very expansion of PEF might be a reason why the issues reflected in the category of high risk are realised – particularly problems with the finance structure. As a final point, in the context of liquidity PEF might be considered 'high risk' in far more significant ways than simply in terms of the invested capital committed to funds. If one thinks of PEF as a contributing factor in unstable liquidity then there is also a link to the significance of the potential instabilities it creates and exacerbates in terms of its worth to institutional investors. On a systemic level PEF may be one reason why asset bubbles occur and collapse. As such the returns it might offer to the small proportion of invested capital from institutional investors may not offset the problems it creates or contributes to in the rest of the investment environment where the majority of institutional capital resides. The irony of this is that it is precisely the growing instability of capital markets and returns on traditional investments that makes investment in PEF, hedge funds, and other forms of alternative investment more attractive over time.

Employment, productivity and wage costs

The effects of private equity finance on employment and wages are a controversial subject. A focus on the constraints created by debt and gearing might lead one to anticipate significant falls in employment and clear cuts in wages. This would be consistent also with increasing productivity – at least if measured as a ratio of profits or revenue to employment. Research in the UK, therefore, primarily produced by CMBOR, has focused on whether in fact LBOs do result in lower employment levels and cuts in wages. The findings tend to reject the idea that LBOs result in significant long term negative consequences for employment and wages. Thorough though the research is it is not definitive. Just as with the issue of high returns to investors there is here scope for looking at the significance of the research in different ways. Those ways can either be based on basic limitations in the data or they can be based on different interpretations of what an LBO means in terms of employment and wage structures within modern management systems. Raising these issues ultimately brings one back to the broader issue of debt vulnerability and to issues of entitlement and returns.

In late 2006 and early 2007 CMBOR findings (Wright *et al.* 2007; Amess and Wright 2007) on the performance of private equity buyouts in the UK were widely reported in the business sections of the press. The main focus of the CMBOR research, however, was not productivity. The Amess and Wright study, for example, begins from a literature review that reports previous findings that productivity is increased after an LBO. The majority of this work relates to the US and the 1980s.[9] However, the claim itself is in many respects an uncontroversial one since productivity gains can be achieved in any number of ways and as I set out in Chapter 5 a GP does have a motive to pursue productivity gains as part of the process of generating returns to the fund (expressed through the p/e relation). As I also highlighted in Chapter 5 this is not all they are doing and as such it is not the only and perhaps not the main source of returns. Productivity can be increased by reducing employment and increasing the amount of work each worker does. It can be increased by generating new technologies and imposing working practices that enable each worker to do more. It can be increased by new incentives and motives for workers to do more work or by encouraging their participation in the design of effective working practices. It can be increased by some combination of these three. It can be increased by changing the ratios of 'productive' to 'non-productive' labour – reducing second line workers, middle management tiers etc. and/or increasing the relative numbers of end-service providers or product-output workers. It can thus involve a net increase or decrease in employment. Returns, meanwhile, can be increased by reducing wage costs in one way or another in order to reduce variable costs with the aim of increasing the margins on revenue at any given level of output based on productivity (and any change in productivity).

As a result of these contingencies, the CMBOR research focuses primarily on the employment and wage effects of LBOs in order to address the issue of whether assumed performance gains are at the expense of employment and/or wage growth. If not, then the inference drawn by the research is that performance gains are not at the expense of labour. In the Amess and Wright research a sample of 1,350 LBOs was drawn from the CMBOR database between 1999 and 2003. The sample was drawn on the basis that each also had at least two years of audited accounts logged on the privately operated Financial Analysis Made Easy (FAME) database and that each could be matched with at least one non-LBO firm deemed to be an industry equivalent. A series of statistical tests were then applied to the sample to compare relative and changing levels of employment and wages. The key findings of the research include that wages per employee were higher for non-LBOs and that LBOs also have lower ratios of employees to fixed assets, as well as inferior labour productivity (measured as profit per employee). Lower wages per employee and fewer employees based on a proxy for the size of the company are not inconsistent with the idea that LBOs rationalise employment and cut costs. However, the research also indicates that where an LBO has occurred, although average wage and employment growth are then less than non-LBOs in all variety of tests, the differences were less than 1%.

The overall findings, therefore, are somewhat ambiguous. On the one hand, the research could be taken to indicate that LBOs directly and adversely affect employees. However, the short time frame of some of the accounts limits the data's capacity to convey anything regarding long term changes. Also there could be various reasons why the LBOs do not compare to 'equivalent' firms in terms of wages, employment and productivity. This is because comparison is based on a highly generalised match for size within a given industry. The differences could be due to the ages, sectors, growth histories, capital intensiveness etc. of the firms. There could be particular characteristics that make a firm a likely PEF target which would then translate to systematic differences with non-LBOs but are not themselves a result of the LBO. For example, capital intensiveness provides a useful source of assets either for disposal or to secure debt.

On the other hand, the research also seems to indicate that an LBO does not have large scale affects on employment and wage growth as a time dynamic. There is, however, some ambiguity in terms of the data here also. The FAME database is an extremely useful information source. It contains headline data in all the key categories used in standard accounting, including also gearing levels, credit ratings and so forth. However, the information on employment and wages in each logged annual company report are general totals for that year. They are not disaggregated into types of employment and sub-sets of wage levels. They are, therefore, not directly informative regarding changes within totals of employment and wages. There could easily be significant changes in distributions of employment and wages and also significant employment turnover (perhaps as part of those changing distributions). As such, the averages derived from the database are not clear indications of how any assumed performance gain is achieved. They are, therefore, not a strong argument for any inference that any assumed performance gain is not at the expense of labour. One might note that FAME company reports also subdivide remuneration into wages, social security costs, and pension costs and provide a further subdivision for directors' remuneration. The full range provides a more complete picture of terms and conditions of employment (though one still hampered by the distributional problem that the totals disguise). Not all PEF acquisitions in the FAME database provide information in all of these subdivisions – particularly directors' remuneration. The relative levels and changes in the range of sub-divisions are not explicitly referred to in the CMBOR research. However, if the matching process of LBOs to non-LBOs is valid one can still sustain the point that in a comparative sense the LBO itself has not resulted in a devastating effect on overall employment levels and on overall wages.

The employment time dynamic of the effect of LBOs is explored in more detail in a further piece of CMBOR research (Wright *et al.* 2007). This research claims that although employment tends to fall immediately after an LBO it then tends to increase over the following years. For MBOs this is net growth within four years. For MBIs it translates into a small overall net fall over the four years that may become a net rise over a longer period. For MBOs employment tends to fall in the first year after the buyout by an average of $2\frac{1}{4}\%$

but rise overall by $21\frac{1}{2}$ % by the fourth year (i.e. around 5% per year over the 4). For MBIs employment falls by $10\frac{1}{4}$% in the first year and just over $3\frac{1}{2}$% overall by the fourth year. At first glance this would seem to indicate a long term general positive relationship between buyouts and employment. The inference is that any productivity growth and, ultimately, any improved financial performance of the acquisition, are not at the expense of labour – at least in the sense of long term unemployment effects.[10]

Three points should however be noted. First, it should be noted that within the general statistical pattern there is also an underlying pattern that it is a minority of firms (around 35% of the dataset for both MBIs and MBOs) that account for the majority of the initial job cuts indicating that in this 35% initial job cuts are liable to be much larger. Second, it should be noted that both the CMBOR and FAME databases are not immune to the biasing effect that reporting by PEF is a voluntary process. As such the statistics are more likely to under-report instances of poor performance or job cuts. This is a problem whose effects are similar to the survivor bias in the reporting of hedge fund performance statistics. Third, it should be noted that the statistics are indicative of effects not causes.[11] They do not explain themselves. Interpretation is still required to make sense of what issues like 'at the expense' of labour mean in a fuller context.

A buyout is not just a concentration of equity in fewer hands it is a refocusing of control and what ownership means. Even if some of the current management are retained, they are retained under new conditions with a new tier of control. Those conditions include a pressure to increase the rate of return on the concentrated equity.[12] Those conditions also include an increase in costs (debt servicing) and, in all likelihood, also include a decrease in after tax net profits. Behind these lies greater debt creation. Greater debt creation constrains choices because of two effects:

1. The business becomes more interest rate sensitive since it is carrying larger absolute volumes of debt.
2. The capacity of the business to carry its other costs or spend, without creating further debt, is reduced.

Constrained choices essentially mean a greater pressure to cut costs elsewhere in order to maintain debt serviceability and reduce risk. If there is any credence in Jensen's control hypothesis for debt creation it must also extend to this idea of cost cutting. In terms of operating costs the most vulnerable is almost always going to be labour. Productivity growth and a restructuring of employment are, therefore, liable to be mutual strategies. Labour is initially shed as the CMBOR data indicates, and the organisational forms restructured on the basis of new working practices. Those practices are liable to be conducive to lower costs both by making each worker do more and by on average rewarding each worker less. The degree to which this is successful would, in conjunction with sales growth on the basis of lower prices, new services or changes in products (all made easier by imposing new forms of 'flexibility'), likely dictate the rate of increase in employment. In MBOs the overall job losses may be less because the management already have in place a plan of changing working practices, and also a degree of political capital that can be used up with the workforce (*trust us this is the only way*) as well as (in smaller or more paternalistic firms) a disinclination for mass redundancies. The absence of redundancies may, therefore, simply mean the more effective introduction of new conditions for the current workforce. In MBIs the initial job losses may be greater precisely because of an absence of these factors. But in both MBOs and MBIs the tendency is one where power is redistributed within the employment relation and in which industrial relations are reconstructed. The issue is, therefore, as the Trade Union Congress and the GMB union have both noted not just one of job losses but also of job security, terms, conditions and benefits, the quality of work and, more broadly, the psychological contract or tenuous trust that sustains the work relation.

This issue of power redistribution and its consequences, however, can be viewed in two ways.[13] One can think of the changes in brute terms and expect a clear distinction between pre and post LBO behaviour that can only be viewed in negative terms. Management armed with a newly liberated right to act translate this into a simple strategy of mass involuntary redundancy and the slashing of wage rates to achieve their goals. This would imply a highly simplistic view of how power operates. It would be a very primitive form of Weberian bureaucratic power (Weber 1978; Lukes 1986). Power flows from the top of a hierarchy along well understood channels to the bottom as a series of edicts. In terms of industrial relations and the employment relation it would be a form of one dimensional and aggressive unitarism based on a strident assertion of the management prerogative (Rose 2004: 26–7). Here there is a simple Manichean division where one can easily draw an ideological distinction between an 'us' and 'them'. Viewed in these terms one might expect that the general weakening of trade unions and of institutional forms of industrial relations over the last 30 years has actually enabled a primitive form of Weberianism that has then translated into aggressive unitarism. However, the very changes in industrial relations and the employment relation that have occurred over the last 30 years can make such a policy counterproductive. If anything is likely to result in the recreation of industrial relations conflict to the detriment of the goal of improving productivity it is aggressive unitarism. Such a policy is likely to be a product of hubris and inexperience or a last resort or desperate measure rather than a first option.

The issue of the redistribution of power and its consequences can then be viewed in a second way. It can be viewed as an instance and opportunity to pursue a further neo-liberal reconstruction of work. Achieving the goal of higher productivity effectively can be done through the newly liberated right to act of management in ways that elaborate on current available management techniques and strategies. If the weakening of trade unions and of institutional industrial relations has already shifted power towards management then it is a better strategy to work within the range of opportunities this provides to limit confrontation in achieving goals. This does not mean there is no longer an 'us' and 'them'. It does not mean that employment will not be cut, that wage costs will not be reduced, that other terms and conditions will not be eroded and that workers will not be induced to do more. Rather it means that the strategies to achieve this will involve a quite different utilisation of the power available to management.

Over the last 30 years the nature of the employment relation has become more individualised and competitive at the same time as the practices of work have articulated new ideas of worker-management communication and team work in general. The goal set forth is one of meeting targets i.e. improved performance and productivity. The milieu in which it is expressed emphasises individual employee achievement – the individual is liberated and empowered to fulfil themselves through work. Flexible working practices enable this. It emphasises common cause – through achieving one also participates in the performance gains to the firm because of target based reward systems. The use of target based reward systems may simultaneously allow basic wage growth to slow at the same time as target based rewards do not grow commensurately with productivity (generating falling wage costs). Through 'common cause' the threat of redundancy is often pushed into the background. It only comes to the fore when one under-achieves targets and suddenly finds oneself exposed as an individual in conflict with the power of the firm. Actual large scale redundancy can become voluntary redundancy. This may involve closing some areas of employment and offering retraining and relocation – which may or may not be a realistic option for those offered it. Individual redundancy can become a slow attrition of demotion, sidelining, reassignment and constructive dismissal.

Overall, this new management environment enables a kind of self-disciplining to which employees are invited to conform or face the consequences.[14] Within the process of work socialisation the degree and personal significance of conformity may be variable. The strategy may not be appropriate to all kinds of work and workplace. It may be more fiction than reality where managers speak the latest human resource management jargon and design work practices that never become a genuine part of work culture. Where they do become part of work culture they may be resented or they may be appreciated. They may result in a reality of work that is highly pressurised, psychologically damaging and conducive to 'voluntary' longer hours. Irrespective of whether this is the case what the new work environment is antithetical to is the equalisation of power between management and worker based on collective action where there may be real differences of interest between employer and employees. The very terms of debate disguise that power has been restructured to focus on the interests of management because these are deemed to be the same as employees. The use of language as part of the strategy is rather like the way New Labour has used the concepts of modernisation and reform in tandem. To oppose modernisation and reform is to support out-dated methods and principles. To oppose empowerment that articulates the achievement of individual and collective performance is to cling to some outdated notion of 'us' and 'them' that returns the terms of debate to the 'bad old days' of strife of the 1970s.

It is what is left unsaid and unjustified that conditions the argument and propels a more sophisticated approach to employment, productivity and wage costs. A useful way to consider this is to look at the results of a joint project between CMBOR and the Erasmus Research Institute of Management (ERIM) in Rotterdam (Bruining *et al.* 2005). The research was based on a survey questionnaire completed by the owner/director of LBOs that occurred in the UK and the Netherlands between 1994 and 1997. The survey received an 18% response rate and highlighted some interesting aspects of attitudes to employment relations and human resource management strategies. The survey indicates that in the UK trade union recognition reduces after a buyout, that management are more hostile regarding the concept of unions, and that new forms of working practices are introduced, as well as target-related pay systems.[15]

Bruining *et al.* interpret this as a reconstruction that is mutually beneficial to employees and employer. The findings are considered to be consistent with the idea that LBOs do not always and simply take a primitive approach to cost cutting and brute impositions of onerous new practices on the workforce (as part of a 'downside' of the operation). Rather the new management structure also introduces new 'high commitment' sophisticated human resource management systems to induce growth by empowering employees and improving their skills and incentives (as part of an 'upside'). They conclude:

> The findings reveal buy-outs have a positive effect on employee relations in both the UK and the Netherlands. The high level of investment in high HR policies and practices and the increase in these investments following a buy-out suggest that buy-outs release their upside potential rather than protect the downside of their operations. (p. 360)

Several points are relevant here. The argument implicitly assumes that a rejection of an overtly aggressive unitarist approach entails a positive effect on employment relations. This in turn implies a sharp division between an upside and downside in operations – sophisticated human resource strategies are about growth only and growth is through positive employment relations. However, based on an interpretation that takes as its context a neo-liberal reconstruction of work one can as easily argue that an upside-downside distinction is not a genuine dichotomy since they are alternative ways to achieve the same goals neither of which need entail 'positive' effects on employment relations. The data itself cannot provide a decisive proof on this question for two reasons. First, the research is constructed on the basis of questions some of which inquire as to the existence of quite general forms of practices. For example, as part of improved communication and empowerment, senior management is invited to respond regarding the introduction of suggestion schemes, attitude surveys, team briefings, employee participation through quality circles etc. The existence of these categories within the workplace is not in itself a good indicator of how they are actually designed, conducted and implemented. Nor is it a good indicator of how employees feel about them. Second, where questions involve assessing degrees of change these are expressed as ordinal ranks provided by a senior manager. Clearly a senior manager has a constrained perspective. One might argue that asking him or her to rank the degree to which the level of trust between managers and workers has improved is of limited use. Similarly, asking a senior manager to state how similar the terms and conditions are between managers and non-managers is a question that invites managers to respond positively. Not necessarily because they are mendacious but rather because the prior questions have a focus on HRM, teamwork and participation, and this invites a mindset for the manager that focuses on similarity rather than absolute differences in scale of pay and remuneration. A fuller picture of the 'upside' would interview employees regarding how they felt about new practices. It would ask them what effect new practices had on hours of work. It might ask them how new target pay systems had affected take home pay. It might inquire into how voluntary any voluntary redundancies were. It might seek to ascertain how many complaints had been brought against the firm by employees and how the firm had dealt with them. It might inquire into how many employees would like to complain but felt they could not. It might provide employees with information regarding the scales of pay of senior managers and how they stood to benefit from any equity share in an MBO/MBI. It might then ask them how they felt about the similarity of terms and conditions between themselves and both managers and GPs – who may only be involved via a holding company. It might ask them what employment relation arrangements and industrial relations institutions they might prefer.

The significance of the available research on employment, wages and productivity is then ambiguous in various ways. At the same time, in so far as the statistics have any validity they do indicate that LBOs have in general lower levels of employment and lower wage growth. LBOs involve varying degrees of at least short term redundancies and introduce employment growth on the basis of new work practices, including a reduced role for unions and what remains of institutional forms of industrial relations in the UK. Any productivity gains, therefore, will involve a combination of mutual strategies of cost cutting and growth. If one accepts the interpretation that this is a further neo-liberal reconstruction of work then the process is a negative one in general for employees. The way in which it is negative is muted by the power shifts that silence and marginalise dissent. If one accepts a 'modernising' interpretation then the reconstruction is simply a manifestation of current good management practice and thus inherently positive.

The general statistics in and of themselves cannot provide a decisive way to distinguish between these two positions. In some respects the answer comes down to whether one accepts the There Is No Alternative (TINA) thesis: the alternative to current management systems is a return to the 1970s and this is no alternative at all given new global competition etc. But this is to replay in a specific form the kind of problematic arguments against regulation I explored in Chapter 6. Here, genuine empowerment and participation is about more than the right to conform to management goals. It requires democratic forums and institutionalised means to equalise power between employers and employees. Beyond this general point there is also a point more specific to LBOs. The long term effect on employment relations and on wages and employment is still highly dependent on the effects of debt creation and then on the capacity for debt to be serviced as capital markets and the general economy change. Nothing in the debate about upsides, downsides, productivity etc. changes the basic fact that the vulnerability to an unknown future has been heightened by debt. There may be immediate consequences involving 'downside' practices but the need to engage in them can also be heightened in an unknown future. This again raises a moral dynamic to the issue of PEF: that of entitlement to the returns extracted from acquisitions. A couple of brief examples highlight this.

The GMB highlight the case of the insurer and vehicle breakdown service organisation, the AA. The AA was bought out by CVC and Permira for £1.7 billion in 2004. The business has had mixed performance figures – losing fleet breakdown contracts with Volkswagon, Seat and Skoda, experiencing slow growth in its core insurance market and a net fall (across the period) in its personal breakdown cover market but increasing its revenue by 5.2% to £794 million and operating profits by 28.8% to an ostensibly healthy figure of £256.1 million (AA Annual Report, 2006). However, after debt servicing costs on debt of around $1.3 billion and other costs are included, net profit in 2006 was just £36 million. Using this measure, in the previous year the firm made a loss of almost £60 million. During the same period the GP had already managed to recoup more than the £500 million in invested equity.[16] In June 2007 CVC and Permira agreed a merger with the insurer and over-fifties service provider Saga, owned by the private equity firm Charterhouse. The merger created a new holding company combining the assets of the two firms – the AA valued at £3.35 billion and Saga at £2.8 billion. The merger represents a case of regearing, combining the debts of AA and Saga at around £2.8 billion and loading an additional £2 billion in debt, which the private equity owners were then reported to be intending to distribute as a dividend.[17] Since the AA owners had already recouped the invested equity their share in the dividend would constitute a clear net return. The return, however, does not appear to be rooted in any direct way in the performance of the business, except in so far as the new debt structure is serviceable.[18] As such one might regard it as a product of being in the right place at the right time and with no clear barriers to prevent the extraction of the return. Such dividends are unlikely to be possible by simply growing a business in the traditional way and relying on greater profits and more revenue – particularly in a four year timeframe where the firm is already laden with debt to finance the initial buyout. Furthermore, the extraction clearly places additional pressures for there to be basic changes in the way the organisation is structured. After the 2004 buyout the AA shed 3,000 jobs mainly through voluntary redundancy from a workforce of 10,000 and replaced union representation with an employer association, the AA Democratic Union. According to the GMB, new performance rules have affected the services the AA provides – the AA no longer fixes 90% of breakdowns in situ, for example.[19]

One could of course respond that the GMB has focussed particularly on the case of the AA because it is an example of heavy job losses, and de-unionisation in a well-known firm whose performance growth is not clearly commensurate with the returns earned by PEF. One could argue that it is precisely chosen to fit the argument rather than because it is typical. Champions of private equity, for example, have in the past often pointed to the clothing and accessory retailer New Look as a counter-example. New Look was bought for £699 million by Permira and Apax in 2004 and earned operating profits of £174 million on a revenue of £862 million in 2006. The firm has expanded in Europe since the buyout and has grown all aspects of the business – increasing employment from 12,000 to 15,000 and undertaking capital investments increasing from £99 million to £230 million, between 2004 and 2006. But even here it is worth considering that the issue is not just the potentially beneficial effects of some aspects of new ownership on performance but also one of the underlying potentials, pressures and temptations (which accumulate to tendencies) of private equity that also occur. The buyout by Permira and Apax was for 66% of New Look (the rest retained by New Look's founder, Tom Singh) with each committing £150 million in terms of equity combined with a total of £400 million in debt. Two subsequent refinancing and dividend payments have already recouped more than the initial equity and Permira and Apax were in early 2007 looking to flip the business in a secondary buyout to another private equity owner for further secondary gearing. In March 2007 they appointed

Merrill Lynch to represent them in an auction process and three bidders emerged. The initial asking price was £2 billion and a reserve price of £1.8 billion was set. However the main bidders, including TPG, were unwilling to go beyond £1.5 billion and the auction process stalled in early July 2007. Even if a sale should go ahead at around £1.5 billion the debt structure built into a secondary buyout is likely to see the business carrying debt of well in excess of £1 billion, alongside which its performance figures will seem significantly less impressive. This in itself, in addition to issues over current interest rate trends and finance prospects may be a reason why the initial £2 billion price was not met – auction bidders are given full access to the accounts. If a sale goes ahead the Permira and Apax funds will then likely share somewhere between £800 million to £1.3 billion. This raises the question, as Froud and Williams (2007) have also noted: has the GP done anything to create the entitlement to this scale of return? One might additionally make the point that it is important not to confuse the capacity for new management to improve a business with the underlying capacity of particular forms of finance and the context in which it operates to also potentially destabilise that business in a broader and longer term sense. This in the end is also an issue regarding employment.

Tax

The BVCA estimates (2006, p. 6) that private-equity backed firms contributed a total of £26 billion in taxes to public revenues in the UK in the tax year 2005–06 on the basis of an estimated £424 billion in sales.[20] What is interesting about these statistics is what they omit. First, they focus on the tax paid by private equity backed firms – presumably including but not differentiating buyout acquisitions where private equity has effective control. Notably they do not state the rates at which tax is paid and what proportions of revenues, earnings etc. are not taxed. The estimation is thus not an explanation and justification of the basis on which tax is paid but rather a simple statement that tax is paid. Second, they make no reference to either the amounts of tax or the levels at which tax is paid by the private equity funds, the private equity firms and the individual executives of those firms. An appropriate set of questions to get a more collective sense of the overall contribution of private equity to public revenues would, therefore, seem to be, what proportions of earnings etc. are paid as tax by:

- Private equity acquisitions.
- Private equity firms and their executives.
- Private equity funds.

The problem, however, is that one cannot easily move from such questions to actual figures that set out how much tax private equity contributes to public revenues compared to what it *could* under the current tax regime and what it might compared to what it does – the difference being based on the degree to which the current tax regime provides private equity with opportunities to be 'tax efficient'. Accurate information on these matters is hard to come by for precisely the same reasons that all statistics regarding private equity are subject to some degree of uncertainty. What one can more readily ask, however, is:

- In what ways, based on a combination of current tax policy as a set of opportunities and current tax strategies available to private equity, can private equity minimise its payment of tax? Put another way, how equitable is private equity? Does it subvert the original intention of the tax policies it uses?

Taxes paid by private equity acquisitions

The UK, as with most advanced capitalist economies has a tax system intended to prevent avoidable business insolvency and intended to promote productive investment as part of growth. For these reasons, interest payments on debt can currently be offset against any operating profits (as calculated using Ebitda). This means that interest payments (debt servicing costs) can be deducted when calculating the proportion of those profits on which corporation tax should then be paid from those operating profits. Non-LBOs, particularly publicly listed companies are rarely highly geared. Their underlying use of debt will tend to remain focussed either on matters of necessity (using it for cash flow purposes during the economic cycle) or on the use of debt for productive investment within a definite timeframe. But for private equity, debt relief on interest payments is essentially an incentive to hold more debt. Net profits are affected to a smaller degree by tax meaning the acquisition can commensurately carry greater debt servicing costs.

The implications for public revenues are twofold. First, the greater the degrees of leverage applied to acquisitions by private equity then the lower the tax liabilities of the firm and thus the lower the overall levels of corporation tax paid in proportion to total revenue and operating profits.[21] This is an effect that is magnified for the larger acquisitions that private equity is now increasingly targeting. Second, tax relief has essentially become a subsidy to the returns on private equity extracted from the acquisitions rather than necessarily a way of maintaining the solvency of the acquired business or of promoting productive investment. The underlying purpose of the tax relief, therefore, has potentially been subverted. It has further been subverted by favouring debt over equity within private equity buyouts and favouring private equity buyouts over public equity in general – since dividend payments to equity receive no such tax relief. One might also argue that the kind of debt generated by private equity is essentially capital used by the new owners in order to become the new owners and might better be regarded as disguised equity to which returns are paid in terms of interest rather than dividends because of the concentration of ownership. All these points raise the issue of whether private equity debt structures in acquisitions should be categorised as debt at all for tax purposes and whether corporation tax relief should be available to highly leveraged private equity acquisitions.

This has implications for how one thinks about the relation between performance, revenue and tax. If, for example, one takes UK corporation tax at 30% and uses the BVCA figures on tax paid in the accounting year 2005–06 compared to total sales revenue – £4.3 billion compared to £424 billion – then either the average private equity backed firm performed rather badly in terms of generating profits from revenue or the average private equity backed firm benefited significantly from tax relief. If tax in full was in fact paid then the entire private equity backed industry generated a total profit of just over £13 billion, which on sales revenue of £424 billion would be an extraordinarily poor performance (around 3%). The implication seems to be that large swathes of public equity operating profits were subject to tax relief. This essentially subsidises the returns to the PEF funds and provides an additional benefit and motive for LBOs.

This argument is neither new nor contentious for analysts of PEF. Its significance is, however, contested. Kaplan (1989), for example, found that the typical LBO based on a sample of US LBOs 1980–86 paid little or no federal tax in the first two years after a buyout and that tax relief on interest was an important source of wealth gains for PEF in an LBO (1989: 613).[22] Graham (2000) later confirmed this general point, finding that the tax benefit of interest rate deductibility was on average 9.7% of the market value of the typical firm but was much higher for LBOs – rising to as much as 20% for highly leveraged cases such as Safeway and RJR Nabisco. Jensen *et al.* (1989), however, published findings that LBOs were in fact a net gain to government tax revenues. This was because LBOs generate a range of tax effects: capital gains tax is paid on the shares that the original equity holders sell as part of the LBO, capital gains tax is paid on the subsequent resale of the LBO, capital gains tax is paid on asset sales, and eventually corporation tax is paid on improved LBO revenues.[23]

Several points need to be stated to place the Jensen *et al.* claims in context. First, the claims do not dispute that corporation tax relief on interest payments is a benefit and subsidy to PEF. As such, the original reason for the policy is still subverted. Moreover, the tax relief encourages greater levels of leverage and thus greater degrees of debt vulnerability. Graham (2000: 1925) acknowledges this in making the point that from a tax point of view, if anything public corporations are under-levered. Second, the evidence for the Jensen *et al.* argument is a set of estimations rather than empirical findings based on IRS tax data – this remains confidential. What one can assert is that the estimates are based on a range of knock on tax effects that are, as Jensen *et al.* note, highly contingent. Many of the institutional investors are tax exempt. Even if they are not, the complexity of the disbursement of tax obligations allows opportunities for the increasingly creative use of tax efficiencies to legally avoid and minimise tax. PEF, beginning with the collaboration of KKR and Deloitte have been pioneers of this. In any case the majority of the knock-on effects are through capital gains tax, which is a 'front-loaded' tax: it is a once only payment triggered by the realisation of an asset. The longer term tax streams particularly revenue growth of an increasingly successful turned around acquisition assumes that revenue does grow in excess of debt servicing costs and/or that debt is paid down. But refinancing and secondary gearing through secondary buyouts mean that this is increasingly unlikely. In a UK context the BVCA figures for total taxes paid would seem to confirm this. The range of points indicates that the estimated net gain is open to dispute.

The current tax system also seems to promote the use of sale and re-lease of property assets by private equity in the initial buyout. The introduction in January 2007 of real estate investment trusts (Reits) has been part of this.[24] If a company owns a large amount of property it can convert itself to a Reit at a cost of 2% of the capitalisation. Once Reit status is given the company is exempt from corporation tax on income and capital gains tax. Reits must distribute 90% of their exempt income (essentially rent) in dividends. Reits were created with the aim of promoting both renewal and improvements in the UK's business infrastructure – office developments etc. – and of promoting broader investment in the commercial property market as a financial structure. But the existence of Reits is also useful for private equity since it adds an additional incentive to split off the property portion of asset heavy acquisitions to create a separate company. The new company is effectively a sale and re-lease strategy in terms of the original company, but for the GP it is an opportunity to concentrate equity in a separate company through securitisation at the same time as benefiting from tax exemptions on the returns the paired company from which it is split pays in rent. This makes publicly listed companies with significant property assets even more attractive to private equity and thus increases the pressure on public equity from private equity.

Again there are two potential effects in terms of public revenues. First, as with corporation tax relief, the overall tax liabilities of the acquisition are reduced. Second, since the existence of land trusts is a further incentive to target particular kinds of publicly listed companies, the existence of the tax policy becomes, as an unintended consequence, a reason why more private equity buyouts may occur, which in turn will reduce total tax revenues in the UK by increasing the number of highly leveraged firms who benefit from corporation tax relief.[25] In terms of this second point then, the underlying purpose of the tax has potentially been subverted. It has also been subverted if one considers that the Reit protected company is not necessarily primarily a vehicle for property renewal (although this is likely to occur as part of the restructuring strategy of the private equity firm) and it is also subverted in the sense that it is subject to the concentration of ownership in accordance with the general strategy of private equity, rather than being intended for the broadening of investment *per se*.

Executive earnings and the taxation of private equity firms and funds

As I set out in Chapters 3 and 4, in 1998 Gordon Brown introduced 'taper relief' on the taxation of capital gains from investments. If investors held onto an asset for ten years they would pay only 10% capital gains tax when the asset was realised. In 2000 this was reduced to four years and in 2002 it was further reduced to two years. The main aim of taper relief was to provide an incentive for entrepreneurs to invest in new businesses, build them up and sell them at a profit. It was thus regarded as an important aspect of the overall policy to create an investment culture in Britain in accordance with the concept of the New Economy. It has, however, also been an opportune tax policy for private equity. Carried interest is characterised as a return on investment. As such it is subject to taper relief. Individual partners within the private equity firm will be paid some proportion of the carried interest. Again, the underlying purpose of the tax appears to have been subverted here.

One might argue that the status of carried interest as a return on investment is a curious one since it is in effect a fee extracted from investment returns rather than wholly a return on the private equity firm's own invested capital. The private equity firm justifies carried interest as a premium over and above its individual fees. It is a premium based on how the returns derived from a specific investment reflect the overall management of the fund and the success of the sale of an acquisition. That is why it is subject to a hurdle. As a fee, however, it is more reasonably considered as income, and as such subject to ordinary income tax at 40% with no offsetting capital gains tax relief. Because it is not, some of the wealthiest individuals in the UK have paid a low tax level of 10% on their main source of earnings. The public revenue implications have been significant. As fund sizes increase and the absolute size of individual buyout deals increases the absolute amounts of carried interest increase. On large acquisitions individual partners may receive tens of millions of pounds from this source. As buyout activity has increased and the scale of buyouts has risen, not only have the individual partners become wealthier, they have becoming wealthier at an increasing rate because they have been able to rely on taper relief at 10%.

It remains to be seen what effect the proposed replacement of taper relief with a flat 18% capital gains tax rate as of April 2008 will have on PEF. Its broader impact on small businesses has been a public relations disaster for New Labour.[26] In some respects removing taper relief entirely fails to differentiate between speculation and investment in the tax regime since it provides no incentive to hold and build up businesses. As such it could foster the kind of short-termism that PEF also represents, despite that it is targeted at PEF. The better solution might be a combination of a longer and more graduated taper rather than the original rapid fall to 10% (i.e. 100% of tax liability first year reducing by a small set amount per year thereafter) and a reclassification of carried interest as income.

It is notable, however, that in December 2007 the US Senate rejected proposals to recategorise carried interest as income rather than capital gains, which would have resulted in it being taxed at 35% rather than 15%. The rejection was not because of any decisive argument that carried interest is a capital gain from investment – many prominent financiers, including Warren Buffett, have expressed concerns over the subject.[27] Rather it was because a strong lobby threatened the broader tax bill to which the proposal was attached.

If PEF cannot rely on the kind of memorandum of understanding it secured in 2003 then it is likely that some firms will respond with more creative approaches to tax efficiency.[28] Private equity firms and executives may undertake additional efforts to reduce their tax exposure. This is something that they may already have been doing. By off-shoring the registration of both the private equity funds and the firm, taxes paid on investment returns can effectively be nullified and taxes on other fees from which private equity create returns can be minimised. In the past the overall tax level paid by private equity could easily have been less than 10%, since it is standard practice for private equity funds to be registered in such tax havens as Guernsey or the Cayman Islands.

As research by the Tax Justice Network indicates, the existence of off-shoring to tax havens is a major source of tax revenue losses everywhere (TJN, 2005).[29] These losses come from a combination of bank deposits held offshore and additional non-cash assets held through offshore companies, foundations and trusts. Based on an initial estimate of $11–12 trillion held offshore earning an average rate of return from investments of 7.5% they calculate that an annual yield of $860 billion is made that is not currently subject to tax and which, if it were taxed at an average rate of 30% would generate tax revenues of $255 billion. Private equity might be placed in this context as both a participant helping to create off-shored returns for others and a recipient of the benefits of off-shoring for its executives. The degree to which this is the case is difficult to ascertain. The Treasury admitted in 2007 that it did not attempt to calculate how much tax was lost to HM Revenues and Customs (Seib, Duncan and Coates, 2007). One way, however, in which one could test the degree to which tax is not paid because of off-shoring, is to require that firms and funds operating in the UK be registered and more rigorously reported in the UK.[30] If this results in a sudden mass exodus of private equity firms and the dissolution or diverting of the activity of their funds, it seems reasonable to suggest that there is a significant degree of tax avoidance occurring. If it does not, the new and clarified accounts of funds and firms will give some indication of the degree to which tax might have been paid in the past as well as at what level it is to be paid now.

The standard response to this approach, as it is with closing off the unintended consequences of other tax policies on earnings and on the debt of acquisitions, is that it risks turning a situation where some tax is paid into one where none at all is paid because the operations simply choose to go elsewhere. However, this 'some tax is better than no tax' argument is a dubious one for private equity in a number of ways.

In terms of the taxable wealth of private equity executives it raises the question of by what strategy they could respond? They could, if they are not already, become non-domiciled or non-resident in the ways I set out in Chapter 3. Some may take the option of becoming non-domiciled. There were 112,000 non-domiciles in 2005 (74% more than 2002), paying a total of £3 billion in tax but with no measure of how much was lost to public revenues because of the categorisation. Since private equity draws its talent from a global pool some of its executives could and many (estimates run as high as 160 of the top 200 earners) do register as non-domicile.

The non-domicile category does not and need not exist to keep private equity executives living and working in the UK.[31] However, this does not make reform of the policy simple. Following the adverse publicity regarding PEF in mid-2007 and the Conservative party's proposals on the subject[32] the Chancellor in October 2007 proposed the imposition of a flat rate fee of £30,000 per year on individuals in order to maintain their non-domicile status (HM Treasury 2007a: 3). This would apply only to those who have stayed in the UK for seven years. If the seven year duration is implemented then short term economic migrants will not be affected. At the same time the £30,000 rate acts as a trigger: those with modest overseas assets and earnings are given a motive to fully opt into the British tax system. For the truly wealthy the £30,000 annual rate is insignificant. What this suggests is that the tax will have limited claw back potential on the tax efficiencies of the most wealthy – including PEF executives. It will, however, cause problems for particular categories of people because of the interaction of tax regimes. It will particularly affect long term UK residents who are not in the 'super rich' category, and who maintain assets abroad in their country of origin. This may specifically affect US citizens of this type. The US has no corresponding tax to the non-domicile levy which means the £30,000 may not be offset against US tax obligations.[33] The tax liabilities of all foreign citizens who fall into this middling group would in any case likely increase substantially. They may be on the borderline in terms of whether it is economically worthwhile to fully opt into the British system. Further, opting into the British system may not reduce their tax liabilities in their country of origin. In any case they are unlikely to be wealthy enough to have shifted their assets to a tax haven. Since the basis of non-domiciled status is an intention to return home then it would also be individuals genuinely intend-ing to do so who would be least likely to have shifted assets to tax havens. The policy reform proposal thus seems both lacking in ambition in terms of the original target (the tax efficient super rich) and counterproductive in terms of its effects elsewhere. It would make far more sense to have an additional gra-duated income tax for non-domiciles that only took effect above a particular income level. This, however, is made difficult by the existence of confidential tax havens and the way in which tax efficiencies in those havens can cat-egorise individual income as belonging to trusts and other entities.

The ultimate problem in introducing a more stringent non-domicile system or stricter non-residency rules then becomes both the existence of tax havens and the threat that PEF might relocate.[34] However, in terms of the threat one should consider that the function of executives within the private equity firm is to do deals for acquisitions and to also manage those acquisitions as sources of returns. The doing of deals and the creation of debt structures are geo-graphically located in major financial centres and the base of operations of any prospective acquisition. Whilst it need not be wholly problematic for any private equity executive to be non-resident whilst striking deals through London as a finance centre it would be at least inconvenient for the exe-cutive in their role as GP responsible for a particular acquisition thereafter. Would most or all private equity executives become non-resident if required to pay the same rate of tax as everyone else on their multi-million pound earnings? Do they value their additional millions (which should more rea-sonably be considered lost public revenues) more than an ordinary person values their modest salary?

This raises a broader issue: should we value the contribution of private equity despite that its tax contributions could be higher? This point can be addressed in straight economic terms. One could make the 'trickle down' case. Private equity creates economic growth and wealth some of which passes down through the system to make everyone wealthier over time. As such we should tolerate PEF as necessary and in some ways beneficial because of its knock on effects on the income of others. This point, however, is sub-ject to counter argument regarding the neo-liberal reconstruction of work. More specifically, the rise of private equity has occurred within the general rise in wage and income inequality in the Western world. As the OECD and other sources continue to report average wages are growing more slowly than GDP or profits. Average real wage growth is also either slowing or falling in most countries in the world, including the richest. One reason for this in the UK is that the overall tax burden has shifted in regressive ways because of the increase in indirect taxes paid by the majority, some of which must surely be seen as compensating for the failure of the very rich to pay an equal proportion on their income and assets.

The economic argument can also be made in a different way. The exist-ence of the current tax regime in the UK provides further incentives for public equity to become private equity and thus for tax revenues from business to steadily reduce over time (as corporation tax is affected). Since the contributions of private equity to public revenues paid from the returns private equity extracts from these businesses are relatively small then the existence of private equity firms and funds is not one that can be justified in the sense that these forms of tax revenue (from carried interest taxed as capital gains etc.) offset its effects on the tax revenue derived from what was once public equity. Put another way, the longer term effects of private equity are not an economically rational argument for the current tax regime, irrespective of whether executives become non-resident or private equity activity reduces. Rather the reverse might be the case – changes to the current tax regime might be justified precisely as ways of reducing either the amount of private equity activity or the nature of it. There is, therefore, an economic argument for greater tax discipline being applied to private equity, irrespective of whether this has negative effects on private equity's contribution to public revenues.

One can also take the question of whether we should value the contribution of private equity despite that its tax contributions could be higher as a purely moral question. As such it entails the norm that we should consider it wrong that the very rich can pay *less* in proportion than everyone else.[35] On this basis a deontological moral principle arises. A deontological approach to a moral principle is one that takes the view that doing what is right is more important than the consequences. From this position we should apply the same level of taxation to PEF even if that means executives decamp from the UK. This is not simply a matter of the kind of argument held between political philosophers such as Nozick and Rawls concerning the fundamentals of socio-economic systems. It can also be a matter of what is equitable once a tax system actually exists and within which irrationalities occur that facilitate unintended inequities. This ought to be considered a powerful argument in itself. Michael Walzer's (1977) concept of just war is a controversial one for different kinds of liberals. Yet, if the decision to fight a war can include moral claims then why not base the decision to tax on moral claims?

This is not to suggest that moral arguments regarding tax are not undertaken. The issue of fairness is often discussed. However, the reality of taxation policy is usually based on pragmatic concerns that essentially put moral issues to one side even if moral language is still used. In any case any moral argument is likely to be one-sided. A moral argument is not likely to elicit a response in the same terms from PEF. Private equity would be unlikely to attempt to mount the argument that it was morally wrong that they should pay the same as others. Such an argument would invite hostility and derision in equal measure. It is far more likely that the issues are returned to pragmatism as a kind of negotiation – what can we get away with paying, what will you dare tax us before we move? In this context the real issues are threefold. The first two imply an imperative to overcome problems of the third.

First, the issue is the continued existence of off-shoring alternatives to which private equity could have recourse. Second, the issue is the existence of differences in the tax regimes of different states which private equity can exploit. These two issues link back into the economic arguments. One might argue that some portion of the returns earned by executives and then taxed derives from investments from funds managed from the UK but buying acquisitions elsewhere in the world – increasingly in Europe. This would be the idea that the tax returns to public revenues in the UK were a net gain since they derived from values extracted in other countries. This, however, is precisely part of the beggar thy neighbour approach to taxation. It results in the existence and reproduction of tax havens and off-shoring. It essentially eschews the responsibility of a state for what it fosters beyond its borders and thus implies that a moral approach to the problem should not be taken because it might have economic implications. This additionally neglects the point that the economic implications are that public revenues are reduced *everywhere* from what they could be. This includes in the UK. One reason for this is precisely that the current tax regime in the UK, as part of financial liberalism more generally is not merely a response to beggar thy neighbour principles but a prime component in the construction and perpetuation of them. Financial liberalism began in the 1970s and the UK and US have been its chief state exponents. States do not have a 'nature' and the psychology that creates the international dynamic within which individual tax regimes occur is not inevitable. It is rather an evolved set of constitutive and regulative rules, written and unwritten. Its social construction has a history and part of that history is precisely the way the UK and US have fostered the dominance of financial capital. Since it has a history it would be hubris to suggest that its future cannot be different than its past.

This leads to the third issue. This is the lack of an effective united front where different states coordinate their tax regimes and also refuse to do business with those that use off-shoring. Such a front would prevent one state being traded off against another to the overall detriment of tax revenues across the advanced capitalist world. All three of these issues arise because of a beggar-thy neighbour psychology. They can only be addressed internationally because it is the activities of states within a permissive international environment that prefigures the problem.[36] This is not to suggest that the UK has lacked a policy and policy development on off-shoring (HM Treasury 2007b). It is, however, notable that the UK is categorised by the OECD as having tax haven characteristics. It is also notable that within the EU the UK is seen as a laggard in developing an effective united front against tax avoidance. Notably, the EU has begun to address the problem in more urgent terms. Following 14 years of negotiation the EU secured an agreement covering 42 jurisdictions, including some of the long standing tax havens such as Monaco.[37] The agreement covers the exchange of information on new cash flows. In early 2008 national tax authorities also began to use informers within the banking system of tax havens to secure information regarding the deposits held by their own nationals.

Conclusion

In this chapter, I have addressed the three main areas in which empirical claims are made for PEF LBOs. I have argued that PEF has created high returns to investors but that those returns are not relatively high and are contingent. I have argued that PEF is not necessarily devastating to employment levels but is a constitutive part of the neo-liberal reconstruction of work with all that this entails. I have argued that PEF does contribute to tax revenues, but its contribution is far smaller than it could be and raises various economic and moral issues regarding tax efficiency. Given these arguments it seems reasonable to conclude that the specific empirical claims made for PEF cannot be used as a decisive counterargument to considering its broader implications in terms of its effects at a systemic level. Retrospectively, making the arguments has also provided additional ways to think about issues like entitlement and whether PEF is a necessary or desirable solution to the problems it claims to solve. The rapid extraction of value through special dividends, the concentration and capture of revenues through gearing and leverage, and the tax efficient strategies that have been open to PEF generate fundamental questions regarding entitlement and necessity/desirability. I now move on to explore a case study of the mechanics of a large LBO. In addition to clearly illustrating how equity is concentrated and returns are focused and accelerated the case study also provides another angle from which to consider entitlement and necessity/desirability in more explicit ways.

8
Alliance Boots as an Illustration of the Dynamics of Private Equity: Issues of Entitlement, Governance and the Values of Value

The buyout of Alliance Boots by KKR in conjunction with one of the board members created a great deal of publicity regarding private equity finance. The buyout provides a useful contemporary case study and illustration of the kind of themes I have been developing in the previous chapters. It was a buyout of a large publicly listed company undertaken by a prominent PEF firm. The buyout was undertaken using the new large funds available to PEF and was undertaken at the height of the last liquidity surge. It involved the creation of a debt structure that was large in absolute terms and also comparatively highly leveraged. As a buyout it illustrates how PEF captures the rights to the returns on large assets based on a proportionately small equity commitment. It illustrates how equity is concentrated and power distributed. As such it raises the basic question of entitlement: should PEF firms and funds have the right to do this, particularly at larger scales and focused on publicly listed companies? This is not simply an empirical question it is fundamentally a moral philosophy question because the implicit 'right' of PEF is founded on a particular understanding of the right to property. That understanding combines the idea that property is a basic human right, that the state should be minimal and that the freedom of markets should be maximised. Exploring how this is so is important because it also reveals how the terms of debate regarding PEF are shaped by these commitments. Having done so, one can also look at entitlement in more specific terms, based on the idea of debt vulnerability. The buyout of Alliance Boots created a debt structure that was possible because of rising liquidity but that was also vulnerable to the collapse in liquidity. As such Alliance Boots provides a useful illustration of how PEF is itself historically dynamic. Looking at the debt structure also raises the issue of governance: why was the buyout of Alliance Boots approved? A buyout creates unique circumstances for governance: it focuses small shareholders on short term gains and it tends to create an ambiguous situation for the board of directors which is ultimately resolved in terms of a focus on shareholder value. The net effect is that corporate governance is rarely an effective constraint on buyout activity targeted at publicly listed companies. Since it is not such a constraint the issue is again raised of whether intervention is desirable. This in effect is also a moral philosophy question because it is about the right of the state to intervene in the disposition of property and thus cuts across the idea of individual right, the minimal state and maximally free markets. This is so even where PEF is in some sense 'value creating' because the moral question remains, should we value these forms of value? One way of addressing this is in terms of broader public interest arguments and, again, Alliance Boots provides a useful illustration here in terms of the issue of pension provision. This is a sub-set of the broader argument regarding the neo-liberal reconstruction of work I raised in Chapter 7. More prosaically, the buyout also usefully illustrates the targeting and bidding processes of a PEF LBO and also the mechanics of the buyout itself.

Background: Alliance Boots as a target for an LBO

In February 2007 Stefano Pessina, a major shareholder and board member of Alliance Boots was privately informed by KKR that they were targeting the company for acquisition. This was potentially the first buyout of a FTSE 100 company. Alliance Boots was an ideal target for a variety of reasons. It had significant disposable assets, and a relatively low share price. It also had good, if disputed, growth potential. The potential existed because it dominated a large share of the pharmaceutical market at all stages of the supply chain in the UK, and also because it had a multinational presence that could be used to improve the supply chain as well as launch a wider growth project. Pessina was an appropriate person to contact to begin the process of an LBO because he was a large shareholder, because of his role within Alliance Boots, and because of his views on the growth potential of the business.

Alliance Boots had originally been created in July 2006 in a £7 billion merger between the European drugs wholesaler Alliance-Unichem (AU) and the high street chemist Boots.[1] The new publicly listed company was a multinational with a particular focus on Europe. It combined retail operations, wholesale operations, and some manufacturing operations (Alliance Boots 2007: 37). The retail operations were located in the UK, Italy, and the Netherlands. The wholesale operations were also located in these places and also in France, Spain, Russia and the Czech Republic, whilst the manufacturing operations were located in the UK, France and Germany.[2] This newly formed multinational was particularly dominant in the UK pharmaceutical market. It constituted 40% of the UK pharmaceutical wholesale market, including supply to its own pharmacies. It quickly moved to secure a sole-supplier distribution deal with the world's largest drug group, Pfizer. Pfizer termed the deal the 'straight to pharmacy' model. The deal cut out other intermediate wholesalers. In 2006, Pfizer had around 15% of the UK medicines market, including the statin Lipitor, and also Viagra. The sole supplier deal was then followed by a similar one, with the second largest drug group, AstraZeneca.[3] This deal, however, also included another distributor AAH Pharmaceuticals, owned by the German wholesaler Celesio. As of mid-2007, Alliance Boots supplied around 15,000 UK hospitals, pharmacies and doctors' surgeries. It also controlled around 17% of the UK retail pharmacy business, operating 3,000 retail stores including 2,700 pharmacies.

When Alliance Boots was created in 2006, Stefano Pessina, who had held a 30% stake in AU, retained a 15% stake in the new company and took a board position. His main responsibilities focused on seeking and implementing cost saving business integration between the two previous organisations. These 'synergies' amounted to £20 million in cost savings in the first accounting year and were projected to rise to £100 million by the fourth. The main source of these savings was a combination of lower wholesale prices, rationalisation of duplicated aspects of the businesses and reduced distribution costs (Alliance Boots, 2007). Pessina was also given responsibility for overseas expansion of the core business. He anticipated that there was strong potential for expansion in different geographical areas for different reasons (Davey, 2007). The combination of an aging population and continuing health market deregulation in Western Europe seemed to indicate a potential for growth in particular lines of privately provided medications. Economic development and the growth in wealth and private health provision also held out the prospect of strong growth potential in East Asia and, to a lesser extent, Eastern Europe.

When KKR contacted Pessina in February 2007 Alliance Boots shares were valued at around £8 and were being consistently categorised by City analysts as a 'sell' i.e. a poor investment. This was on the basis of two trends. First, that Alliance Boots retail business was under threat from new competition from the large supermarkets. The introduction by Asda and Tesco of 24 hour in-store pharmacies created a new source of competition that brought with it significant existing economies of scale. Supermarkets were in any case increasingly encroaching on the lucrative general market for well being and health: the sale of vitamins, supplements and so forth. Proposals to add new general practitioner surgeries to supermarkets could only add to the broad based challenge that Alliance Boots faced in getting customers through their doors. Second, the drug wholesale market in the UK and the rest of Europe had been experiencing a general fall in margins. Western European states, faced with spiralling health care costs because of their aging populations and because of the growing range of medications available for an ever-increasing number of conditions and illnesses had strong motivations to maximise the use of generic versions of drugs and, in the future, place greater pressure on the major pharmaceutical firms, like Pfizer, to reduce the cost of their products.[4] These trends were part of the reason why the main manufacturing firms were responding with a straight to pharmacy model that focused its contracting on the main joint whole-salers and retailers. Pessina and City analysts, therefore, viewed the market for pharmaceutical wholesale and retail in quite different ways. As a result Pessina had expressed public disaffection with the way analysts and equity markets valued Alliance Boots. The scepticism inherent in that valuation had definite implications for the prospects for expansion of the firm. Any rapid expansion based on new investment might trigger a run on Alliance Boots stock, either slowing down the process of expansion or increasing its costs. This provided one motive for Pessina to work with KKR on an MBO.

The bidding process

On March 9th 2007, Pessina and KKR put an indicative offer of £10 per share to the Chairman of Alliance Boots, Sir Nigel Rudd. An indicative offer is a non-binding offer by the bidder. It is non-binding and indicative only because it is based on the available financial information regarding the potential acquisition. In the case of a publicly listed company, an indicative offer need not value a firm at more than the value reflected in its current share price (its market capitalisation). However, since targets tend to be perceived as in some sense 'undervalued' and since at various times there can be increased competition for buyouts, the chances are that the indicative offer will be a premium above the current share price. The point of the offer is to secure the board of directors consent to engage in 'due diligence'. When the offer is received the board convene to consider that offer and vote on whether to allow access for due diligence. Due diligence is a specified period, typically two weeks, during which the bidder has full access to the detailed accounts of the firm. Even for a publicly listed company that registers detailed annual financial information at Companies House such access still creates problems since some information is secret and sensitive.[5] Accordingly, in order to engage in due diligence the bidder typically must sign a confidentiality agreement. At the end of the period of due diligence the bidder must either put a more detailed firm financial offer to the board or end their interest. The firms typically agree a time line between themselves. The time line is however also subject to regulation. In the UK, the process is supervised by the Takeover Panel. Established in 1968 and currently empowered by the Companies Act of 2006, the panel administers the City Code on Takeovers and Mergers. The code involves various degrees of latitude regarding the timing of offers. However, standard practice is that a firm offer must follow within one month of due diligence or the bidder must, if still interested, begin the bidding process again six months later. The time lines are usually imposed to prevent uncertainty about the firm's future, since this is likely to affect the share price. If the board of directors votes to accept the firm offer then they provide their support – recommending it to the shareholders. However, even should they reject the firm offer it can still be put to shareholders as a hostile bid.

The initial indicative offer, especially an MBO offer, creates immediate issues regarding conflict of interest for the board. Executive board members would essentially be voting on their own futures. They would be doing so knowing full well that private equity tends to offer any retained upper management lucrative incentive payments and knowing that any premium on the share price would enhance the value of their share options. As such, in his capacity as chairman, Sir Nigel Rudd excluded the executive directors from the deliberations regarding the offer. Pessina, in acknowledgment of his specific conflict of interest, also stepped down from his active roles in the firm. On March 12th Rudd called an emergency board meeting with the non-executive directors. Rudd and the six non-executive directors voted to reject the offer.[6] The decision was taken not because they were averse to a buyout but because they felt that the indicative offer undervalued the firm. This is a typical first response to an LBO – particularly an MBO. The incumbent management team are almost inevitably aware that the PEF firm perceives a potential acquisition as one with unrealised 'value'.

There were various possible ways in which the indicative offer might be thought to undervalue the firm. Two of the more immediate ones were not directly about any capacity of PEF to improve the business 'organically'. First, the non-executive directors may have been mindful of Pessina's role. As an insider with specific responsibilities for restructuring and expansion, Pessina may not only have been disaffected by the possibilities for the pace of change in a publicly listed company but also intimately aware of the prospects for gearing that a buyout might exploit. For example, the firm had already sold and leased back 312 of its stores as part of the original merger and restructuring process. Boots operated 3,000 retail stores. Its land assets were considerable. Second, given Pessina's interest in the expansion of the firm, he might also have specific knowledge of possible mergers that could occur soon after the buyout. Mergers, as with buyouts, are almost always associated with additional premiums paid on the existing value of a firm. This possibility created the prospect of an immediate cash-in for Pessina and the new owners. Furthermore, any mergers might also create further market dominance for Alliance Boots in particular markets that would work in conjunction with the deals with Pfizer and AstraZeneca. Any growth in market dominance would reduce the competitive pressures that the City currently saw as problematic. This would greatly enhance the potential revenues of the firm and also make it a more attractive future IPO.

On March 30th KKR and Pessina put a new indicative offer of £10.40 per share to the board. This valued the firm at around £10 billion. The new indicative offer was accepted and a period of due diligence was agreed. However, the process was then complicated by the intervention of a counter-bid. The counter-bid came from Terra Firma in conjunction with Wellcome Trust, Britain's largest charity. Terra Firma offered £10.85 per share. On April 14th the Terra Firma bid was also agreed for due diligence. Rudd then informed KKR and Pessina that they had until April 20th to produce a firm bid. On that date they offered £10.90. Terra Firma then offered £11.15 and then £11.26. Finally on April 24th KKR and Pessina raised their offer to £11.39 per share, valuing Alliance Boots' market capitalisation at just over £11 billion. At the same time KKR and Pessina moved to block any further counter-bid by buying up just over 25% of Alliance Boots shares. The capital used to buy the shares derived from an initial £1 billion loan facility provided by the investment banks backing the bid. Ordinary shares carry voting rights. A 25% stake creates an effective veto for any counter-bid. As a result, Terra Firma withdrew form the bidding process and the board of Alliance Boots voted to accept the KKR offer and recommend it to shareholders.

Section 425 of the Companies Act 1985 requires that the takeover then produce a scheme of arrangement document. This provides information on the proposed takeover that shareholders can use in considering their vote and also provides a source for the mandatory court hearing that then considers the vote and approves the delisting of the company. A scheme of arrangement document was published on May 9th and a target date for the scheme to become effective was set for June 26th, with delisting to take effect on June 28th.[7] On May 31st a proxy vote approved the deal by a majority of 93.6% and Alliance Boots duly became the first FTSE 100 company to be bought out by private equity.

Concentrated equity and entitlement

In conformity with private equity practice, a new management company through which the new owners would work was created – AB Acquisitions Limited. The scheme of arrangement also set out an initial financial structure for the deal (AB Acquisitions 2007: 90–2).[8] At the agreed price of £11.39 per share, purchasing the market capitalisation of Alliance Boots would cost £11.1 billion. The deal also took on the current debt of Alliance Boots and allowed for an additional capital flow for operations. The total capital required for the deal was around £13 billion. Of this approximately £9.3 billion was structured as debt – £8.2 billion in borrowings (a 'term facility') and £820 million as a revolving credit facility. This £9.3 billion in debt was provided by a consortium of the Bank of America, Barclays, Unicredit, Citigroup, Deutsche Bank, Merrill Lynch, and Royal Bank of Scotland. The total equity committed in the buyout was set at £3.43 billion. Of this KKR managed funds[9] and Pessina each provided £1.02 billion, with a further £1.39 billion coming from minority investors. Pessina's equity investment was funded by rolling over some of the stock he already held in Alliance Boots. Initially the minority investors were the main debt-providing banks. This kind of involvement has become a more common practice in investment banking in the twenty first century. It enables the banks to profit directly from an equity stake but also facilitates larger buyouts by adding further equity that the banks intend to later syndicate, typically to hedge funds.

The first thing to notice about the new financial structure is that the KKR funds and Pessina have provided less than 10% of the total finance for the buyout but each owns approximately 30% of the equity. Because each owns around 30% of the equity they have a call on 30% of the returns from the acquisition. As I set out in Chapter 5, this is a call on a whole variety of sources of returns: special dividends, ordinary returns based on profits, and the returns from any subsequent resale of Alliance Boots. They thus have a one third call on an £11 billion plus asset based on a stake of around £1 billion each. Furthermore, since minority investors are not given voting rights, effectively KKR and Pessina each control 50% of the company, with just 30% of the equity and less than 10% of the total finance. This voting control, furthermore, is not diluted if Pessina and KKR choose to syndicate some of their equity stake to new minority investors.[10] Not only has equity been concentrated through gearing, but power has also been redistributed and concentrated in fewer hands. This, of course is precisely what PEF claims to do, although the claim is couched in terms of the incentive realignment argument. In Chapter 6, I discussed the issue of human nature and the idea of incentive realignment as an argument based on marginal returns. I made the point that what actually occurs is that a large share of the returns from an organisation are captured through the concentration of equity and that this is not directly about margins but rather about absolute control of proportions of returns. This is made possible by the creative use of debt. Debt is not simply an argument for 'discipline' but is rather about the opportunity to capture control and what that represents. The case of Alliance Boots clearly illustrates this.

For KKR the buyout also represents a stage in justifying annual management fees to its funds. KKR's input of £1.02 billion represents a significant fraction of the main fund used: its $5 billion Guernsey-based KKR Private Equity fund. Capital was also used from their Europe, Quoted, and Asia funds. As I set out in Chapter 5, at a typical 2% per annum the management fee for a mega fund of £5 billion would be £100 million per year whilst at the extreme lower end rate of 0.25% it would still constitute £12.5 million per year. The minority investors' committed capital of £1.39 billion was also subject to a management fee. This was reported to be between 0.5% and 0.7% of invested funds (Pagnamenta 2007). Furthermore, the creation of the holding company AB acquisitions also creates the opportunity for an additional fee structure applied to the acquisition.

For Pessina the buyout also represents the opportunity to make additional immediate gains from his role in the LBO because it was an MBO. The final price of £11.39 per share was over £3 higher than the market quoted share price at the time the initial buyout interest was made known and £1.39 per share higher than the first indicative offer. KKR and Pessina paid over 30%

more for the shares than the original market level and almost 14% higher than their first indicative offer. Pessina was a significant shareholder in Alliance Boots. The higher the premium paid then the greater the value of Pessina's original 15% stake. The final price valued his 15% stake at around £1.7 billion. Pessina put £1.02 billion into the new company. He, therefore, realised over £500 million in immediate returns and still ended up with a greater voting control of 50% and a larger claim on returns of the new company at 30%.

What these points indicate is that a buyout is in essence an extraordinary technical exercise in creating power and accessing and controlling wealth. In Chapter 7, I raised the question: whether the general partner(s) have done anything to create the entitlement to this scale of return?[11] In some respects this seems like a simple empirical question of what they do once ownership is established. But as I also set out in Chapters 5, 6 and 7, returns to investors are not reliant in any simple way on an unambiguous improvement in the performance of the acquisition. In any case, entitlement is more than an empirical issue. It is an issue of whether the right should exist to capture absolute control of the returns to a business organisation – particularly a publicly listed company – in this way.

Entitlement as moral philosophy

Entitlement is a complex area of moral philosophy. It is in the first instance a matter of what is termed 'distributive' justice. Distributive justice refers to how we understand the right to own and dispose of the goods or products of forms of activity within society. Economic goods or products are a prime form of these goods or products. In Chapter 7, in discussing the issue of tax I noted that applying a deontological principle to PEF was not solely an issue of the kind of fundamentals discussed by the moral philosophers Nozick and Rawls. However, the idea that no right should be deemed to exist to prevent the kind of capture of absolute control undertaken by PEF is strongly redolent of Nozick's position on distributive justice. In *Anarchy, State, and Utopia* (1974), Nozick argues that the state does not have the right to intervene to impede the distribution of economic goods. The state exists solely to regulate and expedite the individual transfer of goods. Theft, fraud, slavery etc. are unjust and should be prevented through law. However, thereafter, what is economically just is merely a matter of the individual's decisions. Owning or holding some form of economic good is legitimate. As such, that holding is just in so far as the holding was not obtained through theft, fraud etc. Transferring some form of economic good is legitimate in so far as the individuals offering the good held it legitimately. The distribution of goods is an outcome of these individual holdings and transfers and is, therefore, not a matter for the state. The state cannot justify intervention to prevent particular distributions without violating these individually just situations.

It is important to note that for Nozick these ideas of holding and transfer and their implications are not self-serving, ahistorical, and absurdly abstract. Rather, he argues, any attempt to intervene and upset the way holdings and transfers occur is itself ahistorical and liable to violate his minimal concept of justice. For Nozick, holdings and transfers are a minimal approach to what actually happens and has happened. They do not require us to impose one standard on everyone from one point of view by intervening in what is already manifested as just on the basis of actually occurring distributions. The imposing of a standard is actually a defect of other theories that try to intervene to prevent some transfers and holdings and thus affect distributions. It is first and foremost a defect because it seeks to create a pattern and creating the pattern produces numerous restrictions on the individual. Fundamentally the pattern restricts the right to choose. This will ultimately be oppressive because it is unlikely that the sum of individual choices would ever voluntarily reproduce the pattern that is to be imposed. Moreover, the conceptualisations and justifications that serve to create the pattern (how we should think about justice and the right to dispose of holdings and transfers) inevitably simplify the real complexity of actual individual motives in any action. This tends to produce contradictions in the way that a pattern is argued: socialism valorises loving family relations and seeks to generalise them to society but seeks to restrict the right of the individual to inherit and bequeath. As a matter of consistency Nozick does not think the state has a right to be concerned with whether individuals deserve their holdings. As a result, his argument doesn't turn on whether in fact the outcomes are also beneficial since this would also be an arbitrary principle trying to create a pattern the existence of which would likely be oppressive. He is, however, in keeping with Hayek, the influential Austrian economist and political philosopher, convinced that the outcomes tend to be beneficial within a capitalist society because individuals usually choose to act in ways which benefit themselves and others. His ideas on holdings and transfers are thus argued in conformity with a minimal state and maximally free markets.

If one were thinking critically about Nozick's position the first thing to note is that it is not strictly a moral claim about what is economically just. It is about affirming individual rights in a way that does not presume but does hope that the everyday activity of those individuals has collectively beneficial economic outcomes. As such it is rather a claim about minimising economic injustice for the individual in their holdings and transfers, based on a particular definition of the individual's relation to what *is* individually just. The individual and not the economic is the lever of the argument for justice. The distribution is after the fact. It is a defensive argument that claims the right to choose freely should not be violated. The claim is also that intervention is liable to be oppressive *because* it violates individual rights.

There are two initial counterarguments here. First, as I noted in analysing Jensen's work in Chapter 7, intervention need not be thought of as absolute. It need not be thought of as affecting all aspects of a person's rights in a given domain, like holdings and transfers. It need not be thought of as a rigid for all time imposition. Regulation need not take these forms. It can be, however, applied as a constraint on a particular activity and thus create a specific proscription. This raises the second counterargument: there is no reason why one should think that particular instances of the individual opportunity to act should be allowed on the basis that preventing them violates a general concept of that individual's rights.[12] It might well be in a certain sense 'oppressive' to prevent individuals engaging in certain acts, if oppressive merely means they are prevented from doing what they desire. But this does not mean that as a society we should be committed to allowing those acts. It does not mean that society should value the cumulative 'history' of free individual acts merely because they are historical and fit with an idea of a minimal concept of what is individually just.

It would be a curious notion of oppression if one were to argue that it is oppressive that the very rich have been prevented from using wealth to capture access to even more wealth. No proponent of PEF would be likely to make the argument in quite this way, anymore than they would be likely to make the argument regarding tax that it is unfair that they be taxed the same as everyone else. Rather the argument would have a certain discursive camouflage. It would likely follow two avenues: there should be no right to prevent the right to any given freely undertaken transfer and holding; the new ownership also results in net benefits (returns to investors, including pension funds, employment, economic growth, tax revenues etc.). The latter set of claims, as we have already discussed, are ambiguous and in any case, raise the issue of whether any gains could not have been achieved without PEF. This in itself raises the issue of entitlement. The former point is simply an evasive way of stating Nozick's fuller argument, which is essentially about individual rights and implicitly hinges on the idea that the violation of the individual right is oppression, which is already a problematic use of the term oppression. It also assumes that we all have the actual right to do what some have done. This is not the case. All individuals have the potential to be PEF participants if they had the specific characteristics required. But they simply do not and cannot. The individual right is thus a specific right of some individuals, in so far as it is a right. We are not all wealthy management executives and we are not all administrators of large pools of private equity who also have access to vast pools of debt. One can then reasonably ask why controlling the specific opportunity of some to act in a particular way should be considered 'bad' ('oppressive') in the sense of unjust. It can only be so as a matter of general moral principles if there is in fact a universal human right to property and a further claim that this individual right supersedes that of all other individual concerns and all collective concerns and principles.

The fulcrum of the argument for entitlement as a subject for moral philosophy is, therefore, one of the individual right to property. It is in essence, the concept that property rights are a universal inviolable human right. This argument derives from Locke in his *Second Treatise of Government* (1690; Macpherson 1980). It is in many respects a curious argument. In keeping with his time Locke argues that God gave the earth to mankind in common. However, each individual has a duty to God to preserve his life because that life ultimately belongs to God. Each individual thus has a natural right to life. Since life must be preserved Locke held that each individual also had a natural right to property. Initially property is no more or less than that land and its fruits that the individual has laboured upon and thus legitimately appropriated to preserve himself. In a simple agrarian situation property rights only extend to that which can be farmed and that which cannot be spoiled if retained. However, individuals, still in a state of nature, rather than a complex form of government based on a social contract, invent money. Money becomes an imperishable store of value. Individuals can now appropriate more property than they can individually work or use the product of. Since all individuals use money they have tacitly consented to this. Since wages are in effect the selling of labour that labour and its product becomes the property of the one who pays the wages (labour by proxy). There is, therefore, no limit to the natural right to property based on natural law. For Locke, civil society and a social contract then come into being after the unequal distribution of property and precisely to protect the unequal distribution of property that has developed out of a natural right to that property.

There are, as various moral philosophers have argued, numerous flaws in this argument (Wolff 2006). If one reads it as history it is a curiously unhistorical history – but then so is Nozick's general argument in *Anarchy, State, and Utopia*, despite its claims about history.[13] Once one dispenses with the theocratic element in the argument, as most modern philosophers would, then there is the problem of how one derives a universal right to own. The basis of ownership is appropriation. The basis of appropriation is opportunity. The idea of entitlement based on legitimacy and the individual's conformity with a minimum kind of law that prohibits theft is a focus on certain kinds of individuals and on one side of an artificial idea of pre-social rights that only then exist and operate within societies. It focuses on the equal and inviolable right to use every opportunity to appropriate and amass highly unequal proportions of social goods and products (wealth). But one could as easily argue that all have equal and inviolable pre-social rights to collectively decide to restrict the opportunity to appropriate and amass highly unequal proportions of social goods and products within society. Locke's argument could easily be reconstructed to do this based on a different idea of preservation (collective) and legitimacy (what it means to accept wages). This 'universal' human right would be no less synthetic but it would look quite different. Locke's argument is, as Marx and others have pointed out (Marx 2000; Pike 1999) a defence of the 'rights' of some not all and as such it is a defence of a particular social arrangement that fosters those rights. It is in reality neither universal nor genuinely pre-social in its origins of rights.

We may want to give people the right to property under certain conditions within society but this is a very different idea with very different implications than those that flow from a basic human right to property. The latter creates a justification for why giving and withdrawing rights is not a function of the state and of society. Here I would emphasise that though the line of argument that has got us to this point may have seemed rather abstract it is actually extremely important in considering the theoretical underpinnings and implicit assumptions of PEF. PEF is not just based on empirical claims regarding its benefits. The right to engage in it requires particular views regarding the nature of society and economy: the minimal state, the primacy of markets and the absolute right to property and its disposition. Entitlement is first and foremost rooted in these. What the example of Alliance Boots illustrates is that great gains can be made by individuals based on their access to already existing wealth and based on the use of debt.

The primary moral question for the reader, then, is ultimately: is this just? The subsidiary question is: should it be allowed? More accurately, should it be allowed at increasing scales where the rights to the returns that are captured are larger and where they are larger because those returns are derived from larger companies, particularly publicly listed companies? Once the idea of the minimal state, the primacy of markets and the absolute right to property become rooted these questions are undermined, evaded or ideologically overshadowed. It is, therefore, important to have established the significance of the primary moral question. Doing so introduces the possibility of thinking of PEF as part of an economic distribution that is also a social misalignment. It favours the few – even if it has disputed and contingent benefits for others.

Leverage and debt vulnerability

One of the key aspects of the contingency of the benefits of PEF that I have discussed in several different contexts is the role of debt. As the absolute level of debt rises and leverage levels also increase the vulnerability represented by debt structures also rises. That vulnerability has two dynamics. First, debt expands as liquidity expands. As such, PEF contributes to the change in the conditions under which it accesses debt. It is part of the development of unstable liquidity. It can in this sense be seen as a claimed solution to problems it helps to create. Second, and relatedly, as liquidity expands, leverage tends to increase in each individual deal and LBO deals become larger, paying higher premiums for bigger companies, including, as scales rise, publicly listed companies. More complex debt structures with higher levels of leverage create more vulnerable firms. They are more vulnerable because servicing debt becomes more difficult as liquidity conditions change. Debt servicing costs can rise at the same time as a firm's revenues can fall. Alliance Boots clearly illustrates the rise in leverage and debt levels as LBOs of larger firms in liquid markets occur.

The scheme of arrangement for the proposed buyout of Alliance Boots sets out the initial basis of the debt structure: approximately £9.3 billion was borrowed from the bank consortia. This is specifically referred to in the scheme as an interim facility. It is an interim facility because the intention was that the £8.2 billion term loan would be repackaged and syndicated as senior and junior debt along the kind of lines set out in Chapter 5. The interim facility itself had initial lending conditions: it was offered at 2.99% above LIBOR plus any additional costs incurred by the lenders (AB Acquisitions 2007: 91). If we simplify and take LIBOR at approximately 5% in June 2007 then the £8.2 billion main loan creates an initial interest rate of approximately 8%. At 8% the initial debt servicing obligation would then be £656 million once the full sum had been drawn down. The reported preliminary annual operating profits of Alliance Boots for 2006–07 were £641 million (Ebidta).[14] This was based on an annual revenue of £14.6 billion. Earnings had risen 7% on the previous year, partly due to cost savings made by Pessina in his role as the main executive responsible for integrating Alliance Unichem and Boots after the 2006 merger. If one generously assumes a similar growth in earnings for the following year of 7% then the following year's earnings would be around £700 million. Even so, debt servicing would essentially eat up the whole of current earnings – in 2008 this would likely be a problem compounded by a high and unstable LIBOR that had, because of the credit crunch, decoupled from central bank base rates. That is, unless syndication resulted in much improved terms of borrowing. The Alliance Boots interim facility was agreed just before the credit crunch took hold. Full syndication subsequently proved impossible in 2007. Furthermore, the terms of proposed syndications by the banks were not a significant improvement on the initial provision of debt and would be unlikely to be so in the near future. A junior debt syndication, for example, was initially offered at 4% over LIBOR, and then at 4.25%. The indications as 2007 unfolded were that syndication would require higher rates above LIBOR for all levels of the debt. This was also partly because the original terms of the debt were covenant-lite, making syndication less attractive to investors in the new credit environment.

This problem of syndication did not of course affect the buyout itself. Syndication is more of an immediate problem for the investment banks who are forced to discount the debt in order to try to pass it on. However, the debt is still a problem for the buyout because of its characteristics. In the case of Alliance Boots, assuming no immediate radical change in asset holdings or Ebitda measures then the ratio of debt to earnings would likely be over 12 after the buyout and could easily rise to 15. If one looks at the total level of debt at £9.3 billion as a proportion of the value of the original deal at around £13 billion then one derives a leverage level of approximately 70%. On all measures, then, the Alliance Boots deal was highly leveraged and created an initial debt structure that could be interpreted as vulnerable to precisely the kind of conditions that then began to unfold in late 2007 and that I set out in Chapter 4. Standard & Poor's cut Alliance Boot's long term credit rating from BBB to BB- within two weeks of the buyout because of the change in its financial structure.

It is also worth considering that initially liquid markets foster more vulnerable debt structures in a variety of ways. Higher leverage is possible because banks will lend more. At the same time, larger PEF funds, club deals and/or the use of several funds, and the use of minority investors create the capacity to pay more for a given acquisition. Competitive bidding between PEF firms and also with new entrants like hedge funds, adds to this situation. Premiums paid, therefore, rise and do so for companies of larger market capitalisation because equity markets are also generally rising at a time of growing liquidity. This combination has definite effects on debt and the concentration of equity that then affects possible future decisions about debt.

The premium paid for Alliance Boots was over 30% more than the initial level of the shares and 14% higher than the first indicative offer. This partly reflects how market share prices of a firm undergoing a bidding process tend to rise. Equity investors anticipate premiums and thus buy shares hoping to cash in. The net effect is that the p/e ratio at the time of the buyout rises. At the end of June 2007 Alliance Boots had a p/e ratio of around 24. A rising market capitalisation and p/e ratio has an effect on gearing and the concentration of equity that I set out in Chapter 5. All other things being equal it takes more debt to reduce the p/e ratio to the most desirable level i.e. on or around the time line for returning the committed equity (2–7 years, typically 4). Attempting to achieve the desired level, therefore, requires more leverage in liquid markets. This is another reason why leverage grows at times of liquidity and why PEF firms have motives to exploit all available liquidity. However, though there is a tendency to proportionately larger debt structures for buyouts as part of gearing it is still difficult to achieve the most desirable p/e ratios because of the scales of the acquisition and the original p/e ratio. This is because as more debt is applied to achieve lower p/e ratios and concentrate equity, debt servicing costs also increase eating into earnings. For example, if one looks at Alliance Boots the equity committed was £3.43 billion. If we assume the Ebitda based profit level will be £700 million based on 7% growth then the p/e ratio will be 4.9. But this is based on Ebitda. Debt servicing alone is liable to consume most of the initial earnings of the acquisition. As such the p/e ratio based on net profits is liable to be far higher. Higher even than the longer seven year time frame that KKR claims is typical for its investments, compared to the industry average.

This is important because it implies that alternative sources of return become more important. There is more of a temptation to engage in asset sales and there is more of a temptation to cut other costs since debt servicing costs cannot be cut (especially as the liquidity of debt markets declines). There is more of a need to ensure strong revenue growth. But the degree to which such revenue growth can generate sufficient returns to equity investors is hampered and this is expressed precisely by the way the p/e ratio has been affected. It is unlikely that revenue growth alone can push up earnings from the low post-debt servicing level in order to generate high returns to investors in a short time line. Surpassing the hurdle and achieving carried interest thus becomes more difficult for the PEF firm. As such (particularly if it seems likely that recession will affect equity markets and resale values), special dividends also become more of a temptation. This again has implications for the long term stability of the acquisition. It can result in a cycle of upfront extractions of capital from the acquisition and/or more refinancing creating more debt servicing obligations. Whether this will be the case for Alliance Boots only time will tell. It was reported in December 2007 that on August 6th 2007 Alliance Boots paid £1 billion into AB Acquisitions and on August 20th it paid a further £550 million (Smiddy 2007). This was reported in the financial press as a dividend but KKR stressed that it was not a payment to the owners but rather an inter-company movement of cash. What its ultimate purpose was remained ambiguous. What one can say here is that debt and vulnerability are clearly dynamically related. In this sense Alliance Boots illustrates the way that PEF does not conform to Jensen's general vision of something that responds to historical dynamics but is not itself shaped by them. Not only does this create another impetus to think about entitlement, if one views the process of a buyout as an instance of treating an acquisition as a financial instrument, but it also raises the immediate question: why was the buyout approved? This is an issue of the decision making process within a publicly listed company. It is a matter of governance.[15]

The issue of governance

In mid-2007 Alliance Boots had 82,000 small investors in its equity. Small investors are essentially powerless until the time a vote is taken to approve the buyout. When each does finally vote, it is a private act where each is thinking that the others will in any case act in terms of immediate self-interest and cash in. Thus, even if they had any reservations they may also have good reasons for thinking that a no vote was futile. The large institutional investors, such as Legal and General, notably did not place public pressure on the board to reject any bid. Other investors play a more speculative role in the financial system – some longer term some shorter term. Speculative investment exists precisely to spot and exploit circumstances such as a buyout. One of the longer term speculative investments in Alliance Boots was made by American fund investors Templeton Investment Counsel, who in March 2007 held 66.5 million shares in Alliance Boots, constituting a 7% stake built up over two years and including large buys in January/February 2007. The shares were bought at an average price of less than £7.40 at a total cost of around £500 million. On April 24th as KKR looked to build a 25% stake to stave off the Terra Firma bid Templeton cashed in 60 million shares at £11.39, realising over £680 million. If one factors in their remaining 6.5 million shares realised at the completion of the buyout that figure rises to around £750 million – a return of over £250 million. More short term investments were made by a series of hedge funds in March and early April of 2007 as the bidding war broke out between KKR and Terra Firma. Hedge funds often hold speculative investment assets for as little as a few hours and rarely for more than a few days.

Shareholders voted overwhelmingly in favour of the buyout. Buyouts as with merger activity generally create unusual circumstances for holders of public equity. Buyouts pay premiums on share prices, bidding wars and the rejection of initial indicative offers further push up prices. This creates a strong incentive for shareholders to cash in at what seems the top end of the market. Each shareholder is thinking individually on the basis of the unusual circumstances created by the buyout bid. In a sense all shareholders interests are aligned in terms of a focus on a gambler's scenario of under or over valued stock prices that are in turn framed by a new time horizon for holding the stock created by the bid and defined by the duration that the bid holds good. Under ordinary circumstances different shareholders will be holding stock for different reasons and for different durations creating a more complex governance relationship, which in market forces terms would help to perpetuate the long term viability of the firm as a kind of emergent property.[16] Whatever one thinks of the general robustness of this market based approach to governance the point is that it is substantially weakened by the intervention of a buyout bid. Moreover, this is particularly so the more the offer seems to be overpricing the asset and this tends to be precisely where more leverage is created and more caution concerning the viability of a buyout is warranted.

The existence of this relation throws the issue back on the role of the board of directors. One need not impugn the probity of the board in order to see that there is also a problematic relation here. The board is subject to a dynamic tension. On the one hand, it must assume a sale is imminent and thus take the role of chief bargainer. Here it must consider whether any bid is actually good value for shareholders. On the other hand, it must consider whether the business plan provided in conjunction with the bid ensures the continued viability of the firm. The problem is that these two bases for recommendation are not necessarily compatible. Pushing for higher premiums on current share prices may be good value for shareholders but it can be detrimental to the business when that additional premium is provided through a debt structure.

The board, of course cannot ignore the existence of a debt structure and its implications. But at the same time they are aware that even the most detailed business plan concerning how debt will be serviced through restructuring the business and growing sales etc. is merely a contingency because the future is not yet written. In the case of an MBI this may mean that the Board focuses more on what it can tangibly determine – higher share premiums etc. This is especially so if there is a sense that a buyout is likely to be vigorously pursued in any case – if a share block and voting rights are already being accumulated by the pursuer, if a hostile bid could be made, and if there is a background sense that shareholders (perhaps indicated by canvassing major institutional investors or looking at the structure of more speculative investment holdings) will approve. In the case of an MBO, these issues of testing the psychology of the market are also enfolded in a personal relation and knowledge of some of the bidding participants, who in turn have intimate experience of the business. On the one hand, this invites trust – they are committing their own capital and know what they are doing. On the other, it invites scepticism – the basis of knowing what they are doing and the confidence to invest their own capital is an awareness of hidden value in the firm and/or the opportunities represented by gearing. Again, depending on how these matters are evaluated – some of which can only be intuition, despite that the formal bid to the board and the scheme document and court hearing to approve delisting must be rigorous and clear – the board will again find themselves thrown back on the issue of guaranteeing value to shareholders. But it will often be thrown back on this issue in terms of a more convivial relation with the bidders because they are known.

From the point of view of following a clear procedure intended to militate against a perception of partiality, the Chairman of Alliance Boots, Sir Nigel Rudd clearly dealt with the bid in an appropriate manner. Pessina stood down from his active roles and executive directors did not participate in the initial voting concerning the indicative offers. At the same time, since the approach was an MBO, relations appeared to have been cooperative rather than obstructive. KKR and Pessina, for example, wanted to appoint Richard Girling, a Merrill Lynch pharmaceuticals banker as an advisor on the deal creating a possible conflict of interest since Merrill Lynch was also Alliance Boots' broker. Permission for the appointment was sought from and granted by Alliance Boots. Within 48 hours of the board voting to recommend the April 24th offer Pessina, accompanied by Dominic Murphy of KKR, attended a boardroom meeting to discuss the implications of the offer and assure the directors of the basis of the business plan. The basis of the recommendation seems to have been a combination of trust that Pessina was in fact committed to growing the business and if he was right in his underlying convictions regarding health-related markets in Europe and Asia, then public markets were undervaluing the firm in the long term. As such, the final approval came on the basis of a higher premium both related to this 'undervaluing' as well as because of the intervention of Terra Firma. The board seems to have then focussed ultimately on value to shareholders reflected in the bid. This, as I suggested in Chapter 6 has become the core measure of business organisations in the modern world of financial liberalisation. Many different accounts of 'financialisation' have focused on this (Eerturk *et al.* 2008).

A final aspect of the buyout is that directors also gain. Gains are based on some combination of contracted golden handshakes/parachutes, share options that can be redeemed in the buyout, and new incentive packages for those who are retained in the MBO. Richard Baker, Boots chief executive (CEO) and Scott Wheway, health and beauty retail director, for example, were the only surviving board members from the original Boots plc prior to the Unichem merger. Neither they nor Sir Nigel Rudd continued into the new ten person management team that led the post-buyout company.[17] Baker, having declined a new CEO role, received £6.5 million in accumulated share options from the buyout as well as a year's salary and bonus, amounting to around £10 million. Wheway, received £1.2 million in accumulated share options.

Market based governance, then, does not seem to be conducive to preventing a buyout. Where a buyout is resisted it is usually based on unusual circumstances relating to the large equity holdings of significant investors and board members. In 2007, the supermarket chain Sainsbury's, for example, was the target of a failed buyout in a proposed club deal between CVC, TPG, Blackstone and Goldman Sachs. The bid was eventually blocked by the main shareholders. The main shareholders were members of the original owning family, holding 18% of the equity. In the context of corporate governance of large publicly listed companies the block was therefore unusual because the firm had been a family concern. Even here it was only John Sainsbury who rejected the offer on principle. David Sainsbury thought, rather, that the final offer undervalued the firm. In the more anonymous world of most large publicly listed corporations governance will not reject an offer because of the broader implications of a private equity buyout. But it is the broader implications which are why PEF can be questioned.

In the specific case of the Sainsbury's buyout it is worth noting that the firm was by no means a failing or underperforming company – it had recently appointed a new CEO, Justin King and reported 5% growth in the last quarter of 2006. It was, however, a prime target for buyout because its property assets were valued at a substantial proportion of its market capitalisation. When the club deal's interest was made public on 2nd of February 2007, Sainsbury's stock was trading at just over £5 per share and its market capitalisation was around £7.7 billion. According to a report by the property analysts Numis, Sainsbury's 2006 accounts substantially undervalued its property assets at £5.5 billion. At the beginning of 2006 Sainsbury had raised £1.75 billion through commercially backed mortgage securities, which required an independent assessment of the value of property assets and valued half of Sainsbury's property portfolio at £3.55 billion. Numis doubled this figure and factored in property price rises over the year to calculate that the total value of Sainsbury's portfolio was around £7.5 billion. This meant that, even though the announcement of the club deal's interest pushed up the price of Sainsbury's stock to over £5.30 and shareholders could expect the buyout to pay a premium on top of this – pushing the overall value of Sainsbury beyond £9 billion and its buyout value to around £10 billion – it remained an attractive proposition for private equity. This was because the sale and lease back of property could provide a substantial proportion of the capital required to concentrate the equity. In turn this would mean that there was greater scope for additional debt loading to, for example, pay dividends.

Since market based governance is not an effective constraint except under unusual circumstances the issue is again raised of whether intervention is desirable. This in effect is also a moral philosophy question because it is about the right of the state to intervene in the disposition of property and thus cuts across the idea of individual property rights (to transfer freely), the minimal state, and maximally free markets. Outside of philosophy this kind of interventionist argument has become anathema because of the current dominance of ideas about competition. But there are three responses one can make here. First, there is the argument that competition *per se* is neither a good nor a bad. There are no absolute arguments for the primacy or desirability of competition as such because there are different types and contexts of competition. The problem is that we are invited to think of it as a general phenomenon of the human condition and we are invited to think of it as an extension of liberty (Wolff 1998, 1999). Competition can be a benefit to some and harm to others. It is both liberating and illiberating and sometimes both together (Mill, 1974). Therefore we should not think of competition as an expression of liberty. The issue is which types of competition does society consider worth facilitating?

Second at the heart of economic competition is the relation that winners by winning restrict the capacity of others to compete. As such winning skews competition and increasingly makes it unfree. Winners are the most strident in their claims about the need to preserve free competition at the same time as their very existence and practices restrict others from engaging in such competition. Free competition is not about a level playing field it, like the idea of universal property rights, is about the universal unreal right for all to do what only the few actually have done and can do and where what the few have done actually restricts the capacity of others to do the same.

Third, winners are not in actual fact committed in practice to even this unfree competition, only to winning. When circumstances require it they are quite open to advantageous forms of intervention. The role of the investment banks in the credit crunch illustrates this. They have been happy to receive low interest rate funds from the central banks and to press for lower interest rates and swaps of their CDOs but are less inclined to accept greater regulation because of the failures that led to the need for these advantageous interventions. This kind of relation to competition is general across market participation. The debates regarding PEF and the taxation of carried interest in 2007 and the pressure applied to gain the original memorandum of understanding in 2003 illustrate this. It may also be worth noting that Patricia Hewitt, the former health secretary was reported in February 2008 to have accepted a consultancy worth £45,000 per year with Alliance Boots (Ungoed-Thomas *et al.* 2008). The point is that intervention is encouraged and sought on an interest basis. If this is so for the few that dominate markets then why not for the many that are subordinate to market effects?

Entitlement and the public interest: the broader implications of a buyout

Alliance Boots seems to be a prime example of holdings and transfers that are effectively enabled by free markets but not constrained by debt vulnerability. Market based corporate governance allowed the buyout to occur. Here one might argue that the aggregation of many individual choices need not result in a collectively desirable outcome. This does not mean that there have been no beneficiaries. Clearly there have. Shareholders did realise 'value' through premiums paid, directors did realise gains through payments, Pessina and KKR have achieved control of an £11 billion asset based on gearing and including a number of specific immediate gains and future potentials. An important question is, however: whether this idea of 'value' is one that society should value? Is it one that society should use as a justification for a PEF LBO? One way we have already thought about this is in terms of the general effects of PEF as part of unstable liquidity.[18] Another, more specific way to think about it is to look at the public interest issues created by any given buyout.

A buyout of a large publicly listed company raises numerous public interest issues. In the case of Alliance Boots several specific ones arise. Alliance Boots is a major supplier to the NHS. The collapse of Alliance Boots would create huge problems in the supply of prescription medications. This is a problem of dependency on a private equity acquisition that is subject to debt vulnerability.[19] However, should Alliance Boots prosper then the basis of that prosperity may also be problematic. Boots seeks to profit from simplified supply chains and economies of scale. At the same time it faces sharp debt servicing restrictions on its approach to costs including service provision.

It, therefore, has a combination of characteristics that may affect its future relation with the NHS: growing market concentration and monopoly power but also cost cutting pressures. A poorer delivery service to the NHS and higher prices could easily emerge from this.[20] It is for these reasons that the European Commission and, in the context of the UK, the Office of Fair Trading (OFT) carefully scrutinised the buyout and the implications of the straight to pharmacy model (OFT 2007).[21]

Perhaps the most easily illustrated and generalisable public interest issue raised by the buyout is that of the long term security of private pension provision. UK pension provision by the state is not and never has been intended to be a standalone living income (Morgan 2006b). Private pensions schemes focused around work, where the employer and employee jointly contribute, have traditionally been viewed as the primary source of pension provision. However, in the context of a buyout the maintenance of a pension scheme becomes a problematic issue. This has four dynamics. First, the existence of the debt structure creates long term concerns over the ability of the acquisition to fund its current pension obligations. Second, the existence of the buyout provides an additional impetus to change the nature of pension provision: exacerbating current trends in private pension provision. Third, any failure of an acquisition or failure of the acquisition to be able to fulfil its obligations immediately creates a compensation issue for the state. Fourth, the decline in the terms of private pension provision, to which PEF can contribute, is effectively a shifting of the responsibility for pension provision to the individual and to the state.

Alliance Boots clearly illustrates the first of these four dynamics and is indicative of the significance of the other three. In mid-2007 the Alliance Boots pension scheme had 67,000 members and assets of £3.5 billion. As with many pension schemes in the UK the Alliance Boots scheme was already facing issues of financial uncertainty. The accountancy standard IAS 19, based on current liabilities and assets, placed the scheme slightly in surplus at £20 million. This was a relatively healthy position by contemporary scheme standards. However, an actuarial assessment based on increases in life expectancies placed the scheme in a deficit of £305 million. Furthermore, closing the scheme entirely and buying pensions for its members would cost £4.5 billion (against assets of £3.5 billion).[22] This would become a reality should Alliance Boots go out of business or be unable to meet its future pension commitments because of solvency problems. From the pension scheme trustees' point of view, greater leverage created by a buyout increases the likelihood of this. Trustees can, in principle, be held personally liable if they do not take steps to prevent scheme insolvency on the basis of what can be reasonably known. Accordingly, to guarantee the security of the scheme the trustees made known their concerns on May 3rd 2007 and asked for a capital injection of £1 billion to the scheme in the event of a successful buyout. This would create a capital safety net in the form of a £400 million upfront payment and a guarantee of a series of further lump sum payments. AB Acquisitions responded with an initial offer of £50 million upfront and further annual payments of £10 to £20 million.

The problem for the trustees was that they had no direct power to stop the buyout going ahead on the basis of any inadequacy in pension provision. The pension scheme is a separate entity and there is no legal requirement for the buyers to come to agreement with the pension scheme. Technically, the Pensions Regulator, as the relevant government body, has the power to compel AB Acquisitions to close any deficit, once they become the owners. But the Regulator rarely takes this kind of action and has also been reluctant to intervene in disputes as ownership is considered. In this context the trustees tried to apply public pressure to the buyers in the awareness that Alliance Boots was a major media issue because it was the first FTSE 100 buyout. Again, this seemed to have limited effect. The trustees then hit upon a novel solution. The June 21st court hearing that, subsequent to a confirming vote from shareholders approves the delisting of the stock, must also ensure that all creditors are treated fairly in the transfer of assets. Having taken legal advice, the trustees intended to argue that the scheme was a creditor and that, given the issues of scheme solvency created by the buyout, were not being treated fairly. This was an unprecedented step and whilst it might not ultimately succeed it could at least significantly delay the buyout and bring renewed scrutiny to the issue of the debt structure. On June 20th AB Acquisitions agreed a £418 million cash payment over ten years to the fund and a further £600 million security package as long term cover for the scheme should the company collapse. The solution in some respects was a compromise. It still represented incremental payments but it was now a formula that cumulatively guaranteed the underlying solvency of the scheme. However, though the agreement preserved the security of the accumulated pensions of its members it did not thereby protect the pension rights of all Alliance Boots employees.

First, preserving the pension scheme cannot address the issue of leverage and whether in fact Alliance Boots does become insolvent prior to completing its guaranteed payments. Such an insolvency followed by the collapse of the pension fund would result in the need for the state to compensate employees who have lost some or all of their private pension. So far the state has been reluctant to fully fund this kind of compensation, resulting in significant hardship to retirees who are now in no position to make alternative arrangements. Based on the schemes that have been put in place, however, a GMB survey reported in 2007 that 96 insolvent pension schemes were for workers in private equity backed firms. Two thirds of these were currently being compensated under the government interim Pensions Financial Assistance Scheme and the rest were under consideration by its superseding body the Pensions Protection Fund.

Second, the agreement cannot address the issue of wage levels or of employment security which will form the context within which the majority of current employees will eventually accumulate a level of pension within the scheme. Nor can it address the issue of whether Alliance Boots continues to offer the same pension packages to new employees. The first decade of the twenty first century has seen many companies change the nature of their private pension provision (Morgan 2006b; Blackburn 2002). A combination of longer life expectancies, new tax and accountancy rules and a period of lax contributions by employers have created growing deficits within existing funds at the same time as the costs of funds have been rising. This has given all large firms, pressurised by shareholder value issues, motives to wind up defined benefit contribution schemes that guarantee an income to retirees. Instead, firms have started to move over to defined contribution systems where individual employees accumulate a sum to be used to buy an annuity. This may or may not include employer contributions, and is a far cheaper alternative for the employer. It places the greater emphasis for pension provision on the individual and creates a greater likelihood that any shortfall will result in a greater reliance on the state.

A buyout creates additional debt servicing costs and reduces revenues that might be available to fund better pension provision. It provides an additional motive to view pensions as an unwanted liability because of the sharpened focus on value returned to equity over a short time horizon. PEF and other investment organisations, particularly insurers, have, of course, responded creatively to this. There is now a growing market in buyouts of pension funds – essentially privatising them in ways that reduce them as liabilities for the originating firm. The firm is then better able to become part of the merger and acquisition market that has become such a key area of financial activity in equities. This, again, does nothing to protect the long term conditions of pension provision. As funds become tradable assets they too become financial instruments subject to the pressures this creates.

Conclusion

The pension issue, then, is a specific instance of how PEF is a constitutive part of the neo-liberal reconstruction of work. It is one with definite implications for workers and for the state. As private pension provision is eroded then public pension provision must improve. This has tax implications for the state and for the individual. As private pension provision becomes more individual, tending to be based on accumulating a sum with which to buy an annuity, then the contributions by individual employees must rise. This has disposable income implications for the individual. Since one of the main drivers of economic growth in liberalised economies like the US and UK is consumption then this also has growth implications. The capture of the rights to the returns on large assets based on a proportionately small equity commitment which is at the heart of a PEF LBO has, therefore, far reaching repercussions. That capture raises the issue of entitlement based on the idea of what is just. But it also raises the issue of whether the activity is something we should value even where it creates some kinds of value because the long term distribution of those values is directed at the few and perhaps ought to be directed at the many. This in turn returns us to the terrain of the other sections in this chapter: entitlement, governance, and the context of debt vulnerability created by an LBO of a large company, particularly a publicly listed company. How one views PEF LBOs and whether they should be restricted are questions that arise in conjunction with the issue of entitlement and with the issue of what we should value. These are in one way, matters of distributive justice: the right to intervene to redistribute or to prevent a particular distribution.

The problem with moral philosophy, however, is that there is no trump card when discussing the norms that underpin it. The norms are not simply free-floating. When one asks is it just that the many benefit more than the few or that the few can do what the many cannot, the answers given are not simply based on assumptions and assertions where one voice shouts louder than others. They are based on the analyses of practices that then give grounds for thinking about the norms. The analyses can follow a whole range of forms. One can show the wider relations involved in a practice (liquidity and PEF). One can highlight the mechanics and tendencies of a practice (the use of debt and capture of returns). One can show the inconsistencies of the theorisation of that practice (debt discipline and incentive realignment). One can question the facts and claims used to support a position (the empirical benefits of PEF). One can reveal a practice's hidden assumptions within moral philosophy (absolute rights to property, the minimal state and maximally free markets). One can relate some or all of these to specific examples that help to illustrate and develop the points made and the context they have been made in (Alliance Boots).

However, these simply provide the means to establish that a position is ambiguous, that it is contradictory and that it is unable to justify itself in its own terms. They do not amount to a conclusive argument for an alternative because that is not how norms work. Arguments often state entailments – what necessarily follows from them. But positions on what we should value and what we ought to do are more than just issues of what necessarily follows. They are about what we decide and what we choose on the basis of what we make of the claims we have supported, refuted or questioned. One of the curious things about Nozick's work, for example, is that it seems to undercut the very basis that we might want to choose otherwise: to intervene and redistribute. This is also at the root of the ideological aspect of PEF and of financial liberalisation. That is why one of the founding credos of liberalism has been there is no alternative (TINA). In moral philosophical terms the argument is always more than one of benefits (the pragmatism of TINA) it is firstly about the right to do without restriction that is then beneficial. Realising this is in itself quite liberating because it highlights how one can reject conformity to the unrelenting claims of necessity that often accompany strident claims about the rights of the few.

Conclusion

I have explored private equity finance buyouts in terms of several themes. As:

- A claimed solution (turning round an acquisition) to problems they help to create: the instability of liquidity resulting in periodic adverse economic conditions and problems within the finance system.
- A claimed solution that creates new problems within the dynamics of liquidity and subject to the constraints of changing liquidity: the terms and conditions of work and problems of debt vulnerability.
- A claimed solution that involves issues of entitlement, gains, and regulation.

I have argued that PEF buyouts are part of the unstable growth of liquidity. The size of funds, the scale of acquisitions, the absolute size of debt, and levels of leverage rise as liquidity grows. Thus as markets rise problems of debt servicing and problems of debt vulnerability are created on the basis of the surge in liquidity that is channelled into PEF and which PEF has strong motives to exploit. As PEF grows in scale and significance its mutual relations thereby become one element in the instability of liquidity and thus in the instability of the capital markets in terms of which it is located. This significance reached a new level at the time of the credit crunch. Ironically, the fact that the immediate trigger of the crunch was sub-prime mortgages has tended to overshadow the previous public concern with PEF. There is, however, a case for the regulation of PEF in conjunction with a case for tighter regulation of banking practices in order to control the instability of liquidity growth and the instability of capital markets.

The case is strengthened when one considers that the basic mechanisms of PEF do create additional problems when an acquisition is undertaken. Scales of debt and leverage are translated into specific issues of debt servicing and debt vulnerability. Both rise as the scale of PEF rises. These are not just problems for the finance system. They are problems for what we are used to thinking of as the real economy because they are problems for the individual acquisition and for the inter-connection of those individual acquisitions as constitutive parts of the economy. It is not that PEF is incapable of delivering specific, if disputable, benefits but rather that the basis of those benefits comes at a cost. The cost is debt and debt is a gamble taken with the viability of productive units of the economy. Those units represent employment, tax revenues, and growth sources. Any benefit generated in these terms by PEF can be reversed on the basis of the failure of the gamble. Since PEF can generate returns in a variety of ways and, as scales of acquisition rise, has a stronger incentive to rely on debt creation and special dividends to overcome any hurdle and achieve carried interest, there is a case for regulation of PEF based on debt vulnerability. This is particularly so if the debt control hypothesis for discipline does not hold and one views larger PEF buyouts as situations where improvements to the acquisition could have been made without the generation of debt. The debt was the means to effect the LBO, which itself is a means to concentrate equity and redistribute power in such a way as to capture absolute control of the returns to large capital assets. In the end, PEF is constrained by its relation to its acquisitions as financial instruments.

The case is also strengthened when one considers the further ramifications of what it means to relate to an acquisition as a financial instrument. It is overly simplistic to think of PEF as a primitive asset stripping exercise that must cut wages and employment. However, the basic constraints of PEF as an investment practice clearly have implications for the subsequent development of employment relations and industrial relations. PEF is a product of its time because its very existence and profitability are products of financial liberalisation. But it is also a product of its time in the sense that the constraints and opportunities under which PEF operates (levels of leverage, gearing issues, rates of return, hurdles, the different strategies for generating returns) are additional factors within neo-liberalism that affects the nature of work and the nature of production. The incentive realignment of PEF is focused on the PEF fund. The basis of human resource management systems are quite different kinds of 'incentive'. They are perfectly compatible with, over time, falling real wages, basic wages, job security, collective representation, and broader terms and conditions. The state ought to be concerned about such issues because the long term effects include a greater reliance on the state. This is particularly so in terms of pension provision, where in the end the state will, if anyone does, be forced to make up for the decline in other forms of provision.

The last point returns us to the tax issue. The overall tax burden in major western economies is subtly shifting in regressive ways because of the 'tax efficiencies' inherent in neo-liberalism. PEF is simply an expression of this general trend. At best, PEF complicates matters of tax collection and the prediction of tax revenue for the state.[1] More cogently, individual acquisitions pay less tax than they could. Moreover, the degree to which tax is not paid is related to the scale of debt and the level of leverage and thus to the size of acquisition undertaken. The point also extends to the way PEF firms earn returns. Carried interest, as with other forms of capital gains is, as of April 2007, subject to a flat 18% tax rate. This is still below the income tax rate paid by ordinary employees on their main source of earnings. The existence of the current tax regime in the UK provides incentives for PEF firms to operate and for PEF buyouts to use debt. Since the tax revenues from the acquisition are reduced and the tax levels paid by the firms are low there is, therefore, a case for designing more stringent tax regulations within a tax regime that works in harmony with other regulatory restrictions on PEF. This remains the case even if PEF firms counter that such regulation risks PEF activity reducing and PEF firms decamping, precisely because there may be, on the basis of the current situation, a net tax benefit from them doing so.

These points in turn also move the argument for regulation onto the terrain of entitlement and moral philosophy in terms of distribution and justice. Implicit in the decamping argument concerning tax is the understanding that it is acceptable for the few to pay less in proportion on their millions than the majority do on their thousands. Expressed in this way the implications of PEF seem quite different in moral terms. These terms, furthermore, extend to all aspects of PEF. PEF is an exercise in the capture of absolute control of the returns to large capital assets. It is an exercise that only the few with highly specific characteristics can engage in. At the same time, its underlying justification operates on the basis of universal property rights, the primacy of markets, and the minimal state. It is thereby rooted in a position that has a basis in moral philosophy regarding entitlement but also closes down argument regarding entitlement: there is an absolute and pre-social basis that acts as a proscription on intervention and thus regulation. Implicit in this argument is the understanding that it is oppressive that the wealthy should be prevented from using wealth to capture access to even more wealth. Again, expressed in this way the implications of PEF seem quite different in moral terms.

The terms, however, are not absolute, what they indicate is that the arguments for PEF and the implicit understandings on which PEF is founded are not an impediment to proposing forms of regulation. There can be a normative commitment to an alternative, where the alternative is not simply asserted despite the arguments for PEF but because of the claims and arguments for PEF and because of how those claims and arguments can be reconstructed. In essence that is what this book has been an exercise in. The claims need not be strident or polemical. They need not be seen as a brute attack on profit *per se* or as a wholesale dismissal of PEF. To construe criticism of PEF in these terms is simply a discursive device to undermine the genuine plausibility of arguments for regulation. This is one of the great weaknesses of the positive case as it appeared in the media in 2007. It was often presented as an all or nothing argument. It was also an argument where the brute facts were taken to speak up for PEF in an all or nothing way. This was curious since proponents of PEF also at times acknowledged that PEF had involved misjudgements, errors and mistakes. Phrased in the context of the basic plausibility of PEF these acknowledgements served the same function as Jensen's original take on any defects in PEF practice in the late 1980s: they were anomalies rather than products of the actual dynamic relations of PEF. Moreover, they were anomalies that may well lead to regulatory action in the UK. Since that action seemed likely to take the exception or anomaly as its basis it would be counterproductive. Again this view tends to ignore that what regulation can address and should address is the problems of PEF based on its dynamics. Intervention is not absolute. It can be applied as a constraint on a particular activity in particular ways to create specific proscriptions but where the proscriptions themselves are seen in terms of their cumulative and integrated effects.

An integrated regulatory approach to PEF

The case for regulating PEF begins from the problem of scale, levels of debt and degrees of leverage. It begins from its relationship to unstable liquidity and to capital markets. As such, one aspect of possible regulation relates to limits on the scale of acquisitions, levels of debt and degrees of leverage. Regulation could place breaks on the way PEF expands as liquidity expands and on how PEF is motivated to exploit all available liquidity. This would reduce its role as a constitutive element in unstable liquidity by changing its dynamics.

Here, there is no reason why a specific regulatory ceiling could not be applied to leverage: say 35% of the original deal. There is no reason why measures of debt servicing could not be applied as limitations on the use of debt, such as fixed ratios of debt to Ebitda along the lines of some of the more stringent private covenants. These two measures would directly affect the capacity of firms to undertake larger LBOs and to generate the potential for returns via the concentration of equity and via refinancing that incorporates additional special dividends. They would be disincentives for larger LBOs. Where LBOs do occur those LBOs would carry smaller levels of total debt at lower levels of leverage and subject to wider comfort zones in terms of debt servicing. They would be less vulnerable to debt and this would reduce the gamble taken with the acquisition based on its potentials as a financial instrument or investment asset. Special dividends could also be subject to additional regulatory oversight: they could either be simply prohibited or made conditional on evidence that they were based on cost savings from refinancing rather than simple extractions that essentially increase the debt load of the acquisition.

Lowering leverage and capping debt in terms of debt servicing measures would also have the additional advantage that they would require the PEF firm to concentrate specifically on improving the revenue basis of the acquisition rather than on the use of alternative strategies. They would also likely increase the timeline of any investment. There would then need to be very strong reasons to undertake the acquisition of larger firms because the proportions of equity required would be larger and the capacity to generate rapid returns on the basis of gearing would be lower. In all likelihood this would reduce the returns to funds, particularly mega-funds specialising in larger buyouts. This in turn would likely reduce the size of funds that PEF firms could solicit. The combination of smaller funds and the technical difficulties of creating attractive debt structures for larger LBOs would in turn reduce PEF's contribution to merger and acquisition activity by changing the terms on which such activity occurred.

It is important to note that creating this effect on the basis of regulation of leverage and debt would be different than allowing markets to follow cycles of leverage and debt. The case against regulation would argue that the 'errors' of a period of high liquidity result in large funds creating competitive bidding, high premiums, and accessing more available debt, but that the participants become aware of the problems this creates and new market signals cause the conditions enabling these circumstances to disappear. However, the regulatory counterargument is that the damage has already been done and could have been forestalled. Market 'corrections' cannot retrospectively remove debt from the balance sheets of acquisitions, cannot undo defaults, cannot give back a period of unemployment to an individual or a period of recession for an economy. Markets cannot reverse time or rewrite history and that is why addressing their historical dynamics through regulation is important. One effect of the regulation, for example, would likely be to reduce the problem of premiums paid to equity in a buyout in the sense that the regulation would reduce the capacity to offer premiums and thus reduce the problems premiums create for gearing and the incentives that premiums create that undermine the role of corporate governance.[2]

Corporate governance could also be buttressed by a more effective oversight system for mergers and acquisitions that had a broader remit in terms of how the public interest was interpreted. There could, for example, be a more integrated and interventionary approach to the preservation of pension provision. The Pensions Regulator could be given powers to compel a bidder in an LBO to undertake a legally binding contract to come to an agreement with pension trustees regarding the solvency of the pension scheme. The agreement could also include a commitment to maintain the scheme on its current basis for new members for a minimum fixed duration. Again, this might be a serious deterrent to an LBO. But what it is actually doing is deterring an LBO on a particular basis rather than deterring an

LBO *per se*. As such it addresses the specific question of whether one should value the 'value' created in an LBO because it ensures the LBO is not detrimental to some parties (and thus may be valued by them).

These simple changes could be implemented in conjunction with other aspects of controls on the incentives that banks have to offer debt in ways that foster unstable liquidity.[3] Covenant-lite lending could be banned. Securitisation and originate and distribute strategies could be more tightly regulated. Banks could be prevented from shifting assets off balance sheet to entities that they still have some obligation to (such as a liquidity backstop) or could be required to factor those obligations into their balance sheet. Banks could be restricted in their capacity to reinvest in transformed assets at new higher credit ratings: such as CDOs/CLOs. The credit rating agencies could be paid by the investors not the originator of a securities issue. Regulators could concentrate more on actual absolute capital asset ratios for banks rather than recommended tier reserves. Banks could be audited more tightly based on genuine quarterly data rather than annual sign-offs on the data. The audit could require that the accountants guarantee that the accounts are an actual accurate representation of the solvency of the bank rather than merely that they comply with current regulation. This would be quite a different level of commitment for the auditors. The models banks use as an alternative to mark to market valuations for some assets could be standardised and simplified. Banks could be once again more effectively separated into investment and commercial and retail banking institutions. Regulation could decouple bankers' bonuses from the volume of lending they undertake. Fees could similarly be restructured.

Issues of entitlement could be addressed indirectly. The tax relief on debt used in an LBO could be withdrawn above a particular debt ceiling. The ceiling could be based on the actual size of the debt, or the level of leverage, where the ceiling based on the level of leverage was lower than the additional ceiling on the permitted level of leverage, such as the 35% suggested above.[4] Carried interest could be reclassified as income and subject to (at least) the same levels of obligation as that of employees on their main source of earnings. Both measures would reduce the attractiveness of PEF at the same time as altering the economic distribution that flowed from holdings and transfers. Entitlement and the economic distribution could also be addressed more directly by requiring that the PEF firm provide a specific and significant equity share to employees when an LBO is undertaken. This could be set up as an additional equity fund, administered by trustees on behalf of employees or could involve some form of elected body of representatives of employees that would also form part of the acquisition hierarchy. They could combine the rights of fund limited partners with an additional monitoring role as part of the executive team within the holding company that administers the acquisition. This would ensure a broader more genuine form of interest realignment that would by its nature address the issue of distribution and entitlement, as well as the long term power distribution effects of neo-liberalism. It would help to change the terms in which the acquisition was viewed as a financial instrument or asset for the fund. It would also place a contextual break on some of the negative potentials implied by the imposition of a ceiling on debt. Specifically, it would militate the tendency for lower leverage to result in a concentration on improving revenue that then could become a heightened pressure for cost cutting based on the need to generate returns rather than based on the need to service debt. It would thereby offset any potential for an expression of hyper-neoliberalism.

However, this distributive change would likely be resisted far more than any ideas about taxation or levels of debt. But consider what that resistance implies. At the heart of the positive argument for PEF is that it is based on incentive realignment and that it does have positive effects on employment relations, employment, productivity, and growth. If PEF claims to have these effects then there is no impediment in giving employees an inside track on the mechanisms by which this occurs. It would in fact be an additional interest and incentive alignment that creates a genuine sense of democratic participation that can only enhance the effects that the positive argument claims.[5] The claims themselves, of course, could also be subject to closer scrutiny simply by requiring the same level of reporting of accounts at Companies House for private equity acquisitions, firms, and funds as for public organisations.

None of these changes suggest or require an absolute ban on PEF. They do not prevent larger LBOs but they do control their effects. PEF would likely, therefore, continue at a smaller scale based on smaller fund solicitations and addressing issues like divestment, insolvency, and family succession. Even at this scale, the basis of PEF practice would still be affected by leverage restrictions, reporting requirements and equity stakes. At all levels the terms of each specific regulation could be adjusted in the light of the experienced effects of that regulation. Most of the forms of regulation proposed are simple. The last, however, based on equity stakes and representation is far more complex and would require more design and adjustment. Overall, though the regulation is adjustable the approach is integrated because each regulation would address both an aspect of the overall problem and have a cascading effect across other aspects of the overall problem. The overall aim would be to reduce instabilities of liquidity, reduce debt, reduce debt vulnerability, and expand the entitlements and distributions flowing from PEF based on a broader sense of economic justice. The normative commitment that they all flow from is that capital markets do not effectively control themselves and that the state does have a right to intervene to help control them. That right emerges from the problems created by aspects of economy, such as private equity finance, and from the defects in the justifications of those aspects (universal property rights, the primacy of markets and the minimal state). However, though the right may flow from these and the regulations proposed may be unambiguous and may be simple, implementation is far from simple. This is because political will is also tied to normative constructions.

New Labour's approach to regulating PEF

There is a clear difference between appearing to have solid arguments and those arguments being translated into policy and law of particular kinds. That difference is not just one of the technical complexities of otherwise simple ideas. It concerns the discursive environment and hence normative commitments from within which they are judged. As I set out in Chapter 3, New Labour inherited and elaborated on an economic orientation inherited from the Conservatives. Specifically, The Treasury has maintained a minimal approach to direct intervention in matters relating to capital markets. The UK has gradually become tied into the primacy of finance as an economic sector.[6] Government has tended towards an approach based on voluntary codes of conduct and minor regulatory changes. Most recently, some changes have, of course, seemed less minor to business interests than in the past: changes such as those to corporation tax, to non-domiciled status, and to capital gains tax. The significance of these changes, however, can be viewed in three ways. First, they were not intended to be major changes: they were blunders in terms of design (fostered as they were by a hasty response to the Conservatives) but not intent. In this narrow sense they are arguments against regulation because they show the incompetence of a specific government and the unintended consequences of some regulation. Second, some of the changes were motivated by need: the rapid slide in public finances created by overstretched spending, a poorly designed tax regime, and an incipient recession. Third, and most importantly, the haste, incompetence and need inherent in the recent changes show the limits of the approach that gave rise to them. It was a voluntaristic approach to capital markets, a 'competitive' tax regime designed around attracting all forms of finance and an *ad hoc* approach to subsequent 'minor' regulatory change that created the pressures in the first place. A clearer idea of the need for integrated regulation to control the arising problems would have been neither hasty nor so inadvertently counter-productive. The problem remains, however, that the government, as distinct from parliament, seem committed to reproducing the conditions for these pressures. The Treasury continues to look at the issue of finance starting from the broad idea of financial liberalism and does not want to create broader consequences in its regard. Its overall policy position thus reinforces the autonomy of finance at the same time as being liable to take a limited view of intervention regarding private equity.

Three interventions illustrate this.[7] First, speaking at the GMB trade union conference (a politically canny move) in June 2007, Gordon Brown stated that the ongoing Treasury Review of private equity would provide an analysis of the available evidence on all aspects of PEF and that this would settle the matter. However, the degree to which this meant actions of specific kinds was carefully phrased. The problem would be addressed in terms of whether private equity was exploiting tax loopholes, rather than the broader issue of what the effects of private equity are. Second, on June 26th Sir John Gieve, the Bank of England's Deputy Governor defended private equity in general terms (Duncan 2007). He noted that its earnings are set by global standards and are not specific to the UK. He placed it as simply one element in the development of liberal finance from which the UK has greatly benefited but also warned against complacency regarding the benefits of liberal finance (that careful monetary policy through the Monetary Policy Committee's role on interest rate levels was required to maintain the UK economy and that cycles in finance systems are always likely to occur). Third, in his first interview July 3rd, after replacing Gordon Brown as Chancellor, Alistair Darling noted that he would not be making any populist quick judgements on private equity; that the main issue was a balanced understanding of the way in which some private equity activity had been good for acquisitions and that there were equally some poor examples of public equity; that unintended consequences of ill-thought out intervention had to be avoided; and that the main way forward might be through greater transparency and thus accountability (Barber, Blitz and Giles 2007).

The Commons Treasury Select Committee inquiry of mid 2007 was more critical and more wide-ranging because it was within parliament rather than within government. However, the interim report that resulted, though detailed in its analysis was highly limited in its recommendations (SCT 2007).[8] The problem of rising leverage was acknowledged, as was the issue of debt vulnerability, the issue of corporate governance, and the issue of the tax status of debt. The general finding, however, was that the relevant parties should undertake further reviews relating to the issues: HM Revenues and Customs of the tax issue, the Bank of England of the effects on economic stability of higher leverage, and the Financial Service Authority on the effectiveness of the monitoring of individual debt structures by banks. This was essentially a wait and see policy and also a policy that relied on the existing institutions that already operated a hands-off and voluntaristic approach to most aspects of regulation and enforcement. A previous FSA discussion paper of November 2006, for example, had similarly been motivated by the growing scale of PEF. Its executive summary (p. 5) also articulated similar limitations. It described PEF as a 'compelling business model' making a 'positive contribution to capital markets'. It stated that 'Too much regulation could be detrimental to capital market efficiency and/or cause the private equity industry to move to more lightly regulated jurisdictions'. It acknowledged that its own assessment of PEF was not 'a comprehensive market failure analysis' and that further study was required.

The general approach broadly accorded with the BVCA and thus the private equity industry's own desired approach: a strategy that hoped the public scrutiny would simply decline and a response that emphasised the need for clearer self-regulatory codes of particular kinds.[9] In March 2007 Sir David Walker, formerly of the Bank of England and the Securities and Investment Board was commissioned by the BVCA to produce a report on private equity. The interim report of July 2007 was narrow in remit, tending away from issues of tax and actual leverage in given buyouts, and focused on the need to improve transparency and communication in the context of recent publicity on large buyouts.[10] There were two overall motivating aims: to better persuade the public that private equity should not be vilified and to provide future conditions for effective governance or self-disciplining of the industry because of public scrutiny. The final report was published in November 2007. Recommendations were grouped around the PEF firms, acquisitions and the role of the BVCA. The report recommended that private equity firms publish an annual review disclosing the structure of the firm and its investment approach, the types of investors in its funds and its current acquisitions. It recommended that acquisitions publish an annual report of accounts that included the identity of the owning funds and the GP(s) and board that control the acquisition, as well as a risk management review disclosing policies relating to current leverage and likely business trends. It recommended greater and timely communication between the PEF firm and employees of an acquisition at a time of 'strategic change'. It recommended that the BVCA fund 'rigorous evidence-based analysis of the economic impact of private equity activity' to provide a source of authority for its role as a representative association. Finally Walker also called for an independent monitoring group to oversee the effectiveness of all of the recommendations.

The Walker report is interesting for what it is not rather than for what it is. It is about disclosure but not detail. It thus preserves a core of confidentiality as secrecy. It is about communication but not genuine consultation. It is thus about limited information, it is about minimal standards of conveyance rather than ensuring some mechanism to protect employees that can actually change the basis of decisions. It is about complying with practices that are likely to have no material effect on most PEF firms, funds or their actual relations to acquisitions. The transparencies required are in many respects no more onerous than those that can be found on the current FAME database on which many firms can already be found. A risk management report on leverage can be little more than a graphical analysis of leverage levels and additional time series data regarding revenue streams and Ebitda. This is subject to precisely the same problems that the FSA was revealed to have encountered with risk modelling at the banks in 2007.[11] There is a great deal of leeway in the construction of such models. There existence is not a break on the practices that create risk, it is (at its worst) an exercise in self-deluding optimism. One might also note that the report presupposes the continuation of the entities it analyses: it specifically highlights the need for the BVCA to more effectively represent the larger buyout end of the market. This is a market that the reports own recommendations will not alter in character. This in turn is not because Walker is unaware of the problems larger buyouts can represent. It is rather because he appears to subscribe to the self-correcting markets position in regard of any problems with private equity finance. In a *Times* column at the time of the report he notes:

> [The] sense of uncertainty and ignorance led to a lot of suspicion. I have to say, I think a lot of that was wholly justified, so there was disquiet that had to be addressed [...] private equity at the big buyout end was being fuelled, in particular, by cheap and abundant credit. That's no longer the case and private equity has very substantially slowed down at the big buyout end. (Walker 2007c)

The point then is that the sum total of politically framed analyses of policy at the very height of the interest in private equity finance amounted to a series acknowledgements, deferrals and calls for greater information, transparency and self-regulation. The main actual policy intervention, meanwhile, amounted to some changes in tax law scheduled for April 2008. Those changes encompassed private equity finance in so far as they were focused on taper relief and on non-domiciled status. But, as Chapter 7 makes clear, they were not focused in any effective way on the kinds of issues private equity raised within the tax regime.

In essence, the urgency of the case surrounding private equity seems to have receded. The credit crunch, the collapse of Northern Rock, the beginnings of a housing market crash, a gradual slide into recession and the general emphasis placed on the role of the US sub-prime market have shifted priorities. This is particularly because, as Walker emphasises, buyout activity has reduced since the heights of 2006–07. But to leave matters there is simply short-sighted. It neglects that private equity finance is one reason why current circumstances are as they are. It simply ensures that once private equity finance starts to expand again the same debates will resurface and be replayed – as those of 2007 in the UK replayed those of the late 1980s in the US. It simply ensures that the debate will begin from a terrain where effective regulation has not been implemented. As such it will begin from the dominance of normative commitments that militate against regulation and ensure that any regulation will be hasty, ill-conceived and probably too late. It should not be forgotten that if the UK is a major financial centre it is also dependent and significantly vulnerable to unstable liquidity because of that. Here, perhaps we should think of PEF in the context of a claimed solution to problems that need not exist.

Notes

Introduction

1 This followed on from the Financial Services Authority discussion paper November 2006, which highlighted the risks of growing debt levels (FSA 2006). See conclusion.
2 It cannot for example override common and statute law regarding fraud and does not exempt the fund from investment law, competition law etc.

Chapter 1

1 The term tendency is used here within the broad 'realist' tradition of social theory. Any given identifiable social entity has causal powers based on its constitution and relations. The operation of those causal powers creates further potentials that may be realised, given circumstances that are conducive, including the interaction with other social entities. What exactly a social entity is raises the further issue of agency and structure and various problems of structural determinism dichotomised with methodological individualism. The minutiae of social theory debate on these issues are not strictly relevant here, however. See Harre and Madden (1975), Sayer (1982), Pinkstone (2007).
2 The very first, however, appeared in the early 1960s. I am indebted to Fenn, Liang and Prowse's (1995) extensive study for the Federal Reserve as a main initial source for the early part of this section. The studies bibliography was also particularly useful in tracking down relevant material by various scholars in organisation and finance (Jensen, Kaplan etc.) who took an early interest in the phenomenon. An extended version of the Fenn *et al.* original study is available in *Financial Markets, Institutions and Instruments* 6 (4) 1997: 1–106. Gompers and Lerner (2000: 285; 1998: 151–2) also note the creation of the firm American Research and Development (ARD) in 1946 (See also Cohen 2007: 15).
3 In terms of the role of wealthy families, the change worked in both directions. The Rockefeller family had made venture capital investments in McDonnell Douglas and in eastern Airlines in the 1930s and during the 1960s transformed its *ad hoc* interests in venture capital into a formal organisation Venrock that then provided early stage financing for Intel and Apple in the 1970s and 1980s. (Barnes and Gertler 1999: 276. Rind 1981: 170 and 172) Ferenbach in Jones *et al.* 2006: 17, notes from his own personal experience as one of the earliest fund raisers that this institutionalisation of capital expanded further from 1980.
4 The launch of Sputnik in 1957, for example, helped to spur a whole range of new investment initiatives such as the National Defence Education Act of 1958. The Act helped increase investment across higher education institutions.
5 In a 3:1 or 4:1 ratio to their capitalisation. See Gupta 2000: 7 and 126.
6 'Small' is defined by the net worth of the company (less than $6 million in the late 1970s, for example), its after tax profits (under $2 million) and by employment levels (adjusted by industry) (Rind 1981: 172).
7 In terms of the investment banks the justification of spinouts of PEF have varied over time – one key issue has become conflict of interest between advisory and underwriting functions and competing as a private equity firm.

8 Heizer was unusual both in scale ($80 million – around half the total for all venture capital that year) and in number of investors (35).

9 For the range of terminology – particularly that relating to LBO participants, see Jensen 1989b and 1989c and Jensen in Jones *et al.* 2006: 12.

10 Hedge funds also developed in terms of these laws (Connor and Woo 2003: 5; Lhabitant 2002).

11 For a different taxonomy based on informal-formal forms of PEF see Fenn, Liang and Prowse 1995: 2–3.

12 They have also consistently remained an incentive for individuals to set up partnerships. Cleveland Christopher, for example who had worked intermittently at the SBIC FNCB Capital Corporation (later Citicorp Venture Capital Corporation) since 1971 engineered the spinout of Equico from Equitable in 1990 and recalls: 'Our long term strategy had four components. Step one was to acquire control of Equico and transform it into a mini merchant bank with entrepreneurial spirit that we had total control of and a significant stake in. Step two, once we had Equico was to gain the flexibility to operate outside the regulatory morass of the federal government, or the SBA, because it was too difficult to work within those strictures. Step three was to amass a sizeable pool of capital… The fourth part of the strategy was to gain the capacity to sponsor transactions, taking controlled positions – something we couldn't do under SBIC regulations.' (Gupta 2000: 55).

13 From a high of around 700 SBICs fell to 276 in 1977 (Fenn, Liang and Prowse 1995: 5). As of January 2008 there were 320 SBICs forecast to provide around $100 million in financing in 2008, supplemented by $39 million in debentures offered by the SBA. (Staff Reporter 2008)

14 As Rind (1981: 175) reports only 7% of such venture capital rated itself as particularly successful in a 1978 survey.

15 Gumpert (1979: 178 and 182) reports based on the trade journal *Venture Capital* figures that in 1978 venture capital invested $500 million compared with $400 million in 1977 and $300 million in 1976, whilst new committed investment capital amounted to around $500 million in 1978 compared to $20 million in 1977.

16 As Gumpert (1979: 178) notes, the SBICs, funds and various *ad hoc* venture groupings that had begun to operate through the 1960s faced a new environment: 'Painful changes resulted. Possibly as many as on third of the venture capital firms in existence at the end of the 1960s failed to survive the first half of this decade. Most of those that did became particularly unadventuresome. Some turned totally inward to concentrate all their energy and available funds on existing investments. Others swore off start-up and early stage investments and instead put their money into safer situations such as relatively large and well-established, profitable companies, sometimes even buying stock on public markets.'

17 Also problematic were: 1. the 1933 Securities Act SEC Regulation A allowed a simplified registration procedure for new equity offerings but at a low ceiling of $1/2 million. 2: The SEC Rule 144 limitation on the amount of unregistered stock private investors could sell in public markets to 1% of its capitalisation in a six month period. This slowed the process of a fund divesting itself of assets from investments that it has already IPO'd. See Gumpert (1979: 184) The Nasdaq was opened February 8th 1971 with an index initially set to 100. It provided information on buy and sell prices of 2,400 over the counter (OTC) stocks i.e. unlisted on the main exchanges. Previously information on buy and sell prices for OTCs were only available form the trading desks of dealers or brokers who issued or retailed them – the Nasdaq assimilated information from 500 trading desks using a new computer

system. This made it much easier to trade in OTC issues and thus increased the liquidity of this market. As OTC, the Nasdaq was initially dominated by small and new firms but would ultimately become an alternative exchange as some of the successful hi-tech firms who started there chose to remain rather than shift to the NYSE. (Siegel 2002: 50)

18 The Act was revised 1976, 1985 and 2001 with no material change in this criterion. The 2001 Act is available: http://www.law.upenn.edu/bll/archives/ulc/ulpa/final2001.htm. See also Gompers and Lerner 1998: 152.

19 The Standard & Poor's grading, for example, runs in order of increasing default risk from AAA (premium investment grade), AA (high) A (upper), BBB (medium), BB (lower), B (speculative), CCC-CC (poor), C (highly speculative), D (lowest grade). For the role of rating agencies in the 1980s see Mishkin 1992: 136).

20 As Jensen (1989b: 36) notes investment banks also initially faced restrictions on their activities in public equity markets that would ultimately make PEF attractive. In the wake of the Wall St Crash, the 1934 SEC Act imposed a profit return condition on 'insiders' (those with more than 10% stake or serving as directors of boards) for holdings of less than six months. This and the conditions of the 1940 Investment Companies Act tended to reduce the role of the banks as active investors – agents with significant long term commitment and monitoring/intervention functions in corporations.

21 Capital gains tax was further reduced to 20% in 1981. See, Gumpert, 1979: 182–4; Rind 1981: 171; Fenn, Liang and Prowse 1995: 10–11. Note: the point here is that lower CGT is a commonly cited reason for the growth of PEF. No claim is being made about the efficiency, distributional or moral aspects of taxation at this stage. Historically speaking however, the 1981 tax reduction was part of Reagan's broader emphasis on lower taxes creating higher tax revenues (via an incentive for higher productivity and more hours worked) and resulting in reduced federal deficits – the Laffer hypothesis as part of Supply-Side economics (colloquially referred to as 'Voodoo Economics' and now widely discredited based on its historical record).

22 Department of Labour Interpretive Bulletin 44, Federal regulation 37225, 1979.

23 ERISA may also be seen as part of the long term expansion of institutional share holding from the 1960s onwards. Along with ERISA, there were various attempts from the 1970s to promote retirement savings related to share investment, including the introduction of tax relief on Individual Retirement Accounts in 1978.

24 Fenn, Liang and Prowse 1995: 11. Gumpert (1979: 182–4) also notes that in 1978 SEC Rule 144 was amended to allow 1% of a companies capitalisation to be sold every three months; and the ceiling regarding SEC Regulation A was raised to $2 million.

25 Bond interest rates are calculated through a combination of the default risk of the issuer (the possibility they might suspend interest rate payments or be unable to honour the value of the bond when it becomes due), as measured by the relevant individual accounts of the bond issuer provided in the prospectus for the issue and the credit rating the bond has been accorded by Moody's or Standard and Poor's; the duration of the term to the maturity of the bond and its liquidity (ease with which it can be sold on). The higher the default risk, the lower the credit rating, the longer the term, and the less liquid the bond, then the higher the interest rate. Treasury bonds tend to have the lowest interest rates for any given term because there is deemed to be no risk of default and the bond is highly liquid. All other bonds are compared to Treasury bonds and the difference between the interest rate on those bonds and Treasury bonds is termed the

risk premium. Bonds are issued in fixed sums (e.g. $100) and this is the capital that is repaid when the bond matures. Each bond is issued with a fixed interest rate reflecting the general interest rates of the time and subject to the above variations. A 5% interest rate on a $100 bond would pay a fixed income of $5 per annum. Since interest rates vary through time, when bonds are traded, the price the bond may trade for can be more or less than its face value. This affects its yield. If interest rates and prices never changed – yields would always reflect them (5% of $100 – 5% yield). If interest rates rise, however, then, new bond issues are more attractive than old bonds at old interest rates – demand tends to fall, prices of old bonds fall. If a bonds price falls its yield increases (a 5% $100 bond falls in price to $50 its yield is then 10% – making it more attractive – it cost just $50 for a guaranteed $100 payment and for $5 per annum returns). In theory prices fall until the yield on the old bond reflects the yield on new bonds issued with higher interest rates. The variations maintain a ready market for bonds and therefore help sustain liquidity.

26 The guarantee and the risk they are paid for is that they will absorb the new issue if it cannot be sold on. SEC rules required a prospectus be provided for potential buyers containing accurate material on the issue and relevant accounts of the issuer and that the registration be 21 days before the actual issue.

27 The Act was also intended to restrict conglomeration but was far less successful here, partly because the Act relied on corporate litigation based on how assets were acquired and partly because oversight emphasis was on direct issues of monopoly based on the prior Clayton Act.

28 The 1933 Glass-Steagall Act was a response to the 1929 Wall Street Crash and the subsequent wave of bank insolvencies. There are two reasons for the four year delay. First, legislating takes time. Second, the crash was actually more of a slide from 1929–32. Share prices fell by 10% in 1929 from their 1928 high and 75% by 1932. Share values did not recover thereafter until the early 1950s.

29 This is just one instance of how what we think of as phenomena of the 1980s began earlier.

30 Noting of course that venture capital does not rely on debt creation in the way LBOs do – venture capitalists mainly use majority equity stakes in firms and then also use debt to finance some of the rounds of investment directed into the firms. The debt levels of venture backed firms tend to be less or similar to non-venture backed (Mull and Winters 1996) but the forms of debt used are often of similar varieties to LBOs (see Susko 2003). On average 66–75% of funding is provided by the venture capitalist (Onorato 1997: 7). There are also trends in the size of venture funds and the scale of individual investments that affect the way venture capital operates and the way it approaches ownership and control of firms but these mainly came to the fore in the 1990s – see Chapter 2.

31 As another aspect in their risk management practices, however, pension funds tended to restrict the overall scale of their investment in any given PEF fund to 10% of its total.

32 Also growth in the 1980s allowed many SBICs to pay off their SBA debt and then shift over to become private equity firms structured as partnerships soliciting funds, which then contributed to the number of private equity firms (Gupta 2000). Note: curiously Gompers and Lerner (1998) argue that many of the changes in the investment environment for PEF in the late 1970s and early 1980s created growth through the demand side of the industry i.e. it was primarily lower capital gains tax in conjunction with GDP growth that led many would be venture capitalists, for example, to commit to developing new products and start new firms and this led to

the expansion in investment. However, as various critics note (Blair 1998: 196. Hellman 1998: 201) the data set used cannot effectively distinguish motives for supply and aspects of demand and few start-up venture capitalists would genuinely think to themselves capital gains tax is too high and I might have to pay it in five years if I am genuinely successful...

33 The measures exclude funds under $5 million in size and the averages are based on funds that have been wound up and thus the closure dates run to later than the 1980s whilst the vintage years are dominated by the 1980s for the original data set based on voluntary reporting to the organisation Venture Economics. On a broader measure the average size of venture capital funds was even smaller – in 1985 just $30 million (Onorato 1997: 8).

34 For rise see also Sohl (2003: 7).

35 Again, note there is some discontinuity between different data sets since non-venture PEF funds can include debt funds as well as buyout funds – however, these did not become significant until the end of the 1980s and as such do not affect the general commensurability of the data.

36 It was typical for venture capital firms to be located close to the firms they invested in during the 1980s – larger funds and national and international investment strategies were mainly a product of the late 1990s (Boquist and Dawson 2004: 40).

37 In many respects many of the early venture capitalists were indistinguishable from business angels – relatively affluent individuals who would put their own money into new ideas they believed in and take a close interest in how the firm developed – based on the small beginnings they helped to finance with seed or start-up capital.

38 The point regarding relative returns is a complex one: successful venture capital investments have often tended to generate higher % returns than LBOs but this is usually militated by the smaller size of investments, the greater risk of failure, and the longer term nature of the investment. Again these factors can also be variable – the dot.com boom was predicated on larger investments and quicker turnarounds, for example, (see Chapter 2).

39 As the authors note this affects the nature of venture capital, in much the way it also affects the redistribution towards buyouts, since it tends to result in a shift to larger investment scales in later stage venture capital rather than small scale start-ups. This in itself is a recurring trend in venture capital (Onorato 1997). See also Chapter 2.

40 This does not mean that institutional investors ignore venture funds entirely – they have, for some of the same reasons as buyout funds – become large investors. For example, in 1978 of the $428 million invested in venture funds pension funds supplied 15%. In the height of the PEF boom in 1986, they supplied over 50% of the $4 billion total (Gompers and Lerner 2000: 285).

41 One might also note that in any case the strategy of venture capital funds in response to the conditions of the 1970s was increasingly blurring the distinction between venture capital and non-venture capital on the basis of their approach to ownership. As Gumpert observes (1979: 190) venture capitalists had increasingly begun to take 70% stakes in the invested firms rather than the previous minority 30%. As Fenn, Liang and Prowse (1995) also observe it also became a strategy for the venture capitalists to push out the founding individual in the firm.

42 As Carl Ferenbach, one of the earliest practitioners of PEF recalls the other main source of LBOs were transition or succession issues for family firms: 'At the same time there were a lot of World War II veterans who had founded businesses and reached the point where they needed to make changes in the ownership of those

businesses for estate reasons. Leveraged acquisitions were a way for the companies to remain independent and, in many cases, for a new generation of managers to become owners with us.' (Ferenbach in Jones *et al.* 2006: 18)

43 As Mishkin (1992: 185) also observes based on Fed data, after 1983 (non-financial) corporate debt issue increased from around $50 billion to over $150 billion per year and remained above $100 billion throughout the 1980s with total corporate debt standing at almost 40% of GNP in 1990.

44 Other prominent examples of the time include: Warburg Pincus which began investing through private equity finance in 1971, Thomas H. Lee, founded in 1974, Forstmann, Little and Company, founded 1978, Bain Capital, founded 1984, Hicks and Haas founded 1984 (later to become HM Capital in 1994 under Hicks), Blackstone founded 1985, Carlyle, founded 1987. There are of course also the divisions of the major investment banks such as Goldman Sachs.

45 Though it should be noted that hostile takeovers were in fact extremely rare.

46 Kohlberg was a generation older than the cousins and when KKR was established Kohlberg was allotted a 40% stake compared to the other two partners 30%.

47 For the general issue see Kaplan 1989 and Newbould *et al.* 1992.

48 Baker and Smith have both worked as consultants for KKR and provide an authorised 20 year biography of the firm – it and Anders work are best read in conjunction since they represent different partialities.

49 For example Deloittes proposed revaluing all of Houdaille's assets at higher values than those currently estimated from the original conglomerations of the 1960s – higher values allowed greater depreciation write-offs on tax liabilities – liabilities that could be further reduced by classing the value of Houdaille on the basis of the transfer of the original business into a series of shell companies based on the equity value of the premium paid on Houdaille shares. See Anders 1992: 34.

50 The recession and Japanese competition in industrial processes revealed these to have been highly optimistic.

51 For background see appendix, Anders 1992: 285–95. Wometco was a conglomerate spanning bottling, vending machines and broadcasting. Storer was a broadcasting company that had moved out of radio and expanded into cable television. Owens-Illinois was bottle manufacturer. All three companies had undertaken investment and expansion in the 1960s and 1970s that had increased costs to the value of assets reducing their share value and making them vulnerable to a takeover that could profit by splitting up their assets. Beatrice food followed the same pattern, moving from Nebraska to Chicago in 1913 and emerging as a major dairy corporation, producing milk and ice cream and eventually diversifying into a range of food products, such as Tropicana juices, as well as unrelated businesses such as Avis car rental. As Anders sets out, Beatrice and Safeway fitted the KKR profile, and as Anson, in a standard narrow financial assessment (2003: 289–92) notes: Safeway and Beatrice were prime targets for takeover. Safeway was cross-subsidising loss making stores and unprofitable divisions and paid wages averaging 33% higher than industry equivalent standards (since it had a uniform national wage structure rather than variations by regional differences). Beatrice had conglomerated assets that were valued close to its actual market capitalisation. KKR sold off $7 billion in assets from Beatrice quite quickly, funding the majority of the buyout and justifying the 45% premium paid on the share price (Anson puts the original LBO cost at $6.2 billion – on the basis of which asset sales actually exceeded the initial buyout figure). KKR made asset sales reducing the number of stores and divisions of Safeway and generating $4.2 billion by the end of 1986

that was then partly used to reduce its debt to $3.1 billion (Baker and Smith, 1998: 111). The Magowan family who still dominated Safeway were also receptive to KKR because of the threat posed by a potential hostile takeover by Herbert and Robert Haft – who had gained a reputation as asset strippers that KKR, despite its commitment to asset sales had not. KKR have also been pioneers of the PEF commitment to restructuring businesses and investing in them to produce a new business structure – raising further issues of how and in whose interests that we address later. Duracell was less diversified than other KKR buyouts and did not have the same kind of asset profile but was attractive because of the underlying profitability of the business.

52 See also Markham 2003: 119; Bierman and Bierman 2003: 107–14.

53 'The Street's lingering slump lent a new edge of desperation to the merchant banking game. Windfall profits from LBOs and bridge-loans were the fastest way to shore up a brokerages sagging profits. A single deal could generate upfront fees of $50 million or more, enough to save a firm's quarter.' (Burrough and Helyar 2004: 187)

54 Though scrutiny began earlier – Milken, for example, was under investigation in 1985 – some of his associates in the insurance, savings and loan and mutual funds had been investigated by the regulatory bodies since the early 1980s.

55 Opler (1992), for example, reports that 50% of his sample LBOs paid no tax on earnings after being taken private.

56 In the 1980s senior debt financing for LBOs was dominated by Citibank, Manufacturers Hanover Trust Co and Bankers Trust. Prior to the expansion of the junk bond market and the development of new forms of junior debt – mezzanine debt (see Chapter 2) – senior debt dominated debt structures and was usually lent on a five year basis creating a limit on the expansion of deal sizes since debt servicing would be more difficult (Ferenbach in Jones *et al.* 2006: 18).

57 Typically involving forms of bonds on which interest is paid but where when the bond matures it is converted to an equity stake rather than requiring repayment of the principal or capital sum. Warrants provide the option but not obligation to buy or exchange – the warrant itself can be detached from the debt security and can then be also traded. Preference shares are a form of stock that yields a fixed % dividend.

58 One might also take 1984 since this was the year in which net equity issues by US corporations became negative i.e. repurchasing of stock began to dominate – a trend that continued until 1990.

59 Since the total value of the buyout includes additional expenses like fees and financing for working and investment capital then it is likely that the total is more than the equity capital that was acquired – the leverage level is therefore probably more than nine.

60 Or for international comparability, Libor – see Chapter 4.

61 The interest rate is typically a set rate or spread above LIBOR.

62 As Kaplan and Stein note (1993: 338) the 17% and above are unconditional averages, including buyouts with no issue of public debt – the actual levels are therefore higher.

63 When KKR outbid Kodak for Duracell, creating an initial debt structure of $1.7 billion – $750 billion in senior debt and the remainder in revolving credit and a bridge loan whilst a junk bond issue was prepared for market, 35 of Duracell's senior management contributed a further $6.5 million in exchange for shares and options in the new firm – $1 million was roughly the equivalent of 200,000 shares (Baker and Smith 1998: 116) in a highly concentrated pool of equity (see Chapter 3

on the technical aspects of how this works). This was a potential huge gain, in addition to the gains made on any shares held in Duracell prior to the buyout. If one considers the role of Drexel in the LBO of Safeway, Burnett *et al.* (1991: 126) report that they earned $42.3 million from the deal. Drexel were involved in 13 of KKR's major deals – though by the time of Milken's final prosecution and the demise of Drexel KKR was no longer a client. It should also be noted that KKR bond issues generally outperformed junk bond market averages (Anders 1992). This in itself, however, does not indicate that debt structures do not have inherent instabilities.

64 It is a source of course that can also be put into broader context in terms of a broader range of changes to the creation and flow of credit and investment in the 1980s – Fed policy, flow of debt to other nations, particularly Central and South America, alternative uses of capital available to the commercial banks, and so forth.

65 Primarily the Home Owners Loan Act of 1933.

66 Creating what is usually known as a transformation risk – the potential for adverse outcomes from the time differential between deposits and lending as interest rates vary.

67 A savings product committing the savings for a definite period e.g. six months, 30 months etc.

68 According to the industry representative the US League of Savings Association net new saving fell by 93% in the first four months of 1980 and according to Fed data savings and loan accounted for 65% of residential mortgage money in 1976 but only 37% in 1979 (Glasberg and Skidmore 1997: 76).

69 The aim had been to reduce inflation – in which the Fed was highly success-ful (reducing it from 13.5% in 1980 to 3.2% in 1983, but at the cost of 9.7% unemployment – Stiglitz 2004: 37).

70 40% on commercial real estate, 5% on secured and unsecured commercial loans, 10% commercial leasing, and 30% consumer loans. The complete Act is avail-able from the Philadelphia Fed website: http://www.philadelphiafed.org/src/Garn.html and states 'The Congress hereby finds that – (1) increasingly volatile and dynamic changes in interest rates have seriously impaired the ability of hous-ing creditors to provide consumers with fixed-term, fixed-rate credit secured by interests in real property, cooperative housing, manufactured homes, and other dwellings;' Note: the problem of insolvency was also deferred by the accounting device of allowing the thrifts to assign a current value to expected future profits – thus disguising the decline in their capitalisation.

71 As Bruck notes, (1989: 92–4) Columbia had 26% of its then $10 billion assets invested in junk bond issues by 1986 – how far this could be made to conform to the investment proportions set out in the 1982 Act is perhaps a matter of account-ing nuance. One might also note that the 1982 Act had given the government agencies that oversaw the thrifts – the Federal Savings and Loan Insurance Cor-poration, FSLIC, and the Federal Deposit Insurance Corporation, FDIC – greater powers to turnaround failing thrifts – selling on their mortgage books at a dis-count or consolidating their assets and passing the organisation on to a holding company for administration. This also provided an opening for some of them to be integrated into Milken's network.

72 Fred Carr, for example, ran First Executive, an insurance business offering tax exempt annuity products. From 1978, First Executive invested heavily in junk bonds – buying some proportion of a majority of Drexel underwritten issues from then through the early 1980s. As Bruck (1989: 93) notes: 'By the end of 1981,

Milken and a Drexel group owned 50% of First Executive's reinsurance subsidiary...'

73 Precisely how far the problems of thrifts and junk bonds were actually integrated in a way that made the end problems inevitable is still a matter of dispute. Barth *et al.* (2004) at the Milken Institute argue that junk bonds were only ever 1.2% of the total capital of the thrifts – which would still be many of billions of dollars and quite sufficient to contribute to the liquidity wave in junk bonds that underpinned the buyout boom – but that this was not a genuine source of threat to the thrift institutions. One might question the 1.2% figure in various ways – and also note that the concentration in some thrifts was also an issue – since it created the problem of insolvency triggering guarantees in some large thrifts that would then set of a wave of discount selling of assets across the industry – producing a self-fulfilling market contraction. One must of course also put it in the context of the real estate bubble of the 1980s that was strongly reliant on a rising market and the tax benefits created for real estate speculation in 1981 by Reagan. This in turn of course leads back to an argument as to whether state intervention to prevent a disaster is either a trigger (of underlying vulnerabilities) or the actual cause of them. Barth *et al.* argue that the real problem was the late response in deregulating thrifts and that the later legislation of 1989 and 1990 (see later in this chapter) made matters worse for both the thrifts and the economy as a whole. But this presupposes the efficiency of markets both to structure themselves effectively *and* then unwind the problems that they may manifest (a contradiction in some respects).

74 The Tax Reform Act of 1986 raised top rate capital gains to 28% from the low of 20% after the 1981 cut.

75 The October market crash resulted in a 20% fall in the Dow index in one day.

76 In a hostile takeover the potential buyer tries to bypass the current management by seeking to buy up shares from holders without the support of the board. The potential buyer issues a share tender offering a given price (usually a premium over current trading price) – the offer is good for 20 days. The buyer seeks control of the company in order to gain voting rights to remove the current management and impose its own – which may ultimately be followed by a delisting if the approach is by a PEF firm based on an LBO. Poison pills deter such approaches in various ways. The two main ways created through state legislation are: 1. tender offers seeking controlling share proportions may not be automatically granted voting rights with those shares – a majority of existing shareholders must vote for voting rights to be conferred. 2. An acquirer may be barred for a given duration (3–5 years) from merging the acquisition, selling its assets without prior approval of former directors, or delisting the company. Issues of convertible forms of securities may also be subject to regulations that make them more costly or involve additional rights to other equity holders. Ordinary equity shares may also be subject to restrictions in accepting tender issues (a floor may be created for the minimum premium at a level that is unrealistically high). Corporations are registered (incorporated) in a particular state and thus are legal entities subject to that states law. The nature of that law is one reason why firms choose to incorporate in a given state: 56% of Fortune 500 corporations were incorporated in Delaware in 1987, mainly due to its tax laws. In order to maintain levels of incorporation Delaware adopted a form of 2. above in 1988 (since it is the Board of the firm that decides where to incorporate). State law regarding takeovers, is often tested in Federal court on the basis of its compatibility with Federal law and the constitution – notably the US Supreme Court upheld a use of 1. for the first time in 1987.

77 Complicated by the problem of long term savings products – where current depositors would try to terminate them, activating penalty clauses, and no new depositors would be forthcoming.

78 In the hearings on corporate debt in January 1989, for example, Greenspan began to develop what would become his typical stance on incipient economic crisis – the particular problem (LBOs) is already unwinding under market pressures, warnings (on corporate debt) have already been given privately to the main participants (the banks and bond dealers), and attempting through legislation to halt an upward market is liable to be too late and too drastic. In the context of the recession that followed and the collapse of the thrifts, and his own acknowledgement that 40% of mergers and buyouts involved corporations liable to experience financial distress in adverse economic conditions, this seems overly sanguine. See Greenspan (1989a and 1989b).

79 The network created multiple opportunities for dubious practices – most prominently new bond issues were linked into LBOs where pre delisting equity prices would almost certainly surge. Knowing that a deal was being prepared thus created an incentive for heavy buys in particular equities. Dealers etc. could raise their profile and their fees by investing client's money heavily in these equities. They could also borrow and piggy-back their own buys to personally profit, which if fed through tax havens would remain invisible to the SEC. Milken himself undertook a variety of other dubious practices – particularly siphoning off options and warrants that had been bundled with debt issues and placing these in trusts in tax havens.

80 The 1990 Comprehensive Thrift and Bank Fraud Prosecution and Tax Payer Recovery Act increased penalties for financial institution-related crime. The 1991 FDIC Improvement Act tightened examination and auditing standards and the 1992 Truth in Banking Act required greater disclosure from the banks Jensen 1993). Barth (1991) notes that over half the thrift failures of the 1980s involved fraud (see also Glasberg and Skidmore 1997). However, Barth *et al.* (2004) do also emphasise that fraud was not the underlying problem merely a contributory issue. One might note though that once the problem began to unwind the collapse in prices was essentially unavoidable. When the 1989 FIRREA Act created the US Resolution Trust Corporation (RTC) to try to salvage viable banks out of the failed thrifts it inherited tens of billions of dollars in property – the sale of which (a necessity to meet depositors claims) further reduced property values. (Kindleberger 2005: 84)

81 'The junk bond market was in disarray in 1990 as defaults mounted... Returns to investors in 1990 were negative for the first time (–4.4%) since a small negative year a decade earlier, and spread vs US Treasurys were –14.4%. Indeed the compound average annual return spread from 1978–90 fell to slightly below zero (0.04%).' (Altman 1992: 79)

82 The bailout, furthermore, created immediate federal funding problems in terms of the Gramm-Rudman Act. The Act mandates automatic and widespread spending cuts in situations where deficit targets are exceeded. Thus the bank crisis if brought into the current budget would affect welfare spending at precisely the time that automatic stabilisers were required to offset some of the effects of growing recession. As a result the bailout mainly joined exceptional defence spending (such as the 1991 Gulf War) as an off budget expenditure – though $20 billion was on budget in 1989 (Glasberg and Skidmore 1997: 85).

83 Fed rates did start to fall in July 1989 but were still higher in 1990 at 7% than they had been at the time of the 1987 market crash.

84 Including 2,300 job cuts in the tobacco business.

Chapter 2

1 Though as the Myners Report of 2001 states there were antecedents: 'Venture capital in the UK can trace its origins back to the 1930s at least, with the founding of Charterhouse and the identification of the equity gap for smaller unquoted companies by the Macmillan Report in 1931. The industry took a major step forward with the creation of the Industrial and Commercial Finance Corporation (ICFC) in 1945. ICFC/3i was the dominant venture capital and private equity investor in the UK for several decades. By the mid-1970s there were around a dozen private equity firms rising to two dozen by the time the Wilson Committee on the financing of small firms reported in 1980.' (Myners 2001: 160). Cohen's point, however, still remains relevant since the very point of the Wilson Committee was the absence of innovative new firms. Moreover, 3i has been structured in quite a different way to the LLPs. There were a series of studies regarding the financing of small businesses in the UK from the 1950s onwards, including the 1971 Bolton Committee *Small Firms: Report of the Committee of Inquiry on Small Firms*; the 1979 *The Financing of Small Firms: Interim Report of the Committee to Review The Functioning of the Financial Institutions* by the Wilson Committee and the final report itself in 1980. The general thrust of the reports was that the main banks needed to do more in order to extend finance to new businesses and to enable small business growth. However, despite some change over the period, the clear statistical dominance of nationalised industries and private conglomerates and the very need to revisit the issue over a period of 20 years and more highlighted the general failure of anything concrete to occur (Carnevali 2005).

2 By which I mean the European Community members of that time.

3 As Galbraith notes, the acceptance of Keynesianism in the US was a slow process that developed through the 1940s. See also Galbraith 1977: chp. 7.

4 In 1975/6: 'Nationalised industries are very big business indeed. They include the largest employers in the UK and provide jobs for nearly two million people. The assets of the largest public enterprises are even greater than those of the private enterprise giants. They account for some 11% of gross national output and annually invest as much as the whole of the private manufacturing sector.' (Donaldson 1976: 103)

5 Donaldson notes that though there were many more small firms than large in the UK, employment, output and industrial concentration (averaging 26% for the three largest firms) were dominated by large firms. Growth had, as in the US experience in the 1960s been led by merger and acquisition: '[D]uring the early sixties a dramatic acceleration took place with annual takeover expenditure averaging £300 million a year – ten times the average for the fifties. By 1967, the figure had risen to £800 million. This was again doubled in 1968 and by 1972 reached a new peak of over £2,500 million. AEI and GEC, BMC and Leyland; Tesco and Victor Value; Radio Rentals and Thorn; Boots and Timothy Whites; Schweppes and Cadbury; Imperial Tobacco and Courage; Unilever and Allied Breweries, are just a few examples of the giant enterprises which have become even more massive in recent years.' (Donaldson 1976: 84) As Toms and Wright note (2005: 279) in 1949 small firms accounted for 20.5% of output and 22.5% of employment, falling to 18.2% and 21.7% in the early 1970s. Merger and acquisition were relatively easy since the monopolies and Restrictive Practices Act 1948 was discretionary. Even after the Restrictive Trade Practices Act 1956 and the Fair Trading Act 1973 conglomeration through a holding company form continued.

6 The broader concern of these studies is the 'illiquidity premium' hypothesis – that illiquidity of the LLP and secrecy are necessary for funds to generate high returns on investments and that fund managers seek liquid limited partners to invest – one test of which is if they are able to afford the risk of committing to an illiquid asset like PEF.

7 The requirement that the issue be advertised in two national newspapers would have little bearing on this.

8 There had been regulatory responses to changes in banking practices in the 1960s and these did cause a basic change in the operation of the Bank of England in 1971 and in the regulation of banking. Prior to 1971 monetary policy focused on the largest four commercial banks – Barclays, Midlands, Lloyds and National Westminster – and the other smaller banks that participated in the clearing system at the Bank of England. The central issue was effective monetary policy and control of liquidity and thus inflation. The banks' profit by lending based on their deposits on the assumption that only a fraction of the deposits will be called upon at any one time and that the money lent will then be re-deposited creating both credit and an expanding cycle of deposits in excess of actual cash as money. The banks maintain a cash reserve – partly on deposit at their own bank – the Bank of England – to guarantee that claims on deposits could be met. The function of the Bank of England is to both maintain the liquidity of the banking sector and implement government monetary policy by manipulating the ability of the commercial banks to lend and set given interest rates. Prior to 1971 this was done through setting a central bank interest rate and through open market operations to affect liquidity by influencing the current reserves held by the commercial banks at the Bank of England and also their liquidity asset ratio. If the Bank of England sells securities that are bought by the public then money flows from the commercial banks' reserve accounts at the central bank to the Bank of England's own account – the minimum cash reserve (how much they need in order to meet average calls on their deposits) may then be breached requiring the banks to either have fewer deposits or lend less or liquidate some assets and make fresh deposits at the Bank. If the latter then they may breach their liquidity asset ratio (comprised of short term lending assets which can easily be converted to cash and which must make up 28% of the bank's capital). This again reduces their capacity to lend and tends to push up short term interest rates – slowing down the economy and controlling inflation. The main problem with this mechanism for controlling inflation, however, was that the focus on the main commercial banks caused other financial institutions to offer bank like services causing the rise of the secondary banking sector – which included newly arrived relatively unregulated foreign banks – mainly from the US – as well as building societies, insurers, higher purchase organisations and credit unions – all able to offer credit. This prevented credit creation being controlled by the Bank of England – limiting monetary control of inflation. In 1971 the reserve/liquidity combination was replaced with a single reserve asset ratio set at 12½% with fixed proportions to be held at the Bank of England, the Bank of England interest rate was replaced with a base rate which could not be lent below. This created a more liberalised banking structure with greater leeway for lending at different rates and a simpler intervention process by the central bank. At the same time the secondary banks now became a direct target for monetary policy and for the Treasury. However, liberalised lending resulted in an immediate large increase in the money supply through credit creation, and growing speculative investment, with immediate inflationary effects in 1973. Broad inflationary curbs on property speculation

caused several major secondary institutions to face insolvency – partly precip-itated by a large scale withdrawal of funds by foreign investors.

9 This was also the case with the 1987 Banking Act that followed on from the Big Bang and also from the failure of Johnson Mathey in 1984. The Act gave the bank of England new powers exercised through the Board of Banking Super-vision which included: 1. Auditors could contact regulators without being held to have breached confidentiality. 2. The two tier definition of the 1979 Act was replaced by a single definition of a bank – authorised and regulated to take deposits and subject to a 'minimum net asset requirement'. 3.UK banks were required to inform the Bank of England if an 'exposure' to any single grouping exceeding 10% of its equity-capital and also to seek prior permission if that exposure is likely to be more than 25%. 4. Providing the Bank of England with false information would be a criminal offence subject to a maximum two year imprisonment.

10 As various analysts have noted the total tax burden in the UK was not any larger than the industrialised average and the shift towards indirect taxation had regres-sive effects (Keegan 1984: 118–21). Top rate income tax subsequently fell to 40%.

11 Monetarism is based on the idea that the government should concentrate its economic policy on creating and maintaining low stable inflation as a prerequi-site to economic growth (rather than the Keynesian focus on full employment and demand management). Influential Monetarists such as Milton Friedman began to argue in the 1950s that government deficit spending to stimulate aggregate demand was 'policy ineffective' because 'rational' consumers realise that the increase in wages and incomes it produces are an illusion – more wages and income push up inflation so real wages don't increase – the currently unemployed therefore remain voluntarily unemployed, demand in the economy does not actually increase in the long run and growth is not stimulated. The net effect is held to be inflation (which is bad because it reduces the value of savings, reduces investment confidence, increases the incidental costs of business – more industrial disputes as wages try to catch up – more changes to prices of goods producing loss of con-fidence in the economy etc.). The Monetarist solution is to argue that the govern-ment should reintroduce free markets but also seek to control inflation to prevent escalating problems of wage-price spirals fuelled by rational individuals responding to money illusion (the realisation that money is worth less sets of demands for higher wages and so on). Inflation is to be controlled by: 1. Restricting growth of the money supply (how much is printed) to less than growth in national income (which is a measure of economic growth). If the money supply increases slower than income then the value of money increases i.e. each unit of money buys more goods – this is deflation. 2. Manipulating interest rates: higher interest rates increase the value of saving and reduce spending thus reducing demand and, in terms of the logic of the model, reducing prices. Higher interest rates also increase the cost of credit reducing demand and prices in the same way. The implication of econ-omic models of this kind is that the state should: Withdraw from all forms of owner-ship as an economic intervention – nationalisation, controlling large investment projects, state provision of major services and infrastructure such as health, rail electricity etc. Reduce its role in creating automatic stabilisers to boost or reduce demand and maintain growth – welfare payments, wage hikes or (in times of inflation) price and incomes policies in the public sector. This is argued because the models state that intervention not only prevents the forms of efficiency (implying higher growth and better products) that free markets offer (they 'distort' markets) but also because the very basis of Keynesian demand management is ineffective (resulting in inflation).This minimal state implies far less need for heavy taxation.

Tax revenue would no longer be needed for: 1. A large government bureaucracy needed to administer this intervention. 2. Programmes of subsidy, welfare, employment, investment etc. This means a commitment to the reduction in the Public Sector Borrowing Requirement (PSBR) or state debt and also a move towards more balanced government budgets. Instead the government concentrates on providing a legislative framework that facilitates free markets.

12 The main privatisations include: 1979, British Petroleum; 1981 British Aerospace, British Sugar; 1982 National Freight; 1983, British Ports, Forestry Commission, 1984, British Telecom, Sealink, Jaguar Cars; 1986 TSB, British Gas; 1987 Unipart, Rolls Royce, Royal Ordinance, British Airways; 1988 British Steel, National Bus; 1989 British Water Authorities and in the 1990s, British Electric.

13 As with Cohen, Moulton's biographical details highlight the importance of a US connection: after working as an insolvency auditor for Cooper Brothers in Liverpool Moulton was assigned to their mergers and acquisition group in New York where he worked 1978–80 before joining Citicorp Venture Capital in New York to work on MBOs for one year. He was then sent to set up a division of the firm in London and left in 1985 to set up the UK private equity branch of the pan-European Schroder Ventures organisation. He later worked for Cohen at Apax, 1993–96.

14 Though monetarism and related arguments for free markets focused on a small state and reductions in public spending – the Public Sector Borrowing Requirement (PSBR) tended to rise in the 1980s, partly because of the higher level of unemployment, as a result public spending did not reduce but rather shifted from productive investment and employment maintenance to more primitive automatic stabilisers. BES was replaced by the Enterprise Investment Scheme in 1993.

15 500 companies were listed on the USM by the beginning of 1987.

16 The clarification also resulted in more funds being structured as LLPs and fewer as investment trusts, which had been the case before.

17 As such it provided another useful strategy along with the sale of council houses.

18 One issue was that tax relief on mortgage interest in the 1970s favoured investment in property over securities, reducing the demand for corporate bonds and thus access to investment capital.

19 The point of regulation was to provide a framework to maintain investor confidence. Towards this end investors (who placed their capital in the hands of professional institutions for investment or engaged dealers or brokers) were distinguished from market counterparties in trading. Counterparties received no additional protection since they were deemed to be on an equal footing with each other. Private customers were also distinguished from non-private customers. Non-private was defined on the basis of scale (corporations, local councils etc.) where scale was presumed to translate into expertise and access to professional advice. Private customers were accorded greater protection and the burden of proof on them to show that they were not treated appropriately (informed about risk, interrogated about his situation) was deemed to be lower. The Act also allows for a key distinction between breach of regulation only and breaches resulting in fraud or breach of common law duty. The SIB formalised its expected standards for investment firms in ten Statements of Principle in 1991 (Sharples 1995: 193). These essentially reduce to integrity, know your customer and inform your customer.

20 There were 490 foreign banks and 120 foreign securities firms by 1986 (Galletly and Ritchie 1988: 25).

21 The Eurodollar market began as a deposit denominated in dollars in a bank outside US political jurisdiction – the market took off as a form of tax evasion by multinationals in response to the US interest equalisation tax (1964–73) via which domestic branches of US banks were constrained to charge higher rates for offshore lending – it became more cost effective for corporations to channel dollars into European Banks for further use and for a market to emerge utilising that currency without it returning to the US. The increase in oil prices by OPEC in 1973/4 added the petrodollar market to the Eurodollar market greatly increasing the volume of Dollars available in the European banking system at a time when the major economies were suffering inflationary recession. Surplus Dollars were off-loaded to poorer nations as part of development packages, eventually contributing to the debt crises of developing nations in the 1980s. The Eurodollar market can also be seen as part of the longer series of events contributing to the transformation of securities markets. The market attracted the US banks who then also began to exploit other tax differentials between the US and UK. Share trades in the UK incurred a 2% stamp duty. US securities firms would therefore buy up large volumes of desirable UK equities pay the stamp duty and then effectively trade them through US listings as American Depository Receipts. The emerging large UK institutional investors – pension funds, unit trusts would then buy the ADRs avoiding stamp duty. This increased markedly after the end of exchange rate controls in the UK in 1979.

22 Deferred interest bonds are another similar form.

23 As Mayer 2001:2 notes the specific form of investment delegation takes one of two forms: trustees can either delegate the whole fund including strategic allocation decisions on assets to fund managers or retain strategic allocation decisions within the board of trustees and delegate specific investment functions to a range of specialist fund managers.

24 Forstmann Little & Co developed Mezzanine funds as an alternative to junk bond financing – providing up to 50% of the capital for buyouts from their own debt and equity funds and the rest from senior debt sources (Little and Klinsky 1989: 72). Mezzanine funds in Europe have been provided by a range of institutions. For example, Kleinwort Benson, and the combination of Wasserstein Perella, Banque Paribas, Commerzbank and Amro Bank (Arzac 1992: 22).

25 Exceptions include MFI, bought out from Asda for £718 million in 1987, and the Gateway buyout. Others such as divestments from Cadbury Schweppes (Premier Brands in 1987) would generate less awareness (Boyle 1994: 206).

26 Buyouts could involve some combination of these. For example, the buyout of Leyland Daf in 1993 was of a company that had been privatised and had then failed and was then split into divisions (Boyle 1994: 202).

27 For example, Unipart was bought out in 1987 from the then state-owned Austin Rover (Wright *et al.* 2000: 595).

28 There were 13 such deals in 1989 at the height of the market, ten in 1990, six in 1991 and three in 1992.

29 One aspect that was similar was the way that the growth in merger and acquisition activity in the late 1980s the (few) large buyouts resulted in a new level of interest by regulators in the terms and conditions of takeovers. In the US individual states had enacted poison pill enabling legislation, in the UK the Panel on Takeovers and Mergers began to scrutinise the buyout of publicly listed companies more closely (Renneboog *et al.* 2005: 4).

30 Jensen (in Jones *et al.* 2006: 14) makes the point that this in itself was a reason for the renewed economic growth in the 1990s by restructuring US industry.

31 In a global perspective the greatest effect on the major economies was experienced by Japan where a housing market bubble ended, banks were technically insolvent, the Nikkei index fell by 80% (1990 to 1993) and economic growth drastically reduced, creating a long term problem regarding economic structure and economic policy which is still not fully reconciled.

32 When Clinton came to power at the beginning of 1993 unemployment still stood at 7.3%.

33 See Chapter 3.

34 For a fuller explanation of bond interest rates and yields see Chapter 1 endnotes.

35 The Fed uses interest rates to achieve its federally mandated goals of fostering low inflation and full employment in the service of strong economic growth – the current phrasing was added to the Federal Reserve Act of 1913 in 1977. The twelve members (seven from the Fed in Washington, five from regional banks) of the Federal Open Market Committee (FOMC) meet eight times a year in order to set the interest rate (FRB, 2006) but can also hold extraordinary meetings to change interest rates, though these are by definition rare. The short term interest rate sets the level for inter-bank lending of up to one year and this, in principle, feeds through to longer term lending and commercial lending.

36 Note: a long period of relatively low, and stable interest rates based on a policy of small (if perhaps frequently reviewed and adjusted) and incremental changes is not historically unusual for the US – having been the norm throughout the 1950s and 1960s.

37 Though if inclined to argue for formalisation one might start from 1993 when Greenspan apparently rejected a fixed model of the natural rate of unemployment at 6% (a rule based approach to monetary aggregates had already been rejected in 1987). In 1997 when US growth rose from 2.5% to 4% Greenspan did not increase interest rates. In Fed models 4% growth is an inflation-creating level, moreover, the Fed tends to work on the assumption that to control inflation (and thus maintain economic growth and employment creation) short run interest rates should exceed a level based on GDP growth plus inflation.

38 For example, the upswing in interest rates in 1994 (six small changes in one year) that resulted in the Mexican Peso crisis also caused problems in the exchange rate derivatives markets. Several mutual funds made substantial losses requiring recapitalisation – BankAmerica Corp $67.9 million in two funds, Piper Jaffray $700 million (Roiter 1995: 273). This had knock on effects in terms of the way derivatives were viewed and debated by the SEC and the Fed as well as the UK SIB (Sharples 1995). See also Chapter 4.

39 This is the composite index, the Nasdaq 100 began in 1985 at 250 and was reset in 1994 to 125.

40 Subject to the mandate that the regional carriers provide equal access to all national carriers.

41 Including a series of subsidies to promote access and public welfare benefits – rural services, low-income users, schools, libraries etc.

42 The Bill passed 414 to 16.

43 The Act is available online from the industry regulator, the Federal Communications Commission (FCC) website at: http://www.fcc.gov/ telecom.html

44 More specifically Regional Bell Operating Companies (RBOC).

45 Whether pricing levels that emerged would be restricted was deferred until the outcome of competition could be assessed by the FCC.

46 In 2005 it bought AT&T for a further $16 billion and in 2006 Bellsouth (then valued at $86 billion).

47 There was also the high profile failed attempt to buy Sprint in 1999 for $129 billion. Verizon subsequently bought MCI after the collapse of Worldcom and in competition with Qwest.

48 It is worth noting, however, that selling a service-concept, such as social networking can also be a successful form of business if the system can generate a critical mass of users. This is because social networks rely on numbers of participants to make them viable and there is therefore a first-mover advantage to them so long as they are also competitively updated in terms of what is the current standard for 'user-friendly' technology. Friends reunited and Facebook have both benefited in this way. In 2007 Facebook had a valuation of $15 billion and more than 65 million users. One could also extend the argument to market forums like E-Bay and to information suppliers that provide price quotes for holidays, insurance etc. (which rely on a critical mass of access to those businesses rather than to users *per se*).

49 Insolvency can include: formal bankruptcy; Assignment for Benefit of Creditors (ABC) where all assets are sold to a third party for the benefit of creditors in a legally outlined process that requires no court hearing; the informal process of putting the firm into hibernation; restructuring – the business – selling on aspects etc as spin-offs; or, where 'strip financing' has been applied – creditors may already have fixed proportions of given assets assigned.

50 Though as Stiglitz points out rapidly expanding markets could have been specifically targeted by changing the margin call requirements on equities – higher margin calls and/or shorter periods would make it more difficult to trade in shares reducing the volume of trading and thus the rate of expansion of equities, on average (Stiglitz 2004: 64).

51 Benjamin and Margolis 2001: 259 note that over 20% of Fortune 1000 companies, including Cisco systems, had established venture capital divisions aiming to capture profitable new tech businesses.

52 Numbers increased to 35 1997, 70 1998 and 74 1999 (Toms and Wright 2005: 292).

53 As Credit Suisse First Boston's head of leveraged finance, Mark Patterson, put it: 'The simple early-stage venture-capital model and the simple LBO model have expanded... There's much more variety today. It's harder to say: This is a LBO firm; this is a purely venture firm; this is a growth capital firm.' (Hadjian 2000: 5)

54 A study based on 2001 data, for example, found that average investment for US public and private non-defined contribution plans was 3.4% of the total assets of the pension fund and when adjusted for those that did not invest, the figure was 5.4%, with the largest figure being 23.1% (Chemla 2004. Pension funds accounted for 30–40% of the total solicited private equity funds. Larger pension funds tended to be the main investors. As various analyses, such as Hatch 2003 note allocation proportions by pension funds fell slightly during the market problems of 2000–02 so it is reasonable to infer that they were slightly higher than the Chemla data in 1999. When read in conjunction with Papke's work on the ratios of asset allocation in pension funds based on data from 1981–87 this tends to confirm a long term trend of steadily increasing absolute and proportional levels of allocation with some variation during periods of economic downturn. See Papke 1991. Myners cites a 1999 Goldman Sachs survey that reports an average 4.8% allocation from US public sector pension funds and 6.6% from private pension funds (Myners 2001: 175).

55 In conjunction with more specialist funds PEF firms also started to employ a pool of former CEOs with particular industry-based experience that could then be called upon to help manage the acquisitions (Kaplan in Jones *et al.* 2006: 16).

Chapter 3

1 It should be noted that these firms were not the first examples of trans-Atlantic PEF – some venture firms and some PEF divisions of the US banks opened London-based operations in the 1980s. The arrivals in the late 1990s, however, signal a clear change in the pattern and scale of integration.

2 The Euro served the function of legal currency for transactions from 1999 though it existed in tandem with domestic currencies until 2002.

3 For the structure and indexing of the market see the materials of the trade body, the *European High Yield Association*.

4 The Eurobond market developed as an unregulated trading system not located in any particular country. Companies issued bonds denominated in a European currency and syndicates of banks would buy up the issue and then either rapidly break up the issue and sell it on or hold on to it in expectations of changing demand. As an unregistered market with no physical location trading could be anonymous and free of tax. The bonds could be attractive because they allowed investors to hold assets in alternative currencies (that may be more stable than their own). They were particularly attractive to US corporations investing abroad, for the same reasons that a Eurodollar market arose. Various innovations developed in terms of both. The interest rate volatility of the 1970s led to bond interest rates being fixed as spreads over Libor (see Chapter 4). The different degrees of demand for different corporation's bond issues in different countries also led to a Swap market: US company A issues bonds on the Eurobond market in Francs. US company A does not have any use for the Francs but US company B wants Francs to build a factory in France. B's domestic credit rating is good. It can, therefore, raise capital in the US easily. B uses those dollars to buy the Francs. B gains because no tax is paid on the Franc bond issue. A either gains access to cheap credit in the US for domestic purposes that is cheaper than it could raise itself, or gains from some form of fee. An intermediary securities firm arranging the swap will also earn commission. (Galletly and Ritchie 1988: 48)

5 The main reason for this as I note in Chapter 5 is that PEF buyouts tend to be contingent – and increasingly so as competitive bidding has become more common. As such, there is usually less of an incentive to put together a prospectus and meet other regulatory requirements of the securities exchanges for a public issue of bonds in the initial stage of the buyout. Under Milken, informal and centralised deal making using junk bonds was rapid allowing large deals to be put together by firms like KKR. This was less the case later and viable alternatives now existed in the form of privately placed mezzanine finance and bank syndications based on the originate and distribute model (see Chapter 4). Junk bond issues tend to be more common as a follow on from bridge financing or as part of refinancing.

6 See also Harm 2001: 248.

7 It also involved various policy initiatives to improve venture capital funding of small businesses: the 1994 Enterprise Investment Scheme provided income tac relief (reduced income tax to 20% level) on an individual's investment in common stock of new small firms up to £150,000. The 1995 Venture Capital Trust Scheme was subject to taper capital gains at 10% rather than 40% on investment assets held for two years. (Baygan 2003: 15)

8 The number of buyouts per year actually decreased from 586 in 1992 to 542 in 1995 as the size of individual deals increased (Wright *et al.* 1996: 228).

9 There are limits to this argument in the sense that MBIs also increased in the late 1980s though not on the same scale. The reasoning for the two rises may also be

different. Later 1980s MBIs often reflected the liquidity conditions of the time which enabled hostile outright takeovers or competitive bidding against incumbent management. In the 1990s the issue was more that incumbent management were seen by large investors as the reason for corporate failure and thus were less likely to be seen as part of the post-buyout solution.

10   As well as trade sales i.e. sales to another private company of similar kind.

11   Trade sales were the main form of exit for PEF throughout the 1990s – 40% in the recession period and 50% to the end of the 1990s (Wright, Renneboog *et al.* 2006: 10–11). This to a degree contradicts the point that PEF were an alternative to traditional mergers and acquisitions on the basis that corporations were no longer interested in mergers – unless one assumes that a post-buyout firm was a more attractive/cheaper proposition for the corporation at a later date through private sale.

12   In 1997 Easdaq was also set up in Brussels, consciously following the Nasdaq model (Flowers and Lees 2002: 167). Easdaq never achieved the same kind of prominence and listed only 59 companies at the beginning of 2000 (total capitalisation 56.8 billion Euros with a daily trading volume of equities of just 148 million Euros). The Nasdaq bought a 58% holding in March of 2001 and renamed the exchange Nasdaq Europe.

13   Renneboog *et al.* 2005: 5 provide additional reasons based on both tax issues, propensity for public listings and corporate culture in Europe. See also Wright, Renneboog *et al.* 2006: 15.

14   According to Wright, Chiplin *et al.* (1990) there was some initial trade union resistance to privatisation buyouts in the late 1980s but limited effect. It would be 2006 before serious opposition was mobilised.

15   There have been numerous initiatives to encourage PEF and venture capital at the European level: information regarding the schemes is available via the BVCA website.

16   The main associations are the Confederation of British Industry (CBI), the Institute of Directors (ID) and the Federation of Small Businesses (FSB) and the British Chamber of Commerce (BCC).

17   In 2000 New Labour also introduced the Corporate Venturing Scheme which allows tax relief against corporation tax at 20% for investment in new issues of unquoted small companies shares held for a minimum of three years, subject to the limits that the investment may not be more than 30% of the total of the issue and the gross assets of the company must not exceed £15 million (Baygan 2003: 15). The government also created the UK High Technology Fund and the Regional Venture Capital Fund, both in 2000.

18   More specifically: under the Taxpayers Relief Act of 1997 individual capital gains on assets held for a year for those in the highest income tax bracket in the US fell from 28% to 20% and for the lowest, 15% to 10% – remembering that capital gains on assets of less than a year are taxed at the individuals ordinary income tax bracket level, that endowments and pension funds are tax exempt and that corporations are taxed on the basis of their organisational liabilities.

19   The FSMA supersedes the 1982 Insurance Companies Act, the 1986 FSA, and the 1987 Banking Act.

20   UK PEF is unusual in that it is regulated by the same body that has oversight of the public exchanges and responsibility for protecting the rights of individual investors. Since LLPs are restricted in the way they solicit and thus in the type of investors they attract (see Chapters 1 and 2) this has been a cause of resentment amongst PEF firms (Bushrod 2005).

21 Although the Inland Revenue began to review the non-dom category in 2002, long before it became a political issue in 2006–07.

22 UK pension fund allocation fell from a high of 30% of total investment in PE funds in 1996 (recovering to 40% in 2001). Allocations as a proportion of total assets of pension funds remained low throughout the 1990s: private pension funds contributed 0.5% of their total assets and public sector 0.8%.

23 There were 26 deals in 1998 for a total of £2.5 billion and 46 in 1999 for a total of £4.6 billion (Toms and Wright 2005: 293 and 295).

24 Kaplan (2002: 19) puts the figures at $45 billion and $75 billion.

25 There were over 1,000 venture capital firms (Sohl 2003: 9).

26 The Nasdaq actual peak was 5,132 – the lower figure was its closing level that day. The Dow actually peaked with a close of 11,377 January 11th, the recovery, however brought it almost back to this level.

27 As Clegg (2002: 207) notes the overall dynamic of how markets price equities undermines the founding rational notion that on average markets trade at a real value that represents a rational measure of corporate earnings to prices. One can argue that an efficient market hypothesis is untenable even if one can use statistical techniques for retrospectively smoothing out fluctuations because at no point does such efficiency occur and any temporary correlation that can be constructed need not imply pure rationality as the behavioural basis for its occurrence. In this context 'irrational exuberance' becomes a dubious phrase in terms of its link to the economic theory in which Greenspan was steeped – even if it has a kind of broader public discursive credibility.

28 This can also be guaranteed by 'laddering' agreements where investors offered preferential treatment in the first allocation of the new issue agree to make further buys through the day as particular price levels are reached.

29 There were over 1,000 venture firms by 2000 – around twice as many as in 1997. In 1999 fund size averaged more than $100 million and included $19 billion plus funds – the 19 alone were larger than the entire industry in the mid-1990s. Sohl 2003.

30 As Sohl notes, from 1996 the size of total investment increased faster than the number of companies invested in creating an increase in the size of the average investment – peaking at $90 billion for 5,485 deals at an average of $16.4 million per deal (2003: 13).

31 Brown's argument is considerably more nuanced than Stiglitz's and highlights the way Glass-Steagall was never a full prohibition. Nevertheless, he argues that the repeal then being considered (1995) would be a mistake since it would give monopoly power to commercial banks and cause the final disappearance of any form of independent investment banks.

32 By the Gramm-Leach-Bliley Act.

33 Similarly Bank of America bought Nations Bank, and Fleet Bank merged with Bank Boston. Including the broker Stephen's and Quick & Reilly.

34 Golding's point is that institutional investors became increasingly aware in the 1990s of the conflict of interest of analysts and began to create their own research departments – which of course is a further reason why there is an insider/outsider split in investments – large institutional investors tend to be beneficiaries of some aspects of the investment and banking conglomerate's behaviour and are also in a position to provide a check on where it might have adverse effects on them – without there being an overall check on the tendencies with investment banking.

35 A fallacy deconstructed by Thompson 2002.

36   Aragon's point is that the problem is not one of institutional systems for invest-
     ment but rather overcapitalisation of venture capital funds – the solution to
     which is smaller funds and less capital and thus more care and, presumably,
     fewer hot money effects.
37   Typically 25% of total committed capital is paid up front the fund and the rest is
     called on with around ten days notice (Rand and Weingarten 2002: 31).
38   For a retrospective see also Sood 2003 and Susko 2003.
39   Malik (2003: 171–82) for example shows how Forstmann Little came to grief in
     Telecoms due to lack of market experience and reliance on equally inexperi-
     enced investment bankers, whilst insiders from the telecoms companies made
     large fortunes.
40   The actual process is more complicated since most convertible preference shares
     include dilution clauses that give the holder a priority right to buy new issues if
     they are at the same price as old issues (offsetting 'percentage-based' dilution) or
     includes a conversion price mechanism to adjust for new issues at lower prices
     (offsetting 'price-based' dilution) (Harris 2002a). Three problems arise. First, the
     priority right requires the holder of the original issue to be willing and able to
     commit more capital. Second, the conversion price mechanism can produce a
     'death-spiral' of falling share prices that continually kicks in further conversion
     mechanisms and leaves all un-protected holders of equity worse off. This depends
     on the precise formulation of the conversion based on valuation of the firm and
     capitalisation. Third, the clauses are no protection against default or against the
     continued fall in equity values and/or insolvency of the firm.
41   Distressed refers to both the status of a given firm (illiquid, defaulting, insolvent,
     approaching or in bankruptcy) and debt categories (debts that are traded at a dis-
     count – stated in proportions e.g. 75 cents on the $ – on markets because of current
     credit market conditions). Chapter 11 of the US Bankruptcy Code is a process
     that works in the following way: an indebted corporation files for protection as a
     recognised going concern and then has 120 days to put forward a plan of re-
     organisation that contains proposals concerning repayments to creditors. The
     bankruptcy court then grants a 60 day period for the company to lobby cred-
     itors. Each level of creditor (senior to junior) then votes on the plan – which will
     normally offer larger proportions of repayment to the most senior creditors (bank
     debt), some to junior (bond holders) and typically very little to equity holders.
     In principle acceptance requires a 67% majority in each credit class but the court
     can eventually impose a settlement if the more junior classes try to block the
     plan and the court deems the plan fair on the basis of the current financial posi-
     tion of the firm and its ability to meet its liabilities to the hierarchy of creditors.
     If agreement is not reached in the 180 day period any claimant can file a reor-
     ganisation plan and this can include debt distress firms intervening to meet
     some creditors' demands and effectively gain control of the new firm that emerges
     form Chapter 11. The court imposition of a settlement is likely to occur at this
     stage (Anson 2002: 10).

Chapter 4

1   The TPG office was set up with the potential to use up to $15 billion in funds.
    Carlyle had previously also had a Moscow office but closed it in 2005.
2   TPG's first Asia fund was solicited as early as 1994. Much of its regional activity
    has been focused on Australia. It acquired the airline Quantas for £4.4 billion,
    for example.

3 In 2005 over 50% of the European funds were located in the UK but only 26% of total investments were directed at UK based firms.

4 321 funds closed raising $145 billion.

5 Apax provide an excellent overview of the growth of private equity during the decade in Apax (2006).

6 In 2006 the top five PEF firms (TPG, Blackstone, KKR, Bain and Carlyle) accounted for more than half off global buyouts by transaction value. In 2006–07 PEF LBOs constituted 20–25% of total merger and acquisition activity – thus the top five firms accounted for over 10% of global merger and acquisition activity (Axelson, Jenkinson *et al.* 2007: 1–2).

7 Private equity has in addition become a product that smaller private investors can access in various ways: 1) Private equity investment trusts – that invest your money in a range of funds e.g. HG Capital 2) investment syndicates e.g. Hotbed – which puts the money directly into funds investment in specific firms 3) investment tracking financial instruments that track on performance measures of private equity such as the private equity index (Privex) made of the 25 largest private equity firms.

   Cash offer of $69.25 per TXU share – 15% premium on current market value. As part of the deal TPG agreed to scrap eight of 11 coal projects for power generation, cut prices by 10% and support emission reductions to woo environmentalists, politicians and business opposition. However the agreement also saves them billions on new power plants – up to $1 billion each – a large saving on debt that can be used directly for gearing – and creates a policy problem for power generation strategy in the long run – supply projected to exceed demand 2008. Coal is abundant and cheap (US has 27% of world known deposits) gas currently supplies 70% of Texan demand but price rises in wholesale have been large recently. Since TPG will be out in 3–4 years it will not face the major issue of building the plants or dealing with the failure of not meeting demand...

8 Of the top 100 buyouts tabulated in February 2007 46 were other forms of ownership than publicly listed companies, a further 41 were secondary buyouts (resales of previous buyouts to other private equity groups) and just six were of then publicly listed companies. The leaguer tables are regularly updated: see www.fasttrack.co.uk There are numerous smaller PEF firms specialising in specific sectors of the economy and in particular scales of buyout. For example, ISIS Equity Partners specialises in small firm buyouts.

9 In principle since LLP agreements tend to prevent single investments consuming the whole of fund capital since this greatly increases risk.

10 See also Cohen 2007: 32–3.

11 Thus any protective measures based on insider investment proved ultimately flawed since they presupposed that collapses would be confined to particular companies and sectors.

12 That it did so is of course not unusual in and of itself: the Fed responded to the market crash of 1987 with three cuts in six weeks; it responded to the East Asian/Russian crisis with three cuts in seven weeks in 1998 and made three cuts in seven weeks in 2001. In each case, however, the general context was different i.e. the relation of the finance system to the rest of the real economy was in some respects different based on causes of the crisis, levels of debt in the system, overall levels of interest rates, inflation, unemployment, sources of underlying growth, productivity, and economic vulnerability etc.

13 This was despite the fact that the 1995 Private Securities Litigation Act made it more difficult to hold advisers, analysts and accountants liable for any losses

incurred by investors. In 2001 there was a record 488 class actions for fraud against US firms (Malik 2003).

14   The cut was intended to be temporary and is now set to expire in 2011.

15   The increasing value of housing meant that in terms of housing stock values – wealth was increasing. At the same time, expanding mortgages, equity release, and cheap debt for personal consumption meant that total debt was increasing – creating a potential debt servicing problem. More consumption thus meant a combination of ostentation and austerity. Fed figures report that housing wealth approximately doubled 1999–2006, rising from $10.4 trillion to $20.4 trillion, with the majority of the gains 2001–04. Since no direct form of calculation is made only estimates exist for how much of this has been converted into consumption. Estimates range upwards from $300 billion (based on a 3% extraction assumption). Unsecured debt in 2005–06 stood at around 17.3% of GDP. Household debt servicing costs increased consistently since 1994 to a historically high level of just under 14% of average disposable income in 2005 – indicating a trend increase in the absolute size of debts. According to the industry credit assessment organisation myFico, the average American consumer has 13 credit obligations, four loans and nine credit cards. Credit card usage has expanded disproportionately amongst lower income households (Stavins 2000). According to the research firm CardWeb.com average credit card debt rose from just under $3,000 in 1990 to over $9,000 in 2003. Approximately 60% of US households with credit access have a running balance (not clearing the balance), 37% carry more than $10,000 – though the majority carry far less. Bankruptcy rates rose through the 1990s to around 50,000 filings per million and research indicates that households declaring bankruptcy are likely to also be those defaulting on loans or delinquent in credit card payments (Stavins 2000).

16   Subject to regulatory and legal restrictions: SEC guidelines following on from the intentions of the Investment Company Act of 1940 restrict mutual funds from investing more than 15% of net assets in illiquid assets defined as those that cannot be disposed of within seven days at current valuations.

17   There is no single definitive figure since differentiations occur based on public and private pension funds, insurance providers, mutual funds, foundations etc. This makes comparisons between different sets of data provided in different accounts and studies extremely difficult and also accounts for the range of figures on institutional investment levels that one finds.

18   The 'pension crisis' has been one aspect of a broader social security debate in the US regarding whether the system should be (as Bush Jr has advocated) shifted towards individual investment products and away from a collective system where the current working population maintain the system (including the public benefits of those that have already retired). See Baker and Weisbrot 1999.

19   The Conservatives had also begun to promote institutional investment – though with mixed results: the 1994 Amendment to the Insurance Companies Regulation Act relaxed investment constraints for insurance companies. However the 1995 Pension Fund Act introduced a minimum funding requirement that reduced PEF investment by pension funds – investment began to recover in 2001 (Baygan 2003: 13) – see also later in chapter.

20   For the full argument see Chapter 7 on tax issues.

21   A short/long strategy is the dominant hedge fund method but involves numerous variations. The basis of shorting is for the hedge fund to borrow shares in a given company and sell to generate capital that is then either held or invested. If share prices fall the fund is able to buy shares at the lower price and return these to the

dealer from whom the original shares were borrowed – creating a net gain to the hedge fund. The actual process tends to be more sophisticated using options, contracts for difference and other mechanisms and financial instruments (in turn hedged or offset by placing shorts on the indexes that track the specific investment – which need not be an equity *per se*) The concept of the hedge fund was developed by Alfred Winslow Jones in 1949 and began to grow in popularity after 1966 when Fortune magazine published an article on his strategy. By 2005 hedge fund activity accounted for around 50% of daily turnover (trades) on NYSE and LSE. For methods see Ineichen 2001, for analysis see Lamm 2004, for history see Connor and Woo 2003.

22 This initially created conflict of interest issues for the banks that created problematic relations with the PEF LLP firms, since the investment bank PEF divisions could be bidding against PEF firms at the same time as the investment banks were advising the PEF firms. For example, in 2003 J P Morgan and CSFB acted as advisors to PEF firms and as rival bidders for the UK drug company, Warner Chilcott. The main investment banks/financial conglomerates were earning more from fees (and earning those fees upfront and at low risk) and so scaled back their own fund solicitations around 2002–03. According to Preqin the investment banks amassed record fund solicitations of $13.6 billion in 2000 falling to $600 million in 2004. Thereafter solicitation began to grow again with the banks being more careful to be partners in club deals. Goldman Sachs, for example, began solicitation of a $19 billion fund in 2006.

23 Some of the very largest had done so much earlier when the LBO market was suppressed. For example, Blackstone in 1996. By the end of 2003 Carlyle, TPG and Bain Capital all had hedge funds.

24 According to the Federal Reserve Bank of New York by mid-2007 hedge funds controlled assets pf $1.75 trillion compared to $400 billion in 1990.

25 Research by Brad Hintz at Sanford C. Bernstein provides a breakdown of how investment banks profit from PEF: advisory fees constitute 0.35% of deal size, underwriting a bond issue to finance some of the deal is set at 3% of the issue size, underwriting loans for financing some of the deal is set at 1.25% of the loan size, refinancing debt is charged at 3% on bond issues and 1.25% on loans, organising an auction creates a 0.35% advisory fee and an IPO is charged at 7% of the proceeds.

26 They can, however, also be capital assets – such as whole companies, divisions, capital investments such as machinery etc.

27 Note 'originates' is not the same as original source of the asset. Assets may, for example, be junk bonds and as such the source of the asset is a business. See later in chapter.

28 This is termed 'true sale' creating a 'bankruptcy remote' status – if the SPV is controlled by the originator the legal conditions for true sale become more important to clearly establish at the beginning – having clear contracts, separations of ownership rights, independent directors etc.

29 More specifically, they are not only the last to be paid, and thus the first to experience losses, they will also have absorbed all the losses to which they are exposed before more senior tranches are affected i.e. the returns on their CDO investment will have been wiped out.

30 Note that securitisation is not the same as the creation of a CDO – this depends on the nature of the relation between the SPV and the ownership rights of the underlying asset. The first CDO issue is attributed to Drexel Burnham in 1987. The first CDO based on derivatives rather than a capital/debt asset as an income

stream is attributed to J P Morgan in 1995 (see credit default swaps – CDS – later in the chapter).

31 Nor are SPVs and off-balance sheet strategies. They were, for example, key accounting strategies used by Enron. SPVs were abused to transform liabilities into new income and to recycle revenues as new income, both of which enhanced the apparent valuation of the firm. In the case of the telecoms the firms might originate, issue and buy their own derivatives making debt look like an investment asset. Accounts were also dubious because in some cases no payments were made. If payments were booked these might relate to possible future business of one or more related companies – a 'good will' estimate. Good will estimates were a general feature of the accounting of tech and telecom firms. There was nothing necessarily illegal about this practice – though it could be devastating when good will estimations were not realised. The fibre optics firm, JDS Communications, for example, posted a write down of $50 billion in impaired goodwill in 2001 (Sohl 2003: 10).

32 Duffie and Rahi provide a fascinating introduction to financial innovation focused mainly on derivatives but also including a tabulation derived from Mathews of key economic changes and associated innovations in securities.

33 Also the 1994 Reigle Community Development and Regulatory Improvement Act enabled banks to securitise loans with the intention of freeing balance sheet space for lending to small businesses.

34 The Accord specifically applied to banks that operate on an international basis and has extended from 1992 to the main banks of most nations (before being superseded by Basel II, January 2008). Tier 1 capital reserves consist of highly liquid forms of capital that the bank retains – equity and cash. Tier 1 capital is held against unexpected losses – expected losses based on writedowns on the current valuation of held assets are covered by additional strategies such as profit retention or the creation of additional reserves/provisions. Tier 2 capital are less liquid forms of capital that the bank has retained (junior debt that it holds) forms of capital that are suddenly realised (e.g. a revaluation of land holdings shows them to be worth more) and the set aside provisions for expected losses/writedowns etc.

35 Thus a very high risk asset will have a weighting of 100% a medium of 50% and so forth. The total sum of assets is calculated based on the % weightings and 8% of that sum is required as a capital reserve.

36 That this is the primary function in terms of banking does not of course mean that it is also the primary systemic advantage of the CDO that is constructed – most CDOs involve arbitrage advantages: the transformation of low credit rating debt into higher credit rating CDOs, resulting in improvements in the terms of credit for the original asset sources and originators because of the gains through the spread on the CDO – see later in chapter.

37 As Elizalde (2005a) notes as part of his thesis research, the core problem is one of pricing or calculating the premium (return, interest rate etc.) for the CDO and this is essentially a problem of pricing the tranches in terms of a statistical model of defaults. This is a crucial activity because as defaults increase the returns to the CDO reduce, since the investor is being paid the premium to hold the risk of defaults. If the methods of calculation consistently under-estimate the level of defaults then CDOs are a poor investment and it will quickly become difficult to issue them as securities. The problem, however, is not just that one is estimating the statistical incidence of defaults (a future event from past occurrences) but that there are different models for doing so (structural models and reduced form models). The modeling of each is highly complex and based on assumptions

regarding correlations. Elizalde's 2005a paper explores a structural model. The general problem of risk is addressed in Elizalde 2005b.

38 I've simplified here to clarify the central point that the original assets are discounted in the transfer to the SPV. Matters are complicated if the underlying asset is not the sum of a principal and an interest rate, if the SPV is an off-balance sheet part of the financial conglomerate or if the SPV is also using leverage since these create different and additional issues of how returns are constructed and the transfer of assets is motivated.

39 Again, this is a simplification – the originator may receive payments incrementally. Further, since the bank may have created the conduit precisely to distribute its lending the discount may not manifest significantly in the sale to the SPV but rather in the spread to the CDO/CLO since the bank is still accepting a lower overall return for its lending by paying out some of that return to the investors in the securities in order for them to holding the risk of defaults – see later in chapter.

40 Notably, the proportion of CCC ratings for senior debt increased at the same time as the issuing of lower grade junk bonds (B rated) decreased i.e. banks were lending more money at worse credit ratings and this was reducing the need to issue the least attractive forms of junk bond.

41 The median of the core 8 is actually the Libor. Note also Libor is a guide – effectively a point of reference not the actual rate at which lending occurs through the day – though it is historically a fairly good approximation. The Bank of England is unusual in allowing banks to estimate their own required funds to be held on account at the central bank: 40 banks participate in this system.

42 An SPV must also be capitalised: typically 1–3% of the value of a security issue. It will also typically be guaranteed by a third party who offers bond insurance and/or by some form of rolling liquidity agreement to meet short term cash flow problems – if a conduit then the originating bank will usually be this source (which may include what is termed a liquidity 'back stop': see later in chapter).

43 This is so even though the interest rate on which senior debt and securitisation are constructed are usually floating rates – the float is usually a set spread from Libor and thus as rates fall towards Libor the same issue of reduced margins applies.

44 For example, the First Data deal in 2006–07 had senior debt set at 2.75% above Libor and thus below the usual bank prime rate.

45 Though initially the effect was to unwind the carry as the yen appreciated: a full account of the yen carry is one of successive expansions and contractions as the yen has appreciated and depreciated. Interest rate arbitrage was already a part of this process, since the Bank of Japan already maintained relatively low interest rates by global standards – negative real interest rates simply made this more attractive.

46 At the same time the state began a process of quasi-Keynesian public works programmes and began to underwrite the debts of the Keiretsu.

47 China had been steadily joining the major global and regional political and economic organisations since the 1980s: initially opposed by the US Treasury, China joined the IMF and World Bank in 1980, acquired observer status at GATT in 1984, and made a formal application in 1986. Negotiations for GATT entry were well advanced in 1989 when the Tiananmen massacre caused them to be suspended until 1992. Thereafter various nations worked to delay entry because of China's political significance as the last Leninist state and because of the economic impact of the entry of such a large country (Zhang 1998: 236). China has also been a member of the Asian Development Bank since 1986 and APEC since 1991.

48 China had experienced consistently high levels of economic growth prior to 2001; WTO membership added to this – partly because it stabilised access to US markets (previously China had required periodic renewal of most-favoured nation status).

49 States have in any case been provided with good reasons to begin to diversify out of the dollar, reducing the attractiveness of recycling by buying US Treasury securities. The slow decline in the value of the dollar over the decade devalues dollar reserves and assets (such as securities) and also imports inflation if a state's currency is pegged to the dollar – as the yuan and most of the main Middle East currencies have been (tacitly or openly). As a result China and the main Middle East states have begun to diversify their foreign currency holdings into the Euro – reducing total demand for state securities by reducing overall demand for US securities as part of the global total of desirable state securities to hold. This, in turn increases available capital for other uses.

50 CDS provide the other main source of securitisation: the CDS is essentially an income stream from a holder of a corporate bond. The bond holder takes out a contract with another party and pays them a proportion of the income stream from the bond in order to insure against default. SPVs buy CDSs and sue the income stream to create what are termed synthetic CDOs i.e. based on a derivative. For a clear account of derivatives construction see Karol 1995 and Chisholm 2004.

51 This was reflected in the general sentiment of PEF analysts and PEF trade journals. For example, Krijgsman: '[B]ut the train has to hit the buffers some time. The question is when. PwC's Hemmings reckons it will take more than one failed deal to have a meaningful impact on activity. The collapse of the Isosceles/Gateway buyout in the early 1990s was the last showstopper in the UK MBO market. But back then debt markets were not so deep and liquid, so any change of sentiment was bound to be reflected in a sharp reverse. Today, the proliferation of private equity business models, a more sophisticated approach to debt by the banks and the sheer number of players mean that a number of deals will have to fail before there is a market correction.' (2005/6: 15). See also McCarthy and Alvarez 2006.

52 Even if no equity was released, rising values might mean that the remortgage was now a smaller % of the total value of the property and thus less risky and possibly not sub-prime.

53 It is important also to note that the US and UK have unusually high proportions of home owners. In the US around 70%, of which 38% have no mortgage.

54 A forced sale, typically through auction aims to recoup the value of the loan and can thus be a discount from the current value of the house. This can mean the owners get nothing – losing their initial deposit.

55 An excellent analysis of the emerging problems is provided by William Poole, President of the Federal Reserve Bank of St Louis in a speech 1st week of August.

56 Though created by federal mandate and notionally guaranteed by the state both have been self-financing since floating on the NYSE in 1968.

57 The average is around 55 days. In mid-2007 the US market had around $2 trillion in issued commercial paper (approx 50% unsecured) and Europe around $840 billion (around $300 billion asset backed).

58 As early as July 27th Citigroup was estimating that Fannie Mae and Freddie Mac had suffered $4.7 billion in losses on sub-prime mortgages that it had acquired. Fannie Mae's shares fell form $70 in August to $23 in early 2008 whilst Freddie Mac's fell $65 to $20. Both posted large 4th quarter losses for 2007: $3.55 billion and $2.45 billion respectively.

59 In November Countrywide, for example, reported a reduced year on year mortgage lending by 48% for October 2007 at the same time that it posted a third quarter loss of $1.2 billion.

60 This was a highly unusual form of decline – not because it entailed a housing bubble but rather because the associated circumstances were at odds with a crash: low (if rising) interest rates, high levels of employment, a strong period of economic growth and productivity growth. As such it highlights the core role debt levels can play in a decline (as well as the way housing had become a key driver in the US and UK economy).

61 Axa also posted a 40% fall in value on its US Libor Plus mutual fund, which had a large sub-prime component, and German Union Asset Management halted redemption on one of its funds after investors withdrew Euro 100 million in later July.

62 As of August 30th 2007 the Cantor Index indicated that the largest falls in bank shares over the previous eight weeks occurred at: Bear Stearns (37%), Goldman Sachs 27%, Morgan Stanley (26%), Deutsche Bank (22%), Barclays (21%), Citigroup 17%, Royal Bank of Scotland (16%) and HSBC (8%). Market values continued to reduce throughout the year. For example, from September 13th to November 9th reduce din billions of £'s in the UK: Royal Bank of Scotland 10.3; Barclays 10.2; HBOS 5.3; HSBC 4.9, Lloyds TSB 3.4 NR 2.1; Alliance & Leicester 1.3; and in the US: Citigroup 32; Bank of America 13.5; UBS 8.9; Merrill Lynch 8.9; Morgan Stanley 6.7; CSFB 6.2; JP Morgan Chase 4.9; Bear Stearns 1.

63 This began on August 13th the Bank of England announced that it would make unlimited funds available at its punitive rate of 1% above the base rate. On September 5th the Bank announced auctions for an additional £4.4 billion of funds in overnight markets at the base rate in each of the next three weeks and also widened the margins of acceptable error from 1% to 3.75% on each of the banks account at the central bank used to settle their obligations. On September 19th the Bank offered an additional £10 billion of funds in each of the next four weeks in the three month market and agreed to accept mortgage securities (subject to the mortgages being of 95% or less of valuations).

64 The growing level of cooperation was in some ways unusual. During previous crises the Fed tended to simply organise a market solution with the main US banks (as it did over LTCM 1998). On this occasion, however, Bernanke engaged in increasing degrees of consultation with other central bankers. For example, he engaged in 35 conference calls with central bankers and investment bankers regarding the emerging crisis in August alone (Bawden 2007). Though the Bank of England continued to criticise the need to provide large levels of funds Fed and continually complained in regard of moral hazard it did essentially cooperate with the Fed, ECB and others (though intermittently did not – notably September 6th when the other main parties injected funds) and follow the same general policy of attempting to supply liquidity. In mid-August the Fed also placed pressure on the main banks (and J P Morgan, Citigroup, and Bank of America all comply) to use its discount facility in order to encourage other banks to do so (on the assumption that tapping emergency funds would not be seen as a sign of specific distress to an individual bank). The US Treasury also worked to coordinate market solutions. In October Paulson initiated the organisation of the Master Liquidity Enhancement Conduit: a capital fund to be financed by Citigroup, J P Morgan and Bank of America in order to create a repository for CDOs and other assets particularly of SIVs and hedge funds that are experiencing problems with their CP. The aim was to prevent cycles of distress selling that

further reduced the value of the assets through dumping into essentially illiquid markets. The fund was initially intended to be capitalised at between $80 and $100 billion. It became a subject of dispute between the main parties over the latter half of 2007 and was still not in existence early 2008. On December 12th, five main central banks (Fed, Bank of England, ECB, Swiss bank and Bank of Canada) announce a coordinate series of auction of funds totalling approximately $100 billion.

65 One that the Bank of England was on the verge of attempting in April 2008.

66 This was begun by the Fed since the problems of the banks and of the housing market were acutest there and the pressures on the Fed were greater. On September 18th the Fed funds rate was cut from 5.25 to 4.75% and the discount rate from 5.75 to 5.25%. On October 31st the Fed funds rate was cut from 4.75 to 4.5% and the discount rate to 5%. ECB rates stayed at a consistent 4% in 2007. The Bank of England resists cuts until December 5th when the base rate was reduced from 5.75 to 5.5%. On December 11th the Fed again cut the funds rate to 4.25% and the discount rate to 4.75%. Rate cuts continued into early 2008, the base rate fell to 5.25% and the Fed funds rate to 3%. By March the base rate had fallen to 5% and the Fed rate to 2.25%: with the Fed effectively deviating from the end of 2007 from its previous policy of small incremental changes in rates.

67 On September 10th Libor was actually higher than the Bank of England punitive rate at 6.98%. Euribor meanwhile was 3.5% (actually below the 4% target). As base rates were falling Libor and Euribor continued to fluctuate whilst remaining detached from base rates. For example, November 28th the three month Euribor rose to 4.7%, its highest level since 2001 and the three month Libor was 6.59%. Notably, despite falling central banks rates lending rates to consumers did not fall significantly. For example, though the Fed funds rate was 3% in March 2008, the standard fixed rate 30 year mortgage in the US remained at thelevl it had been in September – around 6.8%.

68 Sachs operated 3 quant funds (see next end note): Global Equity Opportunities (GEO), Global Alpha, and North American Equity Opportunities (NAEO). All suffered large falls in value in July and August. In order to minimise asset sales of the securities used to generate leverage Sachs took the unusual step of recapitalising the funds – providing $2 billion itself and raising another $1 billion from investors.

69 Quant funds: so termed because the decision to buy or sell is made by a computer based on a quantitative analysis. Traders identify a sector for investment and then set up a strategy in that sector (any combination of share price movements, interest rate movements, exchange rates, indexes tracking any of the above etc.) The strategy involves some combination of short and long positions (or market neutral positions). The traders set up parameters – floor and ceiling prices – and then turn over actual trading to a computer based on a programme to maximise the number of profitable trades within the parameters and based on a set of imperatives to unwind positions if the overall strategy is under threat because of breaches of floor and ceiling prices. A number of problems then arise: 1. computer herding: the more computers operating in the same market and programmed to target the same parameters then the greater the amplification of any real market effect by actual trading – a sudden fall sets off instantaneous selling by all computers the net effect of which is greater volatility in markets. 2. If the programme is constantly seeking small differentials for profitable trades on a moment by moment basis then this increases the number of trades per given volume of

capital in the hedge fund – creating further volatility in markets traded in. 3. The underlying problem is that the programme will likely have been designed on the assumption that markets are stable in the long run – which is essentially to say no computers are trading in the way that the quant is. The more computers there are then the less the basis of the programming actually accords with the real time effects of the trading. 4. Since most hedge funds are highly leveraged the programme incorporates a safety protocol for minimising losses by selling liquid assets to cover debts and meet margin calls. Several computers acting rapidly on the basis of the same programming can thus set off a spiral of falling values on any given market as each seeks to deleverage or unwind a position in order to minimise losses. The computer does not have the capacity to step back and assess the rationality of what is occurring in order to realise it is exacerbating its own trading problem. It does not, however, require the quant trading to create volatility in order for the quant to be sucked into a spiral of unwinding positions that exacerbate falling markets. It merely requires all markets to begin new trajectories in ways that undermine a short long strategy (such as all markets falling together or one market falling precipitously).

70   The main data source for hedge fund performance is the Hedge Fund Research Index (HFRX). The HFRX reported its then largest single fall (3%) since its inception in 2003 in the third week of July. This was followed by worse figures for August: HFRX reported average hedge fund losses across funds categorised by 19 of the 20 variants of strategies. Over the full year HFRX also reported that hedge funds posted an average net fall i.e. losses on investments. In July 2007 Sowood's Alpha Fund Limited and Alpha Fund LP, with combined investments of around $15 billion ($12 billion of which was leveraged) fell in value by over 50% and were wound down (both were absorbed by Citadel).

71   Initial examples of losses in August 2007 include: HBOS absorbed £19 billion of debt from its Grampian conduit which was unable to rollover its CP; the German bank Landesbank Sachsen faced capitalisation problems and was taken over by Landesbank Baden-Wurttenburg after its SIV Sachsen Funding I could not renew its debt. On September 4th Cheyne Capital Management's $8.8 billion SIV Cheyne Finance was placed in receivership.

72   As of November 2007 Citigroup had 7 SIVs with assets of around $80 billion. On December 14th 2007 Citigroup announced that it was bringing $49 billion of SIV assets on balance sheet.

73   In August 3 SIVs designed for other investment organisations by Barclays but also guaranteed by Barclays faced capitalisation problems based on CP markets: Cairn High Grade Funding I (valued at $1.8 billion, administered by Cairn Capital), Mainsail II (valued at $2 billion, administered by Solent Capital) and Golden Key ($1.9 billion, administered by Avendis). Barclays subsequently provided liquidity back stops and loans to the three in excess of $3 billion.

74   This is done according to International Accounting Standard 39 (IAS 39).

75   The limit here is created by the Sarbanes-Oxley Act 2002. Sarbanes entails accurate disclosure in accounts and Section 404 requires finance directors and CEOs to take legal responsibility for their accounts. Wilful misrepresentation can result in criminal prosecution and jail.

76   As with housing the problem began to manifest in 2006. Sub-prime car lending amounted to $300 billion in 2006. For 2006, the sub-prime car lenders representative, the National Auto Finance Association reported a rise in delinquencies from 6.8% to 8% for larger lenders (40,000+loans) and from 6.2% to 14.6% for smaller lenders. At the same time the duration of loans had increased to an

average of 65 months and the size of deposits had fallen from an average of 5% to 1% of the value of car.

77   In September Peter Spencer at Ernst & Young had estimated potential losses at $200 billion.

78   The problem then was not just the current level of defaults – which remained initially historically low but rather the accumulation of effects that would mean defaults would grow. In early December 2007 Moody's Kenneth Emery, director of corporate default research was predicting a rise in corporate default rates form a 2007 low of 1.2% to 4.2% in 2008 on the basis that any short run refinancing at higher rates by companies simply delayed and exacerbated an underlying problem. Grant Thornton of PWC was also predicting a sharp increase in defaults through 2008 as the conditions for restructuring firms in financial distress eroded (Stiff 2007).

79   The Bank of International Settlements *Quarterly Review* reported a sharp reduction in bond issues in the 3rd quarter from $750 billion (3rd quarter 2006) to $396 billion. The greatest reduction came in junk bonds.

80   On December 20th MBIA, the largest of the insurers revealed that it had underwritten $8.1 billion of CDOs and its share price fell 27% (against 70% for the whole year). MBIA was forced to seek a new share issue to recapitalise. Over 2007 insurance costs increased from 1% to 6% on a five year debt coverage policy. According to a Bank of England Report, October 1st 2007: the average rate of a corporate loan from a main bank increased by 2% in 2007 for one and five year fixed term lending.

81   Merrill Lynch, for example, eventually posted an unprecedented three consecutive quarters of negative net revenues 2007–08, including losses and writedowns of over $30 billion. Citigroup's losses then stood at $29 billion.

82   Since the Big Bang the UK has grown to have the largest share of all main international financial markets except hedge funds (dominated by US). It hosts 43% of foreign equities measured by turnover, 21% of hedge fund assets, 32% of foreign exchange measured by turnover, 43% of derivatives and 70% of international bond trading (figures 2005–06, Larson 2006). According to International Financial Services London (IFSL) financial services have increased as a proportion of GDP from 6.6% in 1996 to 9.4% to 2007 (22% for London). Manufacturing is still a higher proportion of GDP at approximately 14% but has been undergoing a long term fall. Manufacturing also had a trade deficit of £61 billion in 2007 whilst financial services contributed a £25 billion surplus. Financial and business services has increased at 3–4 times the rate of the rest of the UK economy for ten years and almost doubled its share of economic output since 1980 (from under 15% to 29% on a national basis and rising from less than 20% to 42% if one focuses on London and the South East.

83   Lloyds was again invited to offer a restructuring package on September 16th based on a Bank of England guarantee that the current credit facility would be extended – but by then the damage to Northern Rock's capitalisation and reputation were great. In any case the banks were reluctant to lend to each other because of the underlying problems of the credit crunch – accessing capital to engage in a private bailout was always going to be problematic – this in the end also contributed to the failures of later bids from Virgin, Olivant, J C Flowers etc.

84   A total of $208 billion in Europe (including RNS $18.1 billion, J P Morgan $17.4 billion, Barclays Capital $16.3 billion, BNP Paribas $13.8 billion and Citigroup $10.4 billion) and $269 billion in the US (including J P Morgan $35.1 billion, Bank of America

$32.8 billion, Citigroup $31.1 billion, Goldman Sachs $27.8 billion and CSFB $22.9 billion).

85 And this continued through the rest of 2007. For example, in November KKR and Goldman Sachs walked away from an $8 billion deal for Harman International (an audio speaker maker) and Cerberus activated a $100 million break out clause and walked away from its $7 billion buyout for United Rentals.

86 The banks used the same condition to force the PEF firms to increase the interest rate on portions of its lending and to demand a higher equity stake form the firms of $800 million instead of $150 million.

87 In the UK for example there were 174 buyouts in the 3rd quarter of 2007 but only two in excess of £250 million and these had been set in motion prior to the credit crunch.

Chapter 5

1 With the notable exception of some longstanding firms such as 3i, and also the recent tendency for some of the larger firms to IPO a minority stake in the PEF firm (Blackstones being a prominent example).

2 Fenn, Liang and Prowse (1995: 28) note that 1% is typical, based on the example of larger funds and established firms.

3 The management fee may also be structured as a 'priority profit share' (Douglas 2002: 5 and 9). Here the fee is initially taken from investors but then is taken directly from returns on investments once the fund becomes active.

4 Conversely, when a bid fails much of the work of consultants goes unpaid. For example, the collapse of the CVC led bid for Sainsbury in April 2007 was reported to have cost the main advisor groups more than £100 million in foregone fees (including Lazard and Goldman Sachs for CVC and UBS and Morgan Stanley for Sainsbury).

5 Those returns might then be structured as securities within a unit trust. This can be a useful way of ensuring that the realisation of gains from the investment are eligible for taper relief on CGT.

6 Noting that each fraction of the capital committed by the investor is only invested once and will not be called upon again during the life of the fund.

7 J C Flowers buyout of Long Term Credit Bank in Japan in 2000 for $1.2 billion then floated as Shinsei Bank in 2004 for $7 billion follows the typical timeline. KKR claims to hold acquisitions for an average of around seven years.

8 I am using an example specific to publicly listed companies here. A PEF LBO of a publicly listed company is typically termed a public-to-private transaction or PTP.

9 Equity may also be provided by minority investors. These are additional investors invited to commit capital to the specific buyout but who are not investors in the PEF fund(s). Minority investors are charged similar fees to fund committed investors but also tend to face additional fees specific to the individual investment acquisition they are partaking in. The private equity firm(s) also retain control over the business strategy imposed on the acquisition (i.e. the minority investors will usually have no voting rights in either the acquisition directly or any administrating shell company set up to manage it).

10 The trade journal *Bank Loan Report* is a useful place to find typical examples of debt structures. For other examples see Axelrod *et al.* 2007, Bierman and Bierman 2003: 110–11 and Little and Klinsky 1989.

11 Ebitda defines profits as earnings *before* interest, tax, depreciation and amort-isation. It is the standard industry measure used in PEF.

12 This, of course may be an increase in earnings from the new lower net level created by the initial aspects of gearing rather than an absolute increase.

Chapter 6

1 For example, Mike Wright at CMBOR is the main UK scholar to have focused on PEF and LBOs. In a number of collaborations he has produced a series of care-fully argued contributions to the literature based on the excellent CMBOR data base. In theoretical terms that work has tended to absorb the basic thesis set out by Jensen – albeit adjusted by UK conditions. Wright makes a good case that free cash flow is not a major signaling device in the UK but does tend to reiterate the agency argument, incentive realignment and aspects of the debt hypothesis in an uncritical way. Given that his focus is often econometric and micro rather than on the macro and/or normative aspects of PEF, this is understandable. There are, however, also some curious inconsistencies. For example: 'debt finance is more likely to be used where the desired outcome is efficiency...' (Toms and Wright 2005: 279) This statement seems to entail that debt is taken out in order to create discipline rather than discipline is a possible consequence of debt.

2 For a range of other points of critique see: Opler and Titman (1993), Arzac (1992), Opler (1992) and Rappaport (1990).

3 The point here is not to traduce Jensen's argument by making it appear he is unaware of the difference between a positive and normative argument in eco-nomics. He clearly is and makes use of the distinction in later work (1993/1999: 54) where he seems to place himself somewhere in between as an objective econ-omist with an overall view of the fragmented way in which different branches of economics approach organisations, finance etc. The point rather is that implicit in his argument is a series of normative commitments that structure it but are not addressed by it.

4 It is doubtful that Plato's solution would be very popular: 'First, none of them should possess any private property beyond that which is wholly necessary. Second, none of them should have a house or storeroom that isn't open for all to enter at will... Fourth, they'll have common messes and live together like soldiers in a camp.' (Plato 1997: 1052).

5 Lazonick and O'Sullivan, for example, look at the problem in comparative and historical terms to make the point that the internal learning process of organ-isations that enables innovation and efficiency to have a long term time line is undermined by the way decision making has been increasingly directed towards external financial monitoring: 'What the proponents of market control see as a solution to the dissipation of resources by management, we see as part of the problem. Strategic managers need to have discretion if investments in developing and utilising productive resources are to be made that result in sustained com-petitive advantage for their enterprises and sustainable prosperity for the econ-omy. But who these decision makers are, how they make their decisions, and whom they seek to benefit have profound impacts on whether these companies invest for the future or live off the past... In the presence of a powerful market for corporate control, the use of stock-based rewards aligns the interests of stra-tegic managers with public stockholders, making it all the more certain that the integration of strategy and learning will not occur.' (1997: 27–8).

6   This in turn must be seen in the context of how Schumpeter understood history, prediction, economic theory and politics: 'I do not advocate socialism [public ownership of the means of production and public control of decisions regarding what is produced, for whom and how]. Nor have I any intention of discussing its desirability or undesirability, whatever this may mean. More important is it, however, to make it quite clear that I do not 'prophecy' or predict it. Any prediction is extra-scientific prophecy that attempts to do more than to diagnose observable tendencies and to state what results would be, if these tendencies should work themselves out according to their logic.' (1952: 409) Schumpeter was also no fan of the Soviet system and had definite reservations about the implications of Keynes' work but provided sympathetic accounts of the key insights of both *Capital* and *The General Theory* (1962: chps 1 and 10).

7   This is a common position amongst theorists and practitioners of PEF, as the following from two general partners at Forstmann Little & Co illustrates: 'Political concerns about buyouts have grown at a similar rate [to the scale of the industry] and concern is justified when applied to imprudent transactions. In our opinion, the huge fees that can be had for arranging buyouts and the ready availability of 'junk' bond financing have made unsound buyouts much too common. However, these market excesses are merely abuses of a sound business concept.' (Little and Klinksy 1989: 72). It is certainly the case that Forstmann had a much better track record as a PEF buyout firm than most in terms of financial performance of acquisitions and its funds. It is worth remembering, however, that the means of improved financial performance was one based on rationalisation and asset sales, that it involved special dividends and large returns to funds and PEF firms (raising the issue of whether this is necessary to restructuring and desirable as a social outcome within an economy), and that Fortsmann was not immune to the pressures of the PEF industry model based on the need to guarantee returns – it was for example one of the firms to make large losses on investments around 2000 based on PIPEs etc.

8   Keynes considers the range from the tractable probability of roulette to the basic uncertainty that war might occur. As Philip Roth puts it: 'A gambler at the wheel who bets the colour black because red has turned up ten successive turns may tell himself that he is wisely heeding the law of averages, but that is only a comforting pseudoscientific name that he has attached to a wholly unscientific superstition. The roulette wheel has no memory, unless that is, it has been fixed.' (Roth 1973: 240). Humans of course, do remember and human systems are thus not so regular or so determinable.

9   More precisely: 'The relation between the prospective yield of a capital asset and its supply price or replacement cost, i.e. the relation between the prospective yield of one more unit of that type of capital and the cost of producing that unit.' (1936: 135).

10 For Keynes' the over-reliance on mathematics creates poor method. As he states in his notes on method at the end of his *General Theory*: 'The object of our analysis is not to provide a machine, or method of blind manipulation, which will furnish an infallible answer, but to provide ourselves with an organised and orderly method of thinking out particular problems; and after we have reached a provisional conclusion by isolating the complicating factors one by one, we then have to go back on ourselves and allow as well as we can, for the probable interaction of the factors amongst themselves... whereas, in ordinary discourse, where we are not blindly manipulating but know all the time what we are doing and what the words mean, we can keep 'at the back of our heads' the necessary

reserves and qualifications and adjustments which we shall have to make later on, in a way in which we cannot keep complicated partial differentials 'at the back' of several pages of algebra which assume that they all vanish. Too large a proportion of recent 'mathematical' economics are mere concoctions, as imprecise as the initial assumptions they rest on, which allow the author to lose sight of the complexities and interdependencies of the real world in a maze of pretentious and unhelpful symbols.' (Keynes 1936: 298) The problem as noted in Neilsen and Morgan extends to new innovations in economics such as info-theoretic approaches.

11 For an interesting critique of net present value (NPV) see Magni 2002. Magni deconstructs the modeling assumptions of NPV to show the basic inconsistencies. Specifically: 'The theory of finance tends to cancel the economic, strategic, psychologic, social differences in the events and in the individuals... The principle of additivity, well known in the literature, is then unwarranted, since the way we separate cash flows and then discount them is always arbitrary and based on subjective factors, influenced by the decision makers perception of economic phenomena.' (211–12)

12 Keynes' core point has become a central tenet in the 'heterodox' economic critique of the over-reliance on both statistical techniques in applied economics and pure mathematics in theoretical economics. It is for example, in conjunction with insights taken from the philosopher Roy Bhaskar, central to the work of Tony Lawson (1997; 2003).

13 Minsky was not very complimentary regarding Strange's work. He particularly disliked the 'British' tendency to blame the US for global ills whilst neglecting the culpability of domestic forces in the countries 'affected' by US policy. He also notes that if one is going to appropriate a key Keynesian phrasing (*Casino Capitalism*) then the relation between speculative and efficient/productive investment should be more central to the argument. He is similarly disparaging of elements of the Heilbroner and Bernstein text – here based on the failure to clearly pursue the distinction between conditional deficits and structural deficits.

14 His 1993 paper, for example compares the Roosevelt period with the 'false prosperity' of the 1980s and the challenges facing twenty first century capitalism. Here he highlights the central role played by banking but, given his emphasis on institutional specifics, is remarkably non-specific in his comments beyond some general remarks on the junk bond crisis in the US. Though his short 1996 paper on uncertainty tackles the issue of mutual funds and modern investment forms making the important point that investment strategies have become more short term, there is again, little in terms of overall context and no international dynamic.

15 One curious aspect of the LTCM collapse is that the participants continued to fail to see that the design of the models contributes to the tendency to undermine them. Undermining them is seen as a behavioural tendency that is separate to the risk reducing form of financial instruments. This is central to the original Black and Scholes (1973) model for derivatives and also implicit in the comments of Robert Merton one of the LTCM managers: 'If you invent an advanced breaking system for a car, it can reduce road accidents – but it only works if drivers do not react by driving faster.' (Jones 2007d: 20)

Chapter 7

1 Although a secondary market has started to develop where institutional investors trade their commitments.

2 Specifically the underlying trend across 1998–2003 is one of growth. Some individual years represent a decline on previous years but not in terms of the trend.

3 Barclays along with Deloitte are the main sponsors of CMBOR. Deloitte has a major consultancy interest in private equity, providing for example a comprehensive planning service to tackle the immediate post-acquisition logistics based on a 100 day action plan: an order in which to tackle changes, work streams into which to organise the changes delegated to different sets of key workers/management, monitoring and performance indicators over the period – IT and payroll issues etc. These can also be applied to mergers and spinouts as part of the process. For example, spinout requires new infrastructure – computer networks, maintenance contracts etc.

4 A spectacular example is provided by the Blackstone and TPG club deal for Texas Genco in 2004 which was flipped one year later for $8.3 billion constituting a sixfold return on the original stake.

5 IRR is the usual statistic reported on performance. According to research by Citigroup the average annual return over the ten years to 2006 was 14% in the US. If one breaks that down into averages by year, according to the IFSL, based on Thomson Financial statistics, average annual returns over that time have cycled from 15% to around 30% and back down to less than 5% (Maslakovic 2006a). According to the BVCA average returns in 2005 for the UK were 37% and around 16% over the previous decade. Since averages are for periods not funds *per se* then there not be an exact match between the time duration of a given fund and the cycle over which the average has been calculated. As such there may be some disparity (in addition to problems with IRR as a calculation) between the average % returns to actual investors in funds that overlap the same periods and the averaged percentages calculated that define that period.

6 Which by no means covers all firms or funds – the EVCA identified 1,600 private equity companies managing 2,600 European focused funds in 2005.

7 According to Citigroup, the top performance in the US over the last decade was 36%. BVCA figures for the UK also indicate a variation by investment sector – with an actual negative return on private equity investments in the technology sector over the last ten years.

8 A piece of Citigroup research approaches the problem slightly differently. According to their research an average buyout fund returned 14% per annum over last ten years. Citigroup set up its own basket of publicly traded equities and applied the same degrees of leverage and calculated the ten year return would have been at 38% (36% was the top performing private equity return). Notable underperforming IPOs have included the KKR float of Sealy, and Carlyle float of Magellan Midstream both underperformed the S&P 500 average by more than 12% in 2006. The period was, however, broadly bullish and thus underperformance could still be growth. According to Thomson Financial research, IPOs of buyouts in the US in 2006 averaged 16.4% growth in equity values compared with 23.1% for non-buyouts.

9 For a UK context see Wright, Thompson *et al.* 1992 and Amess 2002.

10 This initially appears to be in line with the various private equity industry associations' claims that private equity is a long term net job creator and improver of work organisation. The BVCA (2006, p. 5), for example, claims that in 2005/6 2.8 million people were employed in the UK in firms that 'have received private equity backing' and that employment growth in these firms was 6%, compared to a net loss of 0.4% in the economy at large. However, there are problems with these statistics and their claims. The BVCA claims, for example, hinge on the

ambiguity of 'received backing'. This is not the same as having been bought out. Here, they provide no data on the period over which that backing was given in relation to the time at which employment growth occurred. In some cases, the backing could easily have been years before the growth and if the backing was not a full buyout with effects on management and organisation it may be entirely unrelated to that growth. They do, however, make the additional estimated claim that the number of people employed by companies currently backed by private equity is 1.2 million or 8% of UK private sector employment. It is also worth noting that John Moulton of Alchemy Partners was publicly critical of BVCA data at the annual Super Returns conference in February 2008. He notes that BVCA employment statistics are not annualised and do not take into account PEF acquisitions that went out of business (the combination he claims would decrease the net employment gain to around 0%). (Kennedy 2008).

11 Which is a different order of issue than the standard problem of significance and the possibility of error. For example in hypothesis testing a type 1 or type 2 error may occur. A type 1 error occurs when we wrongly reject the null hypothesis because of the small probability that the test statistic does lie in the critical region (usually 5 or 1%). A type 2 error occurs when we wrongly accept the null hypothesis when it is actually false. For the broader conceptual issues raised by statistics see Olsen and Morgan (2005).

12 Furthermore, management will also have a vested interest in improving returns by reducing costs because it is a hallmark of private equity strategy to offer large incentives to upper management in the form of performance related bonuses and profit shares.

13 Clark (2007) begins to raise this issue in a recent research note.

14 The concept of self-discipline based on Bentham's panopticon is usually associated with a Foucauldian theorisation of power. I have strong reservations regarding Foucault's social theory but the concept of self-discipline seems a plausible one. See Lukes 1986 chapter 11.

15 Only 34% of UK buyouts recognised trade unions and 40% of buyout managers opposed union membership for employees and union recognition.

16 In March 2006 the AA was refinanced and CVC repaid themselves £500 million. Later in 2006, refinance was again undertaken – replacing £300 million of what is termed second tier or mezzanine debt supplied through specialist brokers with cheaper senior debt (provided by the investment banks) – see section 4.2.

17 In a joint statement June 29th CVC, Permira and Charterhouse set out that funds managed by them would provide the majority of the equity in the new company – 42% (£720 million) from CVC and Permira and 38% (£640 million) from Charterhouse with the additional 20% stake provided by the management of AA and Saga. The statement also noted that CVC and Permira had made a return of three and a half times their original investment in the AA. The valuation of the new company is claimed to be based on advice from float advisors and unsolicited indicative offers for the AA.

18 Perhaps except in so far as it appears serviceable.

19 Reducing the workforce also included the sale and closure of loss-making elements of the firm – its tyre operation and garage network – as well as a reduction in the number of its breakdown patrols (by 600). The AA has since added 200 new patrols but done so on the basis of new contracts and shift patterns.

20 £4.3 billion in corporation tax, £8.7 billion in PAYE and national insurance, £12.1 billion in VAT and £1.3 billion in excise and other duties.

21 If, for example, one takes UK corporation tax at 30% and uses the BVCA figures on tax paid in the accounting year 2005–06 compared to total sales revenue – £4.3 billion compared to £424 billion – then either the average private equity backed firm performed rather badly in terms of generating profits or the average private equity backed firm benefited significantly from tax relief. If tax in full was in fact paid then the entire private equity backed industry generated a total profit of just over £13 billion, which on sales revenue of £424 billion would be an extraordinarily poor performance (around 3%). The implication seems to be that large swathes of public equity operating profits were subject to tax relief.

22 Specifically: a sub-sample of 48 LBOs based on pre 1986 tax regulation created an estimated range of 14.1% to 129.7% of gains based on the median value of the premium paid to the original shareholders. See also Newbould *et al.* 1992.

23 The overall calculation was that gains = $226.9 million, losses = $116.9 million creating a net gain of $110 million and an annualised perpetual gain of $11 million.

24 As well as serving the function of forestalling any sudden crash in a booming commercial property market.

25 One limiting factor in this tendency in general rather than in terms of Reits *per se* is the degree to which securitising property through commercial property markets is possible without affecting the general prices of commercial property and thus the overall yields in terms of rents. If Sainsbury's entire property portfolio had been either sold or securitised the effect on the market of the sudden offloading of a multi-billion value set of assets may have been to drive prices down significantly.

26 The sudden announcement of an end to taper relief created a strong motive for businesses selling up (if they can) to do so before the changes take effect in April 2008. The potential effect is in any case disproportionate for small businesses: they cannot relocate out of country, they are unlikely to be able to offshore tax dealings as PEF and their long term budgeting has been on the basis of prior tax levels. The Chancellor has responded with proposals to introduce measures to protect small businesses from the effects of the change – particularly owners now retiring.

27 Warren Buffett, the 3rd richest man in world ($52 billion) speaking at a fund raising dinner in July 2007 highlighted the curious situation that he was taxed at 17.7% on the $46 million he made in 2006 without trying to avoid tax whilst his secretary was taxed at 30% on her $60,000 salary. Stephen Schwarzman at Blackstone earned just under $400 million in 2006. This was 48 times the $8.3 million average total earnings paid to S&P 500 CEOs and far in excess of the record earnings of Goldman Sachs CEO Lloyd Blankfen ($54.3 million). The 'Blackstone Bill', which if passed was due to become operative in 2012 proposed to increase tax on carried interest to 35%. All the main Democratic presidential candidates spoke in support of the change – Hillary Clinton, John Edwards and Barack Obama. During 2007 the larger buyout firms began to channel a larger proportion of their presidential campaign donations to Republicans (53% in the first half of 2007).

28 On September 13th the BVCA made a submission to the Treasury to begin a lobbying process to oppose any increased tax on carried interest. Notably, the submission based some of its argument on the precarious state f returns to funds and firms: half of the funds do not make sufficient returns to pay carried interest, 1 in 4 loses 25% of its capital and 1 in 10 loses 50% or more, whilst the median returns are about those on market shares. These are curious arguments since it would only be those firms actually succeeding that would be liable for tax on carried interest. The BVCA also made the argument that the economy is

now vulnerable and that deterring PEF would be counterproductive, perhaps causing it to move to other countries.

29 UK tax law on off-shoring is complex and requires extreme care to avoid sudden liabilities and criminal proceedings. If the affairs of an offshore company are controlled from the UK it may be treated as being resident in the UK for tax purposes. As such it would have to pay UK corporation tax on its worldwide profits. If it is not treated as a UK tax resident but the business is trading in this country through a place of business here (a 'permanent establishment') it must still pay corporation tax on the profits derived from that place of business (wherever they arise). This is unless the UK has a tax treaty with another relevant country in which it is situated that gives it the right for this to be waived. If an individual in the UK is deemed to be the controller of a company that is off-shored they could be liable for the tax on its income even if they do not receive that income. Tax efficiency and off-shoring is, therefore, a highly specialised area of tax law and is also one in which the confidentiality and lack of transparency that some locations offer is highly valued.

30 This is not to suggest Customs and Revenue simply ignore the problem but rather that they are aware of the limitations to how they approach it in the current climate. As with all state tax authorities they do research and report on how off-shoring may be regulated as part of the tax regime but have yet to develop their own effective strategy for how this can be done given the nature of the regime. They have recently, for example, been discussing the idea of an amnesty on off-shore accounts if they are reported by the holder. There has also been some move to simplify and redefine off-shore funds (HM Treasury 2007b: 5–6).

31 Given that the argument for retention of non-domiciled status is that the money will somehow be lost to the UK, a key component in the defence would have to be establishing what proportions of the earnings not taxed are retained, invested or spent in the UK i.e. in order to establish what the multiplier effects are. Private equity avoids this argument and focuses on the decontextualised tax paid by acquisitions. Given that marginal rates of consumption are lower for the wealthier – even for those habituated to ostentatious consumption – and given the trans-national nature of the executives and the off-shoring potential for deposits investments etc. it seems reasonable to suggest that the figures are liable to be unfavourable.

32 On October 1st 2007 at the Conservative party conference, shadow chancellor George Osborne announced a flat rate £25,000 annual tax on non-doms. Osborne claimed that the tax would generate £3 billion that could be used to fund two other tax changes. First a rise in the inheritance tax threshold from £300,000 to £1 million, which would then affect the top 2% of income holders only. Second, the abolishment of stamp duty for first time buyers purchasing a property for under £250,000. The figures assumed 150,000 non-doms.

33 The UK tax authorities were seeking clarification on this in early 2008 (HM treasury 2008).

34 The UK tax authorities were considering proposals in early 2008 to abolish the waiver for traveling days I set out in Chapter 3. This would sharply reduce actual possible working days in the UK before non-residency was breached.

35 Adam Smith, for example, though often claimed by the Right as a champion of market forces and of the autonomy of the economic sphere was also a moral philosopher of distinction and held that: 'The subjects of every state ought to contribute towards the support of the government, as nearly as possible, in proportion to their respective abilities.' *Wealth of Nations*, Bk V, Chp 2, part 2 (Of taxes). Complete text: http://www.adamsmith.org/smith/won/won-index.html

One could also look at the moral problem as a rights and responsibilities issue – some moral philosophers argue that there should be no rights without responsibilities and by extension, a differentiation of rights for those who act less responsibly. We seek to impose responsibilities on the poor in order that they have the right to benefits, yet seem curiously averse to imposing responsibilities on the rich in order that they enjoy the 'right' to their wealth. Additional one might consider it in terms of prioritising social goods in terms of functions – Harold Wilson's distinction between making money and earning money is a useful place to start here.

36 The efficacy of the solution of course depends on the nature of the coordination – there is, for example, a tension within EU policy between financial liberalisation in general and the specific tax regime arguments of different countries in regard of private equity. EU coordination is based on tax harmonisation and freedom of movement of capital and labour. In so far as this exists and in so far as it continues to develop, private equity stands to benefit. At the same time, individual states, such as Germany, want tighter restrictions on private equity including tax regulation.

37 27 EU nations, Switzerland, Lichtenstein, San Marino, Monaco, Andorra and 10 former British and Dutch colonies.

Chapter 8

1 Alliance-Unichem was itself created in 1997 in a takeover by Unichem, with Stefano Pessina holding a 30% stake. Boots originated in 1849 when John Boot began selling home-prepared remedies in Nottingham. Boots opened self-service stores in the 1950s, and its then research wing created Ibuprofen in the 1960s. The failure of Manoplax (a heart disease drug) in the 1980s led to the closure of its proprietary drugs wing. The firm employs around 100,000 people.

2 There were also a series of associate businesses across Europe, the Middle East, and in Asia.

3 The deal was initially to begin in 2007 but was delayed until February 2008 in response to Office of Fair Trading concerns. The third major pharmaceutical manufacturer – Novartis – was also considering a straight to pharmacy model as of late 2007.

4 The straight to pharmacy model has been one of a number of strategies. For example, in October 2007 AstraZeneca pushed ahead with plans to outsource production of the constituents in its drugs range. It opened a new sourcing centre in Shanghai and another in Bangalore, India, to help identify low cost producers. Currently AstraZeneca follows an in-house production model: it buys basic materials and then uses its own factories to develop them as active pharmaceutical ingredient production (API), and then processes the API into final products – pills, capsules etc.

5 Companies House is an agency of the Department of Trade and Industry (DTI). The UK has operated a company registration system since 1844 all limited companies are registered there under conditions set by the Companies Acts of 1985 and 1989.

6 Three of these non-executive directors had, along with Pessina, joined Alliance Boots from Alliance-Unichem.

7 The scheme of arrangement document is available from the Alliance Boots website.

8 The buyout of a publicly listed company thus differs from a secondary buyout in the sense that its initial debt structure is subject to public scrutiny. Once bought out this need not be the case for any refinancing – this makes the tracking of

such things as special dividends etc. more problematic unless the private equity concerns choose to disclose them.

9 Reportedly, their Guernsey-based KKR Private Equity fund (a $5 billion fund), as well as their Europe, Quoted, and Asia funds.

10 See AB Acquisitions 2007: 90.

11 A point also highlighted by Froud and Williams (2007).

12 Note: this point might be misinterpreted as implying the classical liberal position of Mill that only issues of actual 'harm' to others should be proscribed and prevented: self-regarding acts should be permissible. This position is fraught with problems as a basis for moral arguments regarding intervention because all acts are at some point removed both a benefit and harm to some. The point also presupposes that the measure of 'right' to intervene is consequentialist, which it need not be.

13 Though in Nozick's terms there is nothing self-serving or ahistorical in the argument about holdings and transfers there clearly is something of this kind from the point of view of critique.

14 Results were preliminary because the tax year was not complete. The measures were also based on accountancy transformations since Alliance Boots was only created by the merger of AU and Boots in mid-2006.

15 There are various ways one might approach the issue of governance in PEF. The PEF firms see PEF as an example of good governance because of incentive realignment. Bad Governance is understood as conflict of interest between investors (e.g. Haarmeyer 2006). Others have argued that PEF involves demonstrable good governance because it has not involved scandals like Enron (Zong 2005). Others have argued that PEF frees the firm from governance pressures created by public equity. But this creates conflicting governance issues in terms of how debt is used and accumulated. The firm is able to make quick and 'efficient' decisions speeding up the process of organisational reform and reducing transaction costs in business decisions. But the flipside of this is that private equity operates in a permissive environment in which there is always the temptation to pay dividends generated through new debts. Publicly-listed companies can in principle concentrate equity by using debt to reduce market capitalisation (buying back shares). But without the pressures created by a four year timeframe there is no *direct* reason to take on the risk of that debt. Investment in a publicly listed company may be a vehicle for profit through dividends but this is not in the same sense that private equity might view the acquisition of that company as a vehicle for debt loading and returns. For example, shareholder governance in a publicly listed company will tend to limit the generation of special dividends from debt. This changes the context and degree of any gearing, as does the market signals that greater leverage sends out concerning the dangers of holding that stock, despite its potential for greater short term returns (if the p/e ratio is reduced). Debt may be created but it may be created to a smaller degree and over a longer time horizon since the management of the firm are not subject to a further tier of control who are thinking of a resale timeframe.

16 For example, one tends to get a variety of responses and groups intervening in a given public equity issue in different ways. Investment banks can downgrade stock in letters to clients who hold that stock if they are unhappy with proposed policy changes. Institutional investor organisations can become involved. For example, the Association of British Insurers (a shareholder lobby group) can issue warnings (amber-top or red-top). The National Association of Pension Funds can approach shareholders to urge them to vote for or against proposals or, just as

damaging, oppose the re-election of directors. Governance research organisations that provide information for institutional investors can become involved
– most notably Pirc in the UK http://www.pirc.co.uk/ All these sources can result
in increased private or public pressure on the Board to consider particular proposals in a different way.

17   The team, finalised at a board meeting 11th July, contains six former directors of
Alliance Unichem, including Pessina and his long term partner Ornella Barra, two
former Boots employees who became directors after the merger with Unichem, and
two KKR executives. Pessina has effectively become executive chairman and no
separate CEO post is now planned. Baker apparently declined the post due to
diminished authority, whilst Wheway wanted a more senior role. Baker's earnings from the previous year were £1.18 million (basic salary of £696,000 and
bonus of £477,000), Wheways £390,000. All of the non executive directors have
departed and as of 12th July had not been replaced. Sir Nigel Rudd declined a
£250,000 charitable payment from the new owners to Derby Grammar School,
of which he is a patron.

18   There is a link here if one considers that the existence of PEF is an implicit pressure on Public companies that can result in higher debt levels for public companies as they respond to the pressures of PEF. Sainsbury's, for example, found
itself responding to its experience as a target for buyout. The first thing the
board did was to announce on April 20th an adaptation of some of the club deal
consortium's restructuring plans, now named 'Project Champion'. The project
involved a commitment of £750 million in capital expenditure on refurbish-
ment and new outlets, potentially creating 15,000 jobs. The financing, however,
was to come from the additional securitisation of Sainsbury's property portfolio
i.e. commercial mortgaging. Mortgaging has the additional advantage of potentially reducing the appeal of Sainsbury's property assets to private equity without
the company losing ownership of those assets. What this suggests is that there is
a pressure on publicly listed firms to be more debt laden and to take more risks.
Sainsbury's, for example, was approached by the property tycoon Robert Tchenguiz
after the collapse of the club deal bid. During the bidding process Tchenguiz had
amassed a stake in Sainsbury of 5%, buying large volumes of shares in three successive transactions. If the club deal went ahead he stood to gain from any premium offered by the consortium. When it did not he was also in a prime position
as a significant minority shareholder to advise the Board to adopt some aspects
of the club deal's property plans. In April he met with the Board to suggest splitting Sainsbury's into two listed companies – an operating company and a property company. Leveraging the property company would create money for
investment and for a special dividend. The strategy was rejected. The CVC bid
was then followed up by a sovereign wealth bid from Delta Two: a Qatari investment firm. Pressure, then, can involve degrees of indirectness but the ultimate
effect is to promote debt. This has been noted as a particular trend amongst
firms with large capital assets, particularly property – which has experienced
great increases in value in the last ten years (Loxton, 2007). In the context of a
publicly listed company, creating debt releases capital for productive purposes.
But it does not thereby follow that a trend towards greater leverage is to the long
term benefit of stable finances. The existence of pressure becomes, in a sense, a
measure of the effectiveness of governance. A problem here is that a publicly
listed company will, as Sainsbury's has, still usually exercise caution in not extending the securitisation of its property assets to a degree that might make its debt
servicing risky. In effect this still leaves it a viable target for buyout. This creates

a certain tension. By definition, effective governance creates limits to what a publicly listed company seeks to do. If it exceeds those limits then it comes closer to the private equity model and thus faces potential problems with its future finances. If it does not, it can remain attractive as a buyout target. Shareholder governance may, therefore, if one accepts the argument that there are problems with the tendencies inherent in private equity, be preferable to private equity but not a solution to it. Shareholders may not be a united body able or willing to marshal effective opposition to a buyout. Members of the board of directors may have reasons for supporting a buyout. The combination raises the issue of whether greater government regulation is needed to alter the context of governance.

19   The whole issue of health provision has been one whose context has slowly shifted. The NHS has gradually shifted in the last decade from being a health-provider to also a procurer from the private sector. For example, from 1999 to 2005 the purchase of acute healthcare services by the NHS from UK private hospitals increased by 400% to a cost of £965 million. The projection for NHS purchase of surgical procedures in private hospitals is 390,000 for 2007. Private healthcare as both an alternative and subsidiary to the NHS has grown in value from £14 billion in 1998 to £20.5 billion in 2006. These changes have occurred within a context of increased public spending on health but also a huge increase in costs. This in turn is increasingly raising the issue of whether a more market based health system, which has in many respects experienced piecemeal privatisation – not least through the creeping effects of public private initiative investments – will face further pressures for actual privatisation. Private equity adds an additional dynamic to this context because private healthcare has been a major target for recent buyout activity. More than 70% of Britain's private hospitals and five of the seven largest are owned by private equity. In June 2007 BUPA sold 26 hospitals to the private equity firm Cinven for £1.44 billion. As with the sale of Alliance Boots, the issues are not reducible to private equity *per se* but rather the further effects of private equity involvement. The introduction of a new tier of control and interests for particular companies in conjunction with the implications of increased leverage again raises issues of the basis (quality and cost) on which services are provided and also of financial and organisational stability. These are exacerbated because private equity is simply not as accountable for its actions as a public company. It thus adds an additional sense in which privatisation is private.

20   There is a clear tension here of another kind: that of monopoly versus monopsony where the potential monopolist is vulnerable to the power of the monopsonist because of their debt servicing costs. On October 4th 2007 the Department of Health cut £400 million from the sum it will pay UK pharmacies for generic medicine purchased on the NHS. It also cut dispensing fees paid to pharmacies for medicines from 36p to 25p per item. The combination affects Alliance Boots margins and thus its revenue base and current debt servicing capacity prior to any savings being made on the introduction of the straight to pharmacy model.

21   The original report was commissioned 4th April 2007 following the Pfizer-Unichem deal March 5th. The initial report 2nd May highlighted that the scheme could result in longer waiting times for drugs at pharmacies due to reduced numbers of deliveries (cost cutting) and also higher prices. It also noted that the Government did not anticipate any adverse changes but would review the OFT findings from the subsequent report of December 11th. The December 11th report found 'significant risk' that the straight to pharmacy model will ultimately result in greater costs to the NHS that could be several hundred million pounds per year at the same time as services were reduced.

22 The problem may even be exacerbated since the pension fund may shift over to more conservative investments (more bonds) to reduce its overall risk profile – more conservative investment mean average lower returns which could in turn increase the deficit but do so in the name of preventing insolvency.

Conclusion

1 If one were, for example, to accept the Jensen argument that combining all sources of tax produces a potential net gain. See Chapter 7 endnotes.

2 One might also consider some kind of oversight body for sanctioning large asset sales after an LBO – perhaps formalising the kind of poison pill conditions written into some corporate structures.

3 And these too could be coupled to further regulatory changes intended to stabilise liquidity in capital markets. Margin calls or the debt used to buy stocks could be controlled or varied to slow down the rate of growth of trading values at times of rapid expansion of equity markets. This could be done in much the same way as interest rates are adjusted by central banks. Volatility could also be reduced for equity markets in various ways. The FSA could actually start to prosecute when unusual trading patterns emerge or when insider dealing is suspected. Shares could be suspended more rapidly when rumours are used or are suspected to be affecting specific equity prices. Computerised trading should also allow tracing of the lines of trades that set off suspicious volatilities. Quants or mechanised trading run by programmes could be banned. Share options and futures could be controlled in various ways: hedge funds for example, could be refused voting rights when buying options on particular equities. Options could be classified as a declarable stake in the firm being speculated in – this could be coupled with the requirement that hedge funds declare their interest and the basis of their investment strategy. The actual cost of options could be increased and the volume of options permissible in any given equity restricted. The creation of credit default swaps could also be restricted: the value of such CDSs could be restricted to the value insured of the underlying asset.

4 In terms of the specifics of the free cash flow argument: if free cash flow is a clear and unambiguous signal that there is a market for corporate control then it is also a clear signal that there is the potential for higher taxation (perhaps a windfall tax) in that economic sector. I argued that free cash flow in Jensen's argument based on the technical definition is more than a matter of the existence of large cash balances but nonetheless the existence of such balances is a tax issue that would also address the initially signalling device for some kinds of LBOs.

5 The sophisticated response is that incentive realignment is based on the narrowing of interests to the few from which benefits to the many flow as an additional consequence. Extending the alignment to representatives of the many undermines the effectiveness of the few. In one sense this is simply question begging since it relies on the empirical fact of extended benefits. Further it tacitly implies that benefits require harsh decisions that other 'stakeholders' would resist. Why would they resist unless the full information available to them about corporate strategy made it clear that their interests were the least concern and the most vulnerable... This in turn is precisely an argument for their incorporation to ameliorate that vulnerability and ensure a focus on genuine forms of 'upside' management.

6 I do not wish to suggest that business friendly or finance related interest representations are necessarily bad – the terms and equalities between these interests and others however must be considered. It is certainly unusual, though not

inconsistent with recent trends that Brown as Prime Minister invited Sir Digby Jones, former CBI Director-General, to become a minister without joining the Labour Party, or that he invited Damon Buffini of Permira to join the new Business Council (eliciting a wave of criticism from the GMB).

7   See also the speech by Charlie McCreevy, European Commissioner for the Internal Market, to the House of Commons All Part Parliamentary Group March 22nd (2007). He makes several points: 1. Private equity is simply exploiting the same cheap debt as anyone else. 2. Private equity executive pay can be seen in the same light as that of professional executives – in so far as it is performance and market driven it is justified. 3. Regarding asset stripping: one investor's asset sale is another's asset purchase' 4. Dividends to investors in funds are then reinvested to create employment elsewhere, at the same time pensioners and other recipients of institutional investment gain.

8   The report is broader than the central media focus regarding the Commons Treasury Select Committee inquiry of mid-2007. The media focus was the tax status of executive earnings and also the corporation tax relief on debt applied to acquisitions. The focus itself, however, was still instructive. The Commons committee, chaired by Labour MP John McFall, called on a range of private equity association representatives, private equity executives, academics and trade union officials to submit evidence. In the first week of submissions to the inquiry, beginning June 12th, Peter Linthwaite, chief executive of the BVCA was called to provide evidence. Linthwaite defended the tax status of private equity, stating that 'There are no special tax breaks for private equity.' This of course neglected two things. It neglected how the actual practices of PEF utilise the tax system in ways for which it was not intended – the tax breaks may not be special but the application of the practice is a special case. It also neglected that the BVCA had in fact lobbied for a memorandum of understanding in 2003. Commenting on the BVCA responses to a range of questions concerning tax and the use of leverage, the Labour MP Angela Eagle stated that the replies were 'the most obstructive piece of evidence we've been given for a long time.' There was also wide ranging perplexity and surprise when many of the private equity executives called to provide evidence could not or declined to say how much capital gains tax they paid as well as what proportions of corporation tax their buyouts did not pay. Subsequent to the BVCA submission and widespread criticism from the private equity firms of the performance of the association Linthwaite resigned and the BVCA began a strategic 'internal review'. A further feature of the inquiry submissions was the general evasion of the moral dimension of the tax argument by private equity representatives. This evasion, however, was not wholesale. In conjunction with trade union activity, part of the initial media attention on the tax issue arose after Nicholas Ferguson, founder of SVG Capital stated that there was something amiss when he paid tax at a lower rate than the low paid (using the example of cleaners). In similar vein John Moulton, head of Alchemy, stated in an interview, 'The tax situation is complicated, but the reality is there's a large chunk of private equity who don't pay any tax at all. There are no means of estimating if most private equity guys are pushing tax allowances to their screaming point, but, put it this way some people in the industry are using tax practices that they wouldn't want their mothers to read about.' (Armistead 2007). Ferguson did not submit evidence. When Moulton was called upon, however, he fell back upon the 'some tax is better than no tax argument': 'You keep saying we are giving you a low tax rate. You should perhaps be looking at it the other way around. You are getting some tax. If you're not careful, you might not get any.' He by no means

meant that he would be likely to take further radical measures to limit his future tax liabilities but he did seem to see this as an industry potential. In this regard Peter Taylor of Duke Street Capital stated that a tax rate of 15–20% would not be a 'material disincentive' and would be 'internationally competitive'.

9 This approach was not new, though the motivation was. In 2002 RCP & Partners, for example, a fiduciary rating agency established an experimental best practice and transparency scheme for PEF to create a rating system that firms could use in solicitation. There was also a move to standardise measures of some aspects of performance in a new set of voluntary international guidelines, in Europe in 2006.

10 Tax is put aside (#6, p. 4) Reports on leverage are proposed but not an analysis of debt creation systems that underpin it (#8, p. 5).

11 And also in terms of PEF specifically: the Discussion Paper 06/6 also resulted in the creation of a specific investment centre of expertise responsible for 'the relationship management of higher impact private equity and hedge fund managers'. This, as the follow up paper of June 2007 makes clear, was intended to work in conjunction with the FSA's routine prudential supervision of banks to maintain a continuing monitoring of the risk levels represented by leverage. The approach and its implementation can only be described as a spectacular failure.

Bibliography

AA (2006) *Annual report 2006* PDF: http://www.theaa.com/aboutaa/annual-report-2006.pdf accessed 10/05/2007

AB Acquisitions (2007) *Recommended Acquisition of Alliance Boots plc by AB Acquisitions Limited* PDF: http://www.irallianceboots.com accessed 20/04/2008

Abdelhamid, D. (2003) *International Regulatory Rivalry in Open Economies: The Impact of Deregulation on UK and US Financial Markets*. Aldershot: Ashgate

Acharya, V. V., J. R. Franks and H. Servaes (2007) 'Private equity boom and bust?' *Journal of Applied Corporate Finance* 19(4): 44–53

Allen, V. (2007) 'The carry trade', *The Hedge Fund Journal* 27: 4

Alliance Boots (2007) 'Alliance Boots Preliminary Results' [Report for the Financial Year April 2006–March 2007] PDF: http://www.allianceboots.com accessed 12/06/2007

Altman, E. I. (1992) 'Revisiting the high-yield bond market', *Financial Management* 21(2): 78–92

Amess, K. and M. Wright (2007) 'The wage and employment effects of leveraged buyouts in the UK', *International Journal of the Economics of Business* 14(2): 179–95

Amess, K. (2002) 'Management buyouts and firm-level productivity: evidence from a panel of UK manufacturing firms', *Scottish Journal of Political Economy* 49(3): 304–17

Anders, G. (1992) *Merchants of Debt: KKR and the Mortgaging of American Business*. New York: Basic Books

Anson M. J. P. (2003) *Handbook of Alternative Assets*. London: John Wiley

—— (2002) 'A primer on distressed debt investing', *The Journal of Private Equity* 5(3): 6–17.

Apax Partners (2006) *Unlocking Global Value: Future Trends in Private Equity Investment Worldwide*. London: Apax

Aragon, L. (2002) 'From the editor: time for a diet', *Venture Capital Journal* 42(8): 2

Arendt, H. (1958) *The Human Condition*. Chicago: University of Chicago Press

Arnold G. and M. Smith (1999) *The European High Yield Bond Market: Drivers and Impediments*. London: LLP Publishing

Arzac, E. R. (1992) 'On the capital structure of leveraged buyouts', *Financial Management* 21(1): 16–26

Ashton, J. (2007) 'Credit storm batters leading banks', *The Sunday Times* November 11th

Axelson, U., T. Jenkinson, P. Stromberg, and M. Weisbach (2007) 'Leverage and pricing in buyouts: an empirical analysis', Working Paper, August

Baker, G. and G. Smith (1998) *The New Financial Capitalists: Kohlberg, Kravis Roberts and the Creation of Corporate Value*. Cambridge: Cambridge University Press

Baker, D. and M. Weisbrot (1999) *Social Security: The Phony Crisis*. Chicago: Chicago University Press

Barber, L., J. Blitz and C. Giles (2007) 'Interview Transcript: Alistair Darling', *the Financial Times* July 3rd http://www.ft.com/cms/s/ebd1ce6a-299d-11dc-a530-000b5df10621.html accessed: 10/07/2007

Barclays Private Equity (2008) 'Secondary exit boom gives way to uncertainty as 2007 falls short of 2006 highs', www.barclays-private-equity.com accessed 28/04/2008

Barnes, T. J. and M. Gertler (1999) *The New Industrial Geography*. London: Routledge

Barry, A. and D. Slater (2005) *The Technological Economy*. London: Routledge

Barth, J. R. (1991) *The Great Savings and Loan Debacle*. Washington DC: The American Enterprise Institute

Barth, J. R., S. Trimbath and G. Yago (2004) *The Savings and Loan Crisis: Lessons From a Regulatory Failure*. New York: Springer

Bartlett, S. (1991) *The Money Machine: How KKR Manufactured Power and Profits*. Clayton Victoria: Warner

Bawden, T. (2007) 'Revealed – the key talks that led to Bernanke's crunch decisions', *The Times*. London October 4th

Batchelor, C. (2008) 'Time to rebuild after firestorm', *Financial Times* London March 3rd

Baygan, G. (2003) 'Venture capital policy review: United Kingdom', STI Working Paper 2003/1 Industry Issues; Paris: OECD

Belderbos, R. and J. Zhou (2006) 'Foreign investment, divestment and relocation by Japanese electronics firms in East Asia', *Asian Economic Journal* 20(1): 1–27

Bellofiore, R. and P. Ferri. eds. (2001) *The Economic Legacy of Hyman Minsky, Volume 1: Financial Keynesianism and Market Instability*. Cheltenham: Elgar

Benjamin, G. A. and J. Margolis (2001) *The Angel Investor's Handbook: How to Profit from Early Stage Investing*. New York: Bloomberg

Bernanke, B. S., J. Y. Campbell and T. M. Whited (1990) 'US corporate leverage: developments in 1987 and 1988', *Brookings Papers on Economic Activity* 1: 255–86

Bernanke, B. S. and J. Y. Campbell (1988) 'Is there a corporate debt crisis?' *Brookings Papers on Economic Activity* 1: 83–139

Biais, B. and F. Declerck (2007) 'European high yield bond markets: transparency, liquidity and efficiency', paper, Toulouse University: IDEA

Bierman, H. and H. Bierman Jr (2003) *Private Equity: Transforming Public Stock to Create Value*. London: John Wiley

Black, F. and M. Scholes (1973) 'The pricing of options and corporate liabilities', *Journal of Political Economy* 81(3): 637–54

Blackburn, P. and R. Sharpe (1988) *Britain's Industrial Renaissance: The Development, Management and Use of Information Technology*. London: Routledge

Blackburn, R. (2002) *Banking on Death or investing in Life: The History and Future of Pensions*. London: Verso

Blair, M. (1998) 'Comment on What drives venture capital fundraising?', *Brookings Papers on Economic Activity. Microeconomics*, 193–7

Blinder, A. and R. Reis (2005) 'Understanding the Greenspan standard,' Princeton University: http://www.kc.frb.org/PUBLICAT/SYMPOS/2005/pdf/BlinderReis.paper.0804.pdf accessed 10/06/2006

Bondt, G. de, and D. M. Ibanez (2005) 'High-yield bond diffusion in the United States, the United Kingdom and the Euro Area', *Journal of Financial Services Research* 27(2): 163–81

Boquist, A. and J. Dawson (2004) 'US venture capital in Europe in the 1980s and 1990s', *The Journal of Private Equity* 8(1): 39–54

Boyle, E. (1994) 'The use of management buyouts as an aspect of corporate strategy in Britain', *Journal of Strategic Change* 3(4): 201–9

Brown, J. R. Jr. (1995) 'The 'Great Fall': The consequences of repealing the Glass-Steagall Act', *Stanford Journal of Law, Business and Finance* 2(1): 129–45

Bruck, C. (1989) *The Predators' Ball: The Inside Story of Drexel Burnham and the Rise of the Junk Bond Raiders*. London: Penguin

Bruining, H., P. Boselie, M. Wright and N. Bacon (2005) 'The impact of business ownership on employee relations: buy-outs in the UK and the Netherlands', *The International Journal of Human Resource Management* 16(3): 345–65

Buckland, R. and E. W. Davis (1989) *The Unlisted Securities Market*. London: Clarendon

Burnett, M., R. Wilson, D. Taorksy, S. Bright and W. Graves (1991) *Case Studies of Selected Leveraged Buyouts*, Congressional report compiled by General Government Division, Washington DC: Diane Publishing

Burrough, B. and J. Helyar (2004) *Barbarians at the Gate: The Fall of RJR Nabisco*. London: Arrow

Bushrod, L. (2005) 'Storm clouds on the horizon?' *European Venture Capital Journal* 123 (supplement): 6–12

Butler, J. E., A. Lockett and D. Ucbasaran (2006) *Venture Capital in the Changing World of Entrepreneurship*. Charlotte N.C.: IAP

Butcher, S. (2005) 'Career path: Alchemy Partners' founder John Moulton', *eFinancial Careers* 20th January

BVCA (2000) 'UK venture capital industry invests almost £8 billion in 1999', BVCA press release, Tuesday 9th May

Canterbery, E. R. (2006) *Alan Greenspan: The Oracle Behind the Curtain*. London: World Scientific

Carnevali, F. (2005) *Europe's Advantage: Banks and Small Firms in Britain, France, Germany and Italy Since 1918*. Oxford: Oxford University Press

Castells, M. (2000) *The Rise of the Network Society*. Oxford: Blackwell

Chemla, G. (2004) 'Pension fund investment in private equity and venture capital in the US and Canada', *Journal of Private Equity* 7(2): 64–71

Chisholm, A. A. (2004) *Derivatives Demystified: A Step-by-Step Guide to Forwards, Futures, Swaps and Options*. London: John Wiley

Clegg, S. (2002) *Management and Organization Paradoxes*. Phil. PA: John Benjamin Publishing

Clark, I. (2007) 'Private equity and HRM in the British business system', *Human Resource Management System* 17(3): 218–26

CMBOR (2005) *Exit Report* 5. Nottingham: CMBOR

Cohen, R. (with T. Ilot) (2007) *The Second Bounce of the Ball*. London: Weidenfeld & Nicholson

Connor, G. and M. Woo (2003) 'An introduction to hedge funds', London School of Economics: Http://fmg.lse.ac.uk/upload_file/190_Intro%20to%20hedge%20funds.pdf accessed 14/02/2008

Coyle, B. (2000) *Venture Capital & Buyouts*. London: Lessons Professional Publishing

CSIS (2006) *China – The Balance Sheet* Washington DC: Centre for Strategic and International Studies, Institute for International Economics

Damodaran, A. (2000) 'The dark side of valuation: firms with no earnings, no history and no comparables, can Amazon.com be valued?' *Working Paper*. Stern School of Business, New York

—— (2001) *The Dark Side of Valuation: Valuing Old Tech New Tech and New Economy Companies*. Harlow: Prentice Hall

Davey, J. (2007) 'Pessina: My vision for Boots', *The Sunday Times* London, April 29th

Donaldson, P. (1976) *Guide to the British Economy*. London: Pelican

Donovan, Lord (1971) *Royal Commission on Trade Unions and Employers' Associations 1965–1968*. London: HMSO; reprint from 1968 edition

Douglas A. F. (2002) 'The limited partnership agreement: explanatory notes'. London: BVCA

Dresner S. and E. K. Kim (2003) *Pipes: A Guide to Private Investment in Public Equity*. New York: Bloomberg

Duffie, D. and R. Rahi (1995) 'Financial market innovation and security design: an introduction', *Journal of Economic Theory* 65(1): 1–42

Duncan, G. (2007) 'Bank chief defends the pay awards of the City's 'Premiership',' *The Times* London, June 27th

Eerturk, I, J. Froud, S. Johal, A. Leaver and K. Williams (2008) *Financialization at Work*. London: Routledge

EIA (2008) 'OPEC revenues fact sheet', US federal Energy Information Administration; available: www.eia.doe.gov/emeu/cabs/OPEC_Revenues/Factsheet.html accessed 10/04/2008

Elizalde, A. (2005a) 'Credit risk models IV: understanding and pricing CDOs', paper: Centre for Monetary and Financial Studies, Madrid; available: www.abelelizalde. com accessed 8/03/2008

—— (2005b) 'Do we need to worry about credit risk correlation?' *Journal of Fixed Income* 15(3): 42–59

EVCA (2006) *Preliminary Activity Figures, 2005* Archived at www.evca.com accessed 18/05/2006

EVCJ (2002) 'Name change for HSBC Private Equity?' *European Venture Capital Journal* 95: 3

—— (2003) 'BVCA lobbies for change', *European Venture Capital Journal* 108: 2

Fenn, G., N. Liang and S. Prowse (1995) *The Economics of the Private Equity Market* Staff Studies Series, Board of Governors of the Federal Reserve System, DC 20551, December

Firla-Cuchra, M. and T. Jenkinson (2006) 'Why are securitization issues tranched?' Working paper, Said Business School, Oxford University

Flowers E. B. and A. F. Lees (2002) *The Euro, Capital Markets and Dollarization*. New York: Rowman and Littlefield

FRB (2006), 'Monetary policy making: Federal Open Market Committee,' Federal Reserve Board: http://federalreserve.gov/fomc/ accessed 2/02/2008

Friday, C. (1990) 'RJR tries to salvage its junk', *Newsweek* 116(1): 38

Froud, J. and K. Williams (2007) 'Private equity and the culture of value extraction', *Centre for Research on Socio-Cultural Change* Working Paper No. 31. www.cresc.ac.uk accessed 10/06/2007

FSA (2006) *Private Equity: A Discussion of Risk and Regulatory Engagement* Discussion paper 06/6 November. London: Financial Services Authority

—— (2007) *Private Equity: A Discussion of Risk and Regulatory Engagement* Feedback on DP 06/6 June. London: Financial Services Authority

Galbraith, J. K. (1975) *Economics, Peace and Laughter*. London: Pelican

—— (1977) *The Age of Uncertainty*. London: Andre Deutsch

Galletly G. and N. Ritchie (1988) *The Big Bang: The financial revolution in the City of London and what it means for you after the crash*. Plymouth: Northcote House

Ganguin, B. and J. Bilardello (2005) *Fundamentals of Corporate Credit*. New York: McGraw Hill

Glasberg, D. S. and D. Skidmore (1997) 'The dialectics of state economic intervention: bank deregulation and the savings and loan bailout', *The Sociological Quarterly* 38(1): 67–93

Golding, T. (2003) *The City: Inside the Great Expectation Machine*. Cambridge: Pearson.

Gompers, P. and J. Lerner (1998) 'What drives venture capital fundraising?', *Brookings Papers on Economic Activity. Microeconomics*, 149–92

—— 'Money chasing deals? The impact of fund flows on private equity valuation', *Journal of Financial Economics* 55(2): 281–325

Graham, J. R. (2000) 'How big are the tax benefits of debt?' 55(5): 1901–41

Grant A. E. and J. H. Meadows (2006) *Communication Technology Update*. London: Elsevier

Greenspan, A. (1989a) 'Statement to Congress March 22, 1989 (Board's views on proposed legislation for the reform and recovery of the thrift industry', *Federal Reserve Bulletin* May: 347–50

—— (1989b) 'Statement to Congress January 26, 1989 (Corporate restructuring)' *Federal Reserve Bulletin* March: 142–6

Greenstein, S. (2007) 'Economic experiments and neutrality in Internet access', NBER conference paper: http://www.nber.org/books_in_progress/innovation8/ accessed 16/02/2008

Gumpert, D. E. (1979) 'Venture capital becoming more widely available', *Harvard Business Review* 57(1): 178–92

Gupta, U. (2000) *Done Deals: Venture Capitalists Tell Their Stories*. Boston, MA: Harvard Business School Press

Haarmeyer, D. (2006) 'The governance problem', *Private Equity Spotlight* 2(7): 1–2

Hadjian, A. L. (2000) 'Wall St. debates future role of private equity', *Venture Capital Journal*, 40(9): 5

Hane, G. (2006) 'Creating entrepreneurs – progress and opportunity in Japan', *The Journal of Private Equity* 9(3): 55–60

Harm, C. (2001) 'European financial market integration: the case of private sector bonds and syndicated loans', *Journal of International Financial Markets, Institutions and Money* 11(3/4): 245–63

Harre, R. and E. H. Madden (1975) *Causal Powers: A Theory of Natural Necessity*. Oxford: Blackwell

Harris, T. J. (2002a) 'The anti-dilution death spiral', *The Journal of Private Equity* 5(2): 35–44

—— (2002b) 'Bridge financing over troubled waters', *The Journal of Private Equity* 6(1): 59–63

Harrison, R. and C. Mason (2002) 'The regional impact of national policy initiatives: small firms policy in the United Kingdom', in M. Hart and R. Harrison eds. (2002) *Spatial Policy in a Divided Nation*. London: Routledge

Hartcher, P. (2006) *Bubble Man: Alan Greenspan and the Missing 7 Trillion Dollars* London: Norton

Hatch, J. and A. Clinton (2000) 'Job growth in the 1990s: a retrospect', *Monthly Labour Review*, December

Hayes, S. L. (1979) 'The transformation of investment banking', *Harvard Business Review* 57(1): 153–70

Heilbroner, R. and W. Milberg (1995) *The Crisis of Vision in Modern Economic Thought* Cambridge: Cambridge University Press

Hellman, T. (1998) 'Comment on What drives venture capital fundraising?, *Brookings Papers on Economic Activity. Microeconomics*. 197–204

Hencke, D. and J. Treanor (2007) 'Unions call for international action against private equity', *The Guardian* March 16th

Hintze, J. (2006) 'Euro Market becomes more American', *Bank Loan Report* 21(36): 1–9

Hirschey. M. (1986) 'Mergers, buyouts and fakeouts', *American Economic Review* 76(2): 317–22

HM Treasury (2004) 'Myners principles for institutional investment decision making: review of progress' December, London: HMSO

—— (2007a) 'Paying a fairer share: a consultation on residence and domicile', December, London: HMSO

—— (2007b) 'Offshore funds: a discussion paper', October, London: HMSO

—— (2008) 'Residence and non-domicile: memorandum to HM Treasury on US Federal Income Tax consequences to US citizens of certain proposed changes to the UK remittance basis of taxation' March, London: HMSO

Huss, M. (2005) 'Performance characteristics of private equity: an empirical comparison of listed and unlisted private equity vehicles', working paper, University of Basel, Dept. of Finance.

IMF (2006) *Global Financial Stability Report: Market Development and Issues* Washington DC: IMF

—— (2007) *World Economic and Financial Surveys: Global Financial Stability Report* April. Washington DC: IMF

Ineichen, A. M. (2001) 'Who's long? Market neutral versus short/long equity', paper, London: UBS Warburg

Jagger, S (2007) 'If you thought that it could not get any worse, think again', *The Times*, London August 20th

—— (2008) 'Citigroup set to sell debt to private equity', *The Times*, London April 9th

Jen, S. (2008) 'Petrodollar tsunami will be at the expense of euro and dollar', *The Financial Times*, London March 4th

Jenkinson, T. (2006) 'The development and performance of European private equity', Working Paper, Oxford said Business School, forthcoming in Freias, X., P. Hartman and C. Mayer, eds. *Financial Markets and Institutions: A European Perspective*. Oxford: Oxford University Press

Jensen, M. and W. Meckling (1976) 'Theory of the firm: managerial behaviour, agency costs and ownership structure', *Journal of Financial Economics* 3(4): 305–60

Jensen, M., S. Kaplan and L. Stiglin (1989) 'Effects of LBOs on tax revenues of the US Treasury', *Tax Notes* 42(6): 727–33

Jensen, M. and R. S. Ruback (1983) 'The market for corporate control: the scientific evidence', *Journal of Financial Economics* 11(1–4): 5–50

Jensen, M. and J. L. Zimmerman (1985) (Editorial summary of symposium) 'Management compensation and the managerial labour market', *Journal of Accounting and Economics* 7(1–3): 3–9

Jensen, M. (1986) 'Agency costs of free cash flows, corporate finance and takeovers,' *American Economic Review* 76(2): 323–39

—— (1988) 'Takeovers: their causes and consequences', *Journal of Economic Perspectives* 2(1): 21–48

—— (1989a) 'Is leverage an invitation to bankruptcy', *The Wall Street Journal* February 1st

—— (1989b) 'Active investors, LBOs and the privatization of bankruptcy', *Journal of Applied Corporate Finance* 2(1): 35–44. Also available from Jensen's Harvard website: http://hupress.harvard.edu/catalog/JENTHF.html accessed 8/01/2008

—— (1993) 'The modern industrial revolution, exit and the failure of internal control systems', *Journal of Finance* 48(3): 831–80. Also available from Jensen's Harvard website: http://hupress.harvard.edu/catalog/JENTHF.html The version used here was revised in 1999. accessed 8/01/2008

Jerram, R. M. Hodges, L. Turner and R. Kurz (1997) *Political Environment for Global Business* London School of Economics http://www.mega.nu/ampp/PEGB/index.html accessed 16/02/2008

Jetter, L. W. (2003) *Disconnected: Deceit and Betrayal at Worldcom*. London: John Wiley

Johnson, H. J. (1999) *Global Financial Institutions and Markets*. Oxford: Blackwell

Jones, S. (2007a) 'Covenant-lie loans hit Europe', *International Financial Law Review* 26(4): 10–11

—— (2007b) 'Europe's second cov-lite loan', *International Financial Law Review* 26(5): 8

—— (2007c) 'Through a glass darkly', *International Financial Law Review* 26(6): 18–21

Jones, A., M. Jensen, S. Kaplan, C. Ferenbach, M. Feldberg, J. Moon, B. Hoesterey, and C. Davis (2006) 'Morgan Stanley roundtable on private equity and its import for public companies', *Journal of Applied Corporate Finance* 18(3): 8–37

Kaletsky, A. (2007) 'The real reason why private equity is under fire', *The Times*, London June 21st

Kaplan, S. (2002) 'Valuation and new economy firms', from Kaplan's University of Chicago website: http://faculty.chicagogsb.edu/steven.kaplan/research/ and reprinted in W. Hunter, G. Kaufman and M. Pomerleano, eds. (2003) *Asset Price Bubbles*, Boston: MIT Press

—— (1989) 'Management buyouts: evidence on taxes as a source of value', *The Journal of Finance* 44(3): 611–32

Kaplan, S. and J. Stein (1993) 'The evolution of buyout pricing and financial structure in the 1980s', *Quarterly Journal of Economics* 108(2): 313–57

Kaplan, S. and A. Schoar (2005) 'Private equity finance performance: returns, persistence and capital flows', *Journal of Finance* 60 (4): 1791–823. Also available from Kaplan's University of Chicago website: http://faculty.chicagogsb.edu/steven.kaplan/research/accessed 8/01/2008

Kaplan, S. (1989) 'Management buyouts: evidence on taxes as a source of value', *The Journal of Finance* 44(3): 611–32

Karol, B. J. (1995) 'An overview of derivatives as risk management tools', *Stanford Journal of Law, Business and Finance* 1(2): 195–207

Kaufman, A. and E. Englander (1993) 'Kohlberg, Kravis, Roberts & Co and the restructuring of American Capitalism', *Business History Review* 67(1): 52–97

Kennedy, S. (2008) 'High profile buyout chief turns on his peer group', *The Times*, London, February 27th

—— (2007) 'Buyout firms ready to pay more tax – but not that much more', *The Times*, London Jul 4th

Kenney, M. (2003) 'What goes up must come down: the political economy of the US Internet industry', 33–55 in Christensen, J. S. and P. Maskell *The Industrial Dynamics of the New Digital Economy*. London: Elgar

Kenny, P. (2007) 'Not good for the companies they buy, the workers in those companies or the British economy', *The Times*, London, June 12th

Keynes, J. M. (1936) *The General Theory of Employment, Interest and Money*. New York: Harcourt, Brace and Company

Kindleberger, C. P. and R. Aliber (2005) *Manias, Panics and Crashes: A History of Financial Crises*. Basingstoke: Palgrave Macmillan, 5th edition

Kincaid, J. (1988) 'The state of American federalism', *Publius* 18(3): 1–15

Kirchgaessner, S. (2008) 'US insiders point to Bain errors over 3Com', *Financial Times*, London March 4th

Krijgsman, P. (2005/6) 'Ride on or wipe-out?' *Corporate Financier* 78, December/January

Larson, P. T. (2006) 'Big Bang still brings much to London finance', *Financial Times* October 25th

Lamm R. M. Jr. (2004) 'The hedge fund revolution', *Journal of Financial Transformation* 10: 87–95

Lamm R. M. Jr. and T. Ghaleb-Harter (2001) 'Private equity as an asset allocation: its role in investment portfolios', *The Journal of Private Equity* 4(4): 8–14

Langley, M. (2003) *Tearing Down the Walls*. London: Simon & Schuster

Lawson, T. (1997) *Economics & Reality*. London: Routledge

—— (2003) *Reorienting Economics*. London: Routledge

Lazonick W. and M. O'Sullivan (1997) 'Finance and industrial development. Part I: the United States and the United Kingdom', *Finance History Review* 4: 7–29

Lerner, R. and A. Schoar (2004) 'The illiquidity puzzle: theory and evidence from private equity', *Journal of Financial Economics* 72(1): 3–40

Lewis, L. (2008) 'Dollar tumble spells trouble for yen trade', *The Times*, London March 19th

Linthwaite, P. (2007a) 'In favour: creating long term value is crucial to what we do', *The Sunday Observer*

—— (2007b) 'Creating a clearer picture', *International Financial Law Review* 26(4): 7–9, supplement

Little, W. B. and S. B. Klinsky (1989) 'How leveraged buyouts can really work: a look at three cases', *Journal of Applied Corporate Finance* 2(1): 71–5

Lhabitant, F. S. (2002) *Hedge Funds: Myths and Limits*. London: John Wiley

Locke, J. (1690) *Second Treatise of Government* edited and introduction C. B. Macpherson (1980) Cambridge, Indianapolis: Hackett Publishing

Lukes, S. ed. (1986) *Power*. Oxford: Blackwell

McCreevy, C. (2007) 'Private equity: getting it right', House of Commons All Party Parliamentary Group Breakfast Meeting London, March 22nd http://europa.eu/rapid/pressReleasesAction.do?reference=SPEECH/07/171&format=HTML&aged=0&language=EN&guiLanguage=en accessed 10/06/07

Magni, C. A. (2002) 'Investment decisions in the theory of finance: some antinomies and inconsistencies', *European Journal of Operational Research* 137: 206–17

Malik, O. (2003) *Broadbandits: Inside the $750 billion telecom heist*. London: John Wiley

Maloney, P. (2007) 'Against: Taxpayers subsidise them', *The Sunday Observer* February 11th

Markham, J. W. (2002) *A Financial History of the United States Volume I and III*. New York: M. E. Sharpe

Marx, K. (2000) *On the Jewish Question*. Milton Keynes: The Open University

Maslakovic, M. (2006a) 'Private Equity, City Business Series, October', International Financial Services London (IFSL) http://www.ifsl.org.uk/uploads/CBS_Private_Equity_2006.pdf accessed 12/03/2007

Mathews, J. (1994) *Struggle and Survival on Wall Street: The Economics of Competition Among Securities Firms*. Oxford: Oxford University Press

May, C. (2002) *The Information Society: A Sceptical View*. Cambridge: Polity

Mayer, C. (2001) 'Institutional investment and private equity in the UK', paper for conference: 'Corporate governance: reassessing ownership and control' Cambridge 19th May: www.finance.ox.ac.uk/Papers/FinancialEconomics/index.htm accessed 17/02/2008

McCarthy, J. and N. Alvarez (2006) 'Private equity: rolling on or rolling back?', *The Journal of Private Equity* 9(2): 13–16

Meltom, W. C. (1985) *Inside the Fed: Making Monetary Policy*. Illinois: Dow-Jones Irwin

Mill. J. S. (1974) *On Liberty*. London: Penguin

Minsky, H. (1982) *Can 'It' Happen Again? Essays on Instability and Finance*. New York: M. E. Sharpe

—— (1986) *Stabilizing an Unstable Economy*. London: Yale University Press

—— (1987) 'Review: *Casino Capitalism*', *Journal of Economic Literature* 25(4): 1883–5

—— (1990) 'Review: *The Debt and the Deficit: False Alarms/Real Possibilities*', *Journal of Economic Literature* 28(3): 1221–2

—— (1993) 'Finance and stability: the limits of capitalism', Working Paper 93, Annandale, New York: Jerome Levy Economics Institute

—— (1996) 'Uncertainty and the institutional structure of capitalist economies', *Journal of Economic Issues* 30(2): 357–68

Mishkin, F. S. (1992) *Money, Banking and Financial Markets* New York: Harper Collins, third edition

Morgan, J. (2003) 'The global power of orthodox economics', *The Journal of Critical Realism* 1(2): 7–34

—— (2006a) 'The US–China trade asymmetry in context', *Working Paper Number 2*, The Centre of Excellence in Global Governance Research, Helsinki: University of Helsinki

—— (2006b) 'The UK pension system: the betrayal by New Labour in its neoliberal global context', *Research in Political Economy* 23: 301–48

—— (2008a) 'How should we conceive the continued resilience of the US Dollar as a reserve currency?' *Review of Radical Political Economics* 41(1)

—— (2008b) 'China's growing pains: towards the (global) political economy of domestic social instability', *International Politics* (3): 1–25

—— (2008c) 'Some contributions on context for Chinese security studies', *Intelligence and National Security* 23(4): forthcoming

Moriarty, G. (1999) 'VC pace unabated in third quarter', *Venture Capital Journal* 39(1): 5–6

Mull, R. H. and D. B. Winters (1996) 'A note on the use of debt by venture capital backed firms', *Journal of Entrepreneurial & Small Business Finance* 5(3): 287–95

Myners, P. (2001) *Institutional Investment in the United Kingdom: A Review*. London: HMSO

Myners, P. and B. Payne (2001) 'Face to face' *Pensions and Investments* 29(15): 20

Nielsen, P. and J. Morgan (2005) 'No new revolution in economics? Taking Thompson and Fine forwards', *Economy & Society* 34(1): 51–75

Newbould, G. D., R. E. Chatfield, and R. F. Ansderson (1992) 'Leveraged buyouts and tax incentives', *Financial Management* special supplement 21(1): 50–7

Nozick, R. (1974) *Anarchy, State and Utopia*. New York: Basic Books

O'Brien, J. (2008) (ed.) *Private Equity, Corporate Governance and the Dynamics of Capital Market Regulation*. London: Imperial College Press

Ofek, E. and M. Richardson (2003) 'Dotcom mania: the rise and fall of internet stock prices', *Journal of Finance* 58(3): 1113–37

OFT (2007) *Medicines Distribution: An OFT Market Study* PDF available at http://www.oft.gov.uk accessed 18/01/08

Olsen, W. and J. Morgan (2005) 'Towards a critical epistemology of analytical statistics: realism in mathematical method,' *Journal for the Theory of Social Behaviour* 35(3): 255–84

Onorato, N. R. (1997) 'Trends in venture capital funding in the 1990s', US Small Business Administration, Office of Advocacy, Washington DC

Opler, T. (1992) 'Operating performance in leveraged buyouts: evidence from 1985–1989', *Financial Management* special supplement 21(1): 27–34

Opler, T. and S. Titman (1993) 'The determinants of leveraged buyout activity: free cash flow vs financial distress costs', *Journal of Finance* 48(5): 1985–99

Osler, D. (2002) *Labour Party PLC: New Labour as a Party of Business*. London: Mainstream

Pagnamenta, R. (2007) 'US-style structure of Boots deal will net KKR and Pessina millions in fees', *The Times*, London, May 12th

Papadimitriou, D. B. and L. R. Wray (1997) 'The economic contributions of Hyman Minsky: varieties of capitalism and institutional reform', Working Paper 217, Annandale, New York : Jerome Levy Economics Institute

Papke, L. (1991) 'The asset allocation of private pension plans', *Working Paper* 3745, National Bureau of Economic Research

Parnass, G. (2007) 'Covenant Lite: An introduction', *Private Equity Law Review* March 25th: 1

Patomaki, H. (2001) *Democratising Globalization: The Leverage of the Tobin Tax.* London: Zed

Philippou, L. and M. Zollo (2005) 'The performance of private equity funds', Working Paper: University of Amsterdam, Faculty of Economics and Econometrics, Finance group, 11 Roerterstraat, 1018 Amsterdam, The Netherlands

Pichinson, M. (2002) 'Weathering the perfect storm', *The Journal of Private Equity* 5(4): 10–14

Pike, J. (1999) *From Aristotle to Marx: Aristotelianism in Marxist Social Ontology.* Aldershot: Ashgate

Pinkstone, B. (2007) 'Tendency', 458–60 in M. Hartwig ed. *Dictionary of Critical Realism.* London: Routledge

Pittman, M. (2007) 'Bear Stearns Fund Collapse Sends Shock Through CDOs', Bloomberg news, June 21st

Plato (1997) 'The Republic' 971–1223 in *Complete Works.* Cambridge: Hackett Publishing

Preqin (2005) 'Global fund raising update', *Private Equity Spotlight* 1(3): 5–6

—— (2006a) 'The emerging markets opportunity', *Private Equity Spotlight* 2(3): 1–2

—— (2006b) 'Investors news', *Private Equity Spotlight* 2(7): 9

—— (2007) *The 2007 Global Fundraising Review* www.preqin.com

Primack, D., M. Copeland and L. Aragon (2002) 'Five more VCs slash funds, is there room for any more?' *Venture Capital Journal* 42(8): 6–10

Primack, D. (2001) 'Mega-funds pump up Q3 numbers', *Venture Capital Journal* 41(1): 16–17

Pwc (2007) 'Why financial reporting valuation matters on private equity deals', *Deal Flash* 6(1): 1–4

Quinn, J. (2007) 'Permira fund will benefit 33 million people', *The Telegraph,* London 30th May

Rand, J. S. and A. L. Weingarten (2002) 'When limited partners default', *The Journal of Private Equity* 5(2): 31–4

Rappaport, A. (1990) 'The staying power of the public corporation', *Harvard Business Review* 68(1): 96–104

Raynes, S. (2003) *The Analysis of Structured Securities: Precise Risk Measurement and Capital Allocation.* Oxford: Oxford University Press

Rind, K. W. (1981) 'The role of venture capital in corporate development', *Strategic Management Journal* 2(2): 169–80

Reed S. (2000) 'New world financiers, old world startups', *Business Week* February 7th

Renneboog, L., T. Simons and M. Wright (2005) 'Leveraged public to private transactions in the UK', European Corporate Governance Institute, *Finance Working Paper* 78/2005, April

Roiter, E. D. (1995) 'Investment companies' use of OTC derivatives: does the existing regulatory regime work?', *Stanford Journal of Law, Business and Finance* 1(2): 271–85

Roth, P. (1969) *Portnoy's Complaint.* London: Jonathan Cape

—— (1973) *The Great American Novel.* London: Jonathan Cape

Rose, E. (2004) *Employment Relations.* London: Prentice Hall

Rosengren, E. S. (1988) 'State restrictions on hostile takeovers', *Publius* 18(3): 67–79

Rozwadowski, K. and B. P. Young (2005) 'Buyout competition: the emergence of hedge funds in the world of private equity', *Journal of Private Equity* 9(1): 67–73

Samuelson, P. and H. R. Varian (2002) 'The New Economy and information techno-logy policy', 361–412 in Frankel, J. and P. R. Orszag *American Economic Policy in the 1990s*. Boston Mass.: MIT Press

Sayer, A. (1992) *Method in Social Science: A Realist Approach*. London: Routledge, second edition

Schumpeter, J. (1952) *Capitalism, Socialism and Democracy*. London: Allen and Unwin

—— (1962) *Ten Great Economists*. London: Allen and Unwin

—— (1997) *History of Economic Analysis*. London: Routledge

Schwarcz, S. L. (1994) 'The alchemy of asset securitization', *Stanford Journal of Law, Business and Finance* 1(1): 133–54

SCT (2007) 'Select Committee on Treasury Tenth Report', Interim findings regarding inquiry into private equity, July 30th Hansard, House of Commons Publications

Seib, C. G. Duncan, and S. Coates (2007) 'MPs plan to investigate loophole used by non-domiciled taxpayers,' *The Times*, London, July 13th

Sennett, R. (1999) *The Corrosion of Character: Personal Consequences of Work in the New Capitalism*. London: Norton

Sethi, R. (2002) 'Review: *The Economic Legacy of Hyman Minsky, Volume 1*', *Journal of Economic Literature* 90(2): 520–2

Shackle, G. L. S. (1990) *Time expectations and uncertainty in economics: selected essays*. London: Edward Elgar

Sharples C. J. (1995) 'The regulation of derivatives in the United Kingdom: A closer look at suitability issues', *Stanford Journal of Law, Business and Finance* 1(2): 191–4

Shepard, Spink, Alvarez and Marsal (2007) 'Distressed private equity', *The Hedge Fund Journal* 27

Sherman A. J. and M. A. Hart (2006) *Mergers and Acquisitions from A to Z*. New York: Amacom

Siegel, J. J. (2002) *Stocks for the Long Run*. New York: McGraw Hill

Skidelsky, R. (1994) *John Maynard Keynes: The Economist as Saviour 1920–1937*. Basingstoke: Macmillan

Smiddy, O. (2007) 'KKR to shore up its listed fund as Boots pays dividend', *Financial News* December 4th *Online* www.financialnews-us.com accessed 11/12/07

Smith, M. D. (2002) 'PIPEs: better for VCs than LBOs?' *The Journal of Private Equity* 5(4): 66–71

Sohl, J. E. (2003) 'The US angel and venture capital market: recent trends and develop-ments', *The Journal of Private Equity* 6(2): 7–17

Sparks, D. (2000) 'Return of the LBO', *Business Week* October 16th

Staff Reporter (2006) 'Seeing the forest for the trees', *Red Herring* February 27th

Staff Reporter (2008) 'Angels of risk', *Time Magazine* January 28th http://www.time.com/time/magazine/article/0,9171,907007-2,00.html accessed 2/02/2008

Stavins, J. (2000) 'Credit card borrowing, delinquency and personal bankruptcy,' *New England Economic Review* July/August 2000

Stelzer, I. M. (2007) 'Politicians will hit dealmakers but not just yet', *The Sunday Times* July 22nd

Stiff, P. (2007) 'Accountants predict rise in insolvencies', *The Times*, London December 10th

Stiglitz, J. (2002) *Globalization and its Discontents*. London: Allen Lane

—— (2004) *The Roaring Nineties*. London: Penguin

Stix, G. (2006) 'Loan volumes remain robust as high yield bonds drop off', *Bank Loan Report* 21(36): 1&7

Subhash, K. B. (2006) 'How to teach the big baby to walk: the case of the Indian Venture Capital industry', *Journal of Private Equity* 9(4): 76–97

Susko, P. M. (2003) 'Restructuring private equity investments', *The Journal of Private Equity* 6(4): 58–67

Tannon, J. M., and R. Johnson (2005) 'Transatlantic private equity: *Beyond a Trillion Dollar Force'*, *The Journal of Private Equity* 8(3): 77–80

Tannon, J. M. (2006) 'Chinese private equity: a paradigm shift', *The Journal of Private Equity* 9(3): 61–5

Thompson, P. (2002) *Skating on Thin Ice: The Knowledge Economy Myth*. Strathclyde: University of Strathclyde

Thomson Financial (2007) Press archive 2006 www.thomson.com/content/pr/tf/tf_priv_equiconsul/2007 accessed 20/05/2007

Thore, S. (1995) *The Diversity Complexity and Evolution of Hi-tech Capitalism*. London: Kluwer

TJN (2005) 'Briefing Paper: The Price of Offshore' available from: http://www.taxjustice.net accessed 10/05/2007

Toms, S. and M. Wright (2005) 'Divergence and convergence within Anglo-American corporate governance systems: evidence from the US and UK, 1950–2000', *Business History* 47(2): 267–95

Tran, V. Q. (2006) *Evaluating Hedge Fund Performance*. London: John Wiley

Ungoed-Thomas, J., C. Newell and H. Watt (2008) 'Ex-ministers cash in on days of power', *The Sunday Times*, London, February 24th

Varian, H. R. (1988) 'Symposium on takeovers', *Journal of Economic Perspectives* 2(1): 3–5

Veblen, T. (1958) *The Theory of Business Enterprise*. New York: Mentor

Walker, D (2007a) *Disclosure and transparency in private equity: consultation document* July, London: walker working group

—— (2007b) *Guidelines for disclosure and transparency in private equity*

—— (2007c) 'Providing a clearer path forward for private equity', *The Times*, London, November 26th

Walzer, M. (1977) *Just and Unjust Wars*. New York: Basic Books

Weber, M. (1978) *Economy & Society volume 1*. Berkeley: University of California Press

Wilde, O. (1987) 'An Ideal Husband' in *The Works of Oscar Wilde*. Leicester: Galley

Wolff, J. (2006) *An Introduction to Political Philosophy*. Oxford: Oxford University Press

—— (1999) 'Marx and exploitation', *Journal of Ethics* 3: 105–20

—— (1998) 'The ethics of competition', 82–96 in A. Quereshi, G. Parry and H. Steiner eds. *The Legal and Moral Aspects of International Trade, Freedom and Trade volume 3*. London: Routledge

Wray, L. R. (2002) 'Review: *The Economic Legacy of Hyman Minsky: Volume 2*', *Journal of Economic Literature* 90(4): 1231–3

Wright, M., Jensen, M., Cumming, D., and Siegel, D. (2007) *The Impact of Private Equity: Setting the Record Straight* CMBOR: Nottingham University Business School; http://www.cmbor.org/index.phtml accessed 05/06/2007

Wright, M., T. Simons and L. Scholes (2006) 'Leveraged buyouts in the UK and Continental Europe: retrospect and prospect', *Journal of Applied Corporate Finance* 18(3): 38–55

Wright, M., L. Renneboog, T. Simons and L. Scholes (2006) 'Leveraged buyouts in the UK and Continental Europe: retrospect and prospect', European Corporate Governance Institute, *Working Paper* 126/2006, July

Wright, M., A. Burrows, R. Ball, L. Scholes, M. Burdett and K. Tune (2006) 'Management buyouts 1986–2006: past achievements and challenges', Centre for Management Buyout Research, paper; June

Wright, M., R. Hoskisson, L. Busenitz and J. Dial (2000) 'Entrepreneurial growth through privatization: the upside of management buyouts', *Academy of Management Review* 25(3): 591–601

Wright, M., N. Wilson and K. Robbie (1996) 'The longer-term effects of management-led buyouts', *Journal of Entrepreneurial & Small Business Finance* 5(3): 213–35

Wright, M., N. Wilson, K. Robbie and C. Ennew (1994) 'Restructuring and Failure in Buyouts and Buy-ins', *Business Strategy Review* 5(2): 21–40

Wright, M., Chiplin, S. Thompson and K. Robbie (1990) 'Management buyouts, trade unions, and employee ownership', *Industrial Relations Journal* 21(1): 30–61

WSJ (2006) 'Who's who in private equity', *Wall St. Journal* July 12th

Yago, G. (1990) *Junk Bonds: How High Yield Securities Restructured Corporate America.* Oxford: Oxford University Press

Zhang, Y. (1998) *China in International Society Since 1949.* Basingstoke: Macmillan

Zong, L. (2005) 'Governance lessons from the private equity industry', *Journal of Private Equity* 19(1): 63–6

Index